THE MIRACLES VERSUS TYRANNY

THE MIRACLES VERSUS TYRANNY

by
Izaak Goldberg, M. D.

Philosophical Library
New York

Copyright, 1978, by Philosophical Library, Inc.,
15 East 40 Street, New York, N. Y. 10016
All rights reserved, including the right to reproduce
any portion of this book, the text or the photographs
in any form.

Library of Congress Catalog Card No. 77-009220
SBN 8022-2213-7

Manufactured in the United States of America

Dedicated to my wife JUDITH,
who helped me in preparation of the book
and to my son JACKIE, who is fortunate to live
in the free, blessed, democratic U.S. of America.

IN MEMORY of my family, murdered by the Nazis.
May their souls enjoy eternal lives with all the other righteous men and women. Conceal them in the mystery of thy wings forever.
May the Lord be their inheritance and may they repose in peace.

Parents

Jacob - Joseph
Chana - Rachel

Brothers

Abraham
Mendel
Moses

Sister

Rosa

This book is consecrated to all those who suffered and perished in Nazi concentration camps and ghettoes, to all those who were tortured and ended their lives with hope and prayer on their lips, that the new world, which was shocked by the atrocities committed by the Germans during the Second World War, will create a new order which will make impossible a repetition of the same outrageous and shameful wickedness.

IN SPITE OF ALL THIS, WE HAVE NOT FORGOTTEN YOUR NAME.
PLEASE, DO NOT FORGET US.

CONTENTS

Preface   xvii

THE YEAR 1941
6/22/41 - 12/31/41
FIRST HALF-YEAR OF RUSSIAN-GERMAN WAR.

CHAPTER I.	The first week of war. Miracle # 1.	3
II.	Strong German advance deep into Russia. Life under German occupation.	23
III.	Fierce fighting east of the Berezina. The Ghetto. Theory of immortality of the soul. Miracle # 2.	40
IV.	The last four months of the year 1941.	58

THE YEAR 1942
SECOND YEAR OF WAR.
RESISTANCE TO GERMAN AGGRESSION.

V.	The special German commandos for genocide. Miracles # 3, # 4 and # 5.	69
VI.	Wolkowysk concentration camp.	121

CONTENTS

THE YEAR 1943
THIRD YEAR OF WAR.
THE MYTH OF GERMAN INVINCIBILITY WAS BROKEN.

VII.	The road to Auschwitz.	149
VIII.	Stalingrad. North Africa. Auschwitz. Miracle # 6.	180
IX.	Miracle # 7. The Krematoria.	219
X.	Germany's retreat. Work in Birkenau.	256
XI.	The Warsaw Ghetto Uprising. The arrest and rescue of Mussolini. The conquest of Sicily.	305
XII.	Maidanek Concentration Camp. The Moscow Conference.	358

THE YEAR 1944
FOURTH YEAR OF WAR.
DEFEAT OF AGGRESSION.

XIII.	The reasons of Germany's defeat. Liberation of Europe.	395
XIV.	Gunthergrube concentration camp. Assassination of Hitler. Miracle # 8.	414
XV.	D-Day. The Polish Warsaw Uprising.	449

THE YEAR 1945
FIFTH YEAR OF WAR.
GERMAN UNCONDITIONAL SURRENDER.
PROCLAMATION OF PEACE
END OF SECOND WORLD WAR.

XVI.	Escape to freedom. Miracles # 10 and 11. Fierce fighting in Germany proper.	467
XVII.	Miracle # 12. Zeilsheim. The death of President Roosevelt.	493

CONTENTS xv

XVIII. The mild sentences in the German courts. 527
XIX. One example of a Nazi trial. 547
   The true story of one survivor.
   Wings to fly. The biblical Job
   and the survivor.

EPILOGUE 585

Index 593

PREFACE

The most important characteristic feature of this book is the fact of telling the truth and only the truth.

Every name, every location, every event, with very few exceptions are real, and represent the way of where and why it occurred.

It is not a fiction, born in the imagination of a writer, but it is a narration of occurrences, episodes, happenings, as witnessed and seen by the storyteller himself with his own eyes.

The hero of this narration is Dr. Harsaw. He is a practicing physician in the city of New York.

He survived the ghettoes in Europe, the concentration camps of Wolkowysk and AUSCHWITZ. He was also a witness for the prosecution in one of the Nazi trials in Frankfort (Germany).

His narration describes the events, day by day, week after week, and in certain instances, even hour after hour.

It is not something which he heard from other survivors, but an authentic story of what he himself experienced, a sort of a true autobiography.

This book was written originally in another language, *immediately after the liberation*, when everything was still fresh in his memory. Therefore the scenes described are vivid, original and unmarred by passing of time. The names of individuals and locations were faultlessly retained, recorded, and remembered up to now, as they otherwise would have been forgotten.

The readers. who were fortunate enough to live in the free and democratic U.S. of America, who were lucky to avoid the Nazi atrocities, who didn't have to look at the wild faces of the Gestapo, will learn to know all the details of those daily occurrences as if they had been survivors themselves.

In reading this book, they'll appreciate more the blessings and freedom of living in the U.S.A., which they have taken for granted up to date.

Many of us had friends and relatives who suffered and perished under the Nazis. We would like to treasure in our hearts the memories of the last days and hours of our beloved kinsmen and fellow human beings. This book will describe the details of the last days and hours as they really occurred.

The truth narrated here has a value for historians and politicians alike.

For historians, the material is an absolute necessity to understand the monstrous structure of Nazism and the devastating effect of its nature, thinking and source.

For politicians—to remember the millions of lives lost, for no reason at all, and to undertake ways and means, that such atrocities and form of genocides should never recur again.

It bestows, also, a warning to all mankind, that the prayers of the Nazi victims uttered in the last minutes of their lives should be honored and entirely fulfilled.

The system of race extermination by the Nazis was similar, with minor variations, in every town, city and even in every concentration and extermination camp. What happened in the ghetto of Rozana or Warsaw, happened in all the other ghettoes. What happened in the concentration camp of Auschwitz, happened in all the other concentration and extermination camps: Treblinki, Maidanek, Chelmno, Osibor, Matthausen and so on.

The regulations enforced by the Germans, and the crimes committed in the occupied territories in the East, were the same in all the Eastern countries.

The rules and regulations in the West were the same in all the Western occupied territories.

The same German experts traveled from camp to camp,

bringing with them and sharing with the Nazis all the latest innovations and devices of mass destructions.

First, mass shootings were used, later the toxic "CARBON MONOXIDE" and finally the lethal gas "CYCLON B."

German experts traveled from location to location, to teach the Chiefs of the concentration camps how to dig out thousands upon thousands of corpses and how to burn them in the most efficient way.

The names mentioned here are real names of people who once lived on this earth like you and me. But, they do not exist any more. They perished together with their entire families and turned to ashes. Their hair was changed to linings for German garments and mattresses, their fat was altered to soap. Nothing remained to remember them. They were forgotten entirely by the world.

This book brings out into the open *some* names of individuals, men, women and children, names of Nazi victims who will never be forgotten and will serve, at the same time, as a memorial to those unfortunate people who disappeared from this world without leaving any remembrance or any reminiscence of their past existence.

The contents of this book comprehend different periods.

1. The ghettoes and the suffering of their inhabitants from the beginning of the German-Russian war (6/22/41) till the end of the year 1941.

2. The concentration and extermination camps from 1942 till the end of the war (5/7/45).

3. The lives of the few survivors after the holocaust and the attitude of the postwar German governments to the Nazi victims.

4. The attitudes to the criminals with their unheard-of atrocities, who are walking freely on the streets of present-day Germany, and who are carrying the seeds of a new genocide.

The above periods are interwoven and intertwined with the happenings of the war proceedings on the battlefronts.

The prisoners, during their incarcerations, were deprived of any news from the battlefields.

How much they desired to find out about the theater of

operations, about the lines of the battlefronts, can be appreciated only by those who survived the German inferno.

By showing the necessary ways and means to be undertaken in order to avoid another Nazi catastrophe, this book is unique.

When you are reading this account, I want to assure you and to give you full guarantee, not only of the full veracity of this description, removing any doubts in your mind, but also that the events described constitute only a pale reflection of the enormous human tragedy caused by the German atrocities.

Dante's "INFERNO" is a small, insignificant poem, in comparison with the real happenings of Auschwitz.

I feel that the contents of this book should be read in every house, especially by the young generation, who will inherit and take over the management of our society and our governments.

Therefore, I decided to keep the price of this book very low, in comparison with the expenses accrued, hardly to cover the cost.

NO PROFIT IS WANTED, NOR EXPECTED.

In this way, every house in the U.S.A. and in the rest of the world will be able to acquaint themselves with the text of this publication.

The reasons of the above decision lie in the following facts:

1. Although the events described represent the truth, as they occurred during the German occupation, they seem very strange and unbelievable to many people, because they never occurred before on this planet.

2. By reading and rereading the occurrences, incidents and experiences of this writing, the people will be better equipped to handle similar events in the future. They'll learn the consequences of neglect and try to avoid them. They'll be better qualified to fight evil and wickedness, because physically and spiritually they'll be better prepared to extinguish the fire right from the beginning.

Our generation, unfortunately, was completely in the dark, and didn't understand the real danger which engulfed them.

They didn't believe till the last moment what the Nazis had in store for them.

They were in the dark when they traveled in the cattle trains.

They were in the dark when they arrived on the infamous ramp of Auschwitz.

Most of the people, of all the races and nationalities, did not comprehend the truth, even when they were lying naked in the gas chambers.

They believed the Nazi lies, that the gas chambers were washrooms and a preparation for a resettlement.

Had they known the truth, as it is known today, had they been cautioned before and possessed a book of truth and warning as this, at the time of the genocide, the results would have been completely different.

Our young generation should learn the veracity of the facts in the schools in order to be able to recognize evil and to fight it right at its inception.

The events, episodes and happenings were of such a magnitude that they failed to adhere to the human minds, because the people were not conditioned to it by past experiences.

Factories of death were created, which operated for many years, under strict supervision and ownership of a freely elected government, and which shook the conscience of the world. As a matter of fact, when Maidanek concentration camp was first overrun by the Soviet army, the Western newspapers refused to print the real happenings in the camp because they were unbelievable. Only later, when the other German camps were discovered: Auschwitz, Dachau and Mathausen, and after they were visited by the Allied leaders and all the crimes perpetrated by the Nazis were detected and seen in all the nakedness, only then did the West broadcast and the newspapers print, with sorrow in their hearts, the enormous crimes committed by the Nazis.

At the beginning, the world was shocked. People talked about it, but still didn't believe it.

Later with passing of time, the events became not clear enough and finally slowly and gradually started on the road of forgetfulness.

The courts in Germany freed many criminals, making it possible for another holocaust to reappear.

This book was written only with the purpose to make another mass slaughter impossible, by constantly reminding the world of the unheard-of atrocities committed for the first time on mankind, and showing the ways of avoiding another terrible genocide by not letting the people to forget.

By reading this true narration, over and over again, the horrible crimes will be comprehended and finally stick to the human minds.

The future generation will learn to resist similar atrocities in the future.

Viewing the world today, the spread of crimes and terror, partially caused by the mild sentences in the present Nazi trials, I am convinced that another evil man, like Hitler, will arise in the not-distant future.

Taking in consideration the new and modern weapons of our time, including the atomic and hydrogen deadly armaments, the chemical and bacteriological warfare, the radio-controlled rockets, the aircrafts flying with supersonic speeds, the emerging of another Hitler would mean the end of mankind.

Don't be like a duck submerging her head under the water and believing that the hunter doesn't see her.

Many Hitlers will appear on the horizon in the future if we don't eliminate the causes of a new emergence of evil.

Don't say it is too terrible to talk about. It is the way to avoid future genocide and future buildings of gas chambers and Krematoria and many other more advanced tools of mass destruction.

The time has arrived when we have to meet the extreme danger face to face.

You must prepare your brains, your muscles, your nerves and every part of your body and spirit to meet the challenges of evil.

You must remember that the unheard-of atrocities occurred a few decades ago on this planet for the first time and will occur again.

You must condition yourselves to the true happenings in order to avoid and to annihilate the schemes of evil in the future.

Tell your children and your grandchildren over and over again the story of Nazism.

My endeavor is to make people recognize evil and to teach them how to make it ineffective, right from the beginning.

By constantly repeating the history of the past we'll avoid the effects and consequences of a devastating cataclysm in the future.

Only by tedious preparation beforehand we'll be successful to prevent another calamity.

The millions of perished Nazi victims are constantly calling upon us to remember everything and not to forget.

This reminder and prayer were on their lips in the last minutes of their lives, right before they died. They warned us, also, of the consequences of another Hitler, who will definitely come.

Germany is ready and ripe for another appearance of an evil man.

I am quoting a recent dispatch from West Berlin: "AN ALARMING INCREASE OF RIGHT-WING EXTREMISM ... AMONG YOUNG PEOPLE ... IS ALARMING TO BOTH JEWS AND NON-JEWS. THEY ARE PARTICULARLY PREVALENT AMONG PUPILS AND STUDENTS OF SCHOOLS AND COLLEGES. AT A NUMBER OF SCHOOLS THERE HAS BEEN AN UPSURGE OF NEO-NAZI ANTISEMITIC ACTIVITIES."

Therefore, it is my duty to tell the story to the world, in order to prevent a repetition of the same atrocities in the future.

The name of Dr. Harsaw is not his real name. It was changed on the insistence of his family, who were demurring because of too much publicity.

The doctor has been practicing medicine for many years in the city of New York. If his real name was revealed, he would have to answer to his numerous friends and patients unnecessary questions, and be compelled to describe details of the Nazi era, which would disturb the further practice of his medical profession.

It is also against the ethical code of a doctor to be on everyone's tongue or lips. Therefore his name was changed.

Arrangement could be made for any responsible individual, institution or department to meet him, personally, for clarification, verification and more details.

So is the name of Mr. Dig, which was altered for similar reasons and mainly on the urging of his family.

I would like to quote here the words of the Hagada. (Germany is substituted for Egypt.)

"We were slaves in Germany and in the occupied territories of Europe. The Nazis did evil to us and they made us suffer.

"All the time, they rise against us and seek our destruction.... God saw our affliction, our burden and our oppression....

"The more one tells the story, the more he is to be praised."

Let me repeat the last phrase.

The more one tells the story . . . the less likely is a repetition of the same atrocities and genocide to occur.

In this book you'll find out also the reasons why the victims died without putting up a strong resistance.

Many are asking this question, and they have to be told the truth and the reasons explained.

You'll learn, also, why the Germans lost the war so shamefully in spite of the fact that the best and most reliable experts in the world predicted a quick German victory.

You'll get acquainted with the methods used by a dictatorship and their effect on human minds.

The author gratefully acknowledges permission from the following sources to reproduce photographs used in this book:

Walka, smierc, paniec, 1939-1945, edited by Stanislaw Poznanski, by permission of Authors' Agency, Warsaw, Poland, for photographs on page 82 top and bottom, 116 top and bottom, 117 top left and right, center left and right, bottom, 118, 208 bottom, 217 bottom, 319 top left, center, and bottom.

We Shall Never Forget, edited by Tuviah Friedman, Director of Documentation Center, Haifa, Israel, for photographs on page 82 center, 94, 118 bottom, 217 top left and top right, 412, 413 left, and 545.

Council for the Conservation of Monuments of Struggle and Martyrdom, Warsaw, Poland (from the collections of the Committee to Investigate the Hitler Crimes in Poland and from the Jewish Historical Institute of Warsaw, Jewish edition) for photographs on page 85, 114, 115, 162, 163 bottom, 164, 165, and 177.

The State Museum, Oswiecim, Poland, for photographs on page 203, 204 bottom, 205 top and bottom, 207, 208 top, 209, 210 bottom, 211, 221, 230, 231, 232, 237 top, 238, 261, 263, 265, 266, 300, 320 bottom, 327, 341, 376, 377, 378.

Scourge of the Swastika, by Lord Russell, Philosophical Library, New York, for photographs on pages 301, 320 top, 344 top left, top right, bottom, 409, and 410.

Library of Congress, Washington, D.C., for photographs on page 62 center and 413 right.

US Archives for the photograph on page 64 bottom left.

The author is also grateful to the staff of the Jewish Division, The New York Public Library, Astor, Lenox, and Tilden Foundations, for their kind assistance in connection with photographs on page 82 top and bottom, 94, 116 top and bottom, 117 top left and right, center left and right, bottom 118, 208 bottom, 217 top left and top right, bottom, 319 top left, center, bottom, 412, 413 left, and 545.

THE MIRACLES VERSUS TYRANNY

Germans invaded Poland from the west and south, and Russia occupied the eastern part of Poland. The border was about 70 miles west from Wolkowysk.

"May be," said Dr. Markus, "that the German planes, by mistake, passed the border."

But it was very puzzling to us and it left an onerous and perplexing feeling. On returning home, we discussed this strange phenomenon, unusual for Wolkowysk. I came home late and went to bed.

At 4 A.M. I awoke to the sounds of exploding bombs falling over the city. I jumped out of bed, turned the radio on and heard the unexpected, which I feared all the time. The war against Russia started. This was 4 A.M., June 22, 1941. The gigantic Nazi war machine surged against the border. Real hell on earth started. German planes roaring in the air spreading devastation and death. Huge tanks were advancing, ripping giant holes in the ground. Artillery shells bursting all around.

Stalin was very much afraid of Hitler, especially after the German victories over France, Holland, Belgium, Norway in 1940, and over Greece and Yugoslavia in the spring of 1941. He delivered raw materials, food, oil to Germany in order to avoid a German attack.

On 11/12/1940, Molotov went to Berlin, on the direct invitation of Hitler. He was summoned to discuss how the world should be divided among the four totalitarian powers: Japan, Italy, Germany and the Soviet Union. Evidently, Hitler wanted to lull the Russians into a false sense of security by promising them a big chunk of the fallen British Empire.

"Nothing will be left of England," declared Hitler, "the downfall of England is imminent. The English empire is on auction. We have to dispose now of the unclaimed assets, which is a block of 40 million square kilometers."

How perfidious Hitler was, can be deduced from the fact that, at this very moment when he spoke to Molotov and asked him what he wished to take from the falling English Empire, at this very instant he was preparing feverishly for the invasion of Russia.

Hitler told Mussolini: "Although we have very favorable

economic and political agreements with Russia, I prefer to use the powerful means at my disposal."

At the beginning of 1941, Hitler told his generals that the struggle against the Soviet Union would be conducted with unprecedented, merciless and unrelenting harshness.

"I do not expect my generals to understand me," he said, "but I want them to obey my orders." He decided first to attack Yugoslavia and Greece. He had contempt for small nations. Therefore they must be attacked with merciless harshness and lightning blows. He had complete contempt for people without Governments: Jews and Gypsies.

They'd have to be destroyed entirely. He hated the Slavs: Polish, Russian, Yugoslavians. They were subhumans and had to be slaves to the victors. This was in accordance with the philosophies of the Super-race of the German National Socialists. It is very interesting and worthwhile to mention that many famous German generals were against the Russian war.

For example: On 5/30/41, Grand Admiral Rueder repeated his demand and urged Hitler to attack Egypt with all the deadly German force and to leave Russia for the future. Had Hitler followed the advice of Rueder, the war would have taken a complete different turn, disastrous to the Allied cause.

It was a brilliant idea! Germany would have occupied Egypt, Iraq, Iran, India and joined forces with Japan. England, deprived of the raw material from her African and Asian colonies, would have to fight on two fronts and would have found herself in a very hopeless and desperate situation. Stalin was ready to supply the Germans at that time with all kinds of food, raw materials, whatever was necessary.

Hitler's crippled mind knew better. He launched instead operation "BARBAROSA," and started the invasion of Russia believing that in a few weeks the campaign will be over.

"Russia had a very hard time fighting small Finland. How could she sustain the mighty thrust of the invincible German forces?" Hitler's aim was to wipe Russia off the map. It was *not* a question of adjusting the frontiers. Moskow, Leningrad, Kiev would be leveled to the ground. The Russians would be slaves, working in industries and on the farms guarded by SS troops.

The First Week of War

And so, the invasion of Russia started against the advice of the best experts and against even any common sense. A three-pronged German attack started. One directed north towards Leningrad. The other aimed in the middle, towards Moscow, and the third was directed to the south, towards the Ukraine and the Caucasus.

In the first weeks of the campaign, the concentrated German onslaught smashed, captured and destroyed the bulk of the western Red Army. In the very first day the unexpected and sudden attack destroyed almost the entire Soviet Air Force in the western areas. The capital of Belorussia, Minsk, was captured in five days of fighting. Shortly thereafter, western Ukraine, Lithuania, Latvia, Estonia and western Belorussia were occupied. *Wolkowysk*, the city where I lived, was not occupied in the first days. I'll describe here the daily happenings in my city, starting from the invasion, as an example of what happened to all the cities in White Russia and Ukraine.

Sunday, 6/22/41, 4 A.M.

The radio announced that the German forces crossed the border, spreading death and devastation. A Russian general lived one flight up from our apartment. I heard quick steps. The general was very nervous, disheveled, came running down carrying with him a pack of documents. I understood that something terrible was taking place. For the first time in my life I started to shiver, a bad omen, because usually I did not react this way. The Germans dropped many bombs over the city. We heard about the first casualties. The son and daughter-in-law of our neighbor Nache were killed. Many fatalities and wounded. Desperation in the city. People were running from one place to the other. They didn't know where to hide.

At seven o'clock in the morning, a radio broadcast, a proclamation by Hitler. "German people! At this moment a march is taking place that is the greatest the world has ever seen. I have decided to place the fate of the German Reich in the hands of our soldiers."

During the first hours of the attack the situation already

became unbearable. The Germans were continuing their air attacks. The bombing was growing in intensity. Terrible bombardment of Belorussian towns. Bialystok, Grodno, Lida, Brest, *Wolkowysk*, Slonim under continuous bombardment.

Soviet planes destroyed on the ground. The "Luftwaffe" were strafing troops and civilians. German paratroopers landed at different places. Dozens of localities were already occupied. At that critical time Timoshenko ordered Soviet troops in the name of Stalin not to undertake any action and not to open any artillery fire.

Stalin still believed at this crucial moment that maybe Hitler would not break the non-aggression pact. He wanted to avoid any kind of action that might be considered in Berlin as a provocation. Evidently Stalin was desperately holding to the peace agreement.

Even he, Stalin, couldn't measure up to the degenerated mind of a Hitler.

Only later, at 7:15 A.M. of the same day, the first directive to the frontier troops came in with an order to resist and to stop the aggression.

In the morning, about 10 A.M., Molotov spoke over the radio. I still remember how his voice was full of sorrow plaintive, almost like whining. At the beginning, the tone was faltering and slightly stuttering.

"At 4 A.M. this morning, without declaration of war and without any claims being made on the Soviet Union, German troops attacked our country. . . . This unheard-of attack on our country is an unparalleled act of perfidy in the history of civilized nations. This attack has been made despite the non-aggression pact between the Soviet Union and Germany, a pact which *was scrupulously observed by the Soviet Union*. The German government had been unable to make the slightest complaints about the USSR not carrying out its obligations."

It was clear from his speech that the Soviet government would have been willing to consider almost any concessions to put off the evil hour.

As we heard the radio broadcast of Molotov, we became very sad and even despondent. We felt slightly humiliated by the announcement of Molotov, that the Germans made no demands on us, insinuating that the Soviets would agree to anything. Just ask and you'll get it.

People were milling around, discussing the speech of Molotov. What will be now? Is it true that the Germans are murdering innocent people, including women and children?

It was impossible to believe. Germany was considered to be a civilized nation. Even the barbarians would not dare to murder for the sake of murdering. Even a wild animal doesn't kill for the sake of killing. It wouldn't help the war. It didn't make sense. It was sheer propaganda!

In the meantime the air raids continued. Many civilians were killed. Rumors were spreading that the Germans were repelled. We felt better. In the night of the same day, June 22, at 9 P.M., we heard Churchill's broadcast.

"No one has been a more consistent opponent of Communism than me. I will unsay no word that I have spoken about. But, all this fades away now. We are resolved to destroy Hitler. We will never negotiate. We shall fight him by land, we shall fight him by sea, we shall fight him in the air, until, with God's help, we have rid the earth of his shadow. . . . Any man or state who fights against Nazidom will have our aid. . . . We shall give whatever help we can to Russia. . . . The Russian danger is our danger! . . ."

This was the speech of Churchill which lifted our spirits. We joked at the famous remark of Churchill.

"If Hitler invaded hell, I would make, at least a favourable reference to the devil in the House of Commons."

2nd day, Monday, 6/23/41.

The German air attacks over the defenseless civilians continued with more intensity. Every 20-30 minutes a new raid, with many civilians, including children, being killed. Terrible confusion. People were desperate. They were running from one shelter to another. In the early morning a bomb exploded in the ambulatorium (city's main clinic). Many sick people killed. Another bomb fell into the house of Dr. Schlakman, the lung specialist. His wife was of very short stature but very energetic. She organized most of the patients for him.. The doctor himself was a tall, handsome man, but a quiet type. When asked why he married such a short woman, he replied that he looked for a shorter one but couldn't find any. Now the doctor was not home. He had been sent to a big city, inside Russia, for additional medical training. His wife and son were in the city, left alone. The house was completely destroyed and his only little son killed in the raid. Terrible!

The city hospital was bombarded. Many fatalities among the sick. Two nurses killed.

Most of the people were running to the basements, because real shelters had not been built as yet.

About 4 P.M. the Germans started to drop incendiary bombs. All the city was on fire. People were taking out of their houses whatever was possible.

At first we desposited many things in our own basement. Later we carried them to the basement of Mr. Press, which was fire-resistant.

I saw Mr. Stolowicki, the flour merchant, running from his house, which was burning, toward us. He was pale, worrying, and asked me whether I had seen some of his family. I didn't see anybody. Both of his daughters survived the war. One was a pharmacist practicing in the U.S.A. She escaped to the forest with her children and later was evacuated deep into Russia. The other daughter survived the war in the forest also, and now is living in Israel.

I kept my medical diploma first in the basement of our house. Later when I saw that the German indendiary bombs were spreading havoc, and that almost all the houses were burned and destroyed, I ran to the basement and took out my diploma, which I still have now with me. I believe that I am the only one who survived such a terrible holocaust, like two years in Auschwitz, etc., who was able to save his original diploma, given to me in Italy.

We took with us the most necessary things and hastened to escape to the house of my cousin Chone, who lived in Karcizna on the periphery of the city. No incendiary bombs were dropped there.

My cousin lived in a big house with his wife and children, separated from the street by a long courtyard. All the surroundings there were like in a farm. Hundreds of people who escaped from the burning city gathered there in the court yard.

We were still able to bring some textile goods there and to bury them deep under the ground. They might later save us from starvation. We were helped by Yosl the vagabond.

There was no place to sleep. So many people were scattered inside and outside the house. Everybody wanted to be on the safe side. We slept on the floor.

Mother returned to the city late at night, to see what was happening to our house. I tried to persuade her not to go. I did not want to let her go by herself and therefore joined her.

In the evening, I saw our house and the other neighboring houses burning. I wanted to come near the house, but the heat from the fire was so intense that I had to go back.

Tuesday June 24, 1941, 3rd day of the war.

Intensive bombardment of the city. Every 15 minutes an air raid alarm. The city was still burning. But not every house was consumed. Our house was burned to the ground. There were smoldering pieces left after the burning and a characteristic smoke was still discernible. One felt it with one's nose, ears, eyes and skin. I stood with my mother near our burned house. She stared only and did not speak. I could imagine what was going on inside her. She was a successful business woman all her life. Admired by friends and foes alike. I said foes. But I could not conceive of her having real foes. Maybe people who envied her intelligence, appearance, energy and decency. She worked very hard all her life and now she looked upon the devastation, caused by an unjust war. She was sad, but accepted the inevitable. We went to the house of Levitt, where we rented a room for ourselves, and which belonged to the very few houses that still remained intact after the conflageration.

My mother went to pray to the Almighty, that the war should end and peace should prevail. On the way, we met Mr. Lachowicki, who complained that he hadn't eaten anything since Sunday. Mother had a piece of bread, which she saved for later. She gave it away to Lachowicki, who thanked her for her good heart, not being able to utter anything more, because of emotion and weakness. We spent the night in our room in the house of Levitt.

My brother Mendel and our relative Chasza went by foot to Rozana, a distance of about 35-38 miles (49 Russian wiorsts).

The road was full of danger and we all wished them well. Russian soldiers were milling around, looking for spies. Many who escaped from the city to nearby villages were shot on the way. The confusion was enormous.

Chasza was my mother's relative and she came to our house to meet her fiance, Mr. Bekenstein. Chasza was a nice girl, about 22 years old. Very intelligent, good and energetic. She and her family lived in Konstantinova, a small village of farmers adjacent to Rozana, where I was born. My mother was born in Konstantinova. All the work on the farm was performed by Chasza. She took care of the cows, horses, chickens, fed them, milked them, etc. She was also a good cook, cleaned the house and did everything that was necessary, performing her work in a diligent, alert and hard-working way.

Lucky Mr. Bekenstein! One had to be very fortunate to meet such a girl. But what was the use? Who knew what was going to happen to all of us? Who knew whether Mr. Bekenstein was seeing his lovely fiancée for the last time?

My brother Mendel arrived from Israel shortly before the war broke out. Israel was at that time under the British mandate. He had lived there for many years, and was a successful business man. He came to Wolkowysk to see his family after so many years of separation. He was a quiet fellow, tall, thin, considered handsome, and was very adept in manual, mechanical work. He was an electrician, mechanic, barber, engineer and what-not. He was also a good physicist and mathematician. He could sit over a mathematical problem for hours till he solved it. I remember

The First Week of War

once, somebody had asked me to solve the following two mathematical equations from algebra.

$$\infty = \text{ad infinitum}$$

1. $x^{y^{x^{y^{x^{\infty}}}}} = 3 \quad y^{x^{y^{x^{y^{\infty}}}}} = 2$

2. $x^2 + y = 28$

   $x + y^2 = 14$

   <u>Answer</u>
   $x = 5; y = 3.$

How to solve it? The #1 equation I was able to solve myself. I substituted $x^{y^{x^{y^{x^{\infty}}}}}$ by 3, then $y^3 = 2$.

The #2 equation was very difficult to solve. I worked for many hours and could not reach the right solution. I proceeded as follows: $x^2+y=28$
$x+y^2=14$, $x=14-y^2$, then $(14-y^2)^2+y=28$
$196-28y^2+y^4+y=28$; $y^4-28y^2+y=28-196=-168$

Using the usual y^4 formulas to solve the equation did not help to find the value of "y." I went to my teacher of mathematics; he could not solve it either in the customary and accepted way. Finally in desperation I went to my brother Mendel, who solved it after two days of very hard thinking.

Mendel had a Palestinian passport. England was, at that time, involved in a struggle of death and life with the Germans. Seeing what was done to innocent civilians, especially of Jewish descent, my brother was afraid to come forward and register with the German police as an English (Palestinian) citizen. He didn't want to enter the tiger's mouth voluntarily. The Gestapo might have killed him on the spot.

The name "Gestapo" frightened everyone, it put a wet blanket and chills in each and everyone of us. We really didn't know at that time that Hitler meant, really, a complete destruction of the Jewish race.

We all hoped and prayed, that Chasza and my brother Mendel would arrive at Rozana healthy, and in best order, in spite of the peril and hazard.

My brother Moritz went to spend the night at the house of my cousin, Chone.

Wednesday, June 25, 1941, fourth day of the war.

Air raids every few minutes. Many killed and injured. Terrible confusion and anarchy. People were running in all directions. Air raids again. Bombs were falling time and time again over the destroyed and burned out houses. Tremendous and horrible desperation and apathy. About 10 A.M. we heard that a bomb exploded in my cousin's house, where my brother slept. We were all very disturbed, disquieted and restless. Who knows what happened to my brother? All of us were hiding in the basement of Pelta. It was a strong brick house and the basement formed a good protection from bullets and splinters. It was impossible to go out from the basement. Bomb explosions all over. It was very unsafe. To walk to my cousin's house took at least 20-25 minutes. It was dangerous. In spite of all the hazard and imperilment, my mother risked her life by leaving the basement and running to my cousin to see what had happened to my brother.

What is danger to a mother when she is confronted with saving her child? What are bombs and bullets when it comes to save her son?

We bowed our heads with esteem, reverence and respect. Later when it quieted down a little, we all went to my cousin. Thank G-d, my brother was alive, not even injured. In the last minute, he escaped to the basement and survived. Many were killed in the house and in the adjacent buildings.

Among the victims was Dr. Berman and his five-year-old daughter. He had his own private laboratory performing analysis of different medical tests. He was such an honest man and performed the tests and analysis of human secretion, excretion, blood and urine in such a perfection, which was unique in the prewar laboratories. He was so diligent and strict in his work that he didn't permit anyone to do the main work. He was responsible and his work had to be perfect. No wonder that all the physicians trusted him 100%. It is almost impossible to find today such dedication and honesty among the laboratory workers. This era has passed.

Many were fatally injured but still alive. I was trying to do my best, working fast under the circumstances. I disinfected the wounds, bandaged, put on splints for immobilization, distributed drugs, analgesics, sulfur and tried to organize transportation to the hospital.

Berman's maid, a young girl of about 25 years old, was very badly injured. A bad wound in the abdomen, through which the intestine protruded. I bandaged her wounds, gave her a Prontosil injection, analgesics and sent her to the hospital as quickly as possible. She was conscious, joked around and thanked me.

Air raids continued again, explosions all around. As soon as we escaped to the basement, we heard the shriekings of the approaching German planes. The sounds got louder, the planes came nearer and nearer. We felt the aircraft fly over our house. Here was the deciding moment—shall we die or shall we live? This was the question. We might all be dead by one direct hit. Fortunately the plane passed and no bomb was dropped. I discovered that, when the plane was near or directly over the house, I lost consciousness for 2-3 seconds.

I asked the others whether it happened to them also. Everyone confirmed the same phenomenon. Medically I could explain it in this way. The supreme danger of imminent death caused a slight shock of short duration in our system. Then the regulatory body mechanism set in, and the senses returned to normality again. This phenomenon was normal, human, and everybody without exception experienced it.

Later, the air raids stopped for a few hours. Evidently the pilots went to eat lunch, after performing their duties in the National Socialistic spirit. By this I mean the murderous attack over civilians. There were no Soviet airplanes in the air. They were all destroyed in the first day of the invasion. We had no protection at all. German pilots flew very low, without fear. Nobody disturbed them. They saw civilians running for cover, children, women, old men.

The Germans had no pity. They dropped bombs on the defenseless and innocent civilian population. Their targets included the city clinics and hospitals, where many were killed. If someone was not fast enough to run to the shelters or was too weak and too sick and remained lying on the streets, the pilots lowered the planes and machine gunned the defenseless people. Such bestialities, rarely to be seen, were constantly practiced by the German pilots and were in accordance with National Socialistic dogma.

Taking advantage of the lull, we went back to our room in Levit's house. We spent the night there. In the morning all seemed to be quiet. We didn't have any food for a few days. Somebody told us that near the railroad station bread was being sold. My brother Moritz volunteered to go there.

Fifteen minutes later an air raid attack again. We worried about Moritz. Fortunately after half an hour he returned lively and happy, because he was able to buy a loaf of bread. He told us that, on the way back, he saw the body of the son of Epstein, our neighbor, killed during the raid.

Thursday June 26, 1941, fifth day of the war.

Air raids continued without a stop. Bombs explosions all over. People were sheltered in the basements which were fire-resistant. All the other basements where people lived previously, were burned to the ground, including our basement. Luckily, I took out my medical diploma in time and kept it with me in my pocket.

We were sitting in the nearby basement of Pelta, which was fire-resistant. Bombs were falling on the top of us. Buildings which were once houses where people lived were now burned-out ruins. When the bombs fell, the temporary loss of consciousness known to us by previous experiences returned.

Many escaped to the nearby village. Some were shot on the roads. The strong brick house of the pharmacist Press was burned, as were all the other houses. Only the basement which was fire-resistant remained. We took some textile packages with us and buried them in the underground of the yard belonging to Levit. My brother Moritz returned to the house of my cousin which was considered more safe than the basements in the city.

My parents and myself returned to Levit's house. Alas! Our room was occupied by the married daughter of Levit and her family. I explained to them that this room belonged to us. We rented it long ago and paid in advance. Even at the present time, when almost all the houses were destroyed, she had no right to occupy our room, she could live with her mother. Justice should be observed all the time and no force should be used. After a while, she agreed and moved to live with her mother. I was satisfied.

Rumors were spreading that the Red Army repelled the Germans, who were withdrawing. It looked this way because no planes were seen for the last few hours. But these were false rumors and false hopes. The air raids returned with a devastating force. We couldn't escape to the fireproof basement because the attack was so sudden and unexpected.

All of us fell on the floor and waited for the onslaught of the German planes. We heard the terrible sounds. We lay down on the floor. Maybe this was the end. The explosions were more intense than ever before. Levit's son-in-law was an orthodox, very religious Jew. I heard his prayers and his begging God for salvation. "Almighty God, He who keeps guard over Israel, protect the remnants of Israel." "Hear O' Israel. God is our God and His name is One." "He who keeps guard over his people, protect the remnants of His people, and see to it that they should not perish. He who keeps guard over the sanctified people, protect the remnants of the sanctified Nation and see they should not perish." Those words, usually recited by the religious Jews every morning, relaxed us and gave us hope to overcome and to survive.

Friday, June 27, 1941, 6th day of the war. MIRACLE #1.

Continuous air raids. They had started already at 3 A.M., which was unusual by itself. Normally, the air raid started about 7 A.M. This was a bad omen.

The Year 1941

We jumped out of our beds and ran for shelter, to the basement of Pelta. We found many neighbors already there seeking protection. Bombs were falling nearby. Terrible explosions! Here, another factor was added. Murderous artillery bombardment of heavy caliber. It was a sign that the Germans were not far away from the city. Some shells were falling nearby. We were afraid of a direct hit. Some fragments hit the door and the walls of the basement. We were in big danger. Women and children cried. All of us trembled from fear.

Russian soldiers came in to our shelter to protect themselves from the terrible shelling. After a while they left.

My poor mother was covered with a cold sweat. Again, terrible bombardment! A bomb fell near the basement. A horrible explosion was heard. A big hole was formed in the ground, no more than three yards from our shelter and five yards in diameter.

The shooting stopped for a while. Somebody came in and asked me to go to a neighbor, who was heavily wounded. He was bleeding profusely. They could not stop the bleeding. I left the basement, went to the injured and stopped the bleeding. I also cleaned the wound and bandaged it.

On my way back to the basement, I met my mother, who wanted to return to our room, at Levit's house. I went with her and tried to get some food for my mother. I was lucky. I got a pint of milk. My mother refused to drink it. She took instead her prayer book and started to beseech God that the destruction should cease. I lay down on the sofa to rest a little because I was very tired, and fell asleep shortly thereafter. Somebody touched me. My mother was standing near me asking me to bring water to my father, who was at Pelta's basement. I was very sleepy, I could not open my eyes. "Go, hurry up," mother urged me, "your father is very thirsty, get up!"

I got up, took with me a jar of water to bring it to my father. It was a very short distance away. Maybe 50 yards. All of a sudden, air raid again. I was near Pelta's basement and quickly jumped in and handed the water over to my father.

Then we heard voices saying that the house of Levit, where my mother was sitting with the prayer book in her hand, and where I was sleeping a minute ago, had received a direct hit from a bomb thrown by a German pilot. Terrible explosion! The house was on fire. I rushed out from the basement and didn't care about the shells, and the bombs. I ran as fast as possible to the burning house, where my mother was. It was impossible to go into the burning house. Explosions after explosions!

I lay down on the ground and waited till the shelling would stop. Shortly the air raid stopped. The house was on fire and collapsed. Soon my father came and my brother Moritz joined us. We tried to throw the burning pieces away. I showed them the exact spot where she was sitting. We worked feverishly.

After a while, we noticed her hand with her golden ring on it under the debris. Alas, we pulled out the hand and recognized also my mother's dress. I pulled further. No use, she was already dead. Many German planes in the sky and another air raid. We hid under the fallen bricks. In a short time the house was completely burned.

My mother! My lovely mother is dead!

Even now, over thirty years later, I remember the scene very vividly. By her death she saved my life. I could have been there in the burning house if she didn't send me out, by some mysterious feeling of a mother, and urged me to bring the water to my father. *This was miracle #1.*

Oh! How my heart was palpitating. I felt body contractions and twitchings around my eyes and face. I was shivering and trembling from the sudden shock and tragedy. I looked at the burning house, the devastation all around, and heard voices.

"Where is my father?"

"Did you see my mother?"

"Help, help, my only child was killed."

Mrs. Levitt was killed also. The old man, her husband, stood near his ruined house, deploring and mourning the death of his wife. Braine was sitting in one of the rooms holding a two-year-old child on her lap. The child was killed and the mother was spared, and remained alive. Again an air raid. People escaped in all directions. Everyone tried to hide as best as he could. I stood near the house, near the place where my mother was killed. I didn't care anymore.

More explosions around. Bombs were falling. But I remained standing like fixed to the place.

Finally, my father came and forced me to leave the place. I started to run away from this G-d forsaken street. Artillery shells all around. The earth was trembling. Fragments of bricks were falling. Real hell on earth.

I didn't see anything. I didn't hear anything. I didn't care, and continued to run. Amazing; so much destruction, devastation! So many corpses lying! It seemed that the sun was dimmed by the devastating dust emanating from the wrecked city. Nothing happened to me. I still had my legs, carrying me across the demolished city, and was running like an object flown, moved and transported by a windstorm. After awhile I found myself in the spacious yard of my cousin's house. All quiet. People were in the basements. They were afraid to go out. I sat on one of the steps of the house, contemplating, considering and mainly brooding.

Finally Mr. Lemon came out, a relative of my cousin who knew me from my studies in Wilna. He looked at my stunned face, my disheveled hair, and asked me what happened.

At the beginning, I was not able to talk, I was in a state of shock. I felt that I was all frozen inside. He looked, sat down near me. He understood that something awful had happened. He didn't want to disturb the silence.

Finally, I told him that my mother was killed. He uttered a sound like grieving or sobbing and disappeared. He couldn't control himself. People all around expressed their compassion and sympathy. I was indifferent. Air raids again interrupted by artillery shelling. People escaped to the basement. I remained sitting. It was the same to me whether I'd live or die. A deep despair and feeling of forlornness engulfed me.

Toward the evening, the air raids stopped. All quiet again. I returned to the basement of Pelta, where my father and brother were supposed to be. I entered inside the basement. Many were lying, surrounded by bundles and packages, sad and forlorn. I asked where my father was.

All of a sudden, I heard voices all around me.

Miracle #7. The Krematoria

"Mr. Harsaw, here is your son."

"He is alive."

My father and brother greeted me with open arms. They didn't see me all day long. I disappeared during the air raid and they assumed that I was hit by a bullet or splinter and was no more alive. Some even told them that I was lying on the street dead. Naturally they were very glad to see me alive. In spite of the terrible tragedy, they were for the moment overjoyed. I felt tears overflowing my face, and was crying. This was the first time in my life that I was shedding tears. During all the devastation and sufferings endured in the ghettos, concentration camps I never wept, nor uttered even a whimper. Evidently I came out of the shock in which I had been submerged all day long.

My father told me of the enormous number of people killed. It was impossible to remain in the city, which was not a city anymore, but a pile of broken bricks, iron and cement. Many escaped to the neighboring villages. We decided to talk it over with our cousin. Maybe he'll go too. We arrived in the evening to his house. He said that at the beginning he wanted to leave the city. But many returned, stating that the roads were full with retreating Russian soldiers. They shot everybody on sight, because German parachutists dressed in civilian cloth were dropped in our neighborhood. It was very dangerous to try to reach the villages.

We left my cousin to return to the basement of Pelta in order to spend the rest of the night there.

On the way back, Russian soldiers stopped us, asking for documents. They let us go. Every few steps we were searched. It was really very dangerous. One of the soldiers pulled his gun and wanted to shoot us. "Don't shoot," I yelled at him, showing him our documents. He looked over our bundles and let us go. Luckily we knew Russian and were able to explain. Otherwise we would have been finished. Life or death depended on very small, unimportant items.

Finally we reached our destination. We got back our corner and spent the night in the basement. All quiet, dark. People exhausted, hungry and tired lay motionless around.

Saturday, June 28, 1941, seventh day of the war.

Calm on the horizon. The air raids stopped. From time to time we still heard some shelling of the guns in the distance. How sweet is the relative quietness! How relaxing to the nerves was the temporary lull!

I tried to go out from the basement and get a little fresh air. By doing so I stepped over sleeping people lying on the floor between our corner and the exit. I tried not to wake up anybody, not to disturb those unfortunate human beings who suffered so much in the last week, completely unnecessarily and innocently, just as the war itself was unnecessary and needless. Maybe they dreamed of peace and quiet and their hearts were filled with the holy joy of stillness. Who was I to alarm them and to wake them up to the reality of our present life. To my surprise, many other people were, already, outside. Everybody was agitated by the news that a bomb fell on the basement of Mr. Margulies, which was considered to be one of the best in the city. A direct hit, one hundred and seventy people lost their lives in this basement alone. Some were killed by the fragments of the bomb, by explosions, and some were choked inside, because the exit was blocked by thousands of bricks and debris which obstructed and locked the door. All of the day was quiet.

In the evening we heard again artillery shells. The shooting intensified all night long, the artillery was very active. Shells and explosions without any stop.

We were lying in the basement fearful of a direct hit, which would make an end to our sufferings. Still we clinged to life, at least to see what will happen later. It is superfluous to say that no one was able to sleep. We were agitated, restless, heads down, and waited for the unknown. Are we going to live or die? Will we be able to get out healthy? This was the question.

CHAPTER II

Strong German advance deep into Russia. Life under German occupation.

THE EIGHTH DAY OF WAR. 6/29/41. SUNDAY. THE GERMANS ENTER THE DESTROYED CITY OF WOLKOWYSK. THE GERMAN THREE-PRONGED ATTACK. TERROR IN THE OCCUPIED TERRITORIES. BRAINE'S HOUSE. INJECTIONS OF NARCOTICS TO ALLEVIATE PAIN. PROPHETIC FORESIGHT OF THE FUTURE TO COME. THE PRAYERS FOR THE DEPARTED. THE GESTAPO IN THE HOSPITAL. FORMATION OF A "JUDENRAT." THE ROAD TO ROZANA. ISABELIN, PODOROSK. DR. SHULMAN AND HIS BEAUTIFUL WIFE. THE ENORMOUS DESTRUCTION OF PROPERTY, AMMUNITION AND LIVES. WAS THE SUDDEN GERMAN ATTACK UNEXPECTED AND UNKNOWN TO STALIN? WHAT WERE THE REASONS THAT THE RUSSIANS DID NOT RESIST THE GERMAN ONSLAUGHT RIGHT FROM THE BEGINNING?

Sunday June 29, 1941. One week after the start of the war.

All night long, I was pondering over our misfortune and misery. I was meditating, pondering, reflecting over and over again about the sudden change in my life. What to do? How to support my family? After all, I was the older one and a doctor by profession. My father was old. He could not accomplish much, under such terrible conditions.

Through the small window of the basement, the first light of the day started to penetrate and to illuminate and brighten first the places near the window and then the more distant points.

A few hours passed. Suddenly, the people near the window informed us that they noticed German soldiers in the city. What was going to happen now? Everybody was asking this question, not with their mouths but with their eyes. Exhausted, depressed and ready for the worse. Some children started to cry. They were hungry and thirsty.

German soldiers entered our yard. They were looking for something. Quiet in the basement. Nobody dared to talk, to move, in order not to call the attention of the soldiers. A moment later, we noticed soldiers' legs and boots stopping near the window. A German was standing nearby, bending and trying to pull out a hand grenade and to toss it into our basement. The women nearby called out in desperation that in the basement were not Russians, but civilians, mostly women and children. The soldier took a good look, put the grenade back and departed.

The Russians' resistance ceased and the Germans entered the city of Wolkowysk. This was Sunday, on the eight day of the war. It was worthwhile to underscore that the Germans had occupied Minsk, the capital of White Russia, a few hundred miles east of us, already on the fifth day of the war. Evidently the Russians put up a resistance in and around Wolkowysk. So the Germans went all around, leaving our city for later.

At this instant, the German vanguard advanced east of Minsk, towards Smolensk, hundreds of miles east of us. This was the *Central German Army* under the leadership of Von Bock and consisted of 50 divisions. Besides this central thrust in the direction of Moscow, there was a *Northern army* under Von Loeb, which consisted of 29 divisions and which advanced in the direction north, towards Leningrad (Petersburg). Another army, the *Southern*, was under the direction of Von Rundstedt, and consisted of 41 divisions, which advanced through southern Poland towards Stalingrad and the Caucasus. In all, considering the reserve divisions and the help they received from Finland, Romania and Hungary, the German strength was composed of 174 divisions. Taking in consideration the armored, mechanized and motorized divisions, it constituted an enormous, huge monstrosity which frightened all the civilized world.

We returned to the burned house of Levit, where my mother was killed by a bomb thrown by a German pilot. We took the remains of my mother to the cemetery for burial. The soil was tough. We worked with almost no equipment, and were helped by another man who evidently knew a little more about digging graves. After laboring for many hours, we succeeded in excavating a grave. We lowered the remains, wrapped in a white sheet, and covered the grave with sand mixed with commingled silica. We put up a temporary sign.

My brother and I recited the Kadish prayer for the departed. This was our first prayer at the grave of our mother, who was killed by the hands of a devil with a human face. We left the cemetery and felt that this was only the beginning of German crimes to follow.

As we can see, Wolkowysk was in a pocket, completely encircled by the German thrust, from Bialystok to Minsk. Wolkowysk was completely destroyed by the frequent air attacks and continuous artillery shelling. Only small parts of the city remained, namely the railroad street, starting from the house of Dr. Kaufman up to the railroad station, and part of Karczyzna section on the other end of the city, including the house of my cousin.

Many of the inhabitants were killed, many left the city. The remainder slept on the streets or in ruined houses. Almost all the food was destroyed. People went around hungry, exhausted and sick.

Some chickens ran around, their owners absent. They were quickly caught. It was unpleasant to see how respected citizens of a month before were running after the poultry with wild eyes trying to catch them. I didn't like these ugly scenes nor the wild eyes and tried to look the other way.

The house of Braine was almost the only house in the center which remained intact. Braine was not home. She had escaped to a nearby village. She was afraid to stay in her house, which was isolated and near the river.

We entered the house, which served us as a temporary shelter, and found there some food, a little flour, and some sugar. There were still many pillows and blankets and we were able to rest our tired bones, muscles and ligaments.

Old Levit was sitting nearby, nibbling a small morsel of bread which he saved for himself in case of emergency. He was 105 years old, a very decent and religious man. He saw a younger person looking upon him with eagerness and desire.

"Take the bread," he said. "You are hungry and young. I am old and don't need much." He handed over the bread, which the young man grabbed and swallowed in a second. Moritz and myself left the house to go to the center of the city to see what was going on there.

As soon as we reached Szeroka Street, we were stopped by a German and ordered to collect all the bricks and debris from the center of the street and put them on the side. We worked very hard. The German stopped many others and ordered them to do the same. We all were very exhausted, hungry and tired from the events of the last week.

I looked at my brother who was very pale and could hardly stand on his feet. "Let's escape," I said, "wait for the right moment." The German was busy arresting other people. "Let's run," I repeated. Moritz and I cleared out. We were lucky and glad this time. Later the German looked for us, but he couldn't find us.

The soldiers of the super-race started to rob the people of all the belongings they could lay their hands on, beating their victims mercilessly. We escaped to the house of Braine, which was isolated. Our father was there, pale, tired and very despondent. He lost everything he had. Mother was killed. My father started to ponder about the death of our mother. How was it possible that such a decent, pious woman should meet such a terrible fate? "It is a bad omen," he said. "I am positively sure about it," he continued. "She was taken away because a more terrible fate was in store for us. She was taken away in order to spare her further sufferings and to avoid the terrible destiny awaiting us. I am certain that we were all doomed to an awful extinction."

STRONG GERMAN ADVANCE DEEP INTO RUSSIA

This prophetic foresight was a divine revelation which foretold the future exactly as it happened. Six million Jews suffered abuses in the ghettos, sustained the most hideous atrocities. Many died of beatings, physical and mental persecutions, malnutrition, diseases. Many committed suicide. Millions were transported in cattle trains, under the most humiliating conditions, to the gas chambers, where they perished. My mother was spared all this, which in my opinion constituted a reward for her extraordinary decency and piousness. She was assisted and aided by a supernatural ruler.

My father became silent and I was sitting near the table, on which many bundles and packages were lying. I was thinking about our future. If my father's predictions came true then life was not worth living.

All of a sudden, I heard my brother's voice. "Watch out!" I turned my head and saw a young thin German soldier, keeping his revolver near my neck. I raised my arms and said that I was a civilian. He looked at me and the bundles, the disorder all around, and left.

Braine returned to her home. Her little boy was killed in the house of Levit. Her husband fractured his leg, when he tried to extinguish the fire caused by German incendiary bombs. He worked for the fire department as a foreman of the fire fighters. He was a courageous young man, who did his best to quench and extinguish the devastating fires. Took active charge in the most dangerous situations and suffered the consequences. His leg had to be amputated because of a severe infection and incipient gangrene. Now he returned home from the hospital and suffered excruciating pains in the amputated leg. Braine received morphine and needles from the hospital to administer to her husband. I taught her how to do it. The pain stopped for a few hours and then it returned again. He suffered enormously. He was one of the first victims of German bestiality.

"Braine" was a very good wife and very intelligent. She learned very quickly, how to sterilize the needle and to inject. She was a big help in those trying days. Later Braine's neighbor returned from the village. We had to move out, and went to our cousin, whose house in Karczyzna remained intact, and took with us our few belongings packed in bundles. Everyone of us carried a bundle. My father, my brother and myself. We took different routes. I walked along the river and didn't stop on my way. People detained me, trying to find out more news. But I was in a hurry to reach my cousin's house. Finally I arrived. Nothing happened to me. But where is my father and Moritz? I waited. They should have been here already. Something occurred on the way. I was very restless.

Finally, I saw them coming. The size of the packages that they carried became small. They told me that they were stopped on the way by Germans. My father was beaten up severely and the most valuable items were robbed. They ordered my brother Moritz to kneel and commanded him to stretch his neck out. A German pulled out a big knife, ready to kill. They expected my father and brother to beg for mercy. To their astonishment and bewilderment nobody begged them for clemency. They saw two people completely indifferent to their fate. My brother was ordered again to remain on his knees and to bend his head and they cut out a part of his hair, making a form of a large cross over his scalp. He took off his cap and showed me the cross excised in the middle of his head. This was one of the dogmas of National Socialism.

We realized the danger that we were in, and discussed that evening our circumstances with my cousin. He was in a much better condition. He had his own home. All the family remained undamaged. He even possessed almost all of his belongings. Thank God for that.

People were milling around his house and yard, dejected, depressed and downhearted. They had lost everything they had. No home, no food, many had members of their family missing. They were worse off than animals in the forest or birds in the sky, who had their usual place of abode and their natural food. So much misery had the Germans brought in, already, to our region.

The tragedy of the people was so deep that they stopped crying and lamenting. They had a certain expression on their faces that told the uninitiated their grief, misfortune and catastrophe.

Ten men were called into one of the rooms to pray. We all recited the prayer over the departed (Kaddish). "Magnified and sanctified be his Name, in the world which He created. May He establish his Kingdom in our life time and in our days, speedily and in the fastest possible way . . ."

"Blessed, praised, glorified, exalted, honored, adored, and lauded be the Name of the Holy One, blessed be he forever. May He deliver abundant peace from heaven to this earth and life for us . . ."

"Oh G-d have mercy on us, because our sufferings reached the impossible. Help us, because we feel very unhappy. Heal us, O G-d, because our bones, flesh, souls are enormously weak, sick and disturbed. Have pity on us and don't deliver us into the hands of the Nazis . . ."

That night we slept in the house of our cousin naturally, on the floor. No other space was available. We were grateful for that.

In the morning, after the usual prayer and Kaddish for the departed, I went to the hospital. The road was scattered with broken tanks, pieces of artillery, shells of all kind. Many corpses were visible. Enormous devastation and ruin all around.

I reached the hospital. The walls were covered with bullet holes. Many sick people lying in beds and on the floor, without much hope to sustain life. Scarcity of medicine and food contributed to the unusual mortality. We discussed the events of the last week.

A Red Cross flag was over the hospital clearly visible to German aviators. In spite of this international sign of neutrality, compassion, pity, no military object, the pilots seemed to be attracted to, rather than diverted from the hospital grounds. They returned time and time again, spreading death and destruction. Many were killed.

All the family of the hospital administrator, including his father, brother, sisters, who looked for shelter in the hospital, were killed by a bomb which exploded in one of the hospital rooms. Only the administrator himself, Mr. Goscinski, who happened to be in another part of the hospital, remained alive. He alone from a large family!

The killed were buried in a common grave, made out of one of the excavations, caused by the falling bombs. The doctors of the hospital met to discuss how to administer help to the needed with our available meager means. Distribution of assignments. I volunteered to work at night, because I had no place to go.
My first night duty at the hospital.
A big building with many rooms which contained numerous sick and injured people, some lying on beds, some on the floor. Dark all over. No electricity. No light available. I sat on one of the benches, glad of having a place to sit.

The injured cried out for help. They complained of enormous pains and sufferings. I administered analgesics, cleaned and bandaged the wounds, in the best way I could. The sick moaned, wailed, mumbled while they were submerged in fantastic dreams and hallucinations.

The darkness was so pitch-black and dense that it seemed to me that I was able to touch it. Real Egyptian darkness. In the meantime, the sobbing, bawling, crying, wailing, hallucinating continued and intensified during the night. Hell, horror, torment in the air. Real purgatory!

I felt very tired, exhausted and dizzy, and sat down to rest a little. No more medicine nor bandages were available. I dozed off and slowly fell in the arms of Morpheus, the Greek God of dreams, son of Hypnos. The sleep was restless. I woke up every 10-15 minutes.

Late at night a man came in, weak, very debilitated, hardly able to stand on his feet. He had returned from a nearby village and was able to pass unnoticed the German guards. He asked me for permission to spend the night at the hospital. I told him that he might stay here for the night. He was lucky to be able to find a place on the floor.

In the morning, all the other doctors arrived and helped as much as they could. We tried to make a little order, to clean up the place. The dead were removed and buried in the hospital grounds.

At noon, Mr. Beilic was brought in with very bad abdominal wounds. He had been shot by a German, and told us that accidentally he had passed by near the place where the City Hall building was standing. A picture of Stalin was supported on a large stone of the destroyed building. The German evidently suspected Mr. Beilic of having put the picture on the stone. Without asking any questions, he pulled out his gun and shot him five times. Mr. Beilic was still alive, but it was clear that his condition was deteriorating from minute to minute.

We rushed him to the operating table. His abdomen was opened. His intestine, liver, spleen were badly injured. The peritoneum was torn and infected. We did the best to repair the tissue, but we had almost no hope to keep him alive. He died shortly thereafter. Many of the hospital personnel envied him when he died. At least he didn't have to suffer anymore.

Next morning, the *Gestapo* arrived. A young German walked in dressed in Gestapo uniform. Cockiness, impertinence, rudeness were visible on his face, manifested by his behavior and movements. His eyes were green, glittering with hate and arrogance. A real member of the super-race.

"The Director should come out right away," he yelled.

Dr. Weinberg moved forward. "You are from now on the Judenälteste [chief of the community]. You have to assemble ten other members. You and the others will be responsible for everything. Any infraction of my orders will be punishable by death." He left, without saying good by. Nobody expected any such amenities from the Eherenvolk. We were glad that he left.

Dr. Weinberg was very frightened of all the responsibilities. We heard previously of the German atrocities in the occupied Polish territories, which were held by the Germans since 1939. The truth was that we didn't believe in the stories and thought them to be exaggerated. How was it possible that a civilized nation should commit so many crimes and under the direction and management of a freely elected Government? It must be propaganda. Now we saw the Super-race with out own eyes and felt it on our own skin, deep in our bones. Evil came into our midst. As we'll see later, the atrocities we heard previously were nothing, a children's play, in comparison to the realities.

Dr. Weinberg was depressed and he asked me to attend one of his own private patients in the city, a Polish woman. I had to administer her an injection. I went to the patient's house, examined her. Gave her medication and administered the required injection. I noticed many loaves of bread on one of the tables. My family was starving. She asked me what was my fee. I said no fee, just give me one or two loaves of bread. She gladly consented. I took the bread, packed it in a paper and rushed home. I was overjoyed and approached my father and brother, who were sitting hungry, pale, not knowing what to do. I handed them over the bread. They were elated, very happy. Death by starvation was postponed for the time being.

I returned to the hospital. From time to time we were getting a little soup and some potatoes. I discovered the place where the potatoes were kept and, after asking permission, brought some home to my family. My brother loved it.

I was the only doctor on night duties. None of the other doctors wanted to work at night. Dr. Kaufman, Dr. Welvelski, even Dr. Weinberg were relatively well off. Some still had their own homes and their belongings. I was in a very desperate situation. My family had no place to be, and we did not know what next day would bring.

We decided to go to Rozana our birth place, about 32-35 miles from Wolkowysk. My brother Mendel was already there. Father would remain temporarily in the house of my cousin. He still had some of the textile merchandise, which was buried in the yard on the first day of the war. He had enough for himself for a long time. He had to join us later. We took farewell from our father, from all our friends, and left.

We had to make this journey by foot. This was on a Sunday morning, two weeks afrer the hostilities started, about the beginning of July. We were going first in the direction of Isabelin, a small village about 10 km. from Wolkowysk, and were trying to avoid the German garrisons. It was early in the morning. Soon we reached the nearby hill which took us to the forest.

I knew this road very well because I used to make excursions on my bicycle there into the neighboring villages in the more happy prewar days. I used to enjoy those trips, traveling through forests and fields.

How different this same road to Isabelin looked now! The same road, the same forest. But at every few steps Russian corpses were lying. Still in their uniforms, lying in the middle of the road, or on the sides. Some were killed at the entrances of the forest. Most of them were young. So many lives lost. Many broken tanks, artillery pieces, mortars, automatic weapons. Some were still in good condition and could be used.

We continued to walk. All the same, hundreds of Russians killed. Huge numbers of all kinds of weapons left. After a few hours we reached *Isabelin*. The village was destroyed only on the periphery. The center was almost intact. We sat down on one of the benches to rest. We were very tired. My brother was thirsty. But he couldn't get any water. The people were behind closed doors, very much frightened. They would not let anyone inside.

We continued on our way, towards *Podorosk*, another village, slightly more populated. We took a side road, in order to avoid the Germans. We walked, approximately 6 km. per hour. I was in front. About 20 yards behind me walked my brother Moritz. We were hungry, thirsty, exhausted. But we continued to poke along.

The Russians lost so much ammunition, war material and human lives that it was unbelievable. I figured, if all the front, all along the battle line, from the Baltic till the Black sea, was covered with as many killed Russians soldiers and lost ammunition, artillery pieces, tanks, etc. as we had encountered on our way from Wolkowysk to Rozana, then my impression was that all the Russian army was vanquished and the road to German victory was clear. The unexpected Nazi attack spelled calamity for the Russians.

Many history books described that Stalin did not know about the German preparations and the following invasion. In my opinion, this was a wrong assumption. Stalin knew everything. He organized a net of spies all over the world. He knew exactly what was going on in London, New York, Berlin and all the other capitals of the world. American and English high military officials often wondered of the great knowledge that Stalin possessed about the American and English business ideas and war preparations. His net of intelligence, helped by communist sympathizers, penetrated all the departments of the Allies. It was in scope, magnitude, second to none. Naturally he had also his spies in the main German cities. He knew everything that was going on the other side of the border. Every movement, every division was known to him, way before.

Stalin was also informed by Churchill, by Roosevelt, and by many others, about the impending Nazi attack.

On 6/14/41, a German soldier escaped to the Russian side and told them that he was a communist, his father was a communist, and he would like to join the Soviets. He was afraid of being courtmartialed because he hit a German officer when he was drunk. He said that everybody in his company knew that the invasion would start on 6/22/1941 at about 4 A.M. This was true because the invasion started exactly at that time. It was incomprehensible that Stalin did not know what was happening. In 1942 Stalin told Churchill that he didn't need any warnings. He knew war would come, but he thought he might gain another six months, or so.

The truth was that Stalin was very much afraid of Hitler. He delivered to the Germans grain, oil and all kinds of material. He wanted to avoid any provocation.

Stalin went to the extreme. He ordered not to fight even when the Germans passed the border, destroyed Russian air planes on the ground, attacked cities, straffing many combatants and civilians. Bialystok, Minsk, Wolkowysk and many other cities, were ablaze, and the order from Moscow was to wait and *not* to shoot. Stalin knew the truth but suppressed it, in order not to provoke Hitler. Even Stalin could not comprehend the sudden attack, at a time when he was ready to deliver to Hitler everything without a war. Even dictators accustomed to cruelty were not able to understand the destructive mentality of the Nazi chief. Hitler wanted only one thing, namely to destroy Russia completely.

This was a characteristic trait of most dictators. Even Mussolini, who was an angel in comparison to Hitler, craved for war.

But Stalin went too far this time. He permitted the sudden German onslaught, he forbade his generals to resist and counterattack. He kept the general staff in the dark, hoping that Hitler would change his mind in the last minute.

The preparedness of the Red Army was not complete, but

Strong German Advance Deep into Russia

had the army known what Stalin knew and resisted the Germans, the attackers would not have been able to break through the frontier defenses so easily. The Russian western air force was almost completely destroyed; 1200 planes were lost the first day, 800 on the ground alone, because the flying corps were assured that no invasion will take place.

Rumors were circulating at that time that even in the first hours of fighting Stalin waited to hear from Hitler that the hostilities had ceased and that the attack was a mistake. Hundreds of thousands of Russian soldiers were encircled by an iron grip, surrendered to the Germans. A terrible confusion dominated the front. Russian troops were in full retreat. Many towns were in flames, people were being killed in the thousands, and Timoshenko, in the name of Stalin, ordered at that very moment *not* to open any fire on the Germans.

Stalin was asked later to explain the initial calamity. He gave two reasons. 1.) Sudden surprise, which was unexpected. 2.) A few mistakes on the Soviet side. He never explained what were those mistakes.

The most cardinal mistake he made was not to disclose to his subordinates, especially to the military, exactly what he knew. This mistake of Stalin, to trust Hitler, cost the Red Army hundreds of thousands of casualties. Another one would have been tried for treason. All elements of betrayal and incompetence were there. But no, not Stalin.

"Quod licet Yovem no licet bovem," as the old Romans said. What I wanted to bring out here is that Stalin knew exactly what was going on. But the Hitlerphobia horrified him to such a degree that he lost contact with reality. He was paralyzed. He waited eleven days, till 7/3/1941, till he was in a condition to talk to the people. Molotov spoke a few hours after the attack.

It was generally assumed that Stalin was an intelligent person and possessed high abilities to organize different structures in many fields of military as well as civilian projects. But Hitler terrified him to a point of anxiety and panic. He saw the smashing German victories in France, Holland, Norway and later in the Balkans, Greece and Yugoslavia. Although he had a strong war machinery, he realized that it took him a long time to subdue the small Finland. He conceived also that after the purges, forced Kolkhonizations, (collective farm in the Soviet Union), the starvation of millions of peasants, the people in Russia did not love him, some even hated him, and his regime was kept in power by terror enforced by the NKVD. This internal unrest was one of the reasons that he was not able to achieve a quick victory over the Finns, as expected. Taking in consideration the above factors, like incomplete preparedness of the Red Army, internal unrest, people's coolness, antagonism and often enmity and hatred towards Stalin and the NKVD, coupled with invincibility of the German army, the brilliant successes achieved in 1940 and spring of 1941, the world at large, including the military experts, assumed with all likelihood that the war will be practically finished in six weeks. No wonder that Stalin was scared to death, and stunned and petrified when his endeavor to stop the invasion became ineffective and useless.

But the world, the experts, even Stalin failed to take into consideration one trait of Hitler's personality, namely his destructive mind, megalomania, and the schizophrenic mentality which all pointed towards unparalleled cruelty. At the beginning, the freshly occupied countries of White Russia, Ukraine, and the Baltic states greeted Hitler as a savior with cries of joy. Instead of treating the people in a nice way and promising them freedom, a better life and justice, Hitler started to apply terror. People, completely innocent without any reason, were murdered in the thousands. Special squads followed the army and spread death, devastation, among the civilians.

Shocked and humiliated, the people realized that the Nazi cruelties surpassed any ruthlessness seen before, and that life under Stalin was still better than under Hitler, who treated them like subhumans. Then and only then, the people stood up united and resolute against the aggressor. The Red Army and Navy and the whole Soviet people fought for every inch of Russian soil to the last drop of their blood. The Germans found out very soon that this was not the same Russian soldiers who fought Finland. This was not an ordinary war but a struggle for life and death.

Finally, in the afternoon we reached *Podorosk*. On the periphery of the village we noticed a Russian tank and an artillery piece. They were not destroyed but abandoned. So much demolition. Peasants were milling around just as before. Somebody told us that in the village was a doctor from Brest-Litovsk. His name was Dr. Schulman. I reminded myself that I studied medicine in Italy with someone from Brest whose name was Schulman. We started, also, the Polish "nostrification" together in Vilna. "Nostrification" in Poland meant complete reexamination of medical subjects for those who studied abroad. If this was the same Dr. Schulman, I knew him well, we were good friends. He was a decent, honest, hard-working fellow who used to smoke a lot. A real chain smoker.

After finding his address, we entered the house. Yes! This was the same Dr. Schulman, my good friend of many years. He had not changed much. The same fellow. He recognized me right away, and greeted me wholeheartedly. He asked me what I was doing in such a little village. I told him everything. He related to me also his story, that he had worked for a long time in one of the best hospitals in Brest, and then he was mandated to Podorosk by the Soviet authorities. He was the only doctor of all the surrounding villages. He had been working here for a few months. It was a very quiet useful life and the people respected him very highly. He did everything by himself. Of necessity he even operated. Spinal taps were a daily occurrence. He introduced us to his wife, who had joined him a few weeks ago and then couldn't return to Brest because of the outbreak of hostilities. She was a young pleasant woman of about 24 years old, very pretty. I didn't know about Brest, but she was, definitely, the prettiest in Podorosk. She made an impression of a very decent, respected human being. A real asset to any doctor. She invited us to the livingroom and prepared for us a nice meal. We discussed our new situation, but we really didn't know what it was going to be. The best thing was to wait and see.

My brother and I were very tired from walking so many hours and we decided to spend the night at the house of Dr. Schulman. Mrs. Schulman prepared for us a nice place to sleep and we went to rest.

We got up early in the morning to continue on our journey. Our direction was towards Rozana, or rather to the nearby village, Old Konstantinova, where we had relatives of my mother.

At the beginning our pilgrimage was nice and pleasant. We were rested, fed, full of energy, and the air was mild, fresh imbued with summer aromas. But soon it became hot and we became again tired, thirsty and hungry. We rested a little and saw bushes of blueberries. We started to collect them and eat, which satiated our thirst and hunger. We felt again cheerful and it seemed to us like being in the desert and being supplied with the "MANNA" (the Bible food provided to the Israelites in the desert).

We met Germans repairing their cars in the middle of the road. They were busy, also, stopping passersby and robbing them of all their belongings. We were happy, because we had no packages, no bundles. They looked at us. Didn't say anything. They let us pass.

We roamed through forests and fields. From time to time we saw a corpse lying, but their number was much less. Evidently not much fighting went on there. Scattered tanks, automatic weapons, artillery shells were scattered all over. We passed many small villages and individual farms, and finally stopped to rest a little.

The villagers came near us and asked about the war and the happenings in Wolkowysk. We told them that the Germans were of another kind of species and that they should be careful and alert.

Moritz told them that I was a doctor of medicine from Wolkowysk. Before long I had many patients complaining of all kinds of diseases. I treated them and advised them how to use domestic remedies. In compensation, they offered bread, butter, milk, cheese. We were hungry no more. We didn't want to spend too much time in the small village and proceeded to our destination.

Far away we saw the periphery of the town Rozana. We went all around, because we did not want to enter into the city, in order to avoid the Germans.

Suddenly we noticed German air planes in the sky, flying in our direction. Remembering the time in Wolkowysk when the

German machinegunned the civilian population from their planes, we tried to hide in the bushes. They didn't notice us. We got up and started to walk again. Soon another group of planes. We fell to the ground, protected by trees and their branches. Apparently the cities and towns were watched better.

We proceeded towards Konstantinovo, reached the nearest hilltop and saw far away the little houses. Swiftly we moved in the direction of the village. We passed the fields which glittered different colors, depending on the seed-plant and the crops.

CHAPTER III

Fierce fighting east of the Berezina. Before and after the Ghetto. The theory of immortality of the soul.

FORMATION OF THE GHETTO, IN ROZANA. THE VILLAGE OF KONSTANTINOVA. STARVATION, CONGESTION, SICKNESSES. PROSECUTION. TERROR. MY MEDICAL OFFICE IN KONSTANTINOVO NEAR ROZANA. THE FAMILY POMERANIEC. MIRACLE #2. THE REASONS THAT THE RIGHTEOUS PEOPLE SUFFER AND THE BAD PROSPER. THE THEORY OF OUR PERPETUAL EXISTENCE. THE PHARMACIST. ROSH HASHANA. DAY OF ATONEMENT.

Finally, we entered *Kontantinovo*. The village was half burned, namely the half which was on the side of Rozana. To be exact, till the house of Mordehai Eshia. We drudged along the road because we were very fatigued. On both sides of our path were rows of houses. This was a small village which had the main walkway in the middle, on each side of which stretched rows of houses. The walkway was called the Concourse, the Avenue or the Boulevard. Behind the houses, there were small gardens with fruit trees like apples, pears, plums, cherries, etc. The garden soil was planted with different vegetables like tomatoes, cucumbers, potatoes, etc.

I knew the house of my relatives, Mr. and Mrs. Pomeraniec. I had been there a few times previously. I remembered the horses, cows, sheep and the nearby river where we used to bathe.

Each time, when I left, I went to the store and bought many gifts for everyone of the family. Mrs. Chaya Pomeraniec used to tell me, "Why do you have to spend money on so many gifts? I'll accept the cash."

Chaya Pomeraniec was a very intelligent, active woman. She had five boys and two girls. The oldest was Jacob, who left later for Argentina. Worked hard and died from complication of diabetes. The next one, Yitzhak, went to the Polish army when the war broke out. He was captured by the Germans and kept in a special camp. He tried to escape a few times but was caught and severely beaten up each time. Finally, he succeeded in his attempt and returned to his family, to Konstantinovo. The third boy was Yosie. He was drafted in the Polish army and never returned. Up to date we have no information about him. The next boy, Berl, was an apprentice to a baker, and escaped from the Nazis when they surrounded the village. He became a partisan and was killed in action. The youngest, Shlomo, escaped also to the forest, fought the Germans as a partisan, and lived to see the Russians returning back to the neighborhood. He volunteered in the army, took part in different battles against the Germans. Finally he fell in combat. The daughter Chasza, whom I described previously, was taken together with her parents to the Nazi concentration camp where they perished in the gas chambers.

This was the fate of one Jewish family. From nine members, only the youngest girl, Michle, remained alive, thanks to supernatural miracles. On the whole, the family Pomeraniec belonged to the more fortunate houses, because thousands of families were exterminated totally, without leaving any one alive. As a matter of fact, the vast majority of the families were obliterated from the earth without leaving any trace, nor any memorandum, that they ever existed.

We continued along the ascending street till we reached the house of Pomeraniec, which was on the left side of the main road. The house itself was erected on a higher platform. Behind the house were the stables for the horses, cows, sheep and also land for the different crops like grain, corn, wheat, potatoes and other vegetables.

Behind the building, there were large fields for seeding, planting, cultivating the agricultureal products. The soil was not good, too black, and did not produce much. The yield, the output, was very poor in comparison with other lands like the Ukraine or around Moscow.

This was also the reason why the peasants in that part of White Russia, were very poor, and they had to supplement their income with additional jobs. Mr. Pomeraniec used to take passengers from Rozana to Wolkowysk and back.

We went up the few steps leading to the interior of the house and soon found ourself in the large living room. Mr. and Mrs. Pomeraniec, Chasa, Michle and my brother Mendel came to greet us. We told them what happened to the city of Wolkowysk. After eating and resting a little, we informed our brother Mendel about the misfortune and the terrible calamity which befell us by the death of our beloved mother.

Mendel listened to everything. He didn't cry nor did he lament. He went on the side without uttering a word, evidently stunned and shocked. During all the afternoon and next morning we didn't hear a word uttered by him. Quiet in his grief and silent in his mourning. Light griefs are lamentable, but great ones are taciturn and silent.

Later we all recited the prayer for the departed, the "Kaddish." From then on, all three of us had to reiterate the prayer, three times daily for one year.

Thank G-d that we had a place to stay temporarily, but food was very scarce, because it was right before harvest. Mrs. Pomeraniec did everything possible to get for us something to eat. Every morning she used to disappear, and came back after a few hours with bread, some flour, grain or a few potatoes. She said that she was borrowing it from neighboring villagers with a promise to reimburse after harvest. She provided us even with meat—of sheep, mutton and lamb. How delicious were those meals, how tasty and delightful! I did not remember having ever savored such palatable food again.

In the meantime life was going on. Mendel helped on the field. Moritz and I in the house.

Rumors about the war were contradictory. News spread

over the German radio that Moscow was taken. I must admit that people believed it. On the way to Rozana, I saw so many Russian soldiers killed, so much ammunition destroyed or left intact, that everything was possible. If this was true all of us were lost.

A few days later, we heard the opposite news. It came from a more reliable source, from a peasant, who came back from as far as east of Minsk. He told us that he was forced to take his horse and travel eastwards. He transported different kinds of ammunition. When he reached the river Berezina, between Minsk and Smolensk, the Russians counterattacked. Many Germans were killed.

Although the peasant was a quiet fellow, compassionate, and never killed a fly, he was glad to see the members of the super-race stopped for the first time in their arrogance. The Germans escaped leaving many dead and losing a lot of ammunition.

It was unvelievable, but pleasant to the ear. The peasant swore with all the Holiness that it was true and that he saw it with his own eyes. These were the first days of July 1941. We heard through the grapevine about a speech delivered by Stalin. Finally he spoke.

"The enemy is cruel and merciless. . . . He wants to destroy the people and turn them into slaves for the German princes and barons. . . . A merciless struggle must be undertaken. . . . The scorched-earth policy must be applied. . . . Partisan units must be formed. . . . All the strength of the people must be used to smash the enemy. Onward to Victory!"

The speech helped to restore the confidence of the people in final victory.

In the meantime I had to watch over the horses grazing in the meadowland. Their front legs were hobbled. I used also to watch the garden for thieves and vagabonds. We used to keep guard also at night. From time to time I carried food to the field workers, who labored hard under the glowing heat of the sun with insufficient food.

The sun's rays are healthy for the skin and circulation if exposed in moderation. In excess they might cause a lot of complications, even cancer of the skin.

I remember from before the war how the father of Mrs. Pomeraniec was afflicted with an ulcer on his face, which didn't heal. The reason was that he had always been in the fields without any protection from the sun. I still remember his face with the ulcer, its edges and appearance. In retrospect, I am sure that this was a carcinoma.

Michle was very pretty and walked around the house in trousers, which at that time was unusual for a small village in White Russia. It fitted her well, she liked it. Next morning I went out on the field to help in the harvest, under the supervision of Mr. Pomeraniec. He was a nice fellow and a good farmer, but very nervous, eager to do the job fast, good, like farmers did. My brothers had never worked on farm fields and never took part in any harvest. Besides, he loved to show his superiority over city people. Mendel and Moritz had a hard time with him. He used to yell, command all day long. For me he had little respect, but after the first day on the field I refused to go out anymore.

In the meantime my first patient appeared, with a common cold. I examined the patient and prescribed the necessary medication. The pharmacy in Rozana (1 km. from our village) still had enough drugs and medicine. The patient took the medicine, which helped him a lot. No charge for the first patient.

Soon I had many other patients from the village. They paid with food.

I remember a patient, Beila, who had a bad abscess of the right breast. She came to me for treatment. I had no equipment, no books, nor medical material. I went to the pharmacist and got from him a few bandages and 3% peroxide. Then I cut out from the gauze a tampon, straightened out a thin metal hairpin, and sterilized everything by boiling in water. The patient suffered enormous pains from the abscess, complicated by fever and chills caused by pus formations. The abscess soon burst. A small hole was formed, through which very little pus oozed. I put the sterilized tampon into the little hole, and enlarged it. Then I pulled it out, cleaned it with peroxide and put a new tampon inside, for 24 hours.

My patient felt immediately relieved and the fever subsided. For the first time in many nights she was able to sleep. Next morning, I was received by the family of Beila, my patient, with open arms. They were very thankful. I repeated the same procedure and left it for overnight.

I used to come every day to treat her. The swelling of the breast slowly subsided, the wound, gradually, healed and my patient was completely recovered.

The news spread all over. Many sick people came to see me. I put on the outside door my medical shield, where had been written with large letters, "Dr. Harsaw."

The peasants used to bring me food like milk, bread, chicken, etc. Since I had no injectable material, I had to improvise. Necessity is the best teacher and is the mother of invention.

There were many cases of fever caused by pulmonary ailments. I used to take fresh 5 cc. of milk, sterilize it in a tube and inject the patient by intermuscular route. This was a kind of proteinotherapy and used to raise the defenses of the body. Probably it worked through the reticuloendothelial system. The results were fantastic.

I was glad to be able to help the people under those circumstances, and we had no more problems with food. Previously Mrs. Pomeraniec used to tell us that she was glad to provide us with food and shelter because of the good deeds of my mother.

They had always been very poor in spite of the hard work. Naturally, her main and only provider was her husband. Once, because of some anti-Semitic machinations, her husband was arrested. She needed a good lawyer and money to take him out on bail. The amount required was way beyond her means.

She went to my mother, told her the full story. My mother gave her all the money she needed, which was life-saving for her and all the family. Mr. Pomeraniec was freed within 24 hours. She never forgot that.

She told us the story years later, with tears running over her face. My mother was a good business woman. To her money didn't mean much, but only as a means of helping others in need. She helped the people with loans, gifts, and was known in the city as a person to whom the poor could turn for help. The loans given, naturally, were without interest.

The time between the First and Second World War presented itself as a very tough period, not only in Poland but also throughout the world. This was the time of the enormous inflation in Europe, especially in Germany, and of the depression in the U.S. of America.

Merchandise was bought on credit by means of checks or notes. When the payment day arrived and the money was not available, it spelled ruin to the business. Bankruptcy and default were widely spread. Although the amounts involved, in a small city, like Wolkowysk, were very small, they still had to be honored. In desperation, individuals used to come to my mother, asking for a loan. Many were helped by these loans. She was, already, so accustomed to distribute money that very often she failed to ask the name of the borrower. Other times, she was too sensitive to ask the name, because the borrower would feel like getting charity instead of a loan. How could it be otherwise?

It is very difficult to conceive today, in the after-Hitler Era, of these kinds of loans, without a signature and without any interest. But at that time, before the 2nd World War, these loans were widely spread, especially in the small towns and cities of Poland.

Although the number of my patients increased, I tried to get on the staff of the clinic of the town of Rozana, which was about 1 km. from the village of Konstantinovo. I was entitled to it because I was born in Rozana. But I had difficulties in being accepted. No vacancy. Maybe jealousy was also a fact. They waited for a meeting of the physicians.

In the meantime, I practiced in Konstantinovo and had many patients from the inhabitants of the village. Almost all of them trusted me. I had also patients from the neighboring villages. Meanwhile, I was informed that the brothers Frenkiel arrived at Rozana. They had a married brother there, who was well situated financially and had a good business before the outbreak of the war. I knew the brothers from Wolkowysk. They were related to us in some way. Their father was a decent man, had a factory in Bialystok. The competition was enormous and after a while he was forced to give it up. His mother and sister were in Wolkowysk, so he came to live there. One of his sons was a teacher, a nice-looking fellow but slightly self-conceited. He had also a weakness in one of his lower extremities and his gait wasn't straight, which probably caused him to be too sensitive. He wasn't married, still looking for the right girl, and moved around in the circle of the more educated class. His brother was a pharmacist and was known as a leftist sympathizer. When the two brothers arrived in Rozana, they asked me, through a messenger, to visit them.

Next Saturday evening I started to walk towards the city. I had reached already the bridge, which divided the town from the terrain of the village. Then, while looking from a distance, I recognized the first streets, which normally were full with people. This time the streets were completely empty, which caused my foreboding and apprehension and a forefeeling that something erratic and queer was going on in the city.

Without thinking much, I returned home, anticipating to see them another time. Next morning we found out that the Gestapo entered the city, broke into many houses, and after robbing the people, beating and pounding most of them, separated the men from the women. Finally, they loaded a number of men on trucks and left.

Nobody knew where the unfortunate men were taken. Some said that they'd be shot and some speculated that they were taken to a concentration camp.

At that time, we didn't realize the real Nazi bestialities and schemes. Many rumors were circulating around but nobody knew for sure what was happening. The men and the Gestapo disappeared and we never saw them again. The two brothers Frenkiel were taken away with the transport. After a few days, I met the businessman Frenkiel in Rozana and he described to me what really happened. The Gestapo came in and, after flogging most of the people, ordered the men to assemble. They asked everybody what was his profession. He said that he was a simple worker. His brothers told the truth, that one was a teacher and the other one a pharmacist. Evidently, they were looking for the educated people only. They left him because he was a simple worker but took away his two brothers.

We have to keep in mind that this episode occurred in the first days of July 1941. Later, the Gestapo didn't separate the sexes, they just took away everybody, including children, and murdered them in cold blood.

This forefeeling, the premonition, saved my life. When I returned to the village Michle was waiting for me and said, "You were very lucky. Some supernatural force was watching over you. It was a good idea. From now on, we'll stick with you."

THIS WAS MIRACLE #2.

I myself was shaken by this experience.

New orders from the Germans arrived. "The Jews must carry the yellow badges on their garments." It was forbidden for them to walk on the sidewalks, but only in the center of the streets. They were not permitted to greet the Germans.

After a few days, on my way to the city, I met a German on a bicycle. I did not greet him, according to the order. He stopped the bicycle and started to yell why I didn't greet a German soldier? I answered that we were ordered by the German Authorities not to greet. He commanded me next time to greet him. I didn't know what to do, and I thought that the best way was to avoid the Germans altogether, which later proved to be an excellent idea.

Right from the first day of occupation the Germans robbed and molested the people. They used to force their way into homes, rob and beat brutally all the inhabitants.

This was in accordance with the doctrine of National Socialism, to exert a terror on innocent people. Many Germans found their way to our village. They robbed everything which was valuable, molested and persecuted the people.

Once, two German soldiers arrived at our village. They were actually Austrian, and stopped at the first house. There were some pretty girls and they loved to spend their time there, behaving like human beings and insinuating that they actually belonged to the leftist party. As soon as they left the house, they used to beat up and rob whomever they met.

This was very characteristic of the German behavior. In one house they had faces of human beings. In the neighboring houses or on the streets they behaved like wild animals. They always wore two masks on their faces.

The same soldiers entered our house and started to beat my

brother Moritz and molest him, because he did not take off his hat when they entered. They made him perform all kinds of sports, like jumping, falling on his abdomen, getting up and running again. In five minutes they took all the strength out of him.

Yitzhak, the son of Pomeraniec, returned home from captivity by escaping from the camp of his retention. He told us gruesome, unbelievable stories of German atrocities. He still wore the Polish uniform and became friendly with the two Austrians. He used to walk around the village together with the Germans dressed in his uniform.

He walked together with the Germans on the street and in the houses, saving a lot of people from being abused. He was respected, because he wore a soldier's uniform. Once he saved me a lot of trouble. All three of them entered the house of Pomeraniec and the Germans lifted their sticks ready to beat me up. Yitzhak intervened and they became more friendly. Other Germans used to come also to our village in order to rob and plunder. Usually we used to run away.

A meeting of the doctors of the clinic of Rozana took place. I was present at the meeting. They accepted me as a member. Dr. Margolis, a woman, was against. I knew her from Vilna.

She was a very jealous woman and didn't understand our deplorable situation. She was afraid that I was going to take away from her some patients. She did not realize that our days of freedom were numbered. Her father was a nice fellow and used to come to the clinic, where we had very useful discussions.

I remember also a tall Rabbi. He was a very handsome man, and still wore a patriarchal beard. He had always been dressed very clean and neat. We debated many times about our ordeal. I asked him:

"What is the reason that we have been so persecuted for generations, culminating with Hitler and the Nazis?

"Why does the Almighty permit such injustices to occur on the earth which He created?

"People with golden hearts, pious, virtuous and immaculate, who sacrificed all their lives for others, are being ridiculed, scoffed and spit upon."

The Rabbi admitted that he could not answer these questions, because he didn't understand them himself.

Our planet is only a very insignificant part of the universe. The Almighty watches, supervises and directs all the stars and planets. He sees everything and He is in everything. All the worlds like ours are under His direct vigilance and surveillance. Their function and purpose are different. In some of the planets (worlds) there is only good. No sufferings, no persecutions and no murder. Other planets and suns are just the opposite. They incorporate all the bad in the universe. Between these two extremes, there are thousands of degrees and grades.

The Almighty created this world of ours, the "Earth," to suffer and to clean and to purify ourselves, after which one would enter a better world. Our world, in which we live, is evil-fashioned, and nefarious. A newlyborn goes through life mostly suffering. He has to overcome different diseases, which constitute the very interior of his existence.

Later in life he meets many disappointments, and a few decades later (70-80 years) he departs from this world, mostly by additional sufferings.

What is the purpose of a man being born, if after a short while he has to disappear from the world? The same is true with the animals and birds.

Let me explain the real substance of our planet. The real nature, the essence of our world, lies in the jungle, seas and air.

What do we see in the jungle?

One kills the other one. The very existence of the wild animals consists of killing and devouring the weak ones. They are not permitted to live otherwise. Nature gave them an ultimatum, kill or die from starvation.

The same is true in the realm of the seas. One big fish must, by nature, swallow the smaller fish. Its very existence and life depend on it. In order to live he must kill.

In the air there is a repetition of the same. The wild birds attack the weak ones. In addition many birds live on engulfing and swallowing small insects or fish, again destroying other creatures, other lives.

As we could see from the above, Nature gave out orders to

its inhabitants, to destroy in order to live. Nature is cruel and human beings, as part of nature, are cruel too. Take off the mask of civilization, culture, and man reveals himself a plain animal. *Homo Homini lupus est.*

The beast in man keeps coming out again and again. All over the town, people were talking about the German atrocities, which took on a form of unheard of evil.

One of my friends a doctor, who worked at the clinic, and who was also a semi-philosopher, asked me:

"What is the meaning of destroying lives? If G-d created everything and He exists in everything, there must be a purpose, a certain design and planning."

"You are right," I said, "there is a design and planning in all of these occurrences.

"G-d is surrounded by millions and millions of souls, spirits, quiddities, vital principles, or whatever you want to call it. If the soul commits a transgression, it has to be punished and purified again, according to the Book of Laws. The greater the transgression, the greater is the punishment. If the transgression is small, the soul is sent to a better world. If the transgression is big, the soul is sent to a bad world. After being purified, the soul returns to the original source, to the vicinity of G-d."

"How does the criminal purify himself? Certainly not by committing more crimes and by murdering innocent people?" asked my friend.

"No! Every criminal suffers also on this world. Some of them are so embittered that they even commit suicide. Their transgressions were so big, that they cannot be purified in one world alone. After they die and their bodies are separated, the souls enter another world, where the process of purification continues. On this world they are the tools of G-d, to make other people, with minor transgressions, to suffer enormously. But when the latter die, they return straight to their original source, to the vicinity of G-d, the Supreme power. This explains also, why the just people, the souls of which committed small transgressions, suffer more on this world than the criminals and murderers, whose souls committed grand, voluminous, large transgressions, and who cannot return to their original source and must continue to pass through different worlds, till they are completely purified."

"How many worlds do they have to pass?" wanted to know my friend.

"There are numerous worlds. Sometimes the souls, after being separated from the bodies, enter other forms of existence, even in the same world. For example, a soul from a human body enters the body of an animal or a fish or even a bird.

"Every creature which possesses life is G-d's creature. Life is soul. When the soul leaves the body, the latter returns to a form without life, to a matter, material or substance which disintegrates and returns to the earth."

"This explains also," agreed my friend, "why the Jewish people is the chosen people."

"Yes! Chosen to suffer more than any other nation on this planet. Chosen to be slaughtered, to pogroms, persecution and lately to the Nazi atrocities."

"When they are murdered," followed up my friend, "they return straight to their original source. To the real *Ziv Hashehina*."

"Yes, only if they are completely purified, otherwise not."

"The malfactors, the ruffians, the real hoodlums, cutthroats and hooligans had to suffer a very long time?" questioned my friend.

"Sure! They have to pass from the grade of 'executioner' to the grade of the 'innocent victim,' which might require many transformations and which is a very slow and gradual process."

"Finally, every soul returns to its source?" inquired my friend.

"Yes! This is correct. Every soul is a part of G-d's surroundings, and must return to its original well."

"Does it mean that the function and behavior of every soul is predetermined, before it descends on the planet in any form or shape?"

"No! The souls have the choice of accelerating or delaying their return to their original fountain or well, by doing good or evil deeds."

For example: There were Nazis who refused to shoot innocent people. They will return to their source earlier and suffer on this or other planets less than the bloodthirsty Nazis, who performed their atrocities voluntarily and eagerly.

I was working at the clinic in Rozana. It was a pleasure to walk from my village to the city. Naturally I had to avoid encountering Germans.

We had many patients in the clinic. The poor were treated for nothing. Most of the peasants used to bring food, which was distributed at the end of every day. I rented also a room in the city, where I practiced medicine.

We had, now, plenty of food. It was nice to see many patients in the clinic waiting only for me, which displeased Dr. Margolis, the woman. Her husband and her father didn't care. I had many patients coming from many villages, except from the village Vola which was a sister village of Konstantinovo having the same Soltys (chief of village). They had old bickerings and arguments among them and didn't like the idea of visiting the doctor of the village Konstantinovo. Only the Soltys used to call me in, for treatment of his wife. Naturally without any payment.

The pharmacist became a good friend of mine. He was a tall nice fellow and had the advantage of having all the medicine, drugs, bandages, cotton, injectables, which were very scarce in time of war.

In addition, the German Commander lived in his house, which was very important. He honored all kind of medications which I prescribed and loaned me some equipment and books. He introduced me to his brother-in-law, who was a medical doctor, a refugee. The doctor was in charge of the hospital. He used to call me in, for spinal taps, which I had learned before, during the epidemic of meningitis.

At the beginning, the doctor and the pharmacist lived peacefully. Later they quarreled and became enemies. Evidently both of them didn't realize the terrible time in which we were living.

The truth was that nobody expected in the year 1941 that

the Germans would, really, go so far and destroy entire races. Suffice to say that the pharmacist suspected the doctor of plotting against him, which compelled him to react in a similar way.

Rosh-Hashaba, Jewish New Year, Monday, Septermber 22, 1941.
    We prayed for peace and hoped that tyranny would soon end. In the afternoon, I walked over to the blacksmith, whose workshop was just on the borderline between the village and the city. They were related to Dr. Marcus, the chief of the medical clinic of Wolkowysk. His wife started to talk to me about partisans in the neighborhood.
    Next day she told me secretly that Dr. Marcus visited them in the middle of the night. His wife and his sister-in-law had escaped on Monday, when the Germans dropped incendiary bombs and all the city of Wolkowysk was on fire. The doctor had to join them later. He was hindered in uniting with his family, and because of the Germans' successful advance couldn't reach the as-yet-unoccupied Russian territories and unite with his family.
    All his family belonged to the leftists. He himself occupied a high position during the Soviet occupation. To return to Wolkowysk meant immediate arrest and execution. He joined a partisan group and fought many battles. His group was one time surrounded by the Germans. They fought with extraordinary courage, but succumbed to the much greater force.
    The last bullet was reserved for himself, because to fall into the hands of the Gestapo meant death, preceded by enormous torture. In this way Dr. Marcus lost his life. Honor to his courage and to his memory!
    The chief of the village Konstantinovo was Mordehai-Eshia. He was a short man, in his fifties. In his youth he lived in America, where he had a very hard life. Later he returned to his birthplace, Konstantinovo. The few thousand dollars which he earned in the U.S.A. enabled him to buy a farm which consisted of a beautiful house with adjacent buildings and a large piece of land, which he cultivated, like the rest of the farmers, with a horse and plough.
    They didn't have at that time the necessary agricultural machinery, like tractors, grain harvesters, combine, etc. It was

very hard work. He was a very sociable person and, although officially under supervision of the "Soltys," actually dominated him. A bottle of Vodka helped to persuade the "Soltys" what direction to take. He was a kind of a trouble shooter. He was married and had one son.

The Germans ordered the formation of a ghetto in the city within a few days. Any Jew found outside the ghetto would be shot.

A terrible confusion took place. People moved their belongings from different parts of the city to one section, designated as a ghetto. Pushcarts had to be used.

Hundreds of people were rushing around the selected few streets named by the Germans to find a place for themselves and their families. Children milled around, lost and crying, parents were running and seeking their lost children, their cries drowned in the tremendous commotion of people uprooted from their homes and seeking a place to put their tired heads.

Life in the ghetto was very difficult. Many familes had to move into one house. The Germans used to come into the houses very often, to rob, persecute and to commit all kind of atrocities.

The Jews and the Poles were deprived of the most elementary human rights. They were forced to perform hard labor, at which they were beaten mercilessly and humiliated.

The Germans imposed huge fines on the people which had to be paid immediately, otherwise they would suffer the consequences.

I had rented a room to treat patients in the house where I was born. The window was directed towards the main street, where the main Gestapo office was located. I remember seeing Jews and even Poles driven to hard labor by the Germans. They were beaten mercilessly without any reason, and were attacked often by vicious German dogs. The victims suffered lacerations, dog bites, and other physical tortures. Their faces expressed anxiety mixed with apathy. They had to work very hard without a rest. To come out alive, after one day of work, was a great accomplishment. People were afraid to go out to work, because of the atrocities committed during work, which often ended fatally.

One morning when I was sitting in my room and watching through the window, I saw Mr. Epstein, the Juden-Alteste (chief of the Jewish community), together with a few members and associates enter the German Headquarters. Mr. Epstein was seventy-five years old and was carrying beer for the Gestapo, as ordered.

I heard barking of dogs. Then, I saw Mr. Epstein running away, pursued by a young husky German, who after catching up with the old man hit him very hard with an iron stick. Mr. Epstein fell, blood gushing out all over him and on the ground. The German then grabbed the old man by the hair and dragged him unconscious to the headquarters. It was a terrible scene. This was the way the Gestapo paid for kindness and obedience.

The Germans took away all the valuables. People were starving. Epidemics were rampant, caused by malnutrition, congested living conditions and continuous persecution. When the valuables were drained out, the oppressors took away furniture, even pillows and blankets. There seemed no end to the sufferings and torment. Terrible scenes at the community center were constantly present.

The inhabitants of the new colony on the other side of the city were ordered at a moment's notice to leave their homes and all their belongings and move into the ghetto, which was, already, very congested. Again heart-breaking scenes.

Our village, the Old Konstantinovo, was in great danger. We were expecting to be thrown out from our houses. The Soltys was invited to the house of Mordehai-Eshia, where he was entertained with food and drinks and also promised money if our village will not be forced to evacuate. I had a nice chatter with the Soltys. He was a White-Russian and lived in the nearby village "Vola." He made a good impression on me and was intelligent enough for his village. He had to execute, strictly, all the German orders.

A few days of anxiety passed. Finally the Soltys came back, announcing the good news, that our village would for the time being remain and would not be evacuated.

I was working in the city clinic, called "Ambulans." It had a different meaning than in the U.S.A., where Ambulance signified a first-aid vehicle. Michle, as the younger girl, went often to the city, to collect my wages, mostly in form of food. She was developing very nicely, and looked very pretty. The fields outside were being cultivated and prepared for the spring.

Old Dr. Kaplinski was beaten up severely by the Germans. He became very sick and was bedridden.

Dentist Abramovski and his wife tried to persuade me to take a room in their office, which would be mutually beneficial. At the beginning I refused, because everything looked to me uncertain. Finally I agreed, because it was nearer to my village.

Day of atonement "Yom Kipur."

The Germans raided the synagogue and murdered a few people. They were forcing themselves into the houses, robbing and torturing people.

CHAPTER IV

The last four months of the year 1941.

THE FIRST MEANINGFUL RUSSIAN RESISTANCE, EAST OF THE RIVER BEREZINA. THE DISAGREEMENTS OF HITLER WITH HIS TOP GENERALS. STALIN SPEAKS ON 11/6/41. ZHUKOV'S COUNTERATTACKS NEAR MOSCOW (12/6/41). HITLER DISMISSED MANY FAMOUS GENERALS. PEARL HARBOR (12/7/41).

Rumors were spreading that the Germans didn't succeed in their war as expected. The Russians were fighting very well. To the surprise of Hitler, the Soviets resisted the invasion with all their strength. In the fighting at the Berezina many Germans were killed and much ammunition destroyed. Sporadic resistance and heroism developed at different areas of the battle line, but the real check of the German advance took place east of Smolensk.

Here the German progress, their forging ahead was halted for the first time. Here it was proven to the world and to the Russian people that the invincibility of the German Army was a myth, a figment of the imagination caused by fear.

The morale of the Russian troops improved enormously. Their artillery was much better, their tanks, expecially T-34, showed to be of higher quality. In addition new modern planes were introduced. The devastating "Katyushka" mortars made their formidable appearance, causing terrible explosions, simultaneously by the dozens, which panicked the Germans.

The main motive of Russian resistance was the realization that Hitler was an irresponsible, destructive maniac, capable of murdering thousands of innocent men, women and children for no reason at all and to no benefit for the outcome of the war.

Although most of the Russians did not like Stalin, it was preferable to live under the Soviet regime than to die under Hitler.

Another important factor has to be added here, namely: Hitler, the ex-Corporal, considered himself much superior in military strategy to his best Generals. Brauchitsch, Guderian, Von Bock, Rundstedt, Harder, all concluded that the best way was to attack the Central Front and to conquer Moscow before the winter sets in, for which they were not prepared, believing previously that the Russian campaign would be over in six weeks, i.e., at the end of July or August. Hitler overruled them and ordered them to attack Leningrad in the north and the Ukraine in the south.

"Moscow can wait," he said.

He decided also to move two armies and one tank division from the center front to the south, weakening the central front. The generals were furious, but powerless to change Hitler's mind.

True, the Russians suffered many casualties east of Smolensk, but the Germans too had heavy losses. Moreover, by arresting the German advance east of Smolensk, the Russian High Command secured a breathing spell for a few months, enabling them to fortify the defenses of Moscow properly by building additional fortifications and by bringing in new reserves.

There were three anti-aircraft defenses around Moscow, with tremendous defensive gunfire. During the first air raid over Moscow, out of two hundred German planes, only ten broke through.

In September, 1941, Hitler suddenly changed his mind and ordered an attack on Moscow. But it was too late.

Hitler yelled at the generals.

"Encircle them, beat and destroy them!"

He ordered the Panzer Group of Guderian and the tank corps to return to the central front.

The famous Russian winter, so well known to Napoleon in 1812 and to the Swedes a century before, started in, which paralyzed the German machinery.

Yet on 10/3/41 Hitler spoke in Berlin.

"I declare today, and I declare it without any reservation, that the enemy in the east has been struck down and will never rise again."

The Germans advanced slowly toward the Russian capital. The Soviet resistance stiffened and the counter-attacks caused heavy losses to the Germans.

Stalin spoke on the eve of the Revolution on 11/6/41.

"The Germans were determined to enslave the world and primarily the Slavic nations.

"They have no honor, nor conscience. They have a morality of animals.... They want a war of extermination.... Very well then.... They shall have it. Our task will be to destroy every German. No mercy! Death to the German invaders!"

On 12/6/41, General Zhukov, who had replaced Timoshenko as commander of the central front, struck with all force at his command (100 divisions) the Germans standing before Moscow. The result was shattering.

For over two years the Germans had achieved victories all over Europe. December 6, 1941 was really the first turning point, when the Germans not only were halted in their advance but were forced to retreat under terrible conditions of winter. Many thousands of Germans were killed and numerous tanks, heavy artillery, and armor were destroyed.

The German General Halder wrote in his diary:

"The myth of the invincibility of the German Army was broken."

The severity of the fighting during the six months of 1941, from 6/22/41 till 12/10/41, could be judged from the following:

In all the German campaign in the west during the year 1940 there were 156.00 losses and *30.000 dead*. During the six

THE LAST FOUR MONTHS OF THE YEAR 1941

months of the Russian campaign in 1941 there were 775,000 losses and *200,000 dead*. By losses was meant wounded, and missing.

As a result of this calamity, Hitler shook up his High Command and dismissed many famous and useful generals.

On 12/18/41 *General Von Bock* was relieved from his duties on the Central Front because he suffered severe abdominal pains when his army was forced to retreat from Moscow. He was replaced by Von Kluge.

General Rundstedt in the South was deposed because he retreated from Rostow.

General Guderian, who was considered to be one of the best tank generals, was discharged on 12/25/41, because he retreated without Hitler's permission.

General Hoepner, who came with his troops within sight of Moscow, was dismissed and forbidden to wear a German uniform.

General Von Sponeck, who during the campaign in Holland was decorated for landing at the Hague, was discharged for pulling back in the Crimea. He was also imprisoned and sentenced on 9/24/42 to death, and executed after the July plot against Hitler.

Field Marshal Von Brauchitsch, the commander in chief of all the Russian front, resigned on 12/17/41. According to Hitler, Brauchitsch was a man of straw.

General Von Loeb in the north was relieved of his duties on 1/18/42 for reasons of health, but actually because he failed to capture Leningrad.

Even Keitel, the main military adviser to Hitler, the chief of IKW (Supreme Command) who had always been in the circle of Hitler, advised his chief to retreat slightly from Moscow. Hitler jumped at him and called him "Blockhead." Keitel felt deeply offended and wanted to commit suicide.

Who do you think substituted the above famous commanders-in-chief? The ex-corporal, Adolf Hitler, himself on 12/19/41. Naturally from then on the German Army suffered enormously. He immediately forbade any withdrawal.

The Year 1941

General Yodl, Supreme Commander.

Field Marshal Keitel, main military adviser to Hitler, Chief of Supreme Command (OKW) wanted to commit suicide because Hitler called him blockhead.

"Fight till the last man, no matter what the consequences," Hitler screamed.

Only Halder remained as chief of the General Staff under Hitler. Franz Halder was later dismissed also, because, as Hitler said, "We need National Socialist ardor, which we can not expect from an officer of the old school, like Halder." Halder was replaced by General Zeitzler, as Chief of General Staff, on 9/24/42.

The results were that armies were surrounded and cut to pieces, causing an unnecessary loss of men and equipment. The German people, in 1939 and 1940, when the Nazis were winning, were very pleased with their chief. Some even idolized Hitler. They forgot about the Nazi atrocities. One factor counted and this was success on the battle front.

But now when the events started to turn around and defeat begun to appear ever more clearly, the Germans were not satisfied. In view of the above, Hitler ordered the Reichstag on 4/26/1942 to pass a law giving him absolute power over every German. He became the supreme power, above the constitution and above the law. He had behaved previously like the highest unquestionable authority in Germany, but now the Reichstag rubberstamped it.

Naturally we didn't know about all these happenings in the village of Konstantinovo. We did hear something from the peasants returning from the battle fronts.

Different rumors were spreading. But being deprived of newspapers, radios, and being compelled to live within or around the city, we actually had no idea of the occurrences in the world and of the real facts.

One time, on the New Year Eve, the Soltys brought me a German newspaper, "Der Völkische Beobachter," dated 12/29/41, in which was written clearly, and to my complete amazement and satisfaction, that the Russians were fighting like real heroes. The bitter cold affected the machines. The telescopic sights were useless. Fuel was freezing and the oil became viscous. Many regiments lost hundreds of men from frostbites. The soldiers were insufficiently clothed and fed poorly. Halder noted in his diary, on 11/19/41, that Hitler realized that neither side could destroy the other and this would lead to peace negotiations.

Even in Rozana we heard of negotiations going on between Russia and Germany to end the war. Germany would have to withdraw to the 1941 border. We didn't believe it but we talked

The Year 1941

Some of the German Generals dismissed by Hitler:
Left: *General Halder*, Chief of General Staff, dismissed September 24, 1942, because, according to Hitler, he "hasn't got the National Sociàlist ardor." Center: *General Von Rundstet* directed the Southern Army of 41 divisions which advanced through southern Poland, Stalingrad and Caucasus, dismissed on November 30, 1941, because he retreated from Rostov (to be replaced by Reichnau).   Right: *Von Kluge*, who replaced Von Bock on the central front on December 18, 1941. Von Bock was desperate and suffered severe abdominal pains because he couldn't enter Moscow. His army suffered defeat. The Russian winter decimated his forces.

L. to R.: *General Guderian*, one of the best German tank generals, was dismissed on December 25, 1941, because he retreated without Hitler's permission.

Fegelein, the brother-in-law of Hitler, shot to death in the last days of World War II, by order of Hitler.

Field Marshal Von Brauchitsch, Commander in Chief of all the Russian front, dismissed (resigned) on December 17, 1941. According to Hitler Brauschitsch was a man of straw.

The Last Four Months of the Year 1941

about it, wishing it were true. But Hitler, the maniac, didn't accept it and the war was going on in full force, spelling disaster to the world and to the Germans as well.

On New Year's Eve we had a little party with the Soltys. After reading such wonderful news in the paper I was elated, and decided to take a little whisky, to celebrate the wonderful moments of approaching German defeat and the slight prospect of peace. I hoped, clandestinely, that the war would be ended in the coming year, 1942. I still had with me my two brothers, my father in Wolkowysk and my sister in Pinsk. I talked to the Soltys and to many other people. This was the first time since the war started that I was a little inspired and even encouraged.

Pearl Harbor.

December 7, 1941, was Sunday in the Hawaiian Islands of the North Pacific.

Pearl Harbor was the chief U.S. base, not far from the capital, Honolulu. It was situated on the shore of the island Oahu and 3500 nautical miles from Japan. It was an enormous harbor and could accommodate the entire fleet of the U.S.A. In the early morning of this fateful day, the harbor contained ninety-four ships, including eight battleships. Most of the crews were sleeping or off on leave during the weekend.

Then, at 7:55 A.M. local Hawaiian time, 1:25 P.M. Eastern Standard Time, three hundred and sixty airplanes, comprising bombers and fighters, attacked mercilessly the moored U.S. ships. Explosives were dropped, causing devastation and huge fires. By 10 A.M. the attack was over. Almost all the battleships were heavily damaged. Some were sunk and others capsized. Two thousand lives were lost, and another two thousand heavily wounded.

The sudden Japanese unprovoked attack was a complete surprise to the world. To start a war against the mighty U.S.A. was sheer madness.

A few hours later, Emperor Hirohito issued a formal declaration of war on the U.S. of America and the British Empire. On 12/11/41, Germany and Italy joined the Japanese in declaring war on the U.S.A.

Hitler was, at the beginning, taken by surprise, but the sudden, unprovoked attack pleased him highly. This was the exact way he was operating.

Now, all three Allied Powers were bound together for a struggle of life and death. Their combined strength was much superior than those of the Axis powers in regards to men power, raw material, industry and potential war production.

After Pearl Harbor, the Japanese landed north of Luzon and later in Lingayen Gulf, threatening Manila (Philippines). They attacked also Malaya and Singapore and even Guam.

THE YEAR 1942
SECOND YEAR OF WAR.
RESISTANCE TO GERMAN AGGRESSION

CHAPTER V

The special German commandos (Einsatzgroupen) to commit genocide.

APATHY IN WOLKOWYSK. FATHER JOINED US. MIRACLE #3. MY RETURN TO WOLKOWYSK FOR PERMISSION TO MOVE TO LYSKOVO. THE SLAUGHTER IN SLONIM. THE EINSATZGROUPPEN. BABI YAR. THE EXECUTION IN ROVNO, AS NARRATED BY ENGINEER GRUEBE. MORE THAN SIX MILLION JEWS WERE MURDERED. LYSKOVO. I SAW MY BROTHER MORRITZ FOR THE LAST TIME. SEVERE FIGHTING ON EASTERN FRONT AND NORTH AFRICA. MRS. YOSOLEVSKA. MR. YANKOWSKY. EVACUATION OF THE INHABITANTS OF THE REMAINING CITIES. MIRACLES #4 & #5. THE ROAD TO WOLKOWYSK.

I continued to work at the clinic in Rozana. I had my private office with the dentist Abramovski, and attended also patients in my village. Michle looked very pretty. They called her "Panienka" or "Princess." She was very satisfied with her changed name and seemed to have accepted it gladly.

I was called sometimes to make a visit to a neighboring village because the patient was too sick to be moved. I had to travel occasionally 20-25 km. from home. Taking in consideration the hard winter, the poor transportation, it was not an easy task.

They used to pick me up with a carriage drawn by a horse. It was not a very convenient voyage, because the carriage used to shake a lot on the road and all the interior used to shake with it. It was still worthwhile if a human life could be saved. No medical help was available at that time of war for many miles around. I had in my bag different kinds of drugs and medications, including the newly available sulfur drugs and injectables like Prontosil, which really could save lives.

I could also perform minor surgery and deliveries, but we did not possess an operating room with the necessary equipment for sterilization and operations.

In these eventualities, we used to refer to Wolkowysk, where they had good hospital facilities and where a good friend of mine, Dr. Velvelski, was working. If necessary, the patient was referred to Bialystok.

I was called once to see a sick patient in a nearby village. When I arrived, I saw a man of about 40 years old who was screaming from severe abdominal pains. He had high fever and the abdomen was hard. No reflexes of the belly were elicited. I diagnosed appendicitis with possible acute peritonitis. Patient was referred to Wolkowysk, where he was operated on immediately and life was saved.

Maybe, he is still alive now, and thinks of the doctor who made it possible for him to live and to enjoy his family and the surroundings for many years to come.

We received a letter from our father, who still lived in the house of my cousin in Wolkowysk. He wrote that he found some money and valuables buried in the basement of our house before it was burned.

One had to be very courageous, diligent and skillful to find it. Many Germans passed by, looked at him and left. Probably they thought that he was ordered to remove the debris. He would like to join us because of loneliness without his children. We arranged transportation. After a few days he arrived.

All of us were very glad to see him. But, alas, how he changed! He had become gray, pale, thin and was very tired. We'd have to do everything possible to improve his health. He told us of the atrocities in Wolkowysk. How the people lost any hope, in view of the German mistreatment and evil.

THE SPECIAL GERMAN COMMANDOS FOR GENOCIDE 71

The Judenrat was forced under threat of death to provide the Germans with money, all kinds of goods. In a burned-out city how could one satisfy the German requirements?

People walked around like shadows. Haunting a world that no more existed. They ceased to greet each other. Everybody was absorbed in his own thoughts. Very little talking. People died like flies, because of lack of housing, because of starvation, malnutrition and persecution.

I continued to work at the clinic. Sometimes I walked to the city. I sometimes was taken by a sled dragged by a horse. In the town, the people were mistreated, abused, oppressed and molested. A few boys accidentally walked near the river. Germans arrived from nowhere. They pounded and knocked the boys down and threw them into the river. The Germans didn't let the boys out of the river, and as a consequence they drowned.

Germans arrived at our village and confiscated many cows and horses. Mrs. Pomeraniec insisted that I should go to the Nazis and ask them politely to give us back the loot. It was a very dangerous undertaking. Looking back in retrospect, I could have been shot on the spot.

"Maybe the Germans would take into consideration the fact that you are a physician and need the horse to come to the clinic," she said. This kind of thinking was very characteristic of the civilian population in the occupied territories. Extreme naiveté in front of German bestiality. The Germans didn't care about clinics or hospitals. I decided to go because it didn't make any difference to me one way or the other.

I went to the office of the mayor, who was a White-Russian. The Gestapo chief was unfortunately there. He wanted to shoot me right away for the impertinence and daring. It was unheard of, to come and ask for the loot back. He drew out the revolver and told me to enter the adjacent building.

The mayor intervened on my behalf. A few councilmen, who were present, helped too. They told the Gestapo man that they needed doctors because of a possible epidemy of contagious diseases which might break out. *THIS WAS MIRACLE #3.* He let me go.

I returned to my village, and was evidently very pale, not

because of fear, but because of the occurrence and the circumstances surrounding my ordeal. It was a clear example of not being able to understand in what world we were living. I didn't tell anybody what happened.

The situation in Rozana deteriorated. We didn't know the reason, at that time. But, now, we know that the calamity on the Russian front irritated the Germans. People were beaten severely, shot, molested. The chief of the Gestapo had a Jewish official, because he spoke and wrote German. He used to write letters for the Germans and perform other necessary functions. He was a nice fellow and helped people as much as he could. One day we were informed that he was shot to death by the same Gestapo man for a minor thing.

A German medical man visited our clinic. He was a fat robust German. Without any reason he yelled, shouted and screamed at the doctors and the rest of the medical personnel. We were the only clinic in the city and performed a very useful job for the inhabitants of the city and many villages around. We prevented or diminished the outbreak of typhus, typhoid, tuberculosis and other contagious diseases. It was very beneficial to the Germans. We were glad when he left.

The family Pomeraniec had relatives in Lyskovo. We were informed that the situation there was much better. The local commandant was more human. I decided to move over to Lyskovo. Permission from the German doctor in Wolkowysk was required. I needed also a separate permission to travel. Since the man who worked for the Gestapo was an acquaintance of mine, he got for me the necessary papers and approval. It was dangerous to travel.

I hired a peasant, paid him a nice sum in advance, and left. I put the permission paper in my pocket and an iron stick to be ready at any eventuality. One could never tell what might happen on the road. Many people were killed by the peasants themselves, who robbed their passengers. Life was very cheap at that time. A Jewish life had no value at all.

The peasant was whipping and flogging his horse and looked at me, obliquely, and crosswise. At the beginning he was rude and disrespectful. I looked at him and was not afraid. I could defend myself very well in case of necessity. The peasant sensed that I was not the right subject for him and became more flexible and more accessible.

We arrived in Wolkowysk without any difficulties, and I told the peasant to stop at the house of my cousin, who had a vast yard and many stables. I myself left for the house of Dr. Kaufman, who was a good friend of mine. His house belonged to the very few houses which remained intact. He lived with his wife, mother and sister. All of them knew me from before the war and they all liked me. I used to visit them very often.

They received me with open arms and were very glad to provide me with temporary shelter. Dr. Kaufman studied in Switzerland and knew well German. He became very friendly with the German doctor and was able to arrange many good things for the community, especially for the hospitals. I told him the purpose of my coming there. He promised me to go in the morning to the German doctor and ask him for the permission to be transferred to Lyskovo. In the morning, we went over and received the necessary papers.

I remained in town another few days to find out what was going on in the big city and in the world at large. The same persecution, beatings, robbings, shootings took place here too. It couldn't be otherwise. The same Germans, the same evil regime. While I was there, the town was shaken by the massacres which were going on in the neighboring cities. We heard of the slaughtering of thousands of Jews in the neighboring town of Slonim. A boy was saved, and he told us the following story:

Slonim was occupied by the Germans on 6/25/41. Ten days later 1,200 people were murdered in the woods. On 11/14/41 thousands of Jews were taken to Pietreskovice and murdered. On 6/30/42, the Germans set the ghetto on fire. Many were burned alive. The rest were taken to the execution place and murdered. Their bodies were thrown into a large ditch, previously prepared. All this massacre was organized and directed by the German Kommandant, *Hick*.

The boy told us that he was shot too. He fell into the pit. People were falling on the top of him. He felt suffocating. By then he realized that he was alive. He struggled upward through a pile of corpses. When the Germans left, he crawled out of the ditch and slowly made his way to Wolkowysk.

Blood was all over him. He had many lacerations and abrasions. Many did not believe him, because such senseless murdering never happened before. But many did not doubt the veracity of the boy's story. His appearance and the German behavior confirmed everything.

People fell into a semiconscious state of mind, because the mind couldn't comprehend such atrocities from an elected government. Some wondered why Wolkowysk was spared. The reason was that some cities, like Rozana, Lyskovo, Wolkowysk, belonged to the General Government of East Prussia, and their extermination took another road. They had to be transferred to the concentration camps and murdered in the gas chambers. Not only Slonim, but people of hundreds of other cities, towns, villages were murdered by *the Einsatzgruppen (Special Extermination Groups)*, which operated in the East.

They did not fight the enemy, but they murdered civilians. They were designated by letters from "A" to "H" and were following the German armies of occupation. Their task was to exterminate people, including women and children, who were murdered for no reason at all. Not because of their religion, not because of their political belief, but because they were born Jews without a country of their own and without a government to protect them. According to Eichmann, these special groups murdered two million people in two years' time.

Group A was commanded by *Franz Stahlecker*, who operated in the Baltic States, like Estonia, Lithuania, Latvia. He was killed by Estonian Partisans.

Group B was led by *Arthur Nebe*, who killed in White-Russia and behind the Central Front advancing toward Moscow. The people of Slonim described previously were murdered by this group.

Here is a letter from one of the killers and cannibals with the name of Kube, dated Minsk 7/21/42.

"To the Reich Commisioner Ostland:

"After discussions with SS Brigade-Leader Zeller and the eminently capable head of the SD, SS-Obersturmfuhrer Dr. J.

THE SPECIAL GERMAN COMMANDOS FOR GENOCIDE   75

Strauch, we have liquidated many thousands of Jews in White Russia. We eliminated all the Jews in the district of Minsk. In Lida 16,000 Jews, in Slonim 8,000 Jews.* The rear section of the *Army* eliminated 10,000 persons in Glebokie district. In the city of Minsk itself 10,000 were liquidated between July 28-29, 1942, among them 6,500 Russians. . . .The district of Sluzk was relieved of 1,000 Jews. The same holds good for Nóvogrodek and Vileika. Radical measures are still in prospect for Baranovicze and Hancevishi. In the city of Baranoviche, there are still 10,000 Jews, of whom 9,000 will be liquidated next month. [Signed] Kube"

I quoted this letter because many towns and cities mentioned there were from my direct neighborhood, like Slonim, Lida, Baranoviche, etc. Similar liquidations were going on all along the battle line and behind the Army rear. It also showed that the Wehrmacht (German Army), and not only the SS, participated actively in murdering innocent civilians.

Group C was commanded by *Otto Rush*, later Thomas. His hordes spread over the Ukraine, carrying devastation, destruction and death. I'll mention here the *slaughter of Babi-Yar*.

Babi Yar was a ravine, not far from the cemetery, outside the city of Kiev. When the Germans occupied the city, there were mostly old men and women and children, because the young adults left for the battle front and were incorporated in the Red Army.

Kiev fell on 9/19/41 and the massacre started a few days later, namely on 9/28/41. It lasted three days, during which 90,000 people were slaughtered.

At the beginning the Germans posted an *unsigned* announcement which ordered all the Jews to assemble at the cemetery with their documents, money and warm clothing. It sounded like an order of resettlement, because most of the people did not believe the rumors of Nazi atrocities.

"How was it possible," they asked, "to murder people without any reason? After all, this government came to power by free and voluntary election of the German nation."

*This was the last execution in Slonim.

The murdering of little children and defenseless women, they argued, would not help, nor be beneficial to the outcome of the war.

How was it possible that enormous, unheard-of crimes should be committed by a nation considered to be civilized and cultured? A nation which gave out Goethe, Schiller, Heine, Mendelssohn and Beethoven? they asked. They reasoned that it was impossible, and that they'd be only resettled, as proclaimed by the Germans, and therefore they followed the orders.

Some others did not believe the Germans and preferred to die by committing suicide.

From the cemetery they moved forward. They were ordered to put their belongings in one huge pile and to pass through a narrow passage, where German soldiers with wild, big dogs stood and waited for them. As they moved through the narrow passage, the Germans started to beat them with rubber sticks, rifle-butts and the dogs were let loose on them. Whoever fell down was shot on the spot.

As the crowd passed the narrow passage, many were covered with blood, screaming and crying. In front of them, was a huge square. They were ordered to undress. Whoever was not quick enough was furiously beaten and often shot. They had to enter into the ravine and soon the massacre started. Not all were killed instantly. Some, very few, were still alive. The Germans shone flashlights on the bodies and fired into those who moved. When the criminals left, in the darkness of the night, very few succeeded in pushing the corpses above them to the side, left the pits and escaped by crawling to the forest or to some Russian peasants' homes. Three days long—9/28/41, 9/29/41, 9/30/41—lasted this senseless slaughter.

Later, this very place, this bloody ravine area became *Concentration Camp Babi Yar*.

Its inmates were Russians and Ukrainian war prisoners and civilians from Kiev proper and neighboring cities. Thousands died of starvation, and beatings, hard labor, and diseases.

Each time a German soldier was killed, 100-300 human beings were taken out from Babi Yar and murdered as a reprisal.

The Special German Commandos for Genocide 77

Here were, as we can see, Russian war prisoners, young, strong and trained militarily. They did not put up any resistance, although they knew that they were going to die. They succumbed, did not rebel, because rebellion was impossible. They were apathetic, exhausted, and they knew that any resistance would be crushed. They had no mental, nor physical strength to start any kind of insubordination, knowing for sure that they'd be massacred in a terrible way. They thought that any day could bring changes. As it goes with the old saying which I myself repeated many times in Auschwitz:

"Even when the blade of the sword lies at your throat, you will not despair from the criminal's actions."

There had, always, been hope. Something might happen. If the war prisoners did not put up any resistance, how could one expect rebellion from old men, women and children, not trained, who even did not know how to use a gun? To say that they went like sheep to be slaughtered is wrong and offensive to the memory of the Nazi victims.

The Germans concentrated their victims first in ghettos. Weakened them by persecution, beatings, hard labor and starvation. Epidemic deseases broke out, which weakened the people still more. In such a feebled and fatigued condition they were brought to the gas chambers or to the ditches and murdered. In addition they had always been cheated and lied to by the "Ehrenvolk," with promises to be resettled.

I assure you, dear reader, that even military heroes would not have rebelled either, because rebellion was impossible. One would not even have believed that the Germans were going really to murder innocent people, because it had never happened before. The crime committed was of such an enormous scale that was unparallel in all the history of mankind. Nobody was conditioned to these atrocities.

I know it, because I was in the midst of the unfortunate victims, and thanks to many miracles was able to survive and to tell the world, whoever wanted to listen, of the wicked happenings and dreadfulness which I had seen with my own eyes. From time to time, special extermination trucks arrived from Kiev at

Babi Yar, fully packed with people. When the gas was turned on within the trucks, screams and frenzied pounding on the doors were heard at the beginning, and then the silence. . . .

One time, Russian women, waitresses in German bars, were brought in, completely naked, to Babi-Yar and killed by gas in the trucks. Perhaps they knew too much.

The final act of Babi-Yar occurred on August 1943, when the Germans were rolling back in defeat. The prisoners, iron clamps on their legs, were ordered to open up the mass graves of people murdered in 1941. The corpses were alternated with logs of wood, doused with oil and burned. Black smoke burst out, terrible and fearful. The stench was sickening, miles around. The bones were crushed into dust and scattered in the air, covering fields of agricultural patches.

Later, the same prisoners were taken to a neighboring ditch where 30,000 Red Army officers were buried. The corpses were dug out and burned. The Germans wanted to remove any kind of a trace of their past criminal acts. The prisoners, the grave diggers themselves, were later shot also. The Red Army recaptured Kiev on 11/5/1943, and they were informed of the enormous atrocities. Here again is a vivid illustration why the Germans lost the war. Instead of being good to the people who hated Stalin and his regime, they killed them for no reason at all. The Russians then realized that Hitler was one hundred times worse than Stalin.

Group D, under the Command of *Otto Ohlendorf*. He was the only one of the above four Group Commanders who was brought to trial in Nüremberg. According to his own recollection his group murdered 90,000 people, including children and women, in one year only, from June 1941 till June 1942. Ohlendorf was following the 11th Army in the extreme south.

Here are his own words:

"The local 'Einsatzkommando' collected the Jews by ordering a registration, on the pretext of being resettled. Then, they were collected in one place and then transported to the place of execution which was, as a rule, an antitank ditch or a natural excavation. The execution was carried out by firing squads, the bodies were buried in ditches. The valuables were handed over

The Special German Commandos for Genocide 79

to the Finance Minister." Ohlendorf declared also at Nüremberg that the German Army also knew about the massacres. In Simferopol, for example, the army requested quick action because there was a great shortage of housing. Not every German soldier was able to murder civilians and children. Therefore, the German Army created a special battalion of professional *criminals*, who had done the job. This battalion was called Dixlewanger Brigade.

The SS men accomplished this ferocious and heinous act willingly and cooperated fully. It was known that an SS man had the right to be transferred to the front any time that he wished.

When I was incarcerated in Günther-grube, which was one of the mines belonging to Auschwitz III, there was a guard from Yugoslavia, probably a "Volksdeutsch," who was shaken by the atrocities and volunteered to serve in the army. He was taken away from his place and sent to serve at the Russian front. Therefore the assertions of the criminals at Nuremburg trial, that they were compelled to commit all the atrocities under threat of being shot, were *false*. The real reason was that they wanted to avoid the front and to be free from fighting the Russians. They preferred to murder other people under the guise of being ordered to do so. Still others preferred to stay on their barbaric jobs in order to accumulate wealth from the innocent victims. One thing was clear, *they did their job voluntarily* for their own dark benefits and not because they were forced to do it.

Here is another description of an execution in Rovno, as narrated by Engineer Graebe, where my sister and her family probably perished.

"The town was illuminated. The people were driven out of their houses.... It was a terrible confusion. Women cried for their children and children for their parents. All the way they were beaten with whips, sticks, etc., till they reached the waiting freight train....

"All through the night, these beaten, hunted and wounded people moved along the lighted streets. Women carried their dead children and children dragged their dead parents by their arms and legs down the road towards the train. I saw many corpses of all ages lying on the streets. The doors of the houses stood open, windows were smashed. Pieces of clothing, shoes, stockings, coats were lying on the streets. At the corner of one house I saw a baby less than one year old lying with his skull crushed. Blood and brains were spattered over the house wall and covered the area immediately around the child."

These savage killings were going on in thousands of towns and villages all over occupied parts of Russia. Would anyone believe that a human being was capable of performing such bestialities?

No! Nobody would believe it. History does not know of such atrocities. The human mind could not absorb, nor comprehend it, and all these atrocities were organized years before, by an elected German government.

I would like to add, also, that in all these criminal acts, thousands of Ukrainians, Lithuanians, White-Ruthenians, took an active part, not under coercion, but voluntarily. Those auxillary foreign units very often reached the level of utmost brutality, equal even to the Super-race. How quickly a human being turns to a wild animal: These young people took for granted the enormous German atrocities and tried to emulate their masters. It is really a short distance between normality and pathology.

The murdering of the civilian population, the shooting in the ditches, had always been an unexpected phenomenon. The people had never seen it before, nor had they ever heard of this kind of murdering. They were not conditioned to this form of slaughter, especially of infants, children, women, and old men. It was unbelievable that a regularly elected government in the middle of twentieth century Europe would become simple murderers, surpassing any atrocities in the past. All this slaughter had, always, been accompanied by severe beatings, shootings, lashings, whippings and floggings.

The people were confused. They did what was demanded of them. They followed orders and walked to their destiny like in a trance, hypnotized by a superior wild, huge prehistorical beast. They did not comprehend what was going on around them. They knew one thing for sure, that the slightest infraction or insubordination would bring immediately a terrible death, for themselves, their children and friends.

This form of hypnotic-trance apathy and depression was part not of one race only. It became a part of every race, religion, civilian or military men. The masses of the Russian-occupied territories reacted just the same way. The same thing happened also to the Czechs, Poles, French or many other nationalities. The Germans massacred all of them at will. People were overwhelmed and did not foresee the true intentions of the Germans, till it was too late.

Even the hardened, trained, young soldiers, taken in captivity, were not immune to the same apathy. For example: On Block 11 of Auschwitz I there was a yard where thousands of war prisoners and young civilians, heroes in their circles, were shot to death without any resistance. They were all of different nationalities. Even hardened Russian soldiers were forced to the gas chambers in Auschwitz, being beaten and flogged on the way and choked to death, just the same as the old men and children were. This happened time and time again.

The victims did not comprehend the degree of German bestialities. Had the victims known, 100% sure, that they'd die, then all of them, even children and women, would have put up a resistance and would have fought for their lives with all their strength. There would have been nothing to lose. "We'll die anyway" would have been the slogan. "By fighting some of us might remain alive. By surrendering, all of us would die."

Had such atrocities, exhibited by the Nazis, happened before, had the people been conditioned to such crimes, all of them would have put up a desperate struggle. The Nazi murderer would have paid for his crime, very dearly. I knew it, I was sure about it. I was in the midst of all these unfortunate Nazi victims. I suffered together with them. I felt what they felt. My thoughts were the same as their thoughts.

On 10/15/1941, four months after the beginning of the war, Stahlecker of Group A reported that his commandoes murdered 118,430 Jews in the Baltic states alone.

On 12/2/1941, Professor Seraphim, Consultant of the Ger-

The Year 1942

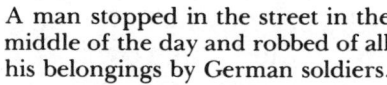

A man stopped in the street in the middle of the day and robbed of all his belongings by German soldiers.

Germans, after murdering many civilians, ordered a Jew to pray to his G-d, to save his life.

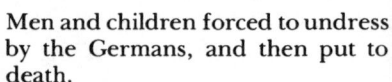

Men and children forced to undress by the Germans, and then put to death.

man High Command (OKW), stated that in the Ukraine were executed about 200,000 Jews. Out of 500,000 Jews of eastern Galicia, only 9,000 survived.

Eichmann figured that about two million Jews were exterminated by these German special Groups alone, totally six million Jews killed. Eichmann did not count the thousands killed at the hands of individual Germans, or the thousands who died as a result of beatings, hard labor, malnutrition, contagious diseases caused by enormous congestion in the ghettos, or the numerous suicides caused by sufferings. The number of those who perished by Nazi atrocities, including the concentration camps, way surpassed the six million given by Eichmann. If we add the number of prewar European Jews living in Poland, Lithuania, Latvia, Estonia, France, Yugoslavia, Italy, Hungary, the vast occupied Russian territories, *plus* natural population growth, and we subtract the number of all the survivors, the number will be much higher than six million. Hitler destroyed the main part of the Jewish nation. His name and the thousands of names of his voluntary helpers should never be forgotten in the annals of history. We have to repeat the narration of the bloody affairs of that time, from generation to generation. Our children have to study it in their schools. By doing this, we'll avoid another Hitler, another catastrophe.

I couldn't stand it any longer, and had enough of those terrible news. I returned to the peasant, who kept his horse at the yard of my cousin's house. I didn't want to waste any time and told the peasant to harness his horse and to return to Konstantinovo.

The peasant was in a very good mood, his mind well disposed. Evidently, he was treated very nicely during the few days while I was in the house of Dr. Kaufman.

It was a sunny, pleasant day. The journey was uneventful. We reached Konstantinovo, and I told my family that I received permission to move to Lyskovo.

Next morning, Mrs. Pomeraniec and myself left for Lyskovo. The road led us through a forest. We had to walk about twenty miles.

After a while, we became tired and sat down at the edge of the forest to rest a little.

In the distance, we saw an approaching car, loaded with Germans. We escaped to the forest unnoticed. Then, after ten minutes we saw another car. This time we didn't escape. We stood at the entrance of the forest and waited. The Germans in the car saw us. To our astonishment, the car did not stop. I noticed one German said a few words to the driver, who immediately accelerated the speed of the car. Evidently the masterrace suspected us to be partisans and they ran for their lives. We laughed at such an assumption, but it dawned upon us that the Germans were afraid too.

We quickened our steps, because they might inform the Gestapo. We arrived in Lyskovo in the afternoon, and found an apartment in the center of the town which consisted of three large rooms with a huge kitchen. The relatives of Pomeraniec promised to loan us some necessary furniture. We returned to Konstantinovo and started to pack. Two good horses were harnessed. Indispensable furniture, cloth, pillows, blankets were all packed and put on the carriage. My father, my brother Mendel walked nearby. It would be too heavy a load for the horses to carry us too. Michle was put on the top of the pillows. She went with us to help us temporarily in the housekeeping. My brother Moritz remained in the meantime in Konstantinovo. We took farewell from all our friends and neighbors and left. The horses started to move. I turned around and saw my brother Moritz standing nearby and waving goodbye to us. It was *the last time that I saw him*. He never came to Lyskovo.

A few months later, all the towns and cities in our neighborhood were transported to the concentration camps. But when the Germans came to Konstantinovo, he was able to escape together with two brothers Pomeraniec to the forest.

In spite of all the announcements, inquiries and investigations, I never heard anything from him.

We arrived at Lyskovo and moved into our previously rented house. Next morning I went to City Hall and presented my permit and order from Wolkowysk to the Mayor's deputy,

The Special German Commandos for Genocide 85

People deported to the gas chambers. (Photographed by a German in 1943.)

Mr. Luka. For reasons not known to me, he didn't like the idea, but had to accept it.

I put out in front of the house the sign of a doctor and was ready to practice medicine.

Lyskovo was a small town. The people had lived here peacefully for many years. Not far from me, on a side street, was the pharmacy. The owner was a very nice, decent fellow. He managed the pharmacy with extraordinary skill and love. He rented out part of his house to a refugee, a lady medical doctor, and her mother, a dentist. The lady doctor possessed a broad knowledge of medicine, in spite of her youth. It was too much work for her, because she was the only doctor for the town of Lyskovo and many villages around it. She needed help very badly. My practice met with an extraordinary success. I worked from morning till late at night. Patients used to come to my office not only from the surrounding villages, but also from many distant municipalities. This was my real first private practice of medicine and surgery. I was needed there and became famous in a very short time.

One morning, the German Commandant walked in. He had a venereal disease and wanted me to treat him. He acknowledged that his disease was chronic and difficult to cure. I wanted to tell him that he should go to his German doctors for treatment, because I did not belong to the Northern race. I treated him with Elendron, which was a new sulfur preparation. This was the first sulfur preparation on the market at that time (summer 1942). Even now we still use similar preparations for gonorrhea and other venereal diseases. The German was very satisfied, because he never achieved such excellent results previously. It was a miracle medicine. He was treated previously by bismuth preparations. After a few days he came back to tell me that his disease was cured completely, which was a pleasant surprise. He asked me to give him some injections to strengthen his system. I advised him of the preparation "Tonophosphan," which had to be administered by injections. He used to come to me 2-3 times weekly for the injections, and confided and trusted me.

He was a German and followed orders. He didn't know much about the Jews. He met them for the first time in Lyskovo, and he came to the conclusion that the Nazi persecution made no sense at all, and it was harmful to the Germans as a nation and detrimental to the war. He treated the Judenrat in a nice way and did not extract any money unjustly.

Robberies were very rare. No ghetto was formed in Lyskovo. There were many partisans around Lyskovo. They lived and acted in the forests, attacking Germans, military trains, bridges, and so on.

Moscow started to organize them in disciplined units. Stalin had ordered his scorched-earth policy already at the end of 1941. Many villages were burned voluntarily, leaving to the Germans vast devastated areas where nothing could be found except destruction and pestilence. The partisans were formed from fugitives, soldiers of the Red Army, civilians who escaped from the Gestapo, citizens who were expecting Gestapo assault on their towns. Many were killed in the forests by different partisan groups. They lived by the law of the jungle, the strong attacking the weak and devouring their prey. Life was in jeopardy all the time by the brutality and meanness of other men.

There were also bands who worked and fought against the Russians, like the "White Poles" in White Russia and Lithuania, or the "Bandrovtsy" or the "Green Bands" in the Ukraine. Dead bodies rotted away with the passing of time, their flesh picked off by hungry animals or birds.

The Jewish partisans had a very hard time. Individuals or small groups were hunted, robbed by some of the villagers and handed over to the Gestapo. For this abominable and wicked job they were paid by the Nazis.

The partisans suffered very much at the hands of the fascist Polish and Ukranian groups. At the end of 1941, Kalinin, the President of the Supreme Soviet, broadcast over the radio.

"The enemy behaves in a beastly, barbaric manner and practices total extermination of soviet citizens of the Jewish nationality. It is hereby ordered to carry through their evacuation to the interior of Soviet Russia, as a matter of priority.

"The life of every human being has to be protected, regardless of race, religion and nationality." Their condition improved slightly, but the anti-Semitism, although subdued, never disappeared from the scene. They fought, died, impressing friend and foe alike by their devotion, self-sacrifice and heroism.

Examples of courage.
Sholem Bass was a teacher in Zhetl, a small town near Wolkowysk. He organized the first partisan groups in the forests between the Niemen and the Szczara rivers. He could have lived all his life as a teacher in a small country school and nobody would have suspected that this man possessed latent military

organizational abilities, to impress the world by its daring and unsurpassed heroism.

Another heroic figure was a physician, Fr. Yechiel Atlas, who shared his command with Eliahu Lipszovitz from Dereczyn, near Rozana and with Eliezer Kovenski from Wolkowysk. They formed a brigade with the name *Pobieda* (victory), which was very popular, inflicting many casualties on the Germans. They attacked German soldiers, burned many bridges and even captured a German Aircraft. Dr. Atlas fell in battle 12/5/42. Mr. Kovenski from Wolkowysk was wounded heavily right before the reentry of the Russian Army and as a result he lost his right arm. He remained alive and resides, at present, in Israel.

Mr. Lipshovitz survived the war and to our humiliation and mortification was assassinated on May 1946 in Lignice (Silesia) at the hands of Polish anti-Semites who shot him unexpectedly from a hiding place. Imagine the tragedy of a hero who survived many dangers in the forests and the war to fall by the hands of a Polish coward, mean and arrogant, who belonged to the group of the "Endeckes." Mr. Lipshovitz fought all the time against the Germans who invaded Poland, and this was his reward by the "Polish Patriots."

Tens of thousands of Jews, men, women and children, escaped to the forest. They formed partisan family groups, under the protection of some of the partisan units. Many were killed and some were saved.

Some of the partisans operated near and around Lyskovo. People who cooperated with the German invaders were taken care of by the partisans. If someone was particularly mean, he was sentenced to death by the specific partisan courts and executed. The good, nice cooperators were respected. This view was a narrow one. To reward the good people and to punish the bad ones.

Soviet-trained guerillas were brought by airplanes and thrown into the partisan cadres. They were supervised, directed and partially supported by Moscow.

Stalin acted in a completely different direction. He ordered partisans to eliminate the good civilians working for the Germans and to save the mean ones. Such an order was misunder-

The Special German Commandos for Genocide

stood at the beginning. Later an explanation followed. The bad alienated the people and such behavior was good for the conduct of the war. The good officials, on the contrary, attracted the people to the Germans, which was not good for the conduct of the war. This was a cruel, but the right decision under the circumstances.

I remember one official was assassinated by the partisans. He was still alive. I gave him an injection of cardiazol to prolong his life. A German standing nearby told me not to give him any injections anymore. This was the reward for serving the Germans well and fighting for them.

Hitler spoke: He heard that the Jews were laughing. He thinks that some of them stopped laughing already. The other part will stop laughing very shortly. The year 1918 will not be repeated, when Germany capitulated fifteen minutes before twelve. "The Third Reich" will never capitulate.

The Germans sent over regular military units to combat the partisans, who became very dangerous by hampering the war effort. They assassinated Germans, taking away their rifles and ammunition, they destroyed bridges, railroads and military trains.

The city of Lyskovo became fully clogged with German soldiers whose task was to fight the partisans. An army doctor was with them in case of injuries sustained in the fighting. He had to leave for the nearby city of Wolkowysk and asked the Commandant whether he knew of a physician, who could substitute for him for 3-4 days. The Commandant, without hesitation, recommended me for the job. The German military doctor came into my office and asked me to take his place during his absence. I had to accept it, otherwise I would pay with my life.

And so, in the midsummer 1942, I became the German military doctor. Luckily, Hitler, Streicher, Rosenberg, didn't know about it. . . . They would have gotten a heart attack or at least a stroke at such abrogation of the Nüremberg Laws. I didn't like to see their faces, but I couldn't help the situation. Very often I told them to go to Wolkowysk because we didn't have the right medication. After four days the German doctor returned and they left Lyskovo for the forest. Thank G-d for that.

The Year 1942

We received bad news from Rozana. The Germans intensified the persecution of the inhabitants. They robbed, stole, murdered and entered the houses, even at night. Food was very scarce. Life was not secure. Epidemics caused by malnutrition, over-congestion of the living quarters, were rampant. Existence became intolerable. Our village Konstantinovo suffered likewise.

Mordehai Eshia was killed. He spent a few years as we know, in the U.S. of America. Returned to his village Konstantinovo and settled down, as I mentioned previously.

The agronomist of the city of Rozana, who was very friendly with the Germans, received many gifts from him. They used to meet each other very often. Each time he prepared for the agronomist a good meal with alcoholic drinks, because the latter loved vodka. It was difficult to provide all the good food in time of war, but Mordehai Eshia got it. Nobody knew the secret. In this way, the village of Konstantinovo was spared a lot of trouble.

One morning about 4 A.M., a German car stopped in front of the house of Mordehai Eshia. A few Germans with the agronomist came out of the vehicle and entered the house. They asked Mordehai Eshia to show them the road to the Jewish cemetery. They took away, also, his only son, about twenty-three years old. All of them entered the car and left in the direction of Rozana. When they reached the outskirts of the city, the Germans took out Mordehai Eshia and his son, chained them to the rear of the car by their legs. The car moved to the middle of the city, pulling the unfortunate victims, whose heads were hitting the rough stones of the street roads. Blood was gushing from those innocent human beings, covering the streets of Rozana where they spent all their lives.

For the Germans it was a play, a public exhibition of their bestiality. But for the civilian people, it was a terrible tragedy, an unexplained, unexpected and unheard-of brutality which called for revenge and hatred. In Lyskovo, such crimes did not happen. I was glad that I left Konstantinovo.

The war was going on, in different parts of the world. Intensive fighting in North Africa. Rommell started to attack on 8/30/42, believing that his thrust would bring him to Cairo.

THE SPECIAL GERMAN COMMANDOS FOR GENOCIDE

Montgomery, the British Commander, foresaw this attack, and when it came, he was fully prepared. Rommel had to withdraw, suffering many casualties in men and huge destruction of armor. Montgomery was a very careful military man. He didn't go after Rommel, but waited. In spite of superiority in men and ammunition, he did not attack and waited till the last week of October, because he knew that very soon the Americans and English would land on the west side of North Africa, which truly was later accomplished and executed.

The Germans had to fight on two fronts. Their army was destroyed and many thousands of prisoners taken. The brilliant attack led by Montgomery started in the east shore of Northern Africa on 10/23/42, followed two weeks later by the landing of Allied forces in the west (Algiers) on 11/8/42.

Rommel, the desert fox, was a very sick man at that time. As a matter of fact, he was ailing at Semmering in the mountains below Vienna, during the month of September.

When the British attack started in October 1942, General Stumme, who took the place of Rommel, died from a heart attack, 24 hours from the assault, while escaping a British patrol. Rommel had to return to North Africa from Germany, a very sick man. The Germans had not sufficient men, armor and fuel. The Allies dominated the Mediterranean sea and many convoys of food, ammunition and fuel were destroyed at sea before reaching their destination.

Rommel fought gallantly and made desperate efforts to stem the British, but he soon realized that the situation was hopeless. By May 1943, all the German and Italian forces were destroyed and North Africa was freed completely and forever from the German plague.

In July and August of 1942, the situation in Russia was desperate. The allies proposed help. They agreed even to send Air Squadrons (pilots and planes) to the dangerous Southern Russian front. They concurred also in sending fighting planes to Russia. Many convoys of indispensable war material were continuously flowing through Iran to the Soviet Union. The Allies promised a second front in Africa and later in Italy proper (the underbelly of the Axis).

But, in spite of all this actual and promised help, distrust and misunderstandings were discernible and visible in the Allied camp. The Russians suspected that the other side was trying for a separate peace. They demanded that those who were imprisoned in England be court-martialed.

From the documents revealed after the war, it became clear that England and America would never had thought of making a separate peace with such a bloodthirsty ciminal as Hitler. Nevertheless, a discord in the Allied camp existed at that time. The Nazis probably tried to make contact with Churchill and Roosevelt, but to no avail. As we'll see later, one thing was sure and documented. Hitler succeeded in making contact with the Soviet Union. Molotov even flew to German-occupied territory in order to discuss the possibility of a separate peace.

The fighting on the Eastern Front.

Hitler decided to attack vigorously on the Eastern Front in the South. His aim was to occupy Stalingrad and at the same time to penetrate deep into the Caucasus, to grab the oil of Grozny and Baku and to reach the Caspian Sea. Against the advice of his generals he tried to accomplish both: Stalingrad and the Caucasus at the same time. His chief of staff, General Halder, who protested such military madness, was dismissed on 9/24/42. The end result was that the Germans reached the Caucasus, but had to withdraw. Paulus' Sixth Army at Stalingrad was encircled on 11/6/42 and destroyed.

Life in Lyskovo was quiet. The German Commandant continued to come for treatment to my office. We heard about terrible crimes being committed in the towns and villages around us. A patient came over to me for treatment, she was in her twenties. She was a refugee from Niesviez, a small town not far from Lyskovo. She told me that many Jews of Niesviez had been murdered already, in 1941. One morning, in the midsummer of 1942, their town was surrounded in such a way that nobody could escape. Germans broke the doors of the houses and by beatings and shootings they forced everybody outside. Then they were transferred by trucks to the nearby ditches, where all of them were killed. Men, women and children

The Special German Commandos for Genocide   93

perished for no reason at all. She was shot and thrown into the ditch. Other people fell on the top of her and then it became quiet. All the Jews were shot. She felt that she was still alive. After a few hours, at night, she was able to crawl out from the ditch and came to her sister in Lyskovo. The same process of murdering, as I mentioned previously, took place in many other cities. The local commandant of Rozana, who lived in the house of the local pharmacist, did not permit them to do their job, saying that Rozana belonged to East Prussia (General Government). All the cities in White Russia, Ukraine, Lithuania, Latvia, met the same fate as Slonim and Niesviez.

Hundreds of thousands of innocent people perished in the summer of 1942. Cities like Baranovicze, Lida, Wilna, Rovno, Sarny, Pinsk, Lemberg had the same tragic destiny.

In Baranovicze was killed one of my friends, Mr. Pacovski, who studied medicine with me in Praha, Checkoslovakia (Carlovy University). He was crippled on one of his lower extremities by infantile paralysis in his youth. He was a very active and joyful fellow and everybody liked him. In spite of his defect, he charmed and fascinated the ladies and all of his friends and had, always, been the center of attraction. He didn't like to study, but his marks at Carlovy University were excellent. He passed the difficult examination of biology under Ruzicka exceptionally well. When he returned for vacation to Wolkowysk, he dressed up himself in the special attire of students with belt and decorations and fascinated the people. Unfortunately, he was not able to continue his studies because of lack of funds. He was married to a woman from Baranovicze, where he settled. After occupation of the city by the Germans, they ordered all the Jews to assemble at the market place. All the aged, disabled, weak and malnourished were set aside and shot. In this way, the pleasant fellow Pacovski died. This sad news was given to me, by relatives of Pacovski, who received a letter from his wife. "Lola is no more among the living. The bloodthirsty Germans took away his life," she wrote, and the letter was drenched with her tears.

The reader will ask, probably, right now, how was it possible that a so-called civilized nation should fall so deep in their morals, as to exhibit atrocities surpassing the wildest animals?

A German fully armed shoots a desperate innocent woman and her little daughter. Instead of fighting his enemies on the front he showed his Nazi ardor and heroism in this cowardly way.

The answer lies in the psychologically established fact that the Germans, more than any other nation on earth, possess sadistic tendencies, well hidden in their subconscious minds by the veil of civilization and culture.

These pathological tendencies were released by Hitler and his henchmen. Once released from the subconscious to the conscious mind, they unleashed enormous amount of energy in forms of evil and dreadfulness, which spread like fire, consuming more and more victims.

The future criminal, at the beginning, while committing his first crime, was still hesitating, because the sadistic and perverted tendencies were not completely released as yet. The first crime, successfully performed, liberated those tendencies completely, causing them to burst out in the open. The criminal, from this moment on, had no scruples any more.

Atrocities, murder, torture, stopped bothering him. They became a part of his life, a pattern of his behavior. They gave him satisfaction and fulfilment. This is what the Nazis learned in their schools, which made it possible for them to continue on their road of crime, always undertaking and assuming more dreadful forms of torture over other human beings, whom

THE SPECIAL GERMAN COMMANDOS FOR GENOCIDE   95

they considered to be subhumans, justifying herewith their crimes.

I was worrying about my sister and her family. They lived in Pinsk. In 1941 they moved to Sarny, not far from Rovno. I didn't hear anything from her. In view of the atrocities committed in Ukraine and White Russia by the German special Commandos (Einsatzgrupen), I had very little hope and expectation.

How had the Germans (Eisatzgrupen) acted in Pinsk and neighboring small towns and villages?

I'll bring here the testimony of *Mrs. Rivka Yossolevska* before the Israeli tribunal. She was a small middle-aged woman, with a gaunt and tragic face.

She had recovered recently from a heart attack and she felt very weak when she started to tell her story. Her physician permitted her to testify. Later her voice became louder and stronger, aided by a strength born out of desperation. She lived in a White Russian village with the name of Zagrovski, near Pinsk, where five hundred other Jewish families dwelled.

The first Nazi action occurred this way:

The Germans entered the house of the Rabbi and told him to put on his prayer shawl. Then they ordered everyone to assemble in the market place, where they commanded the Rabbi to pray and to preach a sermon. Most of the people escaped to the woods, where they heard firing in the village. At night, the shooting ceased and they returned to their houses. The Rabbi's wife told them that the Germans started to beat the people in the market place and drive them to the cemetery, where a ditch was prepared previously. Many were shot at that time. The people thought that the shooting was caused by some Nazi fanatics, without any authorization from the elected German government, who left the village in a hurry. They did not believe that the German authorities ordered it.

Later, on 8/14/42, the first day of Elul of the Jewish calendar, the real holocaust befell the village. The Germans attacked the ghetto and ordered the people out of their homes. Trucks appeared and the Jews were thrown into it. Some had to run behind the trucks. Mrs. Yossolevska had to run on foot carrying her little daughter in her arms. Other mothers had to run with 2-4 children. Whoever stumbled and fell was shot on the spot. They were beaten severely all the way.

After running about three miles, they reached a meadow. Corpses were lying on the way and near the meadow. Her little daughter said, "Mother, why did you make me wear the new Sabbath dress? We are being taken to be shot. What are we waiting for? Let's run!"

Some tried to escape, but they were all brutally tortured and shot.

"It was very difficult," she continued, "to hold onto the children. They didn't understand. We were pushed nearer to the grave, nearer to the end of our torture."

She narrated further how her father, mother and grandmother had been all shot, and how her sister begged for mercy, asking all the time, why? Why?

"Then our turn came, mine and my daughter's," Mrs. Yosselevska said. We reached the edge of the pit and the German said, 'Whom shall I shoot first?'

"I didn't answer. I felt the German tearing the child from my arms. The child cried out and was shot."

Mrs. Yosselevska sobbed. Then she went on.

"He grabbed me by the hair and turned my head around. I heard a shot and fell into the pit."

"Then I felt that I was suffocating. People were falling on top of me. I was still alive."

In a choking voice, she told the tribunal how she struggled upward through a pile of corpses. "Dying victims were biting at my legs and trying to pull me down."

Later, realizing that she was all alone and that her daughter remained in the grave, she returned to the pit and clawed at the fresh dirt that had been thrown over it. She cried, "I was digging with my fingernails, trying to join the dead." She burst into tears again and continued. "I dug with my fingernails, but the grave did not open. I did not have enough strength."

"I thought, why didn't they kill me? What was my sin? I saw them all being killed. Why was I spared? Where should I go?"

Mrs. Yosselevska was wounded in her head. A farmer sheltered her and took her to the forest, where she joined the partisans.

I thought of my sister, Rosa.
Was she, her husband and all his family, murdered in such a terrible way?
I was stronger than iron that I was able to endure it.
All my body was trembling when the atrocities appeared again before my eyes.
In spite of strenuous search and investigation, I never heard of her again.
Could the world survive another holocaust?
Why are the world leaders so silent in front of the present German Nazi courts, which carry the seeds of another more violent holocaust?
One day, I was called to visit a patient. When I arrived, I saw a nice woman about thirty years old crying desparately, lamenting about lost lives. From aggravation she was despondent, forelorn. From agitation she tore out the hair from her scalp and broke everything that came under her hands. I tried to quiet her down by talking to her and by administering sedation. She calmed down a little and from time to time she groaned, wailed, wringing her hands in desperation. Later, I was informed that she arrived from Lida, a town between Wolkowysk and Vilno, escaping from a German massacre. She saved her life by a sheer miracle.
At this moment she had found out that all her family was murdered, and this triggered a nervous breakdown. I was deeply shaken by this terrible scene and was thinking again about my sister.
I returned to my office, evidently pale very upset and stricken.
G-d! I said, how long would these atrocities continue? When were they going to end?
Michle came, asking me what happened. I told her the grim story. She cried lamenting about our fate.
The atrocities committed by the Germans could never be

forgiven. They stood out as a symbol of cruelty unique in the history of mankind.

It served, also, as an illustration of what degree of evil humans could reach.

It was unbelievable, but it was the truth!

If someone will say that it was impossible for such atrocities to occur on our planet, I'll answer only that I myself witnessed some of them, and that they constituted not only the truth, but they presented only a pale reflection of the real happenings, which no human being was able to describe in its entirety, nor were people able to comprehend it.

The horror becomes still worse when one remembers that all the crimes were committed not by animals, not by primitive men, but by human beings of the twentieth century, considered to be normal up to era of Hitler.

When we realize, that most of those criminals are walking free on the streets of Germany today, and that some of the German prosecutors defend the murderers openly in the courts without being ashamed and without regard to the future German history, then we must agree that the holocaust was not ended with the demise of Auschwitz and Treblinka.

Next morning, news reached me, that two of my relatives from Ostrov-Mazovieck saved themselves during a similar Nazi action and had arrived at Wolkowysk, living temporarily in the house of my cousin. This was what happened:

The Nazis packed their trucks with people from their city, who were guarded by armed Nazis, in order to be taken to the extermination places.

My relatives were forced into one of the trucks, where they had to kneel. In the first row was kneeling a man, known for his strength. Two Nazis were standing nearby with their guns ready to shoot. The truck started to move.

After about fifteen minutes, the strong man in the front row, out of desperation, pushed his hands between the legs of the Nazis and threw them out of the moving vehicle. The other Nazis became confused. In the meantime, the other victims attacked the few Nazis left, including the driver, and escaped.

Taking in consideration the circumstances, which I witnessed myself, it was an extraordinary courage and stroke of luck, born out of desperation. Many similar cases occurred, but almost all of the attempts ended in failure. My relatives succeeded in saving their lives temporarily.

Fighting the partisans intensified. The Germans suspected that the local White Russian peasants helped the partisans. Therefore hundreds of peasants were rounded up and sent to concentration camps. Some were being shot on the spot.

One day, while I was busy in my office removing a foreign body from the ears of one of my patients, we heard many rifle shots. We found out that many peasants, from the neighboring villages, were rounded up for no reason at all and locked up in the local church of Lyskovo. They were kept there overnight and in the morning they were all shot to death. From time to time we heard shots, which signified to us that a group of peasants was being killed. My patients, most of them peasants themselves, were sitting in the waiting room trembling from fear. I myself, accustomed to German atrocities, felt unnerved, especially since the peasants were completely innocent.

This was the way, practiced in thousands of villages and towns on a large scale, the Germans terrorized the local people and these were the methods used.

Rumors were spreading that Hitler, realizing that he could not win the war, had contacted the Russians for a possible peace. The Soviets demanded a return to the old borders of 1941 and reparation for damages done. Stalin, at that time, was very angry at the Allies because they did not open a second front in France. The Russians were also very much afraid of a German separate peace with the English. They could not understand either the secrecy surrounding the Hess case. But Hitler, even now, was too bombastic and arrogant and demanded Russian territory as a price of peace.

My office was in the house of Mr. Reznick. He was a nice-looking bachelor, and was compelled to go out to work, every morning, together with other people. Once he came home telling us that his place of work was raided by the partisans. My patients were telling me too about the night visits of the partisans. They were partially armed, very courageous and not too much afraid of the Germans.

Berl Pomeraniec came from Rozana to visit us. He told us a terrible story. Two partisans came to spend a night in one of the peasant's houses. The Soltys of the village Vola denounced them to the Germans. They were taken out in the middle of the night, without shoes, and shot in the yard. The peasants felt sorry for the killing and blamed the Soltys for calling the Germans. The Soltys justified himself, that he didn't know that the Germans were going to kill them right in front of the house, and secondly that he was afraid that the Germans would shoot him for not reporting.

Rumors were spreading that the ghetto in Warsaw was being liquidated. Trains full of people were taken to the Treblinka extermination camp, where they perished in the gas chambers.

In the summer of 1942, a few months after I left Wolkowysk, all the physicians, doctors, dentists, engineers, were arrested, on a suspicion that a wounded partisan was treated by one of the physicians.

The following doctors were arrested:

Dr. Weinberg (the chief of the Judenrat), Dr. Kaufman (who helped me to get the permission to move to Lyskovo), Dr. Velvelski (the surgeon of the hospital), Dr. Siedlecki (the pediatrician), and Dr. Panter (dermatologist, a refugee). The dentists were Dr. Trop and Dr. Einhorn (woman), Dr. Peisakova and Dr. Mant.

Pharmacist Ochron. Engineer Goliatzki, Technicians Rojtman and Pollack.

These were the doctors who lived in Wolkowysk.

Luckily, I practiced medicine in Lyskovo, otherwise I would have been arrested also.

Dr. Kaplan, Dr. Amscibovski and Dr. Mashicki were also from Wolkowysk, but they practiced in different small towns, outside Wolkowysk. In this way they were all lucky not to be apprehended.

The above-mentioned arrested doctors were kept temporarily at the "Koszary," where the Polish cavalry men kept their horses before the war.

Apprehension, fearfulness, anxiety encompassed and took hold of all the inhabitants of Wolkowysk because the arrested doctors were innocent. The technicians and two woman dentists were released later, which encouraged their relatives and friends.

Everything was done to liberate the unfortunate people. The Germans took money, gold, other valuables promising to let the doctors go free.

In spite of all the pledges and predictions, the prisoners were not acquitted.

The frightened populace saw one morning, on 10/13/42, a truck moving through the city. Inside were the poor doctors. They were taken outside the city to the "Burkes," the forest near the city which served previously as a resort place, and all of them were shot in cold blood.

They were all buried in a common grave. Still today, an interested tourist can see the grave, and the sign above it, of the unfortunate victims of Nazi bestiality.

This was a premonitory sign, a portent, of approaching disaster.

October 1942.

I went to City Hall and asked the commandant for wood, because it had become already chilly. My request was immediately granted. Rumors were persisting that the Germans had decided to liquidate also the Jews who belonged to East Prussia, which included Rozana, Wolkowysk and Lyskovo. Officials from City Hall confirmed it. Some heard the Commandant saying that the Jews would shortly be resettled and that other workers would have to substitute them.

Very bad news indeed. Not everybody believed it. It was impossible, to take out people for nothing and to slaughter them. The people simply were not conditioned to such atrocities. The Germans kept one sector ignorant of what happened in the other. Nobody could travel from one town to another town

Left: Dr. S. Markus, Director of Medical Clinics, committed suicide by shooting himself with the last bullet, while fighting against a superior German force. Center, top: Dr. D. Kaufman, graduate in Medicine in Geneva, Switzerland; bottom: Dr. Weinberg and Dr. Kaufman. Dr. Weinberg was chief of the Judenrat. Right: Dr. Siedlecki, pediatrician. His daughter recognized him while he was led to his death.

without permission, under penalty of death. Radios were not in our possession. They were confiscated. People lived in complete isolation.

Different kinds of rumors were spreading. But rumors remain rumors. The Jews in Wolkowysk, Lyskovo lived in a false sense of security, because they were a part of the Third Reich.

One day, I was sitting near my office outside, enjoying the nice weather, the fresh air, and the shining sun. My old teacher Yankovski passed by. I remembered him well. He was living on the first floor above our apartment in Wolkowysk. He was a very intelligent man, and lived together with the principal of the school, who also was a bachelor. One day his sister came to visit him. They lived together in one large room upstairs. The lady was very charming. The principal fell in love with her and they were married in a short while thereafter.

My old teacher told me now that he had moved from Wolkowysk to a nearby residence and was very glad to see me, and enlightened that one of his pupils was a a medical doctor in Lyskovo. He was of Polish nationality and hated the Germans, as all his nationals did. He told me that the Germans would lose the war and that their present success was only temporary. He came to visit me a few more times and then disappeared. Maybe he was arrested or was afraid to come too often.

In Wolkowysk, there was a "Felczer," who like many other Felczers was allowed to practice medicine without having the education of a real doctor of medicine. He was a kind of chiropractor, but not limited to the spine and joints only. This was a reminder of the old times of Russian Tzarism. He was a wise man, but not of very good character. He used to visit our business in Wolkowysk and respected my father highly.

During the Russian occupation, we worked together in the emergency clinic, and were not specifically attracted to each other, in spite of his long acquaintance with my father. I didn't like his behavior, nor his character. In other words, I was disappointed in him. Since he was not of Polish nationality, but a White Russian, he kept himself aloof during the Soviet occupation.

I had all but forgotten about him. One day, somebody called me to the City Hall. I didn't understand the reason. When I came, I saw to my surprise the old White Russian "Felczer," Mr. Gomolovitz, from Wolkowysk. He told me that he had become the supervisor of all the doctors of the county of Wolkowysk, to which also Lyskovo belonged. He took my name and address and departed. After a few weeks, Felczer Gomolowitz called me again to City Hall. This time I was a little scared. Who knows what such a character might connive? He was now at the height of his career under the Nazi regime. Fortunately everything was all right. He asked me a few more questions and I gave him regards from my father. Maybe it helped, because he let me go and didn't bother me any more.

In Lyskovo was a Pollack, who belonged to the "Endekes." He hated the Communists very much, because he possessed a lot of land. He took part in almost all the raids against the partisans. In fact he was the main participant. He was aware of the danger, and always walked around with a machine gun, which he kept also, near his bed, at night. He didn't molest anybody, but people were afraid of him.

Mendel showed me some of the valuables and the place where he buried them in the stable, deep inside, half a yard deep under the surface, covered with earth and a lot of wood. The valuables were protected inside by an iron box.

"Here," he said, "were the valuables. If we all perish and you remain alive, remember the place."

I never returned to Lyskovo. Mendel had a prophetic premonition, because nobody of my family survived.

Although we were surrounded by partisans, I never was able to contact them directly. Maybe, I didn't try hard enough. Another thing in my disfavor was the fact that I never had an occasion to serve in the army. The Polish army did not accept me and had always delayed my recruitment. They wanted only officers of *Polish* nationality in their army. I was a college graduate and, according to the law, they had to accept me in the officers school only. I was not very eager to join the Polish army, which committed a lot of barbarities against the Jews after World War I. The murder of people in Pinsk and Rozana stood vividly before my eyes.

These two factors, the no-contact with the partisans and the lack of regular army training, kept me immobilized in Lyskovo. In retrospect, I was pondering what would have happened had my family, together with the strong, healthy young boys of the family Pomeraniec, organized and prepared a good hidden place in the forests? Maybe some of our families would have remained alive. We could have, even, organized a small fighting unit and done a lot of damage to the Germans.

On the other hand, nobody believed, at that moment, that Hitler would really destroy an entire race, without any reason.

Would the decent part of the German nation permit him to commit such crimes? The living in the forests was combined also with a lot of danger caused by groups sympathetic to the Nazis and imbued with enormous hatred to the Jews. Thousands of escapees lost their lives in the forests or on the way to it. Still, up to now, I have a feeling that our families would have come out much better had we left our warm homes and disappeared in the forests.

November 1st, 1942 Sunday. (The day before the evacuation from Lyskovo).

We heard sounds of approaching horses and carriages. Looking through the windows. we noticed many carriages and

The Special German Commandos for Genocide   105

peasants gathering in the market place. Nobody knew what was the meaning of this. We had never seen in Lyskovo so many carriages on Sunday. The peasants didn't know either. They were ordered by the Germans to assemble.

Rumors were spreading, that the horses and carriages would be used in fighting the partisans. Others thought that the peasants of the villages dominated by the partisans would be resettled and their houses burned. Actually nobody knew for sure.

We became very restless. Some trembled with fear of their lives. Turbulence, unrest and emotional agitation were visible on the faces of all of us. A bad omen! We felt that a black cloud was gathering upon us. Enormous sufferings and maybe annihilation were in store for us.

We felt that belonging to East Prussia did not protect us. In the afternoon, rumors were spreading, that the carriages and the horses, assembled at the market place in Lyskovo, were for the purpose of, and connected with, the evacuation of the Jews from Lyskovo.

I went to the Judenrat to talk with the chief, Mr. Abrahams. He was a tall honest fellow, and had tried his best to postpone the destruction and to avoid the evacuation of his city. At the beginning he did not want to talk, but later he admitted that all the Jews had to assemble next morning in the market place.

I returned home and informed my family of everything. They started to pack the very necessary items and to hide the rest. Maybe we'd be able some day to return home. In the evening, I went to the house of the German Commandant to find out the exact cause of ordering all Jews to assemble. I entered the courtyard. Darkness was all over. I found the entrance door and knocked. Nobody answered. I wanted already, to turn around and leave. Suddenly I heard a woman's voice.

"Who is it?" I answered, "This is the physician, who treated the Commandant, and I would like to talk to him. It was very important."

"We couldn't let you in," the woman answered. "It is night. Come tomorrow."

"Tomorrow will be too late," I yelled in desperation. Nobody answered. The door closed.

I left and couldn't help myself thinking about the successful treatment I administered to the Commandant. He was cured from a chronic bad disease. And now, when I needed him, he didn't want to talk to me.

I noticed light shining through one of the shuttered windows. I came nearer and heard voices intoxicated with alcohol, rejoicing and calling, "Heil Hitler."

Next morning this horde, the bloodthirsty scum of the earth, would come out, armed to the teeth, and murder little children, women and men.

I was careful not to knock on the door again, and looking in retrospect, I was right in not doing so, because they would have killed me on the spot. Here is a real case of entering the tiger's mouth and not being devoured in the process.

This was miracle #4.

The pharmacy, the office of the lady doctor and her mother the dentist were not far away. I decided to visit them. They told me that they were aware of the bitter news. The pharmacist was extremely nervous. The lady doctor, her face expressing extreme nervous tension, proposed to me to take cyanide if necessary. They all chose to commit suicide by poisoning themselves. They preferred to die in their home than to be dragged to some distant execution place.

I left them very heartbroken. Returning home, I found every one was preparing a small package of the most necessary items. I'll always remember this terrible night. Nobody went to sleep. I lay down for a few hours to rest and to prepare myself for the future events, but could not rest. Poor Mendel was among us. He could have been in Palestine and didn't have to suffer so much. A dim light illuminated our apartment and a heavy choking air settled in the house.

November 2nd, 1942. Evacuation.

Early in the morning, I went to see the pharmacist, who was such a decent fellow, a remainder of the old aristocratic generation, and found them all dressed and ready. Every one of them, the pharmacist, the lady doctor and her mother the dentist, had a package of poison in their pockets. They were waiting only for the order to leave their house. Determination, resolution, was written on their faces. The pharmacist was very nervous. I saw him writing a letter. We all heard desperate voices announcing that the dreadful order arrived. Everybody had to assemble in the market place. Anyone found in the house will be shot.

The tragedy made its appearance. Sounds of weeping, sobbing, crying, lamenting uttered by a confused, cataclysmic mass, walking to their annihilation were heard all over. People were shot, beaten, flogged by the bloodthirsty beasts.

The Commandant arrived, accompanied by the Pope's (a minister in the Christian Orthodox Church) daughter. A tall blond girl who worked for the pharmacist during the last two months, probably in preparation for this moment. The German told the pharmacist that he must leave his house immediately and hand over the keys of the pharmacy to his helper, the girl, who would be in charge of the pharmacy.

The pharmacist, pale, lips trembling, the hands shaking, turned over the keys to the girl. He gave over to her also a letter, asking her to mail it to his relatives in France. They should know what happened to him.

The German didn't even look at me. I treated him without any charge, for many months. He was cured of despicable chronic disease, thanks to me. Now, everything was forgotten. This was already the good German.

"I could not do anything," he murmured. "Even shoemakers, tailors, plumbers whom we need here very badly, must go too." I looked at him and would have liked to ask him, why didn't he volunteer for another job? Why did he prefer to stay here and to participate in such criminal acts?

I was overcome with grief, stricken by fear, and returned to my house. They were all waiting for me.

We left the house in disarray. The streets leading to the market place were full with people carrying small packages, beaten on the way by the Germans. Shots were heard all over. Dead people were lying on the streets. Many committed suicide.

The pharmacist, the lady doctor and her mother swallowed

the poison and they were already dead. Their sufferings were finished.

I decided not to follow in their steps. I would fight for my life, as much as I could. It was better, if necessary, to attack a German and even be killed by their bullets, than to commit suicide. Although, under the circumstances I understood fully those who thought otherwise.

Instead of going to the market place, I tried to see whether I could pass through the cordon of the White Russian guards who encircled the city from all sides. I tried all the four corners. It was impossible. They stood with their guns all around the city and didn't let anybody out. They were shooting and ordering us to return to the market place. I was followed by Michle, who at a certain moment continued to walk towards one of the guards.

"Shoot me," she said, "I don't want to live in such a cruel world."

The guard, to my surprise, did not shoot her, but took us back to the city. To attack the guard did not make sense. He wasn't even a German. He was a simple young White Russian, working in the police department as an auxillary force. He didn't know even what he was doing. No! I would wait for a better moment, I would always have an occasion to attack and be killed.

I returned to the city. So many patients were treated, cured in my office. They always had respected and loved me. Maybe somebody will help me in my extreme need. No, they couldn't do it. They were terribly afraid of their own lives. Anyone who was hiding and helping a Jew would be shot. I joined the rest of the people on the market place. The Germans were assembling their victims, beating and flogging them all the time. They lined us up in rows of five. The people envied the pharmacist and the female doctors, who were not among us. They belonged, already, to eternity. We were still here and our suffering was enormous.

We were standing and waiting. Germans all around us, pounding, flailing and banging many of us. I was hit on my back with a heavy stick. Men and women were grouped separately. Children, infants, weak, sick, very old were loaded on carriages drawn by horses. The Germans claimed all the time that we would be resettled to factories, where we'd work for the German Army. The sick and weak would be treated in hospitals.

Suddenly, we heard vehement earth-shaking and ear-splitting voices.

"The doctor's helper is fainting, she is falling."

I went over to the women's group and recognized the helper of the doctor lying on the dirty soil, dying. Characteristic muscular twitchings appeared, stiff neck, muscular jerks, jaws rigidly shut, face livid. "Please don't help me" she said in a low voice. "I don't want to live. I beg my husband to forgive me. . . ."

I couldn't help her. A German was already standing behind me pounding me with a stick, and I had to run away back to my row. I looked at her, she was put on one of the carriages on the top of the bundles. Titanic convulsions set in every 3-5 minutes. Evidently, she had taken a large dose of Strychnine. Attack followed attack and she died soon afterwards.

We were still waiting. Germans and White Russians, armed with machine guns, revolvers, were all around us. I saw Mr. Abrahams, the chief of the Judenrat dragged, bullied and pushed to our group. He was severely beaten over his head and other parts of his body.

The road to Podoresk.

Around 9 A.M., our columns started to move. The men were marching first, followed by the women. Behind them, the carriages with the sick, killed, children and infants, followed by our bundles and packages. On both sides of the column walked the Germans and their local helpers of the White Russian Police. Everyone had a gun, directed towards us. Behind followed a truck loaded with Germans with heavy machine guns. In the middle stood a heavy cannon for firing multiple projectiles.

We left the city Lyskovo, never to see her again. We didn't know where the bloodthirsty beasts were taking us. Some said that they'd take us behind the city and shoot us in the ditches. Others argued that they'd probably take us to the gas chambers.

The day was nice and warm. The sun was shining brightly, and wondering what was going on? The sun's rays were accompanying us, to see and observe our road of pain, our fate and to return to G-d in the evening for a complete reporting.

We continued to march. Evidently, they were not taking us to the ditches. Soon we became tired and exhausted. All of us were thirsty and hungry. Whoever stopped on the way for a little rest was shot on the spot. The road was scattered and disseminated with dead bodies. Some of the Germans who rode on horses entered the columns of the marching people, beating them with sticks and letting their horses step on us and crush us.

I left my row for a moment in order to see what was rubbing my right leg and to pull off my boot.

"Watch out," I heard voices all around.

I turned around and noticed that a German, near me, riding on his horse, was pulling out his revolver, directing it towards me. I jumped right away into the middle of the column, taking my boot with me, and had a very hard time to put it on again.

I recognized the road. It was the road towards Wolkowysk. On the side of our column was walking a civilian, a White Russian. The German nearby pulled out a pistol and wanted to shoot him. The White Russian showed him his documents. He was probably an important man, because the German let him go. He even argued with them.

We passed small villages, fields and forests. Many were shot on the way.

About 3 P.M. we entered Podorosk.

I felt very tired, weary, exhausted and lay down on the naked earth to catch my breath. We were concentrated on a huge place adjacent to the village. The location was surrounded by Germans and the local police.

Near me completely exhausted were lying my poor father, my brother Mendel, and Michle, who joined us.

I was contemplating what to do? How to escape? After a short time, all the Jews from Podorosk and neighboring villages were brought into our place. I recognized Dr. Shulman and his wife, whom I visited about eight months ago. He told me that this was the second time that he was taken away together with other

Jews. On the first time they freed him and his wife, because he was requested back by the village. They were in need of a doctor.

"Maybe," he said in desperation, "they'll let me free now too." I wished him good luck and returned to my family. It showed again the thinking of the people, their reasoning and understanding of the situation. I couldn't rest any longer. I looked for a way to escape and walked all around our place. It was impossible. We were surrounded by devils armed with heavy guns.

I continued to walk around and looked for a possibility to get away. Maybe, all by myself, I could have cleared out. But I would never leave my family all by themselves. This was unthinkable. I was still young, strong, educated and without me, they'd perish.

Darkness started to set in, the sun was sinking at the end of the horizon, together with our heart, strength and hope.

Suddenly we heard gun shots from a distance and sounds of desperation, lamentations and sobbings. In the darkness we listened and recognized sounds of floggings, whippings, lashings. It was terrible! The Jews from Rozana and neighboring localities were pushed in, and shoved into our place. Some of the family Pomeraniec arrived too.

"What happened to the rest of the family?" I asked. "Where is my brother Moritz?"

They told us that Moritz, together with Michle's brothers, Berl and Shlomo, escaped to the forests. Mr. and Mrs. Pomeraniec, Chasa, and Itzl with his nine-month pregnant wife arrived and joined us.

Even now I can not comprehend how she was able to march under such circumstances. Sometimes a human being is stronger than iron.

It happened this way:

Rozana was surrounded. The inhabitants were driven outside the town. In the meantime, the people in the nearby village of Konstantinovo, where my brother Moritz lived, were informed about it. Soon Konstantinovo was surrounded by White Russians also. Some of the people succeeded to escape. Mrs.

Pomeraniec was worrying about them. She didn't let me tell my father that Moritz escaped without a coat, and it was getting cold at night. They were beaten on the road. Many were shot. There was hardly a place to sit after the people of Rozana joined us. The Germans put up a big fire nearby in order to illuminate our place. They shot into the crowd, killing many of us. The multitude of people moved from one to the opposite side causing devastation and more congestion.

Although we were on the outside, under the blue sky, on a cool November night, we felt hot and choking because of lack of air and anxiety. Then the Germans started to shoot on the other side and the mass of people was forced to move to the opposite edge of the camp.

All night was going on like that. No rest was possible. We had, always, to be on alert, lest we be crushed, lacerated or shot. It looked like inferno on earth. The huge fire on one side of the camp, the beatings, the constant shootings made us very bitter and despondent.

The husband of the doctor's helper was lying near us. Finally, he couldn't stand it any longer and swalled the strychnine which he had, evidently, prepared previously. Soon he died, and joined his wife who committed suicide right at the beginning.

The road to Wolkowysk.

At daybreak, although very tired, exhausted, sleepy, we had to get up and march again. As the people gradually left, the congestion decreased. Alas! so many people dead, killed or committed suicide. Hundreds were lying on the field, dead after one night of hell. Not far from us was the body of the doctor-helper's husband. A young, decent man dead because of Nazi bestiality. The Germans were running over the field beating, lashing and shooting everybody on sight. We started to speed in the direction of the main road.

I saw a German beating my father. He ran away, tripped over a stone and fell down. The German pulled out his gun and wanted to shoot. I was ready to jump the ugly barbarian, no matter what the consequences were.

"This is the end!" I said and approached the German. At this moment, my father got up and with all his strength joined the running crowd. My life was saved again. This time by my father. On the road, we were assembled in rows of five. My father, Mendel, myself and two other Jews formed our row. First the men, then the women, followed by carriages with our packages and bundles. Some children who remained alive were also in the carriages.

The Germans were riding their horses and galloping them into the masses, killing and injuring many. The men, who were marching in the front tried to walk more slowly in order to give a chance for the women to follow us. The latter were falling on their feet and many of them were shot, their bodies remaining on the road. Our landlady, Mrs. Reznick, the sister of the bachelor, a decent woman of a very high intelligence, couldn't continue and in desperation sat down to rest for a minute. A German approached her and drew his revolver.

"Shoot me," she said.

The German, to the amazement of all, instead of shooting her, started to hit her with a stick. She got up and joined the crowd. She would like very much to die and get rid of all the sufferings, but she was unwilling to be beaten to death by a savage beast with a German face. She moved further with all her strength.

The German chief asked whether some physicians were among us. Dr. Schulman and myself stepped forward. He asked us whether we had our families here. The answers were affirmative.

"March in front of the column," the German ordered, "and later we'll see."

I didn't know the meaning of his words. Dr. Schulman explained it in his usual optimistic way.

"They need doctors," he said. "No doctors were left in the cities. This is the reason of asking us whether we had families. They'll have to free us."

I didn't answer. Looking back in retrospect, we can see how the people were ignorant of the real facts of life around them, as displayed by the Germans, who wanted to destroy first of all the educated persons. This was the real reason, why the Germans ordered us to step out of the column and to walk in front of the crowd. They didn't want to lose us. A German taxi reached our column and asked for the commanding officer, whom he hand-

Exhausted, despondent, tired, people were taken out to be slaughtered. Note the innocent little children, one with a sack on his shoulder. They didn't understand what was going on. The delicate young women and old men were murdered for no reason at all, by the will of a few criminals. (Photographed by a German.)

The Special German Commandos for Genocide

Civilians taken to the railroad station, loaded in cattle trains, and transported to the gas chambers. See the sadness, apathy and exhaustion of the victims. The German with the gun expresses satisfaction and cruelty.

ed a paper. Dr. Schulman still expressed his hope that the paper contained something to free us. I didn't object. Let him hope. In view of the past German atrocities and the mass shootings on the roads, I gave up all expectations of a change for the better. We continued to march forward, trying to slow down our column in order to give a better chance to the weak ones who followed us, especially to the women.

116　　　　　　The Year 1942

Jews from all over, congregated in front of the trains in special assigned places, to be transported later to their annihilation. (Note the group of children, upper right.)

Men and women waiting for their execution.

THE SPECIAL GERMAN COMMANDOS FOR GENOCIDE 117

A Nazi using his boot on his victim, who couldn't jump into the bus quickly enough; the destination of the bus was death in the gas chamber.

People standing near the wall, to be shot in a short while.

People from Lodz were taken out of their homes (September, 1942) and shot.

People died in the ghettoes from starvation, diseases caused by over-congestion and malnutrition. Some were shot by the Germans or were beaten to death. The bodies were taken outside the cities and buried in common graves.

Civilians caught on the streets of Europe and despatched to the German concentration camps.

118 THE YEAR 1942

Innocent civilians led to the execution.

Poles led to their extermination.

Nazis shooting innocent people for no purpose at all and for no benefit to the conduct of the war. Such senseless killings occurred in cities, towns and villages throughout the German-occupied territories.

Jews from all over Europe were caught on the street and sent to the concentration camps. The lucky ones were sent to Germany for hard labor.

The Special German Commandos for Genocide 119

My boots gave me a lot of trouble, something rubbed me inside, and every step caused me pain. I decided to take off my boots, and leave them on the ground. It was a very hot day and the compulsory march added to the heat. I threw also my coat on the side, in order to get some relief. A White Russian Policeman told us that all the items thrown on the roads would be collected by the carriages in the back.

I walked barefooted on a hard road which was covered with small pebbles. My feet were not accustomed to walk without shoes, naked, on a rough road. Nothing could be done and I continued to walk. The dorsal of my foot, the part on which I stepped on, became painful, apparently caused by a small pebblestone which penetrated the epidermis of my foot. I stepped for a minute outside and was able to pull out the pebble. The Commander pulled out his revolver, stretched out his hand in my direction and. . . .

I quickly jumped into the crowd and blended into the mass. After a few minutes I reached Dr. Shulman and walked on his side in front of the column.

We advanced more and more towards the city of Wolkowysk. We saw, already, the scattered houses on the periphery, and were glad that the end of our tragic march was near. I strained my feet badly, marching without shoes, but I tried to encourage myself, not to give in and to endure the ordeal.

We saw from far away the "Koszary" of the city of Wolkowysk. Dr. Schulman and myself had to stand in front of the gates and count the number of people, entering the large camp, the ex-Polish "Koszary."

The commander stopped in front of us, called in a German soldier and ordered him something important secretly. I did not pay any attention. But, Dr. Schulman was able to hear the order, which was to shoot both of us as soon as all the people entered the camp.

Dr. Schulman became very pale and jittery and told me what he heard. We looked for a way of escaping into the camp to lose ourselves into the masses. But the German was standing nearby watching us. Very bad situation, indeed! Suddenly a civilian, apparently a German too, came over to us and he spoke

to the German, who was watching us. He encouraged us to count and not to be afraid. As soon as we reached the last scores, he told us to run into the camp for our safety. We did so, and became a part of the masses.
This was another miracle. MIRACLE #5.

CHAPTER VI

Wolkowysk concentration camp.

KOSZARY (EX-LOCATION OF POLISH CAVALRY). BUNKER LYSKOVO, BUNKER ROZANA. THE CAMP KITCHEN. THE DEATH OF MR. GALIN. FIRST TRANSPORT (END OF NOVEMBER 1942). SECOND TRANSPORT (BEGINNING OF DECEMBER 1942). THIRD TRANSPORT (DECEMBER 10, 1942). MR. SOLOMON. THE CITY OF BIALYSTOK. THE LAST TRANSPORT (DECEMBER 20, 1942). MY FATHER. THE 1,700 REMAINING PRISONERS. THE GASSING OF THE OLD PEOPLE OF WOLKOWYSK.

Koszary. Wolkowysk Concentration Camp.
This was a huge camp with many dilapidated, broken-down buildings which served as stables to keep the horses of the prewar Polish Cavalry.

The Koszary was encircled by a string of barbed wires and divided in many parts, each of which was encircled, separately, by spikes or barbed wires. Now, instead of horses, it was inhabited by human beings, men, women and children. Each part had a few old buildings, structured like basements. A few steps down led to the interior.

Twenty thousand people were now incarcerated in the Koszary. Thirteen thousand from the towns and villages around Wolkowysk and seven thousand from Wolkowysk proper. In 1941 about thirty thousand Russian prisoners were incarcerated there. All of them perished in a few months.

When I entered the Koszary, miraculously saved previously from a certain death, I saw through the wires other humans, looking at us. They were Jews from Wolkowysk and the nearer villages and towns. They were already living in the stables. For each town, one to four stables were assigned. The congestion, hygienic living conditions were horrible and beyond any description. I recognized a few of the people who were standing and observing us behind the wires. They felt sorry for us, miserable human beings, who suffered so much on the road. Some of us were incapable of standing on our own feet and had to be helped and supported by our friends and relatives. Those who lived, already, in wretched conditions in the stables, deplored those new arrivals, who were in more miserable conditions.

I was very thirsty and asked for water. They handed me immediately a large glass of water. I thanked them, drank the water and returned the glass. They asked me the reason of my walking barefoot. I was so tired, exhausted and broken up that I couldn't answer them. They understood.

Life in Concentration Camp Wolkowysk.

I continued with my wretched people to the part which was assigned for our city Lyskovo, and which was located at the very end of the camp.

This part had eight dilapidated small buildings, which looked like basements, where hay and other fodder to feed horses and domestic animals were kept before the war. The city of Rozana received four buildings. Lyskovo two basements, Podorosk—one basement. The buildings or bunkers were located on both sides of the road. Each bunker had side compartments between which was a small corridor. Each compartment was divided in three chambers (Buksy). Each chamber had 10-12 people who could only sit, but not lie down. But with difficulties it happened, although rarely, that one could lie down on one side, but never flat.

Every bunker contained seven hundred miserable people. The bunkers had small, not usable ovens. Whenever we tried to use the ovens, a black smoke instead of fire came out, which choked us.

WOLKOWYSK CONCENTRATION CAMP

Luckily, at the beginning of November 1942, the weather was not bad, and the presence of so many people in one bunker generated so much heat that the cold did not bother us too much.

My family and myself belonged to the bunker of Lyskovo. The congestion there soon became so great that I felt I was being choked for lack of air. I left the bunker and sat outside to rest and to breathe fresh air.

In the evening the German Commandant of the camp, whose name was Zirka, arrived. He told us that he realized our condition and had compassion for us. We were forced to live in conditions now different than in our own homes. We shouldn't be afraid. We were being concentrated to live here till the end of the war. We'll have to go to work, but nothing was going to happen to us because he, the German Commandant, was going to protect us.

Naturally, we didn't believe a word he said. Soon our forefeelings and premonitions became realities as evidenced by the enormous sufferings of everyday life. We were beaten at work and in the camp. Many were killed and shot in cold blood for no reason at all.

I went to find my boots, because I left them on the road, before reaching Wolkowysk. I couldn't find my own boots, so I took other shoes and a coat, which was better than nothing. My feet were so painful that I was not able to wear any kind of shoes. We were able to recover, though, part of our packages.

It was impossible to enter the bunker, because too many people were there lying one on the top of the other. We spread our covers on the ground outside, put up a few pillows and tried to spend the night under the skies. For me this arrangement was satisfactory, but I didn't know how my father felt. Probably not very well, because in the morning he looked more pale, more emaciated and more depressed.

In the early morning as soon as the first sun rays appeared on the horizon, we got up, bundled up our packages and sat down. I heard my father praying in a low voice.

"Almighty G-d, please save us for your sake. Take a look and see that our strength is gone. The righteous perish every day in the thousands. Please turn Thy mercy upon us and the remnants of the oppressed." Quiet all around. It was still very early in the morning.

My father continued his prayer.

"Look from your heights and see the Nazis are laughing at us and ridicule us. We are being handled like cattle and brought for slaughter, to be murdered and exterminated. The Nazis are scoffing and deriding us. Almighty G-d, have mercy upon us. Our suffering reached the impossible. Help us! because we feel very unhappy. Help us! because our bones, flesh and souls are enormously weak, sick and disturbed."

I listened to my father's prayer and started to feel that we were not alone. A supernatural power was watching upon us. The important thing was not to lose faith, nor courage. People started to get up, milling around. Some were looking for fresh water, to wash themselves and to prepare water for the day. Some tried to get some fire in order to cook something, a few potatoes perhaps, for their starved families. These were people that I knew before, dressed adequately, nice in their behavior. Now they looked wretched, dirty, despondent. How this unfortunate people changed in a few days. They walked around the place surrounded by barbed wires and watched by the Gestapo and the SD (security unit). Any false movement caused immediate death by shooting. The people were hungry, because they already hadn't eaten in a few days, desperate, disheveled, deformed. Their clothes turned to rags, shabby, torn from wearing them all the time the same cloth even at night. People couldn't undress, but had to sleep in their outer clothing. A terrible mass of misery and despair.

I went to find out where to get a little water. I found the well, which was a deep hole in the ground filled with water. One needed a bucket to get to the water. Someone arrived with a pail with a string attached to it, and he pulled up the water. I was able in the meantime to find a water receptacle, which I filled up. I washed myself and freshened up a little. The rest of the water I brought to my family. The family Pomeraniec got some potatoes. They offered me a few. Our condition was deplorable.

There was also Yitzhak Pomeraniec, whose wife gave birth to twins right after arriving into the Concentration Camp Wolkowysk. I still can hear now their vociferous crying and weeping for food, which was not available. They were lying in a stable together with the rest of the people of Rozana. After a few days they died.

Around noontime, our meal for the day was distributed. It consisted of a little watery soup and 300 gm. of bread. This was all the food for the day. I realized that this was not enough and was thinking of malnutrition and the contagious diseases which surely would break out caused by starvation and enormous congestion.

Who could give me wings to fly out from this hell on earth? It was really a very bad situation. Only a miracle could save us. The Al-ty G-d spoke with our patriarchs, with Moses and other prophets, but now, when we were in a very desperate situation, He did not make his presence known. Even the prayers and supplications of the most pious, decent, sanctified men were left without any answer.

I often wondered whether this world was not under complete dominion of the devil. The heavenly beings, the messengers of G-d, were not able to help us. The seraphim, cherubins, archangels were powerless on our planet. The satan and the evil spirits, Lucifer, Beelzebub, Mephistopheles and all the other infernal demons took over our beautiful earth and turned it into fire and brimstone.

The second night in the German concentration camp was spent also outside, under the free skies. At midnight it started to rain. We tried to enter the bunker, our present abode. The congestion was so great, so many people slept on the bare ground, that we were not able even to enter, our own bunker. We spent the rest of the night outside. It was rainy, windy and cold and we waited for the morning to save us from the darkness and misery.

In the morning, I went to a meeting of the doctors. We decided to organize some form of a clinic and a small hospital to help our people as much as possible. Dr. Horn was elected as our spokesman, because his German was very good. Dr. Kaplinski from Slonim was his deputy. One building was given over to us to serve as a clinic and small hospital.

I noticed that the section occupied by the people of Wolkowysk had many buildings, almost empty. Mr. Fucks was the chief of the Judenrat, substituting for Dr. Weinberg, who was shot previously together with all the other doctors. I explained to him that the section occupied by Lyskovo contained only a few stables and that they were overcrowded. An epidemic of typhus would definitely strike the unfortunate victims of Nazi bestiality, which would spread like fire over all the other sections. Since the section of Wolkowysk had empty stables, the people of Lyskovo should evacuate their quarters and move to the region of Wolkowysk.

Mr. Fuchs, who was a nice and reasonable person, agreed with my suggestion. Within one hour, all the people of Lyskovo, gladly moved to the section of Wolkowysk. Podorosk followed next and Dr. Shulman and his wife were near us. It was a life-saving procedure for Rozana, because three more stables became available for them.

My family moved to one small middle chamber in the first side compartment, near the exit. Since I was in charge of administering medical aid to the inhabitants of Lyskovo, my chamber was a little large and was also more convenient to get out of. 6-7 persons occupied each chamber. At least we were able to lie down and stretch even our legs.

The chief was the ex-Judenälteste of Lyskovo, Mr. Abrams. A new order was announced, that everybody had to be in his bunker not later than 9 P.M. Whoever would be found after the announced time would be shot on the spot. Many lost their lives for not observing accurately the above order.

In the camp terrible starvation governed. Many died from malnutrition, beatings and physical and mental sufferings. Every morning many bodies were lain down in front of the clinic. From there they were taken to the burial place outside the camp.

Small two-wheel carriages covered with a rag were used and pulled by the relatives of the departed. The carriages had to pass through the gate of the camp, where the Gestapo guards stood.

They usually ordered the carriages uncovered and pushed the bodies with their rifle butts.

It was very depressing for the relatives to see this German desecration of the dead. The legs and heads of the deceased were pushed and moved in all directions. Nothing could be done, even crying was not permitted by the new regime.

From time to time, a group of prisoners escorted by Gestapo left the camp for the city of Wolkowysk proper. They entered the houses evacuated by the Nazi victims and collected all kinds of food like grain, potatoes, flour, etc., to bring it to the camp in order to feed the people. Naturally the best would be taken away by the superior race.

There were also empty bakeries to bake bread for the people. But the amount distributed was very small. People starved and many died from lack of food. The hunger was so strong that some would not hesitate to eat everything in order to sustain life. Some collected grass, garbage from the kitchen. One day a cart-load of potatoes arrived for the kitchen. The people were so starved that, in spite of the danger of being shot, they attacked the cart-load of food. The result was disastrous. The Gestapo shot everybody who was near the carriage. In one minute, ten were shot to death, and fifteen received fatal injuries. The Germans used dum-dum bullets, which expanded on hitting the target, causing extensive injuries. The use of these bullets was forbidden by international law. But law for the Nazis was worth less than the paper on which it was written.

One of the injured was a man from Konstantinovo, whom I knew well, at the time, when I lived there. He was shot in the arm and in the chest and was bleeding profusely internally and externally. I stopped the external bleeding, as much as I could, and administered the best medication at my disposal, under the circumstances. But the dum-dum bullets caused such extensive internal injuries that in spite of every effort he died, leaving a wife and a few helpless small children.

In the afternoon, I went in the company of Mrs. Kaufman, whose husband, Dr. Kaufman, was shot by the Germans a few months before, to visit the kitchen. Because of the confusion, it was difficult to get in. With the help of Mrs. Kaufman, I was able to enter the kitchen. I found myself in a very large hall full of huge kettles, caldrons, in which the food was cooked and prepared. The hall had no light. Only the fires under the kettles were visible.

Everything was surrounded by vapor and smoke, which choked the people inside. I heard voices, lamentaion and sounds of sorrow. But I couldn't see the people, unless I came very near to the caldrons, which caused an immediate choking sensation. I met there the mother of the late Dr. Kaufman, who was one of the head cooks.

All the kitchen products were under the supervision of Mr. Galin. He was a heavy-set man, in his late forties. Before the war, Mr. Galin, occupied many high social positions in Wolkowysk and served, also, as the chairman of the board of the city hospital. Very intelligent and active person. Not knowing the German order not to buy anything from the Germans, he took a little benzine, for the kitchen use, from a German, whom he paid the asked price. The Gestapo found it out, came to his bunker and beat him up severely with sticks and chains. He returned to his place, lacerated, with a bloody face and broken bones, hardly alive. After two hours, the Gestapo returned and ordered Mr. Galin to come out. He was barely able to move, and only with the support of his neighbors he walked, with great difficulty, to the exit. Before he left, he said, "This is my end, pray for me. Goodbye, friends and neighbors." He left.

Soon we heard sounds of wailing, sobbing mixed with moans and groans. The Germans were beating Mr. Galin fiercefully, vehemently and without any mercy. Mr. Galin, the respected citizen of the city of Wolkowysk, was lying motionless on the ground in a pool of blood. Then we heard two shots and the Germans left. We came out and found the body of Mr. Galin. He could not be recognized. It was a mass of bloody, contused and crushed meat. It was a terrible scene. It made a very depressing impression, even on us, who were accustomed to Nazi cruelty.

His body was taken in front of the clinic and covered with a blanket, to wait his turn for the burial. In this way, Mr. Galin ended his life. G-d have mercy on his soul. Our hopes were completely shattered.

Next morning, I returned to the kitchen to pick up the kettle of food designed for the hospital and clinic. It was the usual darkness, smoke and vapor. I was informed that Mr. Jezierski occupied the place of Mr. Galin. We heard sounds of crying, sobbing, moans and lamentations. Suddenly I heard voices of desperation.

"What happened?" I asked.

"A cook, because of the darkness and dizziness, fell into a boiling kettle. We pulled her out still alive, but all her body was burned. We transferred her immediately to the hospital, but she died because of extensive severe burns. Her name was Hasa Rutczik."

Every doctor took his turn to work at the clinic. I treated patients a few hours daily and was also the only physician in my bunker. My compensation consisted of one meal, which I brought to my family. They were lying in their chamber, starving and exhausted. This was a little help which kept them alive.

In the morning, I returned to the clinic. A young girl was brought in to us. She was dead on arrival. The nurse looked at her and remarked, "How beautiful she looked at her death. Her face expressed supreme calm, resignation and charm! She appeared sleeping. Her sufferings were ended." After a while, a woman entered sobbing.

"This is my daughter. She left our place only a few minutes ago, saying that she was going to get a piece of bread. She was very weakened lately." She fell down, as soon as she left the stable, from exhaustion and died.

At the little hospital, there was the midwife, Mrs. Krol, who took care of the twin boys of Mrs. Trop. She was helped by their aunt Mila Shalakowitz. Dr. Trop, the dentist, was shot by the Germans together with the other doctors. His wife, the most beautiful lady in town, Mrs. Trop, was killed. Her children were taken care by Mrs. Krol. It was a pity to look at these little boys, orphans, without a father or mother, victims of Nazi bestiality. Mrs. Trop previously gave the children to a Polish woman, Palko. The Polish neighbors threatened to report them to the Germans. She became very despondent and went to the Talmud Torah and swallowed a large dose of Luminal (sedative), in order to be able to rest and sleep for awhile. The Germans found her and shot her while she was sleeping. The two children escaped to Mrs. Krol.

Hunger, devastation, despondence intensified. People walked around like shadows. They stopped talking to each other. What was the use?

They died like flies. Every morning the ground in front of the clinic, was piled with dead people. Their bodies lying one near the other. Their faces seemed to be directed toward the skies and asking the eternal question, "Why, what did we do, to deserve such a miserable death?" No answer! Quiet all around.

I still had a few gold pieces in my pocket, and used one five ruble, golden piece for one loaf of bread, which I immediately brought to my family. They cut it into small pieces and handled it like diamonds. It might save their lives. Only he who starved for a few days without any hope and who lost his strength was able to appreciate the value of a small morsel of bread.

Because of malnutrition, severe hunger, congestion, unhygienic living conditions, the dreadful and feared contagious diseases like typhoid, typhus, tuberculosis, erysipela started to spread in the camp. Among the first victims was the pharmacist from Volpe, who died in a few days.

Typhus took a very violent form. The nervous system was especially affected, manifested by semiconsciousness, hallucinations and frenzied behavior.

The only son of the pharmacist contracted the disease soon thereafter. He became delirious and was raving and raging like mad. We helped him as much as we could. There was always a physician near his bed who tried to alleviate his sufferings. He received sedatives and injections of glucose and strophantin to support his strength and to prolong his life. Due to his youth, physical strength, the intensive medical treatment, he overcame his disease.

I met Dr. Volach, whom I knew from the time when I studied medicine during the sophomore years at Karlovy University of Prague. He was a very nice and quiet person, and told me that partisans came over to his office, asking him to join them. He did not realize the real danger, and the real intentions of the Germans to murder everybody without any mercy, and therefore he didn't join them. He was a quiet fellow, a scientist. Life in the forest and violence were strange to his nature. He couldn't imagine that the Germans meant to annihilate entire nations.

I never had such a chance. Partisans never came to my office. I tried myself to find them in the forest, but never succeeded. His wife, Mrs. Volach, was a medical nurse by profession. She was a very nice-looking woman, young and poised. No wonder that she was able to marry Dr. Volach.

She became sick of typhus. Her condition was very serious. Naturally we helped her in every way possible. Her husband stood near her, day and night. Finally she became conscious again, her fever subsided and she regained her previous health. All of us were very glad and proud of her overcoming the terrible disease, which caused hundreds of fatalities. Very few were cured under the circumstances. The vast majority succumbed to the contagious disease.

First transport to the gas chambers.

The concentration camp Wolkowysk was as I explained earlier divided into different sections, according to the cities. At the end of November, 1942, the first transport had to leave for an unknown destination. The Commandant assured us in the name of the government, and upon his honor as a German officer, that the transport would go to the east, work in factories for the benefit of Germany. Later we found out from the railroad men, that the train stopped at Treblinka, which was located not far from the station Malkinia, between Bialystok and Warsaw. This was an extermination camp, which meant that all the people were immediately killed.

To the first transport belonged Rozana, where the family Pomeraniec lived. Mrs. Chaya Pomeraniec came to our section and asked to save her. I advised her to hide herself in some place. She was discovered by Mr. Abrams, who chased her out from our section. All my pleas didn't help. He was not going to risk the life of all the inhabitants, because the Germans would certainly find it out and kill us all. Such a terror, such a fear, dominated us all. Mrs. Pomeraniec returned to her section. At 3 P.M., all the people belonging to the first transport, were assembled in rows of five. They received their portion of bread and waited for their resettlement. At 2 A.M. the following night, we heard desperate voices calling for help, gun shots, very loud screamings and desperate shrieks. It was forbidden to walk out from our stables by threat of death punishment.

The echo of the unfortunate victims yelling at night at a distance seemed to us like hell or bedlam broken loose. We couldn't sleep all night. It seemed to me that somebody was continuously calling the names of the family Pomeraniec, "Hasa, Icl, Haya, where are you?"

In the morning, the Rozana section, was empty. Michle Pomeraniec, the only member of the family, remained with us. Soon, trucks arrived with many persons, who were shot on the way to the railroad station. Michle was looking for some members of her family among the returned bodies.

Second transport.

During the beginning of December 1942, a second transport was assembled. This time the people of other small towns like Zelva, Volpa, etc., were assigned by the Gestapo to be resettled.

Again the German Commandant spoke, assuring the doomed victims that they'd be resettled in the east and everybody would work in his profession. How shamelessly did the German lie. He knew the truth, but lied to the people about their destination. According to the Germans, if somebody lies he has to be shot, but the Germans themselves were allowed to lie as many times as they desired. The old adage was valid here. "Quod licet Yovem, no licet bovem." This was the interpretation of justice of the superhuman race (Ehrenvolk).

The proceedings of the war in North Africa and on the Russian front showed clearly at that time that the Germans were far away from being supermen, not even honorable men, but bloodthirsty criminals, regardless of whether they belonged to the Nazi party or to the army (Wehrmacht),

The martyrs were assembled again at 3 P.M. and were

marched immediately to the railroad station. It was probably a direct order from the Commandant, who was afraid of some disturbances, borne out of desperation.

Next morning the same routine. I went to the clinic to treat the sick. Misery, hunger, apathy, desperation intensified. Still worse, an epidemic of typhus broke out. Every day the number of people who contracted the terrible desease increased. Many died. Very few drugs were at our disposition. Again a meeting of all the doctors. Our situation became hopeless. At the same time, the Judenrat, whose chief was Mr. Fucks, conferred about the new German order to select another transport. I was called by Mr. Fucks, who informed me that, in view of the typhus epidemic, doctors would be excluded from the transport. We needed them here. Their families would remain too.

Third transport.

After a few days, we were informed that a third transport was being prepared for December 10, 1942. All the small towns and villages, except Wolkowsyk proper, had to leave with the transport. Lyskovo, Podorosk, Isabelin, etc., belonged to the third transport. Everybody was ordered to return to their living quarters. A policeman was put in front of every exit. Nobody was permitted to leave.

My family and myself were living in Lyskovo barracks. People started to pack their few belongings to take with them. Misery, apathy all over. Some of the women were crying in desperation. Children looking for their mother, sobbing. Complete pandemonium all over.

Others tried to put fire in the broken ovens. Instead of fire, there was a heavy smoke coming out from the ovens. Some of the people fainted because of weakness and lack of air. We had been living already in this basement for about five weeks. The living conditions were terrible. Starvation, extreme fear, persecution were our daily happenings. I felt being choked myself and tried to reach the exit, which was very difficult, because many people were waiting there already. Finally, I reached the exit, which was covered with a wooden lid. In order to get out from the basement one had to climb up a few steps and lift the wooden cover.

But alas, on the top of the cover stood a policeman, who was ordered not to let anyone out. I told him that I was a physician and that physicians were exempted from the transport, because of the typhus epidemic. At the beginning he didn't want to listen to me, but finally he called his chief, Mr. Sokolski, whom I knew before the war. As soon as he saw me at the exit, he told the policeman to wait and he went to Mr. Fuchs, the chief of the Judenrat, to consult him. After a few minutes, which seemed to me like a year, he returned, and ordered to let me and my family out. And so, my father, my brother Mendel, Michle and myself were saved temporarily from death and were put in an empty barrack.

Later at night, we heard the terrible crying and sobbing of the victims, mixed with German voices, sounds of beatings and shootings. In the morning we found many dead bodies lying on the ground. They were killed by beatings and German bullets.

My family was transferred to one of the barracks belonging to Wolkowysk proper, where my cousin Chone and his family had their shelter.

In the camp was incarcerated a man, whose name was Mr. Solomon. He was crippled on both lower extremities as a result of a disease called "infantile paralysis" which attacked him in his childhood. He was a very intelligent person, and managed his own business in Wolkowysk (Kosciushko Street), which consisted of selling and repairing watches and radios. When the war started, he kept for himself some of the best radios in his collection. This was a courageous deed because, if caught, he would have been sentenced to death.

Even in the camp, he had clandestinely kept one of his radios, and was listening day and night to Radio London, Moscow, and even New York. He knew everything, what was going on in the world, and especially on the battle fronts. The German forces were at that time, at the end of December 1942, in a very desperate situation. It was the beginning of a definite German collapse. In North Africa, Rommel was fighting on two fronts, surrounded in the East and West by allied forces. The end of the African campaign, and the freeing of all North Africa from the

L.: Mr. Galin, chairman of the board of the hospital, butchered by the Germans. R.: Mr. Solomon, clandestinely kept a radio under danger of death, to listen to news from London, Moscow and New York.

German arrogance, was only a matter of time. On the Russian front, Paulus' army was surrounded near Stalingrad, and their complete destruction was assured and their fate sealed.

Under those circumstances, the radios in London, U.S.A. predicted peace in a very short time. Normally and usually a conclusion of a peace agreement was mature at that time. But not Hitler. He knew better! He was not going to capitulate before twelve, but way after twelve o'clock.

The allies did not realize at that time the degree of madness of the Führer, who preferred the senseless massacre of millions of human beings rather than to ask for peace.

We, the people of Wolkowysk, were not aware of anything that was happening in the world, except Mr. Solomon, who predicted that the war would be finished very soon, even at the end of the year 1942. He didn't reveal to anybody the source of his predictions. Since everything which he foretold in the past came true, people trusted him and in those weird times considered him to be a prophet.

The masses, standing on the verge of annihilation, weakened physically and mentally, caused by the ordeal forced upon them by the Germans, started to believe in some extraordinary forces to appear to rescue them.

The ground was ripe for prophecies. People believed in him, especially when he foresaw the imminent German collapse. His words became a balm, which healed their despair. They were able to continue in their hope, for a better future. At the end of

December, 1942, I met Mr. Solomon. I knew him well before the war. His sister used to be a friend of my sister. She came often to our house and fell in love with my brother Mendel.

I knew that many people had full confidence in the predictions of Mr. Solomon. Therefore, I started a conversation with him. He told me that the war would be finished in a very short time. He had spoken with a high German officer, whom he knew for a long time and he assured him that the war would, definitely, end in 1942 or the beginning of 1943.

"Mr. Solomon," I asked, "It is already the end of the year 1942. How is it possible?" "Believe me," he answered, "I can not reveal to you the sources of my information but I assure you that the war will end very soon. You are a friend of my family," he continued, "and I would not dare to tell you something, that is not 100% reliable."

The tone of his assurance gave hope to my battered soul and I felt relieved.

Mr. Solomon related to me a few anecdotes which were circulating in the allied camp.

Here are a few of them:

Hitler couldn't cross the English Channel. He gave it up long ago. Suddenly he found out that a certain old Rabbi knew the secret, how to cross the channel. He summoned the Rabbi and asked him the secret. The Rabbi answered, that Moses had a magic scepter to split the sea.

"Give me the scepter," Hitler yelled. "I must have it. Where is the scepter? Quick; answer!" The Rabbi responded calmly. "In the British Museum in London."

Here was another joke.

We are not going to have Christmas this year, because the Virgin Mary had been evacuated, Saint Joseph was in a concentration camp, the three kings were in London, the Ox in Berlin and the Ass (Mussolini) in Rome.

The name "Hitler" was altered to "Hyckler" (dog shooter). They greeted each other with *Heil Hyckler*.

In spite of the deep tragedy of our situation, I had to laugh at hearing the above jokes. They also lifted my spirit and I thanked heartily Mr. Solomon for telling me these stories, but he refused to reveal to me the sources of his intelligence. Later, after the war, I found out by reading the postwar documents that such jokes were circulating in London at that time. Mr. Solomon must have heard them over the radio of London.

When I returned to the clinic the next day, people were talking about leaflets, which were found by the workers at the railroad station, and which were edited by the underground. In one of these leaflets was written clearly that the Germans were trying to evacuate North Africa, but they met difficulties, because the Mediterranean Sea was completely dominated by the English. Most of the German Army would be destroyed and the rest would be taken to the prisoner camps. The Nazis could evacuate some important officers by air only.

It was very interesting to learn that the few Jews who were caught in Africa by the Gestapo had priority in evacuation before the German Generals. This was convincing evidence to me that the Germans lost the war, without any shadow of a doubt. Proof was furnished by the fact that Hitler did not care about his own generals and that his psychoneurotic disorder dictated him to evacuate first the few Jews to Germany, to torture them and to destroy them. The leaflet described also the German calamity at Stalingrad, and the consequences which would follow in the further conduct of the war operations. Germany must make peace *NOW*, if they didn't want to sacrifice millions of their own people, for no purpose at all, because the war was lost, unequivocally, and the German Army was defeated, overwhelmed and whipped completely.

The conversation with Mr. Solomon and the leaflets lifted my spirit. I started to believe Mr. Solomon's predictions, that peace would come very soon. It didn't make any sense for Germany to continue the war. It was right to assume then that the Germans would conclude a peace agreement, for their own sake, in order to rescue the German nation from a future disaster.

A group of girls, who worked around Wolkowysk, were being transported back to their original city, Bialystok. Some of the young women, who had some money left, tried to join them. It was very difficult. Some succeeded like the daughter of Mr. Chwonik and Mrs. Reznick.

Bialystok was the main city, the capital of Western White Russia. The textile industry was very developed there. The Germans concentrated first and then decided to annihilate all the Jews in White Russia, except Bialystok.

At the time when all the Jews of White Russia were concentrated in different concentration camps, like Wolkowysk, Kosovo, etc., the Jews in Bialystok remained in the ghetto.

The chief of the Judenrat was Engineer Barash from Wolkowysk, who at the Russian occupation escaped to Bialystok. He sent over a special truck to bring over his family and some of his friends. To the fortunate belonged his brother and sister, the family Blacher, Skolnik, Rabinowitz and others. We envied them, because the safest place at that time was Bialystok. His deputy was Mr. Lemon from Rozana, who sent over also a truck to pick up members of his family and some friends. To the lucky ones belonged his sister, Mrs. Berman, whose husband and daughter were killed in the first days of the war, during one of the bombardments of the city.

Next morning, I was informed that another truck arrived ready to transfer to Bialystok some people who were able to pay high prices. Dr. Majzel and his wife and others paid the required price. Rumors spread that Dr. Majzel and his group were caught on the way and shot. Shereshevski and the daughter of Cukierman, his neighbor, joined another truck and reached the city of Bialystok unharmed. His mother and sister remained in the camp of Wolkowysk.

Bialystok.

I'll describe here the happenings in Bialystok, because of the exceptional importance of the city, its unique position, and because some people from Wolkowysk and other towns succeeded in reaching the town. You'll see that even this exceptional city suffered a lot and did not last long.

Bialystok was occupied by the Germans on Friday, 6/27/41. (Wolkowysk was entered two days later). Three hours later the largest synagogue in Bialystok was set on fire. Eight hundred Jews were driven into the burning synagogue where they perished. Many were killed on the streets. In all, two thousand people lost their lives on the very first day.

An order from Berlin arrived to liquidate all towns and villages around Bialystok. On 11/2/42, the destruction began. 120 cities were affected. One of them was Wolkowysk. Many were slaughtered in the ghettos and on the roads. Others were killed in ditches near the towns. Still others were concentrated in the larger towns like Wolkowysk and later transported to the gas chambers and annihilated.

In Bialystok remained only 60,000 Jews which included the ghetto of Bialystok proper, and some of the refugees who succeeded in escaping from the neighboring towns to Bialystok. The Germans declared that this was an important industrial city and must remain intact. Really, there prevailed tranquility in the ghetto of Bialystok, but only for a few months. On 2/5/43, Mr. Barash was ordered to prepare a transport of six thousand, nonworking Jews. Anxiety and restlessness engulfed the occupants of the ghetto. Some put up a resistance. There were some examples of heroism. To mention one case.

Mr. Yitzhak Melamed, who stood guard at Kupiecka 29, poured vitriolic acid on a group of SS-men standing nearby. He blinded one Nazi and scalded another one, who in confusion shot and killed a Nazi.

Melamed escaped. The Germans then threatened to kill every man, woman, and child in the ghetto unless Melamed surrendered. Melamed sacrificed himself and gave himself up to the Gestapo. He was first tortured and then hanged from the gate of his home. Similar episodes happened in many other cities. I'll describe later a very authentic case in Vilna. Six months later the beginning of the total liquidation of Bialystok started.

On 8/15/43 (Sunday), in the middle of the night, the Germans surrounded the city with tanks, heavy armaments. They murdered many people and the rest was transported to the concentration camps. Some of the heroes put up a resistance, fought desperately but succumbed to superior force. Many were killed in fighting and the others were sent to Maidanek Concentration Camp.

Now let us return to the concentration camp Wolkowysk, where my family lived. The living conditions, after the evacuation of all the inhabitants of the smaller cities and towns, were very deplorable.

My cousin, Chone, used to come to my father and talk to him and to consult with us about further possible steps to be undertaken. He told us that the two relatives from Ostrov-Mazovieck were with him. One of them had very high fever and he asked me to visit him.

I went over, examined him and gave him an injection of prontosil. Next day, the fever subsided completely, and the sick relative felt so much better that he came over personally to my barrack to thank me for saving his life. After that, he became my constant companion. Where I went, he went with me. He was afraid to remain all by himself.

On December 20, 1942 a new order arrived. The next transport would be the city of Wolkowysk proper. Only 1,700 should remain and be composed of the youngest and the strongest men and women. Because of the contagious diseases, the young doctors should remain, but *not* their families. The old doctors could not remain either. The old doctor of the town of Volpy and Felsher Podorovski had to join the transport. A new camp had to be formed, from the 1,700 people. All the young people of the camp, whose number should not exceed 1,700, must pass to another segment of the camp and wait till the rest would be taken away. I was worrying about my family, and was thinking how to help them. I went over to the selected camp in order to get a place. Then I returned right away to the old camp to see what I could do.

My brother Mendel told me that he succeeded in avoiding the police and reaching our new camp, but he was caught and sent back. He'd try again tomorrow morning.

I was thinking about my father and contemplating ways of

WOLKOWYSK CONCENTRATION CAMP 141

bringing him over to the new camp. He was old and I would never be able to transfer him officially and openly in the middle of the day. Even if I'd certify that he was a doctor and put on his arm a Red Cross band, it would not have helped because old doctors had to join the transports also. My heart was palpitating and I felt a tension pressure in my head. What could be done? All the police knew him, they would never let him pass. They were afraid of their own lives. Maybe, later at night, I'd try to talk to one of the policemen.

I saw a possibility of saving Michle, but postponed it for the next day, because it was getting dark and the transport had to leave in another two or three days. I returned to the "Life" section where the lucky 1,700 had to stay and which was separated by barbed wire from the rest of the camp. I spent there the first night. I couldn't sleep all night long because all my family remained in the old camp and their lives were in extreme danger every minute of the night and day.

I returned to my family in the early morning. The people there, like in the other barracks, were completely confused and disoriented, because of the fear of approaching transport, which meant death. All of them were despondent because of additional weakness, starvation and constant persecution. Now the people knew that "transport" meant death. The previous transports were still in doubt. Their faces, their behavior, were like those who were condemned to death and awaiting their execution in 2-3 days. Although I was in the same boat with a difference of 1-2 months, I felt enormous pity and compassion for my people. I would gladly sacrifice myself, if I could help them. The situation was without any hope.

I told my father that I was in contact with a policeman, who promised me to bring him over in the middle of the night for the price of fifty gold rubles.

This was all the money that I had in my possession, and I was glad to give him the money, if he'd bring over my father and thus prolong his life for another few months.

What is money? Even millions, in comparison with one month prolongation of my father's life?

My brother Mendel assured me that he'd be able in one way

or another to reach our camp. Really he succeeded in avoiding the police and reached us later in our new barracks.

Now came the time to save Michle's life. I had to take a terrible chance, because the policemen knew all the doctors and the medical nurses in the camp. I found two Red Cross bands and put one on my arm and one on the arm of Michle. We walked, both of us in the middle of the day, towards the gate of our new compartment.

The policeman at the entrance let me pass, because he knew me. But—"Who is this girl?" he asked. "I had never seen her before, working in the hospital."

"She is the new medical nurse," I said. "She was assigned to my section."

He looked at her again and let her pass. Michle was very pleased. She was almost dancing from joy. She was very cheerful all the afternoon. The previous night she spent at the old camp of the condemned people, and now she was enjoying the new camp of "life." It was good to prolong life for another month. Who knew what might happen in another month? When one died, he disappeared from the surface of the earth, never to return again. Why be in a hurry? We'll never avoid our final destiny.

I put her and my brother Mendel in my place and went over to the policeman, to whom I spoke the day before, about bringing over my father. The night was very dark, almost no illumination, windy and rainy. A heavy thunderstorm broke out and I thought that this was the right time. My policeman was almost the only one on the field. I told him, "Go now and you must succeed." He went. I waited very impatiently, anxiously and fretfully for his return. I was wondering that it was lasting such a longtime. Finally, he arrived and told me that he was in the barrack where my father was supposed to be and couldn't find him. He asked Mr. Pidte, who was in the same place with him, and he said that he was not there. I couldn't understand what happened. Early in the morning, I went to my father's barrack and found him there. I asked him, why he did not respond to the policeman's call and why did Mr. Pidte say that he was not there?

WOLKOWYSK CONCENTRATION CAMP 143

My father was very much shaken by the event. He was lying, all the time last night, on his place. Mr. Pidte probably misled the policeman out of jealousy. And so the opportunity to save my father's life temporarily was gone. In the daytime it was impossible, because the place was full of Germans and my father was not a young man. I returned to the camp heartbroken and decided to go to the Commandant and ask him to spare my father's life.

The soldier at the entrance went in to inquire, and he returned after a few minutes saying that the Commandant was not in his room. I waited and waited but to no avail. I was told time and time again that the Commandant was not there. Instead, I heard wild voices of men drinking alcohol. They probably prepared themselves for the next day. Finally, the guard told me to go away, threatening to shoot me. I left still hoping to find the Commandant, or maybe the transport would not take place that terrible night. My going to the Commandant was a desperate action. He would not spare my father's life. There was a possibility of shooting me on the spot. My hope that my father would not be taken away and that I'd have another chance to save him that very night was frustrated also. That same night the worse thing, the exasperated, the unwanted one, took place. The Germans came, fully armed, to the camp and attacked the hopeless, weak, exhausted and undernourished people with such a fury that the wildest animals could hardly emulate. They beat and flogged the innocent and if one was not quick enough to move, he was shot to death. The daughter of Mr. Pidte, who planned to go to Israel with my brother, through Wilno, and later dropped the plan, was murdered on the road, being beaten to death by a wild German. It was terrible, worse than any other previous transport.

In the morning, I rushed to the camp to see what happened. I found drunk German soldiers, robbing the barracks of all the valuables. I entered into my father's barrack and found many packages and goods in disarray.

Disorder was all over. Evidently the people left in a hurry. Some food, even meat was found untouched. I found the exact place where my father was. There were some pots and blankets, which my father used. One was missing. He probably took it with him.

I thought of my father. How miserable he must have been in the last days of his life! His wife was murdered. Not one of his children around him. All alone by himself, old, weak and exposed to the Nazi fury. This was the fate of a pious, decent man.

I, his son, tried hard. All the money I had I offered to save his life for the moment. I was ready to sacrifice myself and to beg the Commandant for mercy to spare him, which I would have never done for myself. I did not succeed. All the doors were closed for me. I knew, that I myself would not last much longer.

I left the barracks broken in spirit and body. Why does the Al-ty G-d permit it? This was the question on everybody's mind, friend and foe alike.

I returned to the new camp. My brother Mendel and Michle were there. The Commandant came in and ordered everybody to assemble in rows of ten. Michle was afraid to go out and to be counted. She knew that she did not belong to the selected 1,700. She preferred to hide herself. Later the Germans declared that all the barracks would be searched and those who were hidden would be shot right away.

I advised Michle to go out and to stand in the regular rows. Finally the Commandant came, counted the assembled people. The number was not over 1,700.

We returned to our barrack. Michle was overjoyed that she did not have to leave with the transport. She made very giant steps forward, excitedly. With a beating heart and glistening eyes she returned to our barrack.

Next morning, we had to prepare other barracks for those who remained. We had to make a disinfection of the barracks, and of the clothing. Every building was hermetically closed. Every fissure and opening had to be covered or eliminated. Later a German arrived and put in a disinfecting gas, which had to remain inside for twenty-four hours.

The German who organized the disinfection started in the meantime to sell bread, charging astronomical sums. I paid him for two loaves of bread. He took the money and gave me only one. Better than nothing! This member of the "Ehrenvolk" was the biggest liar and cheater I had ever met.

The very old people did not go on the transport. They were too disabled and sick to go. What did the Germans do? They transferred the old people to one barrack and closed all the openings and fissures. When the building became hermetically tight, no air could come in or out. They closed the door, fastened it with impregnated paper and let in a deadly gas. The barrack remained closed for forty-eight hours.

When it was opened, a terrible scene was revealed. The innocent old people, men and women, were lying dead on the floor. They were looking up to the sky, their mouths were slightly open, like asking the Creator of the World to explain the reason of their terrible death. What did they do to deserve it? No answer as usual. Quiet all around.

Many Germans were milling around, proud of their accomplishments.

Michla Pomeraniec (Weissmann), saved by Dr. Harsaw, lives in New York City now, has two children.

THE YEAR 1943

THIRD YEAR OF WAR. THE MYTH OF GERMAN INVINCIBILITY WAS BROKEN.

CHAPTER VII

The road to Aushwitz.

THE EVACUATION OF THE LAST 1,700. THE CATTLE TRAIN. TREBLINKA EXTERMINATION CAMP. COMMANDO 1005 (THE MASS BURNING OF CORPSES). CHELMNO EXTERMINATION CAMP. JANUARY 28,1943 (22 SHEVAT TASAG).

In the morning of the New Year, 1943, all of us had to go out to work. We were taken to the railroad station. 1,700 young men and women, who remained from the original 20,000. The rest were taken to the gas chambers and murdered. I received a shovel and was ordered to dig a deep, large hole in the ground. To my group belonged Dr. Shulman. It was raining heavily, and our clothing was drenched and soaked.

Around 10 A.M., a German arrived and took me and other two men for a special job. We were ordered now to shovel coal from the wagons and to accumulate it in one place. We worked with all our strength, because the Germans stood over our heads and forced us to work harder. They were beating us with sticks and iron rods. Droplets of sweat were covering our bodies. This was very hard work, real drudgery.

When we finished this job, we were taken to a small basement where a lot of debris was accumulated around a machine, which was a part, probably, from a generator of electricity. We had to clean the machine, accumulate all the dirt and debris, and throw it out through a small opening above our heads. The basement was very small. We could hardly move. The German inside started to beat us with a heavy iron rod. I looked at Dr. Shulman. He was covered with perspiration, breathing heavily. His forehead was injured. Blood was covering his face. We continued to work under these conditions with all the strength left in us. Fortunately, at noon, we were ordered to get out. The Germans had to go for lunch. We returned to our previous job, to dig the ditches, and were very glad to get out from the murderous hands of the criminal.

Around 2 P.M., the same German returned. He selected ten men including me. This time he took us to the place where a huge pile of coal was lying. We had to transfer the coal to certain shops. The German started to beat us again, yelling, "FASTER, FASTER!" We had to run all the time. Even this didn't help. The German continued to flog us.

I realized that it was difficult to survive till the evening, and slowly started to talk to him. I promised him a golden watch for next morning. The German changed right away his attitude and I was nominated to be the foreman. He left the job to be performed under my supervision. Naturally, as soon as he had gone, we sat on the floor to rest a little from all day of slavery.

This was my first day of drudgery. I returned to my place, very tired and completely exhausted and lay down to rest. I felt shivering and realized that I had very high fever. My sleep was restless and interrupted.

In the morning I went to the clinic. I was headachy and my temperature was 103°F. I was hospitalized immediately. They gave me a bed and a cover. Near me was lying another patient, Dr. Marek Kaplan and his wife.

A terrible epidemic of a severe form of typhus broke out in the camp. Shortly, my brother Mendel and Michle contracted the same disease.

Dr. Kaplan had hallucinations. He cried and yelled for help. He was disoriented and had delirium. This epidemic disease was called *"Typhus exanthematicus"* and was characterized by malaise, high fever, headache, preceded by anorexia and chills. The accelerated pulse rate did not correspond to the very high fever.

This relative bradycardia, in relation to the fever, was very characteristic of typhus.

In our camp where the outbreak of the disease was caused by overcrowding, very poor hygienic conditions and malnutrition, typhus attacked mainly the nervous system. All the cases which I had seen had neurological phenomena: delirium, prostration, headache, violence, hallucinations, crying, restlessness, muscular contractions and in many cases coma (unconsciousness) and death. In the concentration camp of Wolkowysk, every other patient suffered also of *carphology* (involuntary picking at the bedclothes caused by high fever and exhaustion) and subsultus tendinum (twisting of muscles and tendons).

I had very high fever right from the beginning, severe headache, weakness, no appetite. Otherwise, I was very quiet, no delirium, no crying, completely alert. The fever reached 105°F., the headache increased, but no violence and no carphology. I was lying quietly in my bed.

I remember how the medical nurse, who checked my temperature, became very alarmed. The temperature reached over 106°F and I lay quietly, alert, complaining only of headache. The attending physician ordered aspirin, pyramidon, other salicylic preparations, cold compresses to my head and other symptomatic treatment. I received also injections of cardiazol. Glucose injections were very difficult to get and were used only in extreme cases. This time the physician got from someplace glucose, and administered it to me, by intravenous route, together with cardiazol. Immediately after the injection, I felt very bad and experienced extreme weakness, prostration, heart palpitation, dizziness. Everything became black around me. I thought that I was going to die. The end of my life was approaching. In desperation, I called the doctor to help me, but he disappeared. He couldn't help me and preferred not to be present at my agony. The headache increased in intensity and I had the feeling that my head was bursting. Luckily, all this lasted only a few minutes. Later it started to subside gradually. The danger of death was lifted.

My condition returned to my previous state, similar to the status before the injection. In retrospect, I surmised that the physician, introduced by mistake some air into my veins, which caused all the dangerous symptoms. It might have ended, also, fatally. My constitution had always been in excellent physical and mental condition, which helped me now to overcome the perilous and hazardous attack.

The disease lasted about two weeks longer, accompanied by high fever and headache. One day, I felt that my body was covered with unusual perspiration and I started to feel more relaxed and the headache was less intense. I felt very weak and fell in a deep sleep. When I woke up, I felt completely relaxed and the headache almost subsided entirely. Every day I felt better to the amazement and satisfaction of the medical personnel.

Michle and my brother had the same course of the disease as mine. Evidently all of us were infected by the same bug. After another few days, my temperature dropped to 98.4°F in the morning, but 100-100.5°F in the evening. My condition improved and I started to feel better, but very weak.

After another ten days, I was transfered to the convalescent barrack. Before leaving the hospital, I tried to put my clothes on, by myself, and to walk over to the convalescent place. I did not realize, how weak I became. I was not able even to make a few steps. I felt ringing in my ears and noise in my head. Two medical helpers took me under the arms and assisted me to the convalescent barrack.

My brother was already there. He told me that he felt well, but was very weak. Michle came in later. The chief of the convalescent barrack was my friend, Dr. Shulman. The food was a little better, but not enough, and not sufficient to recover fast. I bought from my own money additional food and distributed it to my brother, Michle and myself. I was buying additional bread, sugar and even meat and fat. We felt that we were getting every day better and better. The walking improved and we tried to walk outside. The typhus epidemic intensified. Many were contracting the disease, which course was assuming more severe forms, attacking especially the nervous system. Some were cured like Dr. Marek Kaplan and his wife. Some were not able to overcome the disease. Their number increased. They were lying one near the other, because of lack of space. Some were very violent, lying in delirium, crying and twisting and picking their bedclothes. Mr. Akiba Ain was very violent. We couldn't quiet him down, and had to strap him to his bed so he shouldn't fall on the floor and injure himself.

I knew Akiba well. He was a son of a wealthy family, who came to their richness after the First World War. He had been a pleasant youth. When he fell in love with a poor girl and married her, his father told him that he would have to make a living by himself. He became an electrician and had very mediocre means to his disposal. Now he was lying strapped to his bed, crying and hallucinating. His movements sometimes were very violent.

Fuks came to me and asked me to start working. He realized that I wasn't completely healthy as yet, and that normally I would need an additional few weeks of rest. But taking into consideration the fact that many doctors became ill, and that the contagious diseases were spreading like fire, it would be very beneficial if I returned to work. I agreed and started from then on to treat patients at the clinic and at the hospital.

Most of the doctors while treating their patients contracted the dreadful disease, typhus. Among them were Dr. Shulman, Dr. Teichner, Dr. Epstein and the doctor who gave me the injection. Among the other people afflicted by the disease were: Engineer Pszenicki, the brother-in-law of Dr. Mozes Einhorn of New York City, Mrs. Kaufman (the wife of Dr. Kaufman, who was shot in Wolkowysk), Mrs. Niemczyk (the wife of Dr. Niemczyk who was drafted at the beginning of the war into the Polish army and now has been practicing medicine in Israel— Ramath Gan, under the Hebrew name of Dr. Askenazi).

How strangely fate plays with us. Dr. Niemczyk was assimilated completely with the Polish people. He couldn't speak Jewish, nor Hebrew. His only language was Polish. Mr. Galin, who was murdered, as I described previously, by the Germans, brought him over from Warsaw and engaged him as a director of the hospital. He lived on the top of our apartment. I met him later in Israel. He spoke Hebrew and acted like a born Israeli. The war brought him back to his stem, ancestry and stock.

I worked very hard, day and night, to alleviate somewhat

the enormous sufferings of my people. My presence alone encouraged many sick persons not to give in, but to fight for their lives. The reasoning was that, if I could come out completely healthy from such a dreadful disease, then they had a good chance to do likewise.

My two relatives from Ostrow-Mazowieck, who escaped miraculously from the death van, described previously, lived with my cousin Chone. They were among the last 1,700 young men and women left. The others were sent to Treblinka, where they perished. They joined me in my new barrack.

Both of them contracted the disease. The older one overcame it and joined me, becoming a part of my family.

The younger, whose constitution was not very strong, became more ill, and finally he became delirious and very violent, and finally he died.

I noticed that the persons who contracted the disease late suffered more and the illness became more intense and violent. We, all the medical personnel, worked day and night, with all our strength. Finally the dreadful disease started to subside. We noticed a definite improvement. Many returned to their work and very few became ill. Our intense work resulted in stopping the epidemic.

Some doctors contracted the disease very late, like Drs. Shulman, Teichner, Epstein. Some of the doctors vaccinated themselves before the war, and they became immune, like Dr. Kaplinski who remained immune and did not contract the disease. Some contracted the disease, right from the beginning, in a very light, quasi-ambulatory form, and were able to recover without even going to the clinic.

Up to now, all the transports went to the terrible extermination camp of Treblinka. My father, my cousin Chone and his family, and all the people concentrated in the camp of Wolkowysk, were transferred by cattle trains to Treblinka.

What was Treblinka?

Treblinka was a German Concentration Camp, whose only aim was to destroy human beings. It was a factory to destroy lives. The camp was located about 2 1/2 miles from the railroad station *Malkinia*, which was in the middle of the railroad line. The camp was cut out in a forest and covered about 33 acres. The killed were from Warsaw Ghetto, Siedlce, Chenstochova, Radom, Bialystok, Grodno, Wolkowysk, etc.

Treblinka Conc. Camp

WARSAW ↗ BIALYSTOK
Malkinia Station

Treblinka camp was set up at the end of 1941. Different prisoners were kept there. At the beginning, there were brought Polish peasants who did not pay taxes or deliver enough of their products, who avoided forced labor, all kind of people who in one or in another way resisted the Germans.

The guards who watched the camp consisted of Germans and Ukrainians.

The above prisoners were compelled to build gas chambers, barracks to live in, railroad tracks, and to dig large ditches. All the camp was enclosed by barbed wires.

In the *spring* of 1942 there were 13 gas chambers where the Germans murdered their victims.

Each gas chamber could kill two hundred persons in half an hour. All the thirteen chambers annihilated about 2,600 victims at one time (half hour) by the deadly *carbon monoxide gas*, which was produced by special motors near the gas chambers. The gas was conducted by special pipes, which discharged through openings in the ceilings of the chambers. After half hour, the doors of the gas chambers were opened and the corpses pulled out. The rings were taken off, the gold teeth extracted and the bodies buried in large ditches. The deportations of the Jews from Warsaw started on July 22, 1942, which was according to the Hebrew calendar, the ninth of the month of Av (Anniversary of the destruction of the temple).

This first Warsaw transport reached Treblinka in the morning of July 24 and consisted of twenty cars (about 2,000 people). From the station of Malkinia, the train moved on the side line to the station of Treblinka proper, where the extermination camp

Treblinka was located. It was covered from all sides by trees in order not to make it visible from the outside. Beside the barbed wires, there were watchtowers, where Germans with machine guns stood on the top, ready to shoot and kill. The victims didn't know that they were going to be exterminated. The master-race did everything possible to cheat their unfortunate victims and to mask the factory of death. When the trains arrived, the victims were driven with whips, sticks and iron rods to the first building, which looked like a railroad station. Signs were visible with directions and timetables to other cities like: Bialystock, Wolkowysk, Warsaw, etc., signs where train tickets were sold, a big clock showing 3 o'clock. People thought they were at a railroad station.

Behind the station, in the camp itself, was a street called *"Paradise Street"* (Street of death), which led straight to a large shed, labelled *"Wash house."* There was also a sign reading, "Take a bath, after which you'll be resettled to the east for labor."

There was also an exit to the hospital. Whoever entered the hospital was shot immediately in the back of his neck by an SS-man. The weak, crippled, were sent immediately to the "HOSPITAL."

When the first transport from Warsaw arrived, the men were separated from the women. The latter were taken right away to the gas chambers, after cutting their hair, which was sent to Germany.

The men had to undergo a "selection" because the Germans needed two hundred young strong men to work in the camp. The "selection" occurred as follows:

The *first order* of the Nazis sounded like this: "The skilled workers to step forward!"

Most of the people stepped forward. Only the desperate, the weak, who gave up everything in life, the hopeless, remained standing. They were sent immediately to the gas chambers.

2nd order—"All those who speak German step forward!" Many stepped forward. They were assembled in rows of five. Then the Germans and the Ukrainians started to beat them over the head and body, with heavy sticks, whips and rifle butts. Whoever fell was shot on the spot.

The last 200 who survived were divided in two groups. One group had to transfer the dead bodies from the gas chambers to the ditches. The other group had to carry the accumulated clothing to one place. All the work had to be done running. Whoever stopped or didn't move fast enough was shot to death.

In this way the Germans selected the workers from the first transport of Warsaw. Later they created different commandos.

The *blue* commando collected the baggage of the arriving victims and cleaned the cars.

The *red* commando carried the clothing to the sorting square, where the goods were segregated like valuables, gold, diamonds, money, clothing, linen, dresses, stockings, shoes, machinery, etc., and sent to Germany.

The victims, not expecting death and believing the promises of the Germans, that they were only being resettled, brought with them all kinds of tools, domestic chores, etc.

The people were forced to travel in cattle trains, 100 persons in one wagon, without food nor water. Many died on the way, because of lack of air and terrible unhygienic conditions. When they arrived at Treblinka, they were in no condition to put up any form of resistance. When the unfortunate entered the simulated, ungenuine, sham railroad station, they saw all the signs of a real station. A large poster was hanging.

"Do not worry about your future. All of you are going to the east to work. Your wives will take care of the households. Before going to the east, you must leave all clothing for disinfection. Deposit all the valuables and money with the cashier, for which you'll get receipts. Take a bath to clean yourselves. You'll get everything back later unharmed."

Many believed them. After all, these Nazis were fulfilling the orders of a government which came to power, not by revolution, but by a simple, ordinary election. This was in the middle of the twentieth century. The Germans were considered a civilized nation, in the middle of Europe. It was unthinkable, that they were going to murder in cold blood innocent civilians, including women and children. It was unreasonable to assume, that they were going to kill for the sake of killing without any cause, it would not even help the war effort. On the contrary it might even make a peace settlement in the future more difficult. All logic and common sense, led them to believe the Germans.

Some were so exhausted, despondent, so dispirited and downhearted, that they didn't care to stay alive, they preferred to die, rather than to continue their miserable existence. Death will come anyway, sooner or later. It was inevitable. Why suffer? They walked like in a trance, hypnotized, without any will of their own. The crime was so monstrous as to be without parallel in history.

In spite of all the atrocities known to the West, the world was silent. G-d's representative in the Vatican was silent. London and Washington were silent. It was horrible, not understandable, and at the same time astonishing..

Later, the prisoners were divided into two sections.

Treblinka I, where the victims were taken off the trains, undressed, and forced to the washing rooms, which were actually gas chambers. The unfortunate walked first on the *"PARADISE ROAD"* (Street), which was lined by SS-men, empowered with whips, sticks and guns.

When the victims were driven to the gas chambers on the road of death they were severely beaten by the Germans and the Ukrainians. Wild dogs helped the criminals.

The women were forced first into a building where their beautiful hair was cut and sent to Germany. Then they were driven to the gas chambers, where they perished.

Later, the men were forced to enter the gas chambers. Each chamber could contain two hundred persons but later they increased the number, by packing the victims very tightly, so that they had to stand with their hands above their heads. Because of the increased number of people, it was difficult to close the doors. Two Ukrainians known as *Ivan* and *Nicolai* managed to close the doors, by jabbing the last arrivals with bayonets.

The people reacted differently Some repeated loudly psalms, asking G-d for help and praying for forgiveness. Others cursed G-d lamenting that they didn't deserve it. Others doubted of His existence. "G-d is dead," they cried. Mr. Eliahu Rosenberg worked in the corpse disposal squad. He heard very often cries and lamentations and prayers emanating from the gas chambers.

"Hear oh Israel, G-d is one and His name is one." Or frantic voices, "Father!"—"Mother!"—"Help! Help!"

After thirty minutes all were dead. The doors were opened and the people inside were still standing like columns of stone. Some children would still be alive, especially those who were close to the floor. The Germans would take the children and shoot them.

Treblinka II. The corpses were separated and taken out with special hooks. The special squads who disposed of the bodies were active for only a short time. The Germans would murder them and select a new squad from the new arrivals.

Some of the prisoners of the disposal squads, after the first day of this ghoulish work, couldn't take it any longer and committed suicide.

The gold extracted from the corpses was sent to Germany. The weight of the gold per week from Treblinka alone was 18-22 pounds.

Therefore any golden pieces received from Germany, like monetary pieces, medals distributed to athletes or rewards to other persons, might contain some traces from the robbed gold extracted from the corpses.

Beware of the German gold!

The commandos had always been beaten, furiously, by the Germans at their work. They had to run, and at the same time they were flogged with sticks and whipped over the face and body. If the beatings left a mark on the face of a prisoner, like a black eye, or a bruised cheek or a cut on the face, he was called *"Clepsydra"* and had to die.

If the prisoner stepped forward, he died normally without suffering. He was shot in the back of his neck.

If he did not come out voluntarily, the prisoner suffered enormously before he died. He was hacked to death by a shovel. Many of the prisoners committed suicide. They could not endure any more. They craved to get rid of their sufferings, to free themselves from the evil of this planet, from the madness and wickedness, and to enter into a better world or to nothingness and voidness.

Here is a scene of *"Father and Son."*

The father was old, the son still young. Both were working in Treblinka, as prisoners. The son wanted to live, in order to continue the name of his family. One day the son was beaten at work and received a mark on his face. He felt blood on his hand when he touched his face. He became a "Clepsidra" and had to die.

Later in the barrack the son asked his father:

"Tell me Father, is my face marked?"

"Nothing is there," answered the Father.

"Please let me know Father," insisted the son. "I don't want to be hacked to pieces by a shovel."

The father took his son into his arms. He kissed him, hugged him, tears running over his face. He held his son tight in his arms for a long time.

"There is no G-d," said the son. The father didn't answer. Suddenly he got up quietly and said, "Son, there is a bad mark on your face. Prepare to die. Better now than to be hacked to death in the morning."

The son got up, stretched his neck ready to die. He climbed on a box. The father took his belt and fastened it around the neck of his son. The other end he attached to the ceiling. The father pushed the box, in a sudden movement, and the son remained hanging. After a short while, he returned, took off the body and laid it down on the earth.

Then the father himself climbed the box, put the same belt on his own neck, kicked the box under him and remained hanging. In this way, father and son died in the terrible camp of Treblinka.

G-d Almighty! why did you permit the criminals to commit such atrocities? Why did you allow to continue their unlawfulness even after the war?

Why did you let the land which is drenched with blood of millions of innocent people have a prosperity that they had never had before?

Is there a reward, on this world of yours, for crimes committed on infants, little children?

The bigger the crime, the greater the reward.

It is very difficult for a survivor of a Nazi concentration camp—who saw with his own eyes the atrocities and the murder committed on mankind, and who saved his life, not because he wanted to live, but because he wanted to tell the world, everything that he saw himself—to witness and watch the injustices in the German courts of today.

The evil perpetrated was of such a magnitude that became unbelievable, and he wanted to be a living eye-witness to the crimes. In the name of millions of people, who lost their lives for no reason at all, I the survivor am demanding justice, so that such madness should not be repeated again, and that the victims can rest in their graves.

In the summer of 1943, Himler arrived. In view of the approaching Red Army, he ordered to liquidate the camp, to kill all the prisoners, to dig out all the bodies previously killed, and to burn them. He wanted to eliminate all traces of German atrocities.

By July 1943, over one million people were exterminated. The digging out of the bodies and burning them constituted an enormous, difficult task. The Germans were experts in this too.

A new commando was created, *Kommando 1005*, under the leadership of *Plobel*, whose assignment was to remove old traces of atrocities and exterminations committed by the Germans. They operated from autumn, 1942, till September, 1944. They opened all the graves, removed and cremated all the bodies, using special incinerators.

The German Floss arrived at Treblinka to help the burning of the bodies. He discovered that the longer the body was buried, and the more fat the body contained, the better they burned. Females burned better than males. So the best body to be burned was the old, long-time buried, fat female body. He built an incinerator from cement, on the top of which he put railroad tracks. The fat bodies to be burned, he put on the top of the railroad tracks and on the top of them he put the bodies who

162				The Year 1943

Open mass graves in Treblinka. The bodies were later burned. (Photographed by a German in 1943.)

burned worse. Below he put wood under the grills, which resembled small campfires. The incinerator was big enough to put in one thousand bodies. When the fire from the wood caught the bodies, the flame shot up releasing a cloud of smoke.

The Germans were sitting near the tables and alcohol was served to celebrate the moment.

By putting up ten large incinerators, he was able to burn 10,000 people at one time.

Franz Kurt, called "Lalka" by the prisoners, was very satisfied. He served liqueur and whisky to his fellow criminals, who yelled "Heil Hitler."

This was a spectacle of a real inferno. Huge fires of burning

Treblinka II after occupation. Here the bodies were placed after their removal from the gas chambers. The gold teeth were extracted and the body openings searched for valuables.

Paradise Road—The Road to Death
The victims walked on this road from the trains to the gas chambers.

bodies, the cracking of human flesh in the air, the characteristic smell of the black smoke, the drinking of alcohol by the Germans among shrieking wild voices of "Heil Hitler." All these represented an unusual, unearthly scene which made people shiver.

The commandant received the order from Himmler to kill all the prisoners. But in the meantime, to avoid trouble, he tried to lull them into a false sense of security. He arranged entertainments on Sundays, he formed an excellent orchestra, and he even permitted some of the capos to choose from the newly arrived transports pretty girls and marry them. But the prisoners themselves could not be deceived any more. They saw that

Treblinka
The most terrible Nazi extermination camp. Most of the Warsaw Jews perished there. My father, my relatives, my friends, were murdered in this camp. The Germans destroyed all the camp before evacuation. Now, on the grounds of the place are stones, large and small, on which are written the names of countries and cities as a memorial to the inhabitants who lost their lives here. Nothing remained from Treblinka, only stones.

the number of transports diminished. It came almost to a standstill. They watched the fires of the uncovered graves, which consumed hundreds of thousands of bodies. Pretty soon, when the last bodies were burned, they'd be liquidated also, in order to eliminate all kinds of traces of Nazi bestialities.

The prisoners—workers whose number in both camps reached one thousand men, prepared to revolt.

A locksmith, a prisoner, made skeleton (duplicates) keys to the armory. They took out many automatic rifles, pistols with cartridges, hand grenades, etc.

The revolt broke out on 8/2/43. Twenty-five Germans and sixty Ukrainians, henchmen, were killed. Out of 1,000 prisoners 600 reached the nearby forest. From the six hundred left, many were killed later by the Ukrainian bands, by the Polish fascists, like the A.K., by the peasants, by the retreating German soldiers, and also on the front battle lines, fighting the Germans. Only about forty remained alive after one year when the Red Army arrived. Now they live in different places.

They told the world the unbelievable story of Treblinka. Their hope was realized. They survived, not for the only purpose to be alive, but to be living witnesses of unbelievable German atrocities.

Before evacuating Treblinka, the Germans destroyed all the buildings, the gas chambers, the ditches, the incinerators. Nothing remained.

I visited Treblinka in September, 1973, where my father and most of my relatives perished in December, 1942. The Camp Treblinka did not exist any more. Only an accumulation of thousands of large stones remained. On each stone was written the name of a city as a memorial to the inhabitants who were destroyed there. Some watch towers and some wires were still visible. Quiet all around. A dreadful silence engulfed everything. No human beings, no criminals, no demons. All the place looked like being still in a shock, unable to free itself from the burden of guilt, and unable to look straight into the eyes of those who came to see Treblinka.

Now let us return to our camp in Wolkowysk. In January,

1943, Fuks told me that our camp was going to be liquidated in a few days, and probably we'd be sent to Auschwitz. We were completely isolated from the world, because there were no newspapers nor radios. We were completely ignorant of what was going on, except rumors. Taking in consideration our deplorable situation, when death was lying before our eyes, every day and every minute of our lives, we had no strength nor willingness to find out the real happenings in the world. No matter what the war proceedings were, our personal life was not worth anything. We had no hope to come out alive, no matter who the winner will be.

Most of the people in the camp of Wolkowysk did not know what "Auschwitz" meant. Some said that it was an extermination camp, where everybody gets destroyed right away. Some thought that it was a simple concentration camp. The prisoners had to work very hard, but no senseless killing.

Whatever it was. we were certain that this was a place where only a miracle could save us.

The commandant came in to our clinic and told us that we'd be only resettled.

"You don't have to be afraid. You'll be only resettled to work for the German Reich. It will be hard work. I'll assure you, in the name of Germany, that you'll arrive healthy to your place. The sick people will be transferred to the hospitals in Auschwitz. After recovery, they will return to work."

This was the way one of the main agents of destruction of the "Ehrenvolk" spoke to us, the innocent victims of Nazism. Every word was a lie and we knew it. Some started to cry and to lament over their fate.

I went over to the hospital and spoke to Dr. Shulman.

"I feel better," he said, "but I am very weak. I need at least a few weeks more to recover. I don't know whether I'll be able to walk to the railroad station."

I encouraged him and told him that I passed the disease also, and that the main thing was not to lose confidence and to be courageous. Once he'd start to walk, his condition would improve by the hour.

Dr. Tauchner felt better too. He was two weeks in a coma, and right now he regained consciousness. He was too weak to walk.

Dr. Epstein had very high fever, but he was quiet and completely alert. He had a strong constitution, but how would he be able to walk to the station and to survive the first days in Auschwitz? It would require extraordinary physical strength.

Mrs. Kaufman had a violent course of the disease. But she felt better now, very weak. As soon as she noticed me, she called me to her bed.

"This is the end of my life," she said. "Shortly I'll pass to another world, a better one, free from Germans and free from atrocities. I'll meet there my husband, who was brutally murdered a few months ago."

I tried to perk her up and to encourage her to live.

"You are still young, beautiful, intelligent and possess a strong constitution. Please, don't give up. A whole useful life is waiting for you. You'll overcome everything, just don't lose the faith in yourself."

Nothing helped. She did not want to live in such a world. The sooner, the better.

Mrs. Niemczyk was elated when she saw me. She witnessed the time when the doctors were alarmed about my disease.

"Now," she said, "seeing you I hope to survive too."

"Excellent," I said, "this was the right attitude. I hope to see you and your husband alive and in a liberated free world."

The second expression of hope came true. After the war, in 1955, I met her husband alive and healthy in Israel. His name was now Dr. Askenazi (Hebrew translation of Niemczyk).

When I returned to my barrack the sick people stood before my eyes. The Germans didn't know what pity, mercy, compassion meant. They didn't have this kind of words in their vocabulary. I felt sorry and my heart was bleeding for them. But the poor young doctors, who sacrificed their own lives by extinguishing the epidemy of typhus in the camp, now they themselves fell victims to the same disease which they helped eradicate. Now they were were surely to be the first victims of Nazi bestiality. How fearful and frightful, dreadful and unjust. But justice, in any form, didn't exist any more on our part of the world.

I was very thankful to the forces who managed my fate to make me contract the disease very early. Now I felt completely cured and was able to resist the rigor of the future much better. I was healthy mentally and physically, and was ready for a strong fight, not because I wanted to live, but because, as other victims of Nazi bestiality, I desired and craved to tell the world, what happened to us.

The atrocities and the crimes in all their nakedness, should be revealed before the eyes of the world. In this way the necessary steps, would be undertaken, and it would made sure that such crimes could not be repeated again.

January 25, 1943. Late in the evening, we heard voices at the Judenrat. What could that be? At such a late date? I left my barrack and went to the place where the protesting voices came from. In front of the building, many stood guarding protesting the selfishness of their superiors. Shymka Daniel, who was the deputy of Fuks, organized and prepared a truck to take him, his family and his friends to Bialystok. They wanted to save themselves from the approaching and inevitable catastrophe. They paid for the truck with heavy funds taken by force from us. I heard voices. "You are not going to save yourself and leave us to die! You'll have to go together with us! No exceptions!"

Mr. Daniel was a tough man. Although he was only a deputy to Fuks, he was the main person who oppressed the people, by taking out all their money, by forcing them to work for the Germans. He was good to the Germans, fulfilling all their wishes and demands, but he was not just to his own people.

Fucks himself was a just, decent fellow. He was nominated as a chief of the Judenrat, but left everything to be done to Shymka Daniel. He was not able psychologically and physically to execute German orders. Now the people protested and nullified the foul play of Mr. Daniel and his friends. It served him right. Most of the people tried to save themselves, by any means at their disposal, just and unjust. Mr. Daniel was, certainly, no exception.

January 26, 1943. It was very cold, freezing. The temperature dropped to $-15°c = -5°F$.

Taking in consideration the wind factor, it felt even more freezing. The temperature kept dropping and the wind accelerated.

At 2 A.M., the Germans came into the camp and ordered everybody to assemble on the road. Whoever would remain in his barrack would be immediately shot. We left our barracks, taking with us only the few indispensable items, like a warm blanket, some food, water, etc. We had to assemble in formation of tens.

I stood with my brother Mendel, Michle, my relative from Ostrow-Mazovieck, the sister of Dr. Amscibovski, her brother and other four people in one row. We were standing and waiting.

In the meantime, Dr. Horn and Dr. Kaplan returned from the railroad station. They accompanied the sick, the disabled, to the station believing our commandant that the sick will be transferred to a hospital.

"As we arrived at the station with the sick people, we were met by the SS men," related Dr. Kaplan, "who started to kick, and beat us with sticks, rifle butts, rods of iron. They shot the disabled and many of the sick and threw their bodies into the cattle wagons. It was terrible! Real hell on earth! The wagons were illuminated and behind us was darkness. The criminals were beating their victims, shooting many of them and throwing them into the wagons. All this created an unusual, terrible scene on earth. Dr. Horn was beaten very severely. His face and many parts of his body were bleeding profusely. I am not sure whether Dr. Horn will survive the beatings.

"One of the doctors was weakened by the ordeal and couldn't jump fast enough into the wagon. A German shot him on the spot and threw his body inside. It was terrible! Unbelievably cruel."

An order arrived to begin marching.

We started to move in the direction of the central railroad station of New Wolkowysk.

Out of very large families counting over two hundred people each, we the survivors remained very few, able to be counted on the fingers of one hand. Their premature and innocent death, as well as the death of millions of other victims of Nazi bestialities, should never be forgotten. They should all be remembered as saints who by their death made it possible for others to live. The world should always remember the innocent millions of lives who were lost for no reason at all. By their death they made it *impossible* for other criminals and psychopaths to repeat the same evildoings and atrocities.

The cold intensified. In spite of the tension and masses of people following us, we felt the freezing weather especially in our faces and fingers. The Nazis started to beat us. Some were shot on the road. Pandemonium ensued.

Finally, we reached the station, which was partially illuminated. From this moment on, they started to beat us more furiously with heavy sticks, truncheons, iron rods, whips, and rifle butts. Some couldn't reach the wagons, stumbled and fell. They were shot immediately.

Finally, with difficulties, hardly alive, the few members of my family and myself succeeded in entering one of the wagons, and were among the first to get inside and to choose a corner (west south) in order to put down our packages.

We were now all together, my brother Mendel, Michle, and the relative from Ostrow-Mazowicek, whose brother died of typhus in the camp. Soon other victims came in or thrown in. The Germans counted one hundred persons and locked the wagon. The train had about twenty wagons, used previously to transport cattle. The last wagons were occupied by German guards. The congestion was enormous. In spite of the biting cold, we felt very hot, perspiring profusely. Our wagon had a little opening, like a window at the top of one wall. We heard desperate voices outside, sounds of beatings, gun shots and understood that the other wagons were being loaded. We were sitting on the floor contemplating what was going to happen now? Would the Germans kill us? Or would they resettle us, as proclaimed and promised by the "Master Race" so often? Some were trying to look through the little opening. We felt bitter in our hearts as nothing could be done. After a while, the train started to move very slowly in the direction of Bialystok.

Are we going to live or not? That was the question in everyone's mind. Taking in consideration the atrocities at the railroad station, the murdering and shooting, I assumed that this was the last road to death. We were all condemned to die, not by a court, not because we had done something wrong, but because of the will of the Nazi party. Here I was thinking again about the old expression of hope, in order to avoid a total mental collapse.

"Even if a sharp sword is pushed against your throat, you should not despair of the criminal."

Some inner thought kept telling me—

Maybe, we will not be killed this time!

Maybe, we'll remain alive as promised!

The train was moving with the unfortunate human beings. Darkness was all around us, and inside us. From time to time, we saw a flickering light appearing at the window, which soon vanished. Suddenly one struck a match and I saw the following inscription on the wall.

"December, 1942, 4,500 people brought to Treblinka."

"Everywhere, but not Treblinka," I prayed. "G-d help us!"

Near me, a man was praying.

"G-d Almighty, look upon our misery and plead our cause. Destroy their design.

"Look from Thy heights and see how the Nazis are murdering us, ridiculing your name. We are being handled like cattle brought for slaughter.

"Have pity on us, don't deliver us into the executioner's hands. Why should the Nazis boast by saying,

"Where is your G-d? Let him come now and save you.

"Let him show his strength.

"Don't wait any longer, because we reached the breaking point.

"Come and help us for your sake.

"What are you going to have, if we'll be massacred?

"When our flesh and bones will turn into ashes in the Krematoria, who is going to sanctify your name?"

This was how the man prayed to his G-d whom he trusted and believed in without any shadow of a doubt.

The fellow, who was standing near the window, declared that the train stopped at the station "Bialystok."

Civilians were walking at the station or nearby, like nothing had happened. Here were hundreds of innocent people, living in the trains, in the most miserable conditions, condemned to die, by a bunch of criminals, and you men of the railroad station move around undisturbed? How was it possible?

Some of those near the window asked for water, a little snow from the ground, because we were very thirsty.

"Please give us a little water, we'll use it only for our children. Please help us, don't let us die!"

It was forbidden. The Germans declared that they'd be severely punished, if they gave us water or a little snow to cool our burning bodies. No water was given.

The train moved again in a western direction, we were approaching the station of Malkinia. Darkness had started already, by that time, to melt away and the prime of the morning began to brighten the horizon. Finally the train stopped at the station of Malkinia.

The fear of death engulfed us all. We knew that not far from the station the terrible extermination camp Treblinka was located.

Were we going to be murdered in this factory of death or not? This was the question on everyone's mind.

Was this last transport from Wolkowysk going to share the same fate as the previous transports?

Lamentations, cryings were heard all around.

From what direction will come our aid? I wondered.

Some were very weakened from the ordeal, heat and excessive thirst, and were lying motionless on the floor. Some were in agony.

My brother Mendel, Michle, my second cousin from Ostrow-Mazowick were sitting near me, on the floor of the train, like paralyzed, half-dead already.

The Year 1943

Over one hundred people were in our wagon. All the talking, crying, praying stopped. Not a sound was heard!

A heartbreaking silence and internal darkness engulfed all of us. Our brains refused to function. We were, already, a part of another world, but still holding the edgy sharp corner of this planet. We were very fatigued physically and mentally by the ordeal of the previous concentration camp in Wolkowysk, by the constant beatings, starvation, contagious diseases of the last three months, by the ordeal of the last night.

We knew, that there was a side line from the station Malkinia, direct to the death camp of Treblinka. It took only 20-30 minutes of travel. The train was still waiting at the station of Malkinia and inside were enclosed the unfortunate victims of Nazi bestiality.

Why did not the train move? We were taken to be murdered. What were the Nazis waiting for? To prolong our agony? To increase our pain and torture? It is clear that the train did not stop at Malkinia for no reason!

Go ahead, kill us! You Nazi murderer! Nobody was going to protest anyway. The world was paralyzed today, as far as our fate was concerned.

The train still stood on its original place. It did not move. It seemed to us a very long time. Maybe, in the face of death, inevitable horror, every minute appeared to be a year.

Suddenly, like a bolt from the blue, the train started to move. We heard sounds of metallic connections, wagons joining wagons, wild German shootings. The train was continuing on its way, probably moving on the side line towards Trablinka. Another 20-30 minutes and we'll be there. Another two hours, and our lives will be taken away from us. Our lungs will be choked. Our flesh and bones will turn to ashes. How terrible!

What happened?

Twenty minutes passed, thirty minutes, one hour, two hours, and the train was creeping forwards. We had to be at Treblinka long ago. What was going on?

Suddenly, we realized that we were being taken, not to Treblinka, but to some other concentration camp. Any place was better than Treblinka.

We woke up. Our brains started to function again.

Maybe we'll live a little bit longer. Maybe we'll survive this terrible nightmare and be able to tell the world what happened to us.

Hour after hour passed and our train continued on its way. My pious neighbor said, "I have a feeling that we are going to survive. I am positively sure of it. You can see for yourself the miracles of G-d. The train stopped at Malkinia, at the gates of death. Normally everything would have been over by now. See! We are still alive. It is difficult to understand the ways of G-d. I feel it in my bones. Angels of salvation are around us, on my right side is the angel Michael, on my left side is the angel Gabriel and over my head—G-d himself."

The man started to cry and pray.

"It is better to trust in G-d, than to put confidence in man. It is better to trust the Lord, than to put confidence in princes.

"All the nations encircle, encompass and beleaguer us.

"In the name of the Lord, we will cut them off.

"They encircle and engulf us, in the name of the Lord, we will thrust them off. They encircle us like bees, they shall be quenched as the fire of thorns. In the name of the Lord we will cut them off. . . .

"The Lord is our strength and He became our salvation."

People recovered from the deep shock of being so near to Treblinka, the camp of death. All were talking and thanking the forces which managed their fates. Most of the people wanted to know where the Nazis were taking us.

Shelkovitz, the tailor, a very distinguished and intelligent man, said.

"I know. This road is leading us toward Warsaw, the capital of Poland."

"That is right," said my cousin. "We are going in the directionf of Warsaw. From there, probably, we'll continue to the concentration camps of Chelmno or to Auschwitz. In Chelmno, the Nazis use poison vans. I know it, because I was caught in one of these vans and escaped together with my brother."

"Please tell me about Chelmno," I said. "I heard very much

about Auschwitz, Treblinka, etc., but I had never heard anything about Chelmno."

"I am ready to tell you everything about Chelmno. Maybe we'll find a way to save ourselves."

Chelmno was located between Poznan and Lodz. The camp was an extermination camp. People were killed in gas vans. It existed from the year in 1941, when a transport from Lodz arrived and all perished there.

Many Russians, Poles and Gypsies were exterminated there. Hundreds of thousands of Jews lost their lives in Chelmno. As usual, the victims were cheated by false promises. People believed the treacherous Germans, because it occurred at the beginning of the war or even before the Germans attacked the Russians. The victims never heard nor read before of such bestialities. They believed the "Ehrenvolk," that they'd be resettled and followed the orders of undressing and taking baths. Many doubted. Nobody was sure of anything. The masses were confused. Any slight resistance meant death, not only for the individuals who resisted, but to the entire transport. An enormous responsibility, especially since one always nurtured a thought: "Maybe the German promises represented the truth."

They were severely beaten and driven to the vans. When the door was closed, the driver started the engine and the poisonous gas, carbon monoxide, filled the interior of the vans. Anguished screams and frantic knocking at the walls and doors emanated from the vans.

In a very short time all were dead. The victims were brought to the forest a few miles away and burned in the pits. Three vans operated. Each one was able to murder one hundred victims. One thousand people perished in one day.

"This is the truth about Chelmno," continued my cousin. "I want you not to have any doubt about it, and act accordingly when necessary."

The train continued to move forward. The journey stretched endlessly, the wagons were jerking, shaking, twitching and jolting. The sick groaned, the weak lay on the floor not able to move.

The trip was morbid and gloomy, people were dying.

The Road to Auschwitz 177

One of the wagons of the cattle trains, where about one hundred human beings including children, even infants, were packed and transported to the concentration camps. No food or water was given. Many died on the way. Through the small window in each wagon some victims could look out and observe the passing stations on the way to the extermination camps.

Through the open small window, we could see German soldiers at the railroad stations. They cursed us, sneered and threw insults in our direction. They certainly had no sympathy for us, the victims of Nazi bestiality. They probably did not understand what was going on. They surmised that we were enemies of the Third Reich, that we were the ones who started the war, and therefore were guilty of their defeat. They did not blame Hitler and the Nazis, but they blamed us. How surprised they would have been in finding out that the train was filled with people completely innocent, and that the majority did not know even where Germany was located.

All of a sudden, the train stopped at a big station with many lights. The man at the window announced that we were at Warsaw (Capital of Poland). How strange!

We saw many people milling around, talking, laughing, like nothing had happened, no misery, no war.

We were sitting inside, waiting to see what our fate was going to be. After a few hours, the train started to move again and, it seemed to us, in the direction of the South. This was the night of January 27, 1943. We were sitting on the floor and suffering. No water, no food, lack of air. We were very crowded. Sanitary disposal was out of the question. The little window was a big help.

In spite of enormous exhaustion and tiredness we couldn't sleep.

The train continued on its way slowly but surely. This was the second night of our journey locked in the wagon. We passed the station of Czenstochova. I tried to get through the window, but it was too small. We passed many stations on the way but the train did not stop at any of them.

The day of January 27 arrived and passed with no change in our miserable condition. My neighbors were lying without any signs of life. Some of them were dead. The bodies could not be removed. They remained with us all the time.

January 28, 1943.

It was already the third night of our wretchedness and our agony. In the morning the train stopped at Katowice. A railroad man passed near our window.

"Please, tell us, where our train is going to?" asked one of the prisoners, who stood near the window.

"You are going to be killed! Save yourself if you are able to!

Trains are passing here very often," the man answered, looking around in all directions to make sure that nobody was watching.

He continued further. "Yesterday another train passed. A small boy of about nine years old got through the window and he wanted to escape. One of the SS men caught him and shot him on the spot. It was terrible! Escape, extricate yourself! Don't have any illusions!"

We asked him for a little water or snow.

"I am afraid, they might shoot me. To them life, except their own, has no value."

He looked around and took snow from the ground, and in spite of the danger quickly gave it to us. He ran away hastily, to avoid being caught by the guard.

Other civilians and trainmen passed by. They looked at us but didn't talk. Our questions remained unanswered. Nobody dared to give us a little snow or water. They were afraid, or maybe they didn't care.

I looked through the window and recognized the station. I remembered it from the time of my studies, when I used to pass the station on my way to Czechoslovakia or to Italy, where I studied medicine at the universities of Prague or Bologna.

I was wondering whether my friends in the cities were still alive. Whether they exercised their profession. They certainly didn't know that I was here in the bottomless deepness of hell.

CHAPTER VIII

Stalingrad——Aushwitz——North Africa

THE INFAMOUS RAMP OF AUSCHWITZ. THE FIRST SELECTION. MIRACLE #6. MY BROTHER MENDEL. MRS. KAUFMAN. NORTH AFRICA. STALINGRAD. BIRKENAU. BLOCK 22. ZONA. THE FIRST VICTIM. TATTOO #94430. MY DIPLOMA. BLOCK 26. THE NIGHT OF JANUARY 29, 1943. SECOND DAY IN BIRKENAU. PFLEGER OF BLOCK 26. BLOCK #7 (DEATH BLOCK). DR. ZENKTELLER.

Finally we reached the station of "Auschwitz," which was called in Polish "Oswiencim."

Auschwitz was a small town in Silesian Poland which had existed since the first kings of the Piast family, who organized and formed their independent Polish state.

At the end of the 18th century, when Poland was divided among its neighbors, Prussia, Austria and Russia, Auschwitz belonged to Austria.

The barracks outside the town served as stables for Austrian cavalry.

At the time of the German occupation, in the year 1939, Auschwitz had a population of 12,000. All the terrain was flat and surrounded by stagnant ponds. When Poland was occupied by the Germans, some villages were evacuated by force and their inhabitants expelled.

In April, 1940, Himmler ordered the establishment of the

STALINGRAD. NORTH AFRICA. AUSCHWITZ.

concentration camp "Auschwitz," and in June, 1940, Rudolf Hoess was nominated commandant of this terrible camp.

Thirty prisoners from other concentration camps, professional criminals, were sent to Auschwitz to serve as kapos (chiefs at work), Lager-älteste (chiefs of all the camp), Blockälteste (chiefs of a bunker) and Stubendienst (orderlies).

In all the German concentration camps, the camps were administered by: 1.) Germans, who had the suffix Führer, and by 2.) prisoners nominated by the Germans for their cruelties, who had the suffix älteste.

For example: Lager-Fuhrer, (chief of all the camp) Block Fuhrer, (chief of one building). All of them were Germans, mostly SS men. There were also guards.

Lager-alteste, Block-alteste—as explained above—were prisoners. There were also kapos and foremen who, although prisoners themselves, were nominated by the Germans to their positions for their special cruelties. The German guards, the Kapos and foremen were supervising the work. The camp in Auschwitz was separated for men and women. Camp for men (Manner-Lager) and Camp for women (Frauen-Lager). The prisoner supervisors were almost as cruel as their German masters, for they believed that extreme ruthlessness and heartlessness might save their own lives. Of course, they were wrong because, at the end, the Germans tried to exterminate all their prisoner helpers, the kapos, the foremen, and all the other prisoner chiefs.

The Nazis wanted to erase any trace of mass murder in the concentration camps in order to get rid of all the eyewitnesses.

The female camp was not better off. Female criminal prisoners from Ravensbruck were transferred to Auschwitz to serve as supervisors. Most of them were prostitutes and real beasts. Himmler regarded them as particularly well suited to act as Kapos in the women camp.

Auschwiz was later expanded and finally devided in three parts.

Auschwitz I (Stamlager). The original camp.

Auschwitz II was called *Birkenau*. It was an extermination camp. Most of the krematoria were built there.

Auschwitz III, called *Buna*, to which belonged many small mine camps, where the prisoners worked in mines or factories. On January 28, 1943 at 4 P.M. (22 Shwat, Tasag), we arrived on the famous ramp of Birkenau. We had been sitting in the wagons half dead, without food nor water for three nights. Many died of the ordeal. We heard noises around us and we assumed that some of our people were getting off the wagons.

Sudenly the doors of our wagon were unlocked and wild voices accompanied by beatings were heard.

"Heraus, Heraus" (get out)!

We left the wagons in a hurry. Some tried to take their packages with them.

"Leave the packages!" We heard orders accompanied with beatings. The sun and the fresh air refreshed us a little. We saw men dressed in stripes, jumping into the wagons and taking out our packages and the dead, which were assembled in different piles.

Wild Germans with guns were running around, beating us without any reason. Some had dogs, to be used when necessary. Trucks were standing not far away. We were told to assemble, men and women separately. We said goodbye to Michle, who remained standing alone, all by herself, tears running over her face. The Germans continued to beat us with truncheons, clubs rods and canes. We dispersed in all directions, and finally joined the group of men, who were standing in front of a German.

This was the Nazi doctor who was to examine us and make decisions who shall die and who shall live. The examination was not a medical examination. The Nazi doctor looked at his victims and usually asked two questions.

How old are you?

What is your profession?

Then he directed the innocent, confused, and tired prisoner to the right or to the left.

Right—meant life. Left—meant death.

With all the chaos, muddle and mix up, I kept my composure and absolute coolness, watching our men passing in front of the Nazi and answering his two questions.

I saw Dr. Marek Kaplan passing.
What is your profession?
A medical doctor, answered Dr. Kaplan.
How old are you?
Thirty-one years was the answer.
Dr. Kaplan, who was a husky fellow, was ordered to go to the right.
Then I saw Dr. Schulman standing before the Nazi.
How are you?
Thirty years was the answer.
What is your profession?
A medical doctor.
Go to the left, said the Nazi.
Dr. Schulman, was thin, depressed, convalescent from the typhus illness. Three days ago he was still in the hospital bed in the concentration camp of Wolkowysk.
I understood that the profession didn't play a major role under those circumstances, but the appearance, behavior, exterior were the main components which decided whether one remained alive or not.
I looked all around the unfortunate masses of people. All of them looked exhausted, despondent and very pale. I straightened out myself, struck and rubbed my face to make it appear more colored.
When I appeared before the German executioner, I knocked one heal to the other and stood to attention. My heart was palpitating and I waited for the decision. Right or left. Life or death.
The German asked: How old are you?
Twenty-five years old.
What is your profession?
Medical doctor and mechanic.
I didn't know what to say. Is the profession of a doctor good for the Nazi, who was a doctor himself, or not?
The right answer would decide whether I was going to live or die. The German laughed. It was extraordinary and unusual to see a German smile under the circumstances.

All the time he stood stiff, morose.

He said, "How is it possible? If you are a medical doctor, you have no time to be a mechanic."

I replied, "During my medical studies I had to supplement my income by working as a mechanic."

The German looked at me again and said, Go to the right!

This was *Miracle #6*.

I was safe for the time being, not knowing what was going to be in the future.

I saw my cousin being sent to the left.

My brother Mendel was sent also to the left.

Instead of going to the left, he went to the right and joined our group. A Nazi noticed it, took him out from our group and sent him to the left, beating him severely with a truncheon. After a while, my brother slipped away and joined our group again. The same Nazi saw him in our group and chased him away again. In all the pandemonium he kept an eye on my brother. It was very unfortunate.

The Nazi doctor continued his gruesome and ghastly job of sending people to the right and left, to life or death. After a short time the majority of the prisoners were still waiting in front of the examiner for his decision. Then the Nazi moved on the side and all the people strong or weak, young or old, were driven to the left.

The selection was finished. Less than 22% were selected to enter the camp, the other 78% were sent straight to their death, many without any selection.

Our transport originally counted about 1,700 strong, young men and women. Only 366 were selected, 279 men and 87 women. The rest, the vast majority, more than 1,300 people, were loaded on trucks and sent to the special designated places near the camp Birkenau (Auschwitz II) where they all perished. In front and back of the trucks, which took the people to be exterminated, Red Cross cars were visible, the normal sign of compassion, pity and help. For the Germans, they served as cars of death.

Michle told me after the war that she was chosen to go to the left, but seeing the column of women selected to the right, she pushed herself in, and remained standing there. She had better luck than my brother Mendel. Michle is married, lives in New York and has two children.

We were standing, assembled in rows of five, waiting. We were the lucky ones, selected to enter the camp of Auschwitz. The others were driven to the waiting trucks, and were beaten severely with rods, sticks, gun butts. Some were fatally shot. Men separately. Women separately. The children and their mothers were sent right away to the trucks (left). The crying, sobbing, screaming and lamentation of those destined to die were terrible, defying any description. Mrs. Kaufman and her daughter Liba, whose son and brother Dr. David Kaufman, was shot in Wolkowysk, were standing in another open truck, pressed from all sides, by other unfortunate women and children. Their heads were tilted down. The mother, Mrs. Kaufman, called out.

"You, young men from Wolkowysk, retain the memory of our suffering. Our innocent blood should constantly remind you to tell the world what you had seen with your own eyes. You should never forget us."

I remember also Mrs. Panter from Wolkowysk, standing in the open truck, calling on us.

"Remember, all of you, who remain alive. What the Germans did to us! You should never forget us, the innocent victims of German bestiality!"

I never forgot it. This awful, terrible, horrible scene, I will, always, remember.

In the days or nights, in my wakeful hours, in my dreams, in my work and leisure, I will, always remember it. I will fulfill your demands! I will tell the world what happened to you Mrs. Kaufman, Mrs. Panter, and to all the other unfortunate millions of human beings, who perished for no reason at all, victims of a pathological fury of the super-race. I will not rest, regardless of sacrifices, financial, professional, physical and mental effort and exertion, until all the world knows what happened to you and to all my loved ones.

The trucks moved away, loaded with people—men, women and children.

From about 20,000 people gathered in the concentration

camp Wolkowysk, in November 1942, only 366 remained alive, exposed to the hard labor and chicanery of Auschwitz, 279 men and 87 women were standing on the ramp of Auschwitz waiting and hoping on this cold day of January 28, 1943. Then we were ordered to march towards *Birkenau*, which was called an extermination camp because an average person could not live there longer than 1-2 months.

What happened on the battle front on this day of January 28, 1943, when I was incarcerated in Birkenau, the only one who still, remained alive, from a very large family? On this day, January 28, 1943, the German 6th Army under the leadership of General Paulus lost any hope of extricating themselves from the vises of Russian encirclement. Thousands of men were killed in battle. Most of the armor was destroyed. In fact, on this day, January 28, there was no army anymore, but only three small pockets of soldiers hiding and trying to survive the strong Russian bombardment. Paulus was lying in a cellar of the southern pocket. On January 31, all the 6th Army surrendered and was sent to captivity.

From 300,000 men, only 150,000 survived. Among them twenty-four generals. On the way to Siberia, most of them perished from exhaustion and sicknesses. An epidemic of typhus broke out in the spring, which decimated the number of Germans. Only 6,000 remained alive.

Hitler fell into a furious rage.

"Paulus is a traitor, he should have committed suicide instead of surrendering!" After the war he was going to courtmartial him and order him to be shot!

"He should have freed himself from all sorrow," continued Hitler, "and ascend to national immortality by committing suicide. But no! He preferred to go to Moscow! What a shame! There was a beautiful woman," continued Hitler, "a real beauty of the first rank, who felt insulted by some words, nothing of any importance. She went to her room, wrote a farewell letter and shot herself to death."

"Na!" Hitler said, "here was a soldier, a field marshal, who was frightened to do the same thing, but preferred to go to captivity."

STALINGRAD. NORTH AFRICA. AUSCHWITZ. 187

This was an allusion to his neice Geli Raubal, whom Hitler drove to commit suicide, when he lived in one household with his sister.

On February 3, 1943, the German radio announced, "The battle of Stalingrad has ended. . . . The 6th Army, under the exemplary leadership of Field Marshal Paulus has been overcome, by the enemy."

Three days of national mourning was proclaimed. All theaters, movies were closed.

According to the German historian Goerlitz, "Stalingrad was the greatest defeat that a German army had ever undergone."

On this day, January 28, 1943, the world knew, unequivocally, that the Germans lost the war, in spite of the tyranny or maybe because of it.

Rommel in North Africa was also severely beaten.

Anglo-American troops landed a few months previously in Algeria and Morocco, creating a double front for the Germans. The complete collapse of the Nazi "1,000 year Reich" was now only a matter of time. By the end of spring, North Africa would be freed completely. On the Russian front, the Germans were running back to their old frontiers.

The German radio, unintermittently announced "The strategically withdrawal" of their armies to the west.

The functioning of Hitler's mind could be judged from the fact that he threatened at that late date to courtmartial his General Paulus for surrendering to the Russians. It was clear that Hitler and his henchmen had lost all contacts with reality.

Let's return to the time when we arrived on the famous ramp of Auschwitz.

We, the selected ones, stood and waited in this cold afternoon of January 28. The rest of the people, men and women were beaten, massacred and loaded on the trucks, which left for the special extermination places and gas chambers, where they perished.

We, the fortunate ones for the moment, were ordered to march, accompanied by wild Germans and dogs. The road was clean, on both sides were piles of snow. After 20-30 minutes of marching, we reached the gates of Birkenau.

We saw barbed wires, watch towers, where men with machine guns were standing, watching and ready to shoot.

The main camp gate was illuminated. On the top of the gate was an inscription in German.

"Arbeit Macht Frei." (Work makes you free.)

This was another one of the Nazi lies. Work never freed any one in Auschwitz or in any other German concentration camp. Even the ex-Commandant of Auschwitz, Rudolf Hoess, when he was imprisoned after the war, confirmed the falsehood and cynicism of this inscription.

We passed the gate and entered the proper terrain of Birkenau. Dante's inferno and the inscription on the top of the purgatory was more suitable here.

"Abandon hope all ye who enter here."

We found ourselves in the midst of the M.K.L. (Männer Koncentracions Lager), which signified—men's concentration camp. Two hundred seventy-nine young, strong men, but enormously tired, exhausted and despondent.

The barbed wires around us were charged with high electrical voltage. Many inmates committed suicide by touching these wires. Touching the wires meant death.

Birkenau was previously a Polish village, under the name of "Brzezinka," a few miles from the town of Oswiecim (Auschwitz).

On March 1, 1941, Himmler visited the villages around the town of Auschwitz. He stopped at the village of Brzezinka and decided to remove all the inhabitants from the village, to destroy the houses, and to build the extermination camp Birkenau there. The place suited the German well. It was out of the way, far from populated centers and separated by about 2½ km. from the old camp, Auschwitz I. It is very characteristic that Himmler decided to build an extermination camp a few months before the outbreak of the German-Russian war. He had it already in mind to use prisoners, and especially Russian prisoners, for this purpose.

The building of the camp started in October, 1941, by

prisoners of war brought in from Auschwitz I. The physical state of the prisoners was disastrous. They were very weak, because of hard work, very bad living conditions and lack of food. Their shoes were torn. Some had no shoes at all and no coats. Under those conditions, they were dying in the hundreds, especially in the cold weather and high humidity of Auschwitz.

The prisoners, according to the ex-Commandant Hoess, could stand the cold better than the dampness and humidity. They were constantly drenched to the skin.

About two thousand prisoners were forced to build the barracks of Birkenau.

It is difficult to realize now under what conditions the building of Birkenau was going on at the end of 1941 and 1942. Weak and starved prisoners in the freezing weather were forced to work with their last strength, pulling wheelbarrows, wading knee-deep in mire. Many were killed during work or just fell dead from exhaustion.

There was a revolt in one of the barracks, where the penal company was kept. It happened on June 10, 1942, when fifty prisoners revolted. Next day, on June 11, 1942, the camp leader Anmeier, together with Hoessler, shot twenty prisoners in the yard of the barracks, and about 520 prisoners were driven to the gas chambers, where they perished.

At the end of 1941, there were 13,775 Russian prisoners alone, beside the prisoners of other nationalities. Four months later only 5,400 prisoners remained. On 1/17/45, at the evacuation of Auschwitz, only 92 Russian prisoners remained alive.

German industries, like G.I. Farben Industry, built plants near Auschwitz, because of cheap labor and the forced hard work of the prisoners, who built and operated the plants.

While the building of the men's camp of Birkenau was taking place, another camp started for women prisoners. The latter lived till then in Auschwitz I (Blocks 1-10, separated and surrounded by a wall).

On August 10, 1942, they were transferred from Auschwitz I to the newly built camp of Birkenau for women.

They lived in terrible conditions similar to that of the men in the Birkenau camp for men. The dignity of womanhood was destroyed by the inhuman German arrogance and brutality. Many committed suicide.

The newly built camp for women was later, in July, 1943, enlarged. They occupied the men's camp. The men were transferred to another camp.

The women prisoners were under supervision of German women called "Wardresses (SS-Aufseherin)," whose morality was very low. They were on the same level as the SS guards in regard to cruelty.

Here is a description by an ex-prisoner of the above German wardresses:

"Happy are those who never had to observe the expressions on human faces. The sweet, subtle face of a woman—full of an intense desire to enjoy tormenting the defenseless, the condemned. The face of a staid matron—distorted by a violent urge to inflict still greater pain.

"A calm, noble face—changing into a face as if carved in stone, cruelly cold, when the people tormented and baited to death were begging for mercy."

During work hours, the women prisoners were supervised, not only by SS women, but also by SS men, who, wishing to enjoy themselves, beat them and harassed and tormented them by baiting attacking dogs on them.

The barracks in which the prisoners lived were called "Blocks." They were made of bricks or wood. The later were actually stables where previously horses were kept.

Each barrack had four rows of boxes. Each one of the latter was divided into three berths, upper, middle and lower.

It had always been damp and cold inside. The aisles between the berths were covered with a slimy mire. The straw in the births was rotten and had a bad odor. Primitive stoves running along the length of the interior of the barracks failed to keep it warm.

The blocks were numbered. First, we were taken to Block #22, where the new arrivals were fetched. It was a large stable or hangar. All of us were forced into one corner. A German came in and announced that all the valuables, like money, gold watches, should be handed over immediately, for which we'd get receipts,

Stalingrad. North Africa. Auschwitz.   191

called "Bony." The possessor of the "bonies" would be able to buy in the camp anything he desired, like food, drinks, cigarettes, etc.

One of the Stubendienst (an orderly) came over to our corner and advised us to give the valuables to him. Later he'd return one half to the owner. Otherwise we'll lose everything.

Many of us believed him and handed over the valuables which we possessed. Mr. Fuks, the Judenälteste, the chief of the Jewish council of Wolkowysk, gave him a beautiful gold watch and a lot of money.

Shamke Daniels, his deputy, did not enter the camp. He was taken from the ramp, straight to the gas chamber and exterminated. He had probably more valuables with him than any one of us.

Then, we had to pass in front of the old inmates and be searched for possible hidden valuables. When my turn came, I was ordered to put any valuable on the table and not to hide anything. I put both hands over my head and said, "Go ahead and search. It doesn't make any difference to me. I consider my life to be at the end anyway."

The old inmate looked at me, didn't search and let me pass.

SS men were milling around, watching and searching, examining the gold pieces and other valuables.

Their greedy eyes were glowing with desire. I noticed one of the criminals was examining a ring with diamonds very eagerly. His face showed enormous satisfaction. After a while, he put it in his pocket.

After the search was finished, we were taken to the washing and bathing building called "ZONA." But where were the receipts, the "BONIES," which the Germans promised to give us for our valuables and which would enable us to buy additional food?

What happened? Instead of an answer we were beaten with truncheons, clubs, kicked with heavy German boots. Why did they lie? We were in their hands anyway. But this was the way the Germans operated. Lies upon lies. The bigger the lie the more truthful it seemed for the uninitiated victims.

"ZONA," the bathing building, was a huge hangar where

the new arrivals had to undress, bathe and receive new clothing. We were waiting in front of the "ZONA." Only fifty prisoners could enter at one time. We waited. Menkes from Swislocz, not far from Wolkowysk, who studied the first year of medicine in Praha, Czechoslovakia, gave me a piece of bread. You see, he said, "I am dividing my bread with you because I know you from Praha as a decent and courageous man. I want you to be my brother. I have a feeling that you are going to survive."

It became dark and very cold. We were also hungry, depressed and tired.

The brother of Dr. Kaplinski walked around and between us, murmuring something to himself. Then he stopped in front of me and said, "You are a medical doctor, like my brother, who escaped from the camp of Wolkowysk and is hiding in some place. He is a very intelligent person. I am sure that he will survive. If you meet my brother, after the war, tell him that I was very thankful to him for giving me the cocaine, which was supposed to kill in one hour. My brother told me so. I have taken the poison already, and I'll be dead shortly. What is the use of suffering? Most of us will be killed in a few days anyway. It is better to die now than to go on with such a miserable life. My brother did me an enormous favor. Tell him that I thank him for that."

He paused for a while and said, "Tell my brother everything, what you saw with your own eyes, how we suffered, how tha Germans murdered us."

He became very excited and with a loud voice continued, "You have an obligation to find my brother, search for him all over, and tell him that I couldn't do otherwise. I saw how the Nazis took away my wife and child. I am not able to live without them. I want to die at the same time when my family perished."

I was shaken and uttered, "I promise you to find your brother, and to tell him everything what you said."

He started to cry and continued further, "I had a very nice and good brother. It is amazing how he foresaw everything. In the last minute he handed me the cocaine. What would I have done without the drug? I would have suffered another few days and be killed in a terrible way by the hands of the criminals. Isn't it better this way? Pretty soon, I'll close my eyes peacefully and forever."

We all looked at Mr. Kaplinski and envied him, that he possessed the cocaine and that he was to die peacefully and not be massacred by the Nazis.

I looked all around and saw the electrically charged wires and the nearby canal. It was dark and cold. But I didn't feel any cold, nor was I hungry, because the cold and fear, probably, produced adrenalin by stimulating the suprarenal glands.

The wires and the canal were illuminated very strongly. Every small item was visible as in the daytime. Every one who would come near the canal or the wires would be shot immediately by the SS men in the watch towers.

We saw in the canal a dead man, lying flat with his face down. One fellow sufferer said that the dead man was Mr. Kaplinski's close friend, the son of Dr. Shmutz, and he shared the cocaine with him. The poison worked and he died shortly after the intake. Most probably his organism was less resistant to the action of the venom and maybe he received a larger portion. This was the first dead man from our transport.

Mr. Kaplinski walked around us, talking to himself, murmuring some words which we couldn't understand. The cocaine did not work on him the way he expected. We assumed that, after sharing the venom with his friend, his remaining portion was too small to get the desired result.

Finally, we entered inside the building. First, we found ourself in a small room, where we had to undress and leave all the clothing except the shoes, belt and one personal document. I took with me my doctor's diploma, which was given to me by the medical faculty at the university of Bologna (Italy). We'll see later whether this diploma helped me and how I was able to conserve it and keep it with me in Auschwitz for two years under the very noses of the Nazis.

Then we entered the adjoining room, where the barbers were working, cutting the hair from the heads and bodies of all the new arrivals. Suddenly, I noticed that one of the old inmates walked around with my stethoscope. He played around with it, making an earnest and thoughtful face, like a real doctor.

He stopped one prisoner, and told him, to breath deeply while he was listening with the stethoscope. Then, he stimulated palpation and asked the patient where he felt pain. He was, evidently, very satisfied with his new role.

He turned to us and asked: "Whose stethoscope is it?"

"It is mine," I answered.

"Are you a real doctor? All my life I wanted to be a doctor. I ended up, instead, here. We are going to help you to get some work. Otherwise you'll succumb in a very short time." This was true. Nobody was able to survive longer than one month in any German concentration camp. The food was very scarce. The hard work and severe beatings diminished the number of the prisoners in a frightful way. Most succumbed in 1-2 weeks. The only way to prolong life was to be fortunate enough to get some kind of a function in the camp, like stubendienst (orderlies) or any other function.

For me, the only salvation would be to become a doctor in the little clinic or hospital. A pfleger (doctor) in anyone of the blocks would save me too. But it was very difficult, under the circumstances, to get such a job, because of the great number of the newly arrived physicians, and because these jobs were already occupied.

Later we were taken to another large room called "registration room," where many tables were standing. Near every table were sitting inmates, who were registering the new arrivals by writing down the name, address, profession, education, the number of languages one can speak and write, etc. I asked him, in my ignorance, whether a physician could get a job here. The registrator, a pale, undernourished prisoner, looked at me. He didn't answer. I understood everything. No additional explanation was necessary. When the registration was over, the tattooing started, which consisted of puncturing the skin with a needle and inserting indelible colors, which left permanent marks. Every puncture caused a formation of a point under the epidermis. Different numbers or letters could be made out of the points, which remained forever. In this way the Germans marked every prisoner with a number.

My number was 94430, which is still impressed permanently now on my left forearm, on the dorsal part, between the wrist and elbow. This job was performed by two young Hungarian prisoners, who did it very fast and skillfully. I heard a noise and looked around. One old prisoner, evidently, a privileged one, who had more food and was dressed better, was beating another prisoner who had arrived recently. I couldn't understand such a behavior. Both were prisoners and both were destined to die. Why then the fighting? In my naiveté, I still did not understand fully the German concentration camp.

Later, we were rushed into the bathing barracks. At the door stood an inmate who painted and smeared every prisoner with petroleum.

The bathing barrack was a large hangar which had inside steps, arranged like in a theater. We were hastened in, and ordered to wait. I sat down on one of the steps. It was very hot in the barrack. Most probably, in this way, the skin disinfection after the petroleum was enhanced. I was sitting and looking around.

"Maybe this was the gas chamber," I thought. "Who knows?" After the ordeal, we did not trust the Nazis. I searched the walls and looked at the ceiling to see whether they contained openings. There were none. We waited. The fellow who smeared our bodies with petroleum was a physician by profession. He asked us for news in the world and how the war was progressing. Here in the concentration camp they were not informed about anything. They were kept in the dark. He lifted his hand toward us and said, "Brothers! You should know, that you arrived at a very terrible place. Hell is a paradise in comparison. Most of the people perish in 1-2 weeks and in very miserable circumstances. Although I have here a small function and not exposed to atrocities, common to all the prisoners, my life is very miserable. Cursed should be the day when I was born, and damned, execrable, should be the day when I was brought in here. Death would be a salvation for me. My heart is bursting, my brain is being shattered every day, when I see the new transports arriving here. God! Why do you permit it?"

Mr. Kaplinski was sitting on one of the steps. The cocaine did not work. The dose was too small. A kapo approached him and said, "You wanted to kill yourself. Come and we'll help you." He started to hit him very hard with his fists and with a club. When he started to kick him with his boots he fainted. He grabbed his legs and dragged him to the neighboring room where cold water was running. The water was icy. Mr. Kaplinski, under the crispness and briskness of the frigid water, opened his eyes and closed them again. Later he was taken out and put in a corner of the bathroom. He was alive, but extremely weakened and exhausted. It was already late in the evening, and every one of us had to go under the shower of freezing water. Previously we were sitting in a very hot room and suddenly we were compelled to submerge in icy water. It was far from being pleasant. In addition the windows were broken and cold winds were crossing the room. I was sure that many were going to get sick. Contracting pneumonia was a possibility. This was the way a bath, shower, and disinfection looked at Birkenau.

Then we were forced to enter another large room, where clothing was distributed. We had to form a row and everyone received a jacket and trousers, regardless of size. A short fellow received long trousers and a tall fellow short ones. The same happened with the jackets. The clothing was actually torn rags and tatters. On the back of each garment was a red heavy line painted, which served as a precaution for the Nazis in case some prisoners should escape. We walked around like comics in a circus, a real masquerade. Luckily, I received a normal jacket, but the trousers were short.

In spite of the very cold weather, we were pushed outside, without overcoats or caps to cover our heads. It was already, around 11 P.M., and we were ordered to march to Block 26. We were freezing and shivering from the extraordinary cold. They let us wait for additional two hours in front of the block. After two hours, we were permitted to enter the barrack. It was 1 A.M. They started to beat us and every one who was able to move pushed himself speedily into one of the berths (boxes). Some were so beaten up in the process that they fell on the ground, completely exhausted and not being able to stand up.

STALINGRAD. NORTH AFRICA. AUSCHWITZ.

* * *

January 29, 1943, First night in Birkenau (Friday).
I forced myself into one of the middle berths where other prisoners were sleeping. Normally two or three people could sleep in one berth. We were on the average about 12-15 people in one berth, and therefore couldn't lie, nor could we sit comfortably. One on the top of the other. The slightest noise was punishable very severely. The block was a dilapidated stable without windows. Holes in the ceiling and walls, through which winds were penetrating. It was a rickety building made for those who entered the purgatory.

Eight hundred tired despondent people already slept in this block before we arrived. Our transport counted 279 men (one committed suicide). All together, our barracks contained one thousand seventy-eight unfortunate and miserable human beings.

In spite of the exhaustion, we couldn't sleep. Near me was sitting an inmate from Pruzany (near Wolkowysk) whose transport arrived a few days earlier. He asked me: "What place did your transport arrive from?"

"From Wolkowysk," I answered.

I tried to get from this fellow sufferer more information about our new place of abode.

Was it possible to survive? Was it really so bad as we experienced in the first hours of our arrival?

"It is an extermination camp", commented my neighbor. "People from all over the world are fetched and brought here. Most of them are taken to the gas chambers on the day of arrival, where they perish. The rest (10-15%) are transferred to the camp for hard labor and enormous mental and physical sufferings before they are killed. Some of the new arrivals are murdered in a few days and without any selection. It depends on such strange factors as the mood of the commandant Rudolf Hoess, or the course of the war and many other components. A few hours ago, a train arrived loaded with people from Czechoslovakia. Very often people from France, Holland, Poland, Russia roll in. All the transports are treated with the same atrocities, the same mishandling and final annihilation."

"How long is the average, healthy young man able to live under these circumstances? I asked.

"Women, children, old men, as you had seen at the ramp, are not taken to the camp at all, but straight to the extermination places. Only the strong, robust, young people are selected, whose survival is calculated to be 2-4 weeks. The criminals want hard work performed with the little strength still left in us.

"Your transport," my neighbor in misfortune continued, "counted 279 strong young men, selected from 1,700 people. I assure you that after 1-2 weeks about 80% will perish. They'll be murdered in the block, during the roll calls and in the course of hard labor. You arrived last evening, Thursday. Today is already Friday, January 29, 1943 (23 Shvat, Tasag). In the early morning, you'll experience the first roll call. You'll go to work on Monday. Three days you'll stay in the camp. Do you know, what it means not to go out to work for three days?" asked my neighbor. His face was pale, tense, his voice trembling.

"Thousands of people will die or be killed in those three days. To survive one day is an attainment. I wish that I could stay in camp for three days. In reality, it doesn't make any difference," reflected my neighbor.

"We'll all disappear from the earth pretty soon. My advice is to try to get yourself some job in the camp. You are a physician, maybe you'll get something. A pfleger (male nurse) in one of the blocks would be your salvation. For the rest of your transport, there is no hope."

We stopped talking because the night watchman walked by near our berth. I was sitting like in a daze.

Suddenly, the gong with its loud, resonant tone was heard all over Birkenau. This was a sign to get up immediately. Whoever remained lying or sitting was severely beaten up, or even slaughtered.

The time was 3 A.M. when the day started in Auschwitz. Since we were dressed in our tatters and rags, we jumped off from our boxes in a hurry. The prisoners of Auschwitz slept in their working clothings and did not undress at all at that time.

We ran with all our remaining strength to the exit in order to avoid catastrophic beatings and possible crippling.

But, alas! the senior of the block (Blockälteste) stood already at the door exit with a few of his henchmen equipped with trancheons, clubs, and hit every one who passed through the exit.

It was very dangerous.

Finally we reached the yard, and started to assemble outside in front of the barrack.

Imagine, dear reader, more than one thousand miserable men, hungry, tired, running towards the door and trying to assemble in a row of ten, accompanied at the same time by severe blows. We were running for our lives, like a herd of domestic animals attacked by wild beasts.

Every one received a portion of bread, 250 gm., for the entire day of hard labor, a tiny piece of margarine and the so-called coffee, which was actually a thinly colored substitute.

Our transport did not get anything, because we did not go out to work as yet.

It was very cold at 3 A.M. in Birkenau. The actual roll call (Appell) took place at 5 A.M. During the two hours we had to be assembled and were severely beaten. Then started the training of "MUTZEN AB" (caps down) and "MUTZEN AUF" (caps up).

Nobody was sure whether he'd remain alive, after the roll-call. Heavy blows with clubs or iron rods over the heads and backs fell on us all the time. If somebody was not exactly in line, he was beaten, often to death.

Then the Blockälteste took over the training.

"MUTZEN AB," shouted the block chief. All the prisoners had to take off the caps from their heads. All the thousand men of our block had to do it at the same time. If someone was late, he received a blow over his head.

"MUTZEN AUF" was the next order. Everybody had to quickly put his cap on his head. This kind of training went on till 5 A.M., till the German came for the inspection.

Finally, a fat arrogant German, arrived. *"MU—T—Z—EN AB!"* (caps down) yelled the Blockälteste. All the caps went down. The German counted us. The number should be 1,079, including the dead of the night before, and the sick who couldn't stand on their feet. He left. *"MU—T—Z—EN AUF!"* (caps up) shouted the Blockälteste and the caps were put on again.

Our transport, luckily, did not receive any caps as yet. So the training with the caps was omitted with us and a few lives were temporarily spared.

When I saw the dead prisoners lying in front of the barrack, completely nude, with the number written over their chests, I couldn't believe my own eyes. Was it a bad dream, a nightmare or a reality? Could such a condition exist on our planet? The sick prisoners, not dead as yet, were lying nude near the dead bodies on the snow. They did not receive food nor water, and remained there till they died. Later in the day, the corpses were transferred to the so-called "DEAD HOUSE" (Leichen Kamer), where the bodies accumulated in piles remained till taken to the pits for cremation.

I observed the people who were lying, completely naked, but hadn't died as yet. Some of them tried to sit up, or to turn over on the other side. Their lips were trembling, their eyes half-closed, looking into the far distance. They couldn't make it and fell backward. They tried again to lift themselves up and fell again. I was shaken, not by fear but from the unexpected scene, which I had never seen before, and had never imagined that could happen. I was in a shock. Darkness engulfed me, my head was turning all around and I felt like fainting. My neighbor grabbed me and said: "Don't worry, you'll get accustomed to it." He explained further: "The blockälteste receive orders from the Germans to murder, every day, a certain number of prisoners. Otherwise they'll pay with their own lives. Some of the blockälteste or Kapos achieve a certain degree of dexterity in killing people. The victim destined to die is hit over the head: when he falls, they put a long stick over his neck and two people stand over both ends of the stick. The blockalteste presses the abdomen inside. The prisoner can't breathe, loses consciousness and is dead in 1-2 minutes.

After the roll call, we heard the order:

"ARBEIT—KOMMANDO FORMIEREN." (Form labor

commandoes.) The prisoners started to run in all directions, like ants, to join their groups (commandoes).

There were different "COMMANDOES," like: "PLANIER KOMMANDO," which had to straighten out small hills. This work was completely unnecessary, because after a few days they had to return the heaped earth to the original place. "BAU—KOMMANDO" had to build barracks or Krematoria. "KOMMANDO BANASH" to work for the proprietor Banash. "KOMMANDO CANADA" had to sort out the merchandise and the packages brought in with the new transports, and so on.

The valuables and the good pieces were taken away by the Germans and sent to Germany. Thousands of wagons filled with clothing, shoes, machinery robbed from the new arrivals were sent from the concentration camps to Germany. The articles which were not good were taken to the clothing barracks (Bekleidungs Kammer).

The best "KOMMANDO" was "CANADA," because the prisoners, while sorting out the goods, could nourish themselves better from the food found, and therefore were able to resist the ordeal much longer.

Among the relatively more fortunate who belonged to "CANADA" were two from our transport, Mr. Koss, the tailor, and the sister of Dr. Kaplan, Nuna.

Lets now return and see what happened to us, the transport from Wolkowysk, on this first morning in Birkenau (January 29, 1943).

When the "COMMANDOS" left, we remained in the camp, and were not allowed to enter the block. It was very cold outside. We were standing in the yard, trembling from cold since 3 A.M. We had no overcoats, nor caps. The scarce and miserable food was not given to us at all, because we did not go out to work. We were clinging to each other like sheep.

Somebody found out that by rubbing our backs one against the other we were able to warm up slightly. Soon we formed circles, one circle inside the other. The back of one circle was directed against the back of the other circle, and so we rubbed our backs one against the other and felt much warmer.

We continued in this practice till we received small quadrangular strips of linen cloth, upon which were stamped our personal numbers, which were previously engraved on our left forearms. The strips were 4 inches long and 2 inches wide. We had to fasten it by sewing, on our jackets above the left upper pockets, and on our trousers (upper thigh, left). Later, after receiving our overcoats, we had to put similar strips on the upper left sides.

The strips had triangles with different colors. Green—for criminals. Black—for asocials, prostitutes. Pink—for homosexuals. Violet for clergyman. Jews had a Star of David (Zion emblem) on their strips. Letters showed the origin of the prisoner. P—for Poles, J—for Jew, etc. The German prisoners usually had green (criminals) or black (asocials) triangles. The Russians had black triangles (asocials) for reason unknown to me. The Germans considered the Russians to be asocials (subhumans—"UNDERMENSCH").

The prisoners who went to work found themselves outside the camp proper. The supervision of the camp was accomplished as follows: Besides the charged barbed wires and the encampment there were two systems of chains. "Gross kette," which functioned in the day time, watching the workers, and "klein kette," which functioned only during the night time, watching the barracks.

Suddenly, the Blockälteste, whose name allegedly was Leon Stachoviak, appeared on the yard. He found out that Mr. Kaplinski had swallowed poison because he wanted to commit suicide.

"Come to my room," he said to Kaplinski. "I'll help you".

After a few minutes, I saw the body of Mr. Kaplinski, carried outside. He was lain on the ground completely naked and was dead.

I observed the body and wanted to find out the cause of his death. No wounds, no signs. How did he die? It was a mystery to me. Later I found out that they pressed his upper abdomen with the knees, preventing the movements of the diaphragm. In this way was killed the nice, decent, intelligent man, Mr. Kaplinski. No traces of violence were visible on his body.

Respect and honor to his memory!

Women and children led to gas chambers at Birkenau. (Photo taken by the SS)

Every block had its own **Pfleger** (male nurse or sanitary man). His main function was to write on the chest and thighs of the dead, with large letters, the number which he received on arrival. In addition he had to perform other chores, like cleaning, carrying the heavy kettles of food and water. If someone became sick, he helped him to go to the clinic or to the hospital.

Terror reigned in the camp. Danger was all over.

A prisoner could have been attacked by a foreman, stubendienst, and murdered. No questions asked.

The male nurse of Block 26 was a doctor of medium height, very pale, thin and very depressed, about thirty-five years old. He was dressed like the rest of us. His trousers were torn and long and his jacket was very short. Red paint was smeared on the

Trains arriving at Auschwitz. Each wagon contained 100 miserable human beings. Many died on the way.

Arrival of a transport at the ramp, at Birkenau. (Photo taken by the SS)

Transporting the "loot" to Canada (Birkenau). (Photo taken by the SS)

Auschwitz. Magazine with clothes.

back of the garment. He looked like a comedian and clown in a circus.

The Pfleger told me that he was very sick at present. When he arrived at the camp, one month ago, his health was excellent. Almost all the people who arrived with him had perished already. Very few remained alive. Thanks to his function as a Pfleger, he was still among the living. He felt that his life was now at the end. He would not last much longer. Life had no meaning to him after seeing all the atrocities with his own eyes.

The senior prisoner (Blockälteste) and his henchmen caused him a lot of trouble. They ordered him around, they beat him with clubs and sticks, and his life became very miserable. The only escape was death. The barrack orderlies felt a special hatred towards the educated people. A medical doctor was a good target, especially if he was undernourished and weak. A few days ago he was battered and hammered so severely that he had difficulties in breathing. Maybe some of his ribs were fractured or some ligaments torn.

On Block 9, the Pfleger had been choked to death not long ago. This was the general attitude in Birkenau. One had to be endowed with exceptional moral stamina to remain decent and honest.

I felt a lump in my throat and asked my fellow professional: "What do you do with the sick people on your block?" "I am taking them to the clinic, where they get a few tablets and are sent back to their barrack."

I questioned him further.

"What kind of hospitals are here?"

"Two kinds of hospitals," he answered. "One is a small room, behind the clinic, where only privileged people are being admitted, like German prisoners, political, asocials, thieves, murderers, enemies of the state, Blockältesre and his henchmen.

"Here, the sick are able to rest in a bed, receive their food and sometimes some medication.

"The other hospital is actually not a hospital but an extermination barrack.

STALINGRAD. NORTH AFRICA. AUSCHWITZ. 207

Fabrics made from human hair.

"*It is Block 7.*

"This block", he continued, "is a barrack like the others. Most of the sick people are transferred to this block, where the living conditions are even worse than in an ordinary barrack. In one berth are packed about 15-20 prisoners. They do not receive any medication, nor any attention. Very little or no food at all. They are beaten and flogged many times during the day. Many die during the ordeal and are left lying on their places. Twice weekly a truck comes in and collects all the sick and dead and transfers them to the krematoria.

"An average transfer is constituted from 1,000 people. Weekly—2000 men. It is very difficult to imagine such a hell, but

Prisoners at work, in Birkenau. (Photo taken by the SS)

Civilians unloaded from the trains. The prisoners in the stripes belonged to the commando unit "Canada" whose task was to take away all the packages and valises and to sort out all the goods.

STALINGRAD. NORTH AFRICA. AUSCHWITZ. 209

This is barrack No. 26, where my transport entered on January 28, 1943. On the grounds were lying hundreds of corpses, taken away by trucks daily. New corpses always filled up the space.

The bunkers in Birkenau. A series of two holes and one on top making three rest places. In one hole 12 to 15 prisoners had to sit, often one on top of the other. In the middle is the so-called oven.

The Roll Call Square, where thousands of prisoners had to stay for many hours during the roll call. (A: the gallows, where the prisoners were hanged; B: the watch tower, where the German Rapport Führer stood.)

The main camp gate of Birkenau (Auschwitz II) called in Polish Brzezinka. Birkenau was the terrible German extermination camp where most of the gas chambers and crematoria functioned day and night, operated by criminals, unheard of in the annals of mankind.

it is the truth. I had seen it with my own eyes many times. Whoever enters block seven will never come out alive. It is the gate to death."

I was shaken by this information and asked the Pfleger, "Why do sick people go to the clinic or hospital for help? From your story it is clear that nobody should declare himself sick and go to the clinic."

"Sure," said the sanitary man. "Tell all the people from your transport that they should hold out. They should never go to the clinic and they should never mention about sickness. Because sickness means death by poisonous gas. The Germans have no pity nor any compassion. The more a person is sick, the faster they destroy him."

"I had seen inmates who were here for one week, and they certainly knew the significance of the clinic and of block seven, and yet declared themselves sick." I said in desperation.

"The reason was that certain people were not able to suffer any more and decided to give up and to make an end to their miserable lives. Others had wounds on their legs which became swollen and painful, and they were not able to walk anymore. They preferred to die like the rest of their family instead of being put down naked in front of the barracks to die in agony."

I did not understand one thing," I insisted. "Why didn't the physicians of the clinic help the inmates as much as they could. A few sulfa tablets, a few days of rest in the nearby hospital would succor and aid a lot. Aren't the doctors in the clinic prisoners too? Weren't they destined to suffer at the hands of the Germans just the same? Why not to help each other?"

"This is a very good question," answered the Pfleger. "The main doctor over the clinic and the little hospital, both of which are located on block 12, is one Polish prisoner from Poznan, *Dr. Zenkteller*. I could never understand myself his behavior. He treats the sick inmates like the Germans do, although he himself is a prisoner. He beats severely the sick, drags them by the hair, kicks them over the heads, and bodies. When the unfortunate falls, he pulls him by the legs and leaves him outside the building to die.

"Dr. Zenkteller is the angel of death in Birkenau, and as a

result he is the most trustful person in the eyes of the Nazis. He walks with the Nazi doctors and takes part even in the selections.

"Dr. Zenkteller is the terror and fright of the inmates of Auschwitz. He is sending almost everybody to block seven. An insignificant cold, a slight headache are enough to be sent to block seven, which means death. Only the Nazi era could give out such a product."

"How is it possible, that a human being, a Pole, should be so degenerated and fall so deep morally?" I asked.

"He speaks a perfect German, and I assume, as his name Zenkteller implies, that some of his ancestors were Germans, which would explain, in part, his cruelty."

"Was it possible, that Dr. Zenkteller was compelled by the Germans to commit atrocities?" I asked.

"Nothing of that kind", said the Pfleger. "He did it from his own volition. The murdering of human beings excited him. It was like blood to a shark."

The doctor stopped for a while, looked at me and continued: "I believe that if, instead of Dr. Zenkteller it would have been another prisoner doctor, the number of killed would have been much diminished. He himself caused the death of many prisoners, who were afraid to go to the clinic and preferred to die rather than to go to block seven. He prevented the prisoners by his behavior from coming to the clinic for treatment. They did nor want to enter voluntarily into the tiger's mouth. They walked around sick, went to work, when a few sulfur tablets, a few salicylic preparations, one or two days of rest could have made a world of difference to the victims. These were prisoners who, in spite of the enormous sufferings, did not want to give up and preferred to stay alive as long as possible.

"The privileged, prominent, strong prisoners went frequently to the hospital for a few days of rest. Dr. Zenkteller was afraid of them. Like any other tyrant, he had enormous respect for the strong and contempt for the weak."

"How did Dr. Zenkteller treat his own fellow physicians, colleagues?" I asked.

"Could not be worse. He treated them the same and sent even many of the doctors to death. He beat and kicked all of them. The Doctors were afraid of him. He maltreated not only the doctors, who worked in the clinic or hospital, but also, and especially, the block pflegers who accompanied the sick to the clinic. There wasn't a day when he did not kick me. I felt it was dangerous to accompany the sick, but I could not help it. Nothing could be done to change the situation, because the Germans loved and trusted him. He was one of them."

"What else did he do?" I asked.

"He walked over the camp, entered the blocks and made selections on his own, by sending all the musulmans to block seven."

"What is a musulman?" I wanted to know.

"It is a man or a woman prisoner, malnourished, very weak and temporarily not capable of work. Instead of sending him to the hospital for a few days of rest, he sent him to block seven. Sometimes he selected healthy inmates because he didn't like how they stood in front of him, or their faces did not appeal to him. Small insignificant items were sufficient and decisive to take away their lives."

"Did somebody try to stop him to talk to him and to see he should change his conduct?"

"Many tried without success."

"Is it possible to get some little job in the camp, as a physician?"

"It is possible, but very difficult. As usual, one needs friends who occupy high positions to help him. In addition good luck is important."

This was the sad news which I received from my friend on this gloomy morning of January 29, 1943 (Friday).

This morning, when all the inmates left the camp for work, we, the transport of Wolkowysk, remained on the yard of our block. In the midmorning we received our caps, which were round and stripped.

After two hours we received our overcoats. The caps and overcoats were of different sizes. One received a large cap, another one a small cap. One received a short overcoat, another one a women's coat.

I received a normal cap but a short and tight overcoat, which

Prisoners beaten, starved, maltreated and later murdered by the Germans who fled, leaving the bodies unburied.

had on the back a heavy red line. My coat had fresh traces of cement smeared in different places, which was proof that the prisoner before me was alive a day ago and worked with cement. I found in the pockets socks and ear-muffs. I put on the coat and felt warmer.

We stood outside and were not permitted to enter inside the barrack. The yard was flooded with water. We were ordered to clean out the yard, to remove the water with our soup dishes. Two hundred seventy-six men gathered the water with their

A prisoner escaped and was caught by the Germans. He was severely beaten and returned to the concentration camp carrying a placard with the inscription Ich bin Wieder Da! (I am back here!) Later, at the end of the day, the prisoner was hanged in the middle of the camp. All the other prisoners were compelled to watch the hanging.

dishes and emptied it into the nearby canal, accompanied by the usual shoutings, beatings, floggings.

When this job was finished, we had to carry bricks and cement. Everything had to be accomplished while running. We worked very hard this Friday afternoon, but no food nor water was given to us. The first day we had to work without any nourishment.

Finally, the time for the evening roll call arrived. We assembled again in rows of ten.

This time, the condition was different. We already had our caps and had to participate in this crazy "MUTZEN AB" and "MUTZEN AUF." Heavy blows were distributed from all sides.

STALINGRAD. NORTH AFRICA. AUSCHWITZ.

The railroad lines leading to the gate of Auschwitz.

Selection at the ramp of Auschwitz. Left, to death; right, to the camp for very hard labor, terminating, usually, with a terrible death.

The ramp of Auschwitz, after most of the people had been sent to the gas chambers and perhaps ten to fifteen percent of the Nazi victims sent to the interior of the camp to suffer and perform very hard work. The units of the "Ehrenwolk" return from their job. Their task was accomplished. I recognize the middle Nazi (marked with an X) who was especially cruel.

Barracks where people suffered and died for no reason at all, by the will of Nazi criminals.

One could have been beaten to death any minute. Finally the German (Block-Führer) arrived. "MUTZEN AB!" a loud voice in the air was heard, which resembled thundering in a rain storm. A thousand men took off their caps in a jiffy. The German counted, wrote the number down on a piece of paper and left.

"MUTZEN AUF!" was the next order. Everybody put their caps on. The same procedure was repeated at every barrack. The number was brought to the Commandant or "RAPORT-FUHRER," who counted all the numbers together, the living, the dead, and ths sick lying in front of their corresponding barracks.

CHAPTER IX

The Krematoria.   Miracle # 7.

THE DISEASES IN BIRKENAU. ACTION REINHARDT. THE GAS CHAMBERS AND KREMATORIA. RUDOLF HOESS, THE COMMANDANT OF AUSCHWITZ, AND HIS AUTHENTIC STORIES. JANUARY 30, 1943, THIRD DAY IN BIRKENAU. JANUARY 31, FOURTH DAY IN BIRKENAU. FEBRUARY 1st, FIFTH DAY IN BIRKENAU. FEBRUARY 2nd, SIXTH DAY IN BIRKENAU. FEBRUARY 3rd, ONE WEEK IN BIRKENAU. MIRACLE # 7. FIVE DOCTORS ASSIGNED AS PFLEGERS. MY SHOES WERE STOLEN. THE WHIPPING OF A PRISONER. BLOCK 17. FEBRUARY 8, 1943, MONDAY, I GOT THE JOB.

If one was missing, the hell on earth broke out. We had to stand on our feet and endure the hardship till the escapee was found.

It was very difficult to escape from Auschwitz because of the following:

1. The camp was surrounded by high voltage, electrically charged, barbed wires. Touching the wires meant immediate and violent death. Outside the wires were the watchtowers, where Nazis stood on the top with machineguns.

2. Wild dogs were running outside, specially trained to attack the fugitives.

3. The guards were rewarded for shooting escaped prisoners.

4. Once outside the camp, it was very difficult to hide,

because the Germans had many spies among the local population who reported any suspected person.

5. Reprisals. The arrest of members of the family of the non-Jewish escapees (the Jewish families had been exterminated long ago). Parents and children were brought to Auschwitz and kept there till the prisoner surrendered.

6. Arrests of the inmates, who were kept in solitary confinement and left there to starve till the prisoner was caught. Very few agreed to take the responsibility and to be the cause of sufferings and torture of their relatives and friends.

The reason for escaping was not only the will to live. The main thing was to tell the world all the atrocities perpetrated in Auschwitz, which were unbelievable and unheard of in all the annals of mankind.

The first reaction after one was missing was the sirens, which wailed with deafening sounds. Patrols with police dogs prowled the region immediately.

All the prisoners had to stand at the roll call place and were not allowed to move. Wild Germans penetrated our ranks and beat us mercilessly. Terror and fear dominated our heart. In spite of that, every one of us wished or prayed to his G-d that the escapee should not be caught. We hoped that the fellow sufferer, who succeeded in his undertaking, would tell the world what was happening in Auschwitz.

The atrocities, as we had seen them, were of such unusual and unnatural degree that all of us were sure that the Allies didn't know about them. Otherwise, they would have bombarded the extermination place, the houses of the guards and the Krematoria.

The gassing, killing and burning of humans would have been stopped for a while, till the buildings and the other murderous tools of Nazi bestiality had been restored. We, the masses of prisoners, did not know, at that time, that the English and American radio reported the crimes.

Roosevelt and Churchill did not believe or did not want to believe the enormous scale of crimes perpetrated by the Nazis—murdering millions of people, annihilating entire races—because they were very unusual and difficult to believe.

Miracle #7. The Krematoria

Entrance to Auschwitz. On top is written Arbeit macht frei (Work makes you free.)

Stalin thought the atrocities to be beneficial to the conduct of the war, for the people would realize the consequences of a German victory and their resistance would harden. Stalin considered the German crimes to be directly proportional to the resistance of the occupied territories. The greater the crime, the more formidable the resistance and the determination to fight the Nazis.

If the escapee succeeded, our hope rose and we debated the results for many days, expecting some future changes in our ordeal. We didn't mind the flogging, whipping, the prolonged standing, and crude exercises.

If the escapee was caught, he was returned to the camp carrying a placard with an inscription: "I AM HERE."

The prisoner was hanged, in the middle of the camp, and all the prisoners were compelled to watch the hanging.

Once upon a time something unusual happened. A prisoner escaped and was caught. He was brought into the camp and ordered to carry the placard with the inscription. Knowing that

A row of bunkers.

he was going to die anyway, the unfortunate prisoner refused to carry the placard, which shocked the inmates and the Nazis alike. It was unheard off, something extraordinary, to refuse a Nazi order in Auschwitz.

When the Germans started to beat their victim with truncheons, he attacked one of them with such a fury that it startled all of us, the unwilling spectators and the Nazis.

Like Samson he screamed: "LET ME DIE TOGETHER WITH THE GERMANS!"

His head was smashed with heavy boots. Then he was taken to the gallows and hanged.

The roll call (Apel) lasted usually about two hours in February, 1943. Sometimes it lasted four to five hours regardless of weather conditions, rain or shine, snow or wind. The Germans wore good and warm raincoats or leather overcoats, and were able in stormy weather to run for shelter in one of the buildings.

Only we, the victims, had to stand all the time, exposed to the cold, wind, snow, and freeze.

If the escapee was not caught, we had to stand over twenty-four hours, being beaten all the time and being continuously exposed to the Nazi fury.

After the roll call, on that particular evening of January 29, 1943 (Friday), we had to return to the barrack. At the entrance stood the "Stubenälteste" with the orderlies, and like in the

Miracle #7. The Krematoria

morning, flogged every one who entered. One had to be very lucky not to get a few blows. Every one had to run inside and push himself into one of the berths as quickly as possible.

Every night another berth and other neighbors. 12-15 prisoners to one berth. We were sitting one on the top of the other.

I jumped this time into one of the upper berths, occupied by fourteen other prisoners, and was sitting at the edge, my right elbow supported by the margin of the board. Suddenly, I felt a very severe pain in my exposed elbow caused by a heavy blow from an orderly. The pain was so severe that I thought that the bone was fractured. Luckily I was able to move my elbow, but the malaise and distress lasted for many months.

At 6 P.M. we had to be in our berths. At 7:30 P.M. we received colored water, called coffee. One receptacle of one and a half liters was given to fourteen prisoners. All of us were very thirsty. It was interesting that in the first days of our presence in Birkenau we were more thirsty than hungry. In desperation, some used snow or ice to quench their thirst, although we knew that the snow in Birkenau was contaminated. As a result, diarrhea developed, which usually was fatal.

A few diseases were prominent in Birkenau which caused a lot of suffering and many deaths. I'll enumerate the most frequent ones:

1. *Swelling of lower extremities,* caused by long standing on the feet. In my opinion, it was aggravated also by lack of food, especially proteins (Hypoalbuminemia). The swollen legs impaired the movements and caused a lot of suffering, misery and even death.
2. *Diarrhea,* which weakened the body still more, and if not corrected ended fatally.
3. *Frequent urination* (Pollachiuria). Urination 40-50 times daily caused by bladder infection and exposure to cold. It was a real pestilence.
4. *Malnourishment* (Musulmanizm), caused by lack of food and the essential elements to maintain life.
5. Diseases like thyphus, typhoid, tuberculosis and gastro intestinal afflictions, and others.

Any one suspected of the above illnesses was immediately and unequivocally transferred to the famous BLOCK SEVEN, from which he was taken to the extermination places.

The gassing, at that time, before the construction of the four big gas chambers and adjacent Krematoria at Birkenau, took place in farm houses called "RED HOUSE" and "WHITE HOUSE." Sealed and adapted especially for the purpose of mass murder.

The bodies were first buried, but later, at the end of 1942, the Nazis started to excavate the bodies and to burn them, first on wood pyres and later in pits. 1,000 bodies were burned in one pyre or pit. In the early days, oil refuse was poured on the bodies, but later methanol was used. The burning continued day and night. By the end of November, 1942, over one hundred thousand bodies had been burned.

Later the gas chambers and Krematoria were used. The stench of burning flesh was carried for many miles away. The entire population around Auschwitz knew about the mass extermination of human beings. The fire from the pyres was visible at night, far away.

The first attempt to exterminate Soviet prisoners of war, by gassing, took place in September 9, 1941, in Auschwitz I, where six hundred prisoners of war and two hundred fifty civilian inmates were killed by gas.

FIVE KREMATORIA

Krematorium I was built in Auschwitz I, and was active during the years 1940-1943. It was turned to a shelter in 1943. The other four Krematoria were built in Auschwitz II *(Birkenau)*.

Krematorium II started to function on 3/31/43.

Krematorium III was opened on 5/2/1943.

Krematorium II and III had underground gas chambers. Both were blasted by the SS men on January 20, 1945, two days after the evacuation of Auschwitz.

Krematorium IV started to function on 3/22/1943 and was destroyed in 1944 during the revolt of the "SONDER KOMMANDO" in Auschwitz.

Miracle #7. The Krematoria

Krematorium V started to function on 5/4/1943 and was destroyed by the SS men on the night of January 25-26, 1945, on the eve of the Russian occupation of Auschwitz.

All the Krematoria had gas-tight doors, and the gas chambers had observation windows made from unbreakable glass, through which the SS men could look and see the agony of their victims. The new arrivals were ordered to undress and go to the "WASHROOMS." They were promised they would be resettled afterward and work in factories or on farms.

They were driven to the gas chambers, which looked like washrooms, by whips clubs, truncheons, gun shots and, especially, by trained dogs. About two thousand people were packed in one chamber, where shower-like devices were affixed to the ceiling.

The chamber had an area of about 300 square yards.

The door was locked, air pumped out, and the gas, cyclon B, was discharged through special vents. Cyclon B was prussic acid (crystalized), which caused death in 15-20 minutes, according to weather conditions, preceded by fear, dizziness and vomiting. Death came when the lungs were paralyzed. When the doors were opened, the most macabre scene appeared. Two thousand corpses were standing, one attached to the other. It was difficult to separate them.

The Germans used special hooked, tipped poles, which were thrust deep into the flesh of the corpses, to separate them apart. The victims in their hideous suffering tried evidently to crawl one on the top of the others. Some had their nails in the flesh of their neighbors, and the Germans looked through the peepholes to observe the dying and agony. The gold teeth and bridges were extracted, the hair cut off, the corpses dragged to the pits or to the Krematoria, where they were burned. The drained fat was accumulated and soap from human fat was formed.

The gold and platinum were melted into ingots and sent to Germany. The hair was sold at the price of fifty pfenning per kg. to the Bavarian factory (Firm of Alex Zink), where the hair was processed. Mattresses and tailor's linings were made from human hair.

The entire property of the prisoners, as I mentioned before, which was brought to the camp, was taken first to the store barracks, called "CANADA." Hundreds of prisoners sorted out the clothing, shoes, etc. day and night. Many trucks were loaded with the robbed property (often as many as twenty trucks per day) and sent to Germany. It was impossible to cope with the merchandise and the property.

The looting was called "ACTION REINHARDT." Watches were sent to Oranienburg; spectacles to the sanitary office; articles of everyday use like towels, suitcases, rucksacks to Volksdeutsche Mittelstelle; furs to Ravensbruck; gold, diamonds, platinum, valuable papers to the Ministry of Finances.

Some of the SS men used to apply in writing, asking for baby carriages for their children from the robbed goods. Objects which had no value were left for the prisoners who entered the camp.

The immense amount of articles and goods found after the liberation of Auschwitz constituted only a small amount in comparison to the loot sent to Germany, but it gives testimony to the number of murdered, and reveals also some names of the victims. (The names were written sometimes on the articles, valises, etc.)

In addition to those prisoners who were selected and entered the camp, there were millions who perished without being registered.

The soil of Birkenau covered the ashes and bones of millions of such victims. One of the first exterminations of Jews in Auschwitz by gassing occurred in the spring of 1942, on Jews from upper Silesia (Beuten). This transport, according to Hoess, was conducted by Palitzsch and Anmeier. They talked with their victims about their qualifications and trades in order to mislead them. Later they forced them to enter the gas chambers (washrooms) to be murdered.

Here are some of the stories as told by the commandant of Auschwitz, Rudolph Hoess, after his imprisonment: "One woman approached me as she walked past me and, pointing to her four children, whispered:

Miracle #7. The Krematoria

'How can you bring yourself to kill such beautiful children? Have you no heart at all?'

"One old man passed by me, and said: 'Germany will pay a heavy penalty for this mass murder.'"

"If this man would have gotten out from his grave now, he would have had said: "Unbelievable!

"Germany, who committed so many crimes, is now enjoying a big prosperity, encouraging herewith a repetition of the same crimes. How is it possible? Is the world really so foolish?"

Many prisoners in the concentration camps were driven to despair. Some were so desperate that they committed suicide by taking poison, or by running towards the electrical wires, which surrounded the camps, and being electrocuted. Others attempted to escape, knowing that it was impossible, but hoping that they'd be shot, and in this way they'd end their misery. Some hanged themselves in their respective blocks. Life in the women's camp was so terrible that suicide by hanging was a daily occurrence.

Hoess continued his story. "By the will of Himmler, Auschwitz became the greatest human extermination center of all time...."

By direct order of Hitler, the Russian politruks and commissars were taken out from the prisoners camp and liquidated. The first smaller transports were executed by firing squads. Later they were gassed with Cyclon B. The Russians were ordered to undress and to enter the gas chambers. The doors were closed and the gas was shaken through the holes at the ceiling. For a little while a humming was heard and the trapped prisoners hurtled themselves against the doors, which were able to hold.

After half an hour the doors were opened and all the prisoners were dead.

Thousands upon thousands of civilians were brought to Auschwitz and murdered.

Many women hid their babies among the piles of clothing. But the Nazis always found them and pushed the unfortunate children to the gas chambers.

Many children, feeling the upcoming horrible death, were

crying and fighting. But, the Nazis always forced them into the gas chambers.

The crying of the children and the brutal voices of the Nazis filled the air with unusual sounds of terror and fear. It seemed like hell coming to this planet. Never before in history were such scenes described. As I said before, even Dante's "INFERNO" seemed like child's play in comparison with the realities of the German concentration camps. It was impossible to imagine that such cruelties would be performed on this little piece of earth called "AUSCHWITZ." The Germans were watching it. They were fulfilling orders.

Rudolf Hoess, the Commandant of Auschwitz, made the following remark in his book on page 122, and I quote. "THE EMOTION OF HATRED IS FOREIGN TO MY NATURE. BUT I KNOW WHAT HATRED IS.... I HAVE SEEN IT AND I HAVE SUFFERED MYSELF." (Probably, as a prisoner—author.)

A typical Nazi, blaming everybody but not himself. Hoess blamed the atrocities committed in Auschwitz on the guards and the prisoners themselves. He never sanctioned it. He himself never maltreated any prisoner....

Such an approach was not only a lie, but a cynical denial of what everybody saw and experienced in Auschwitz. He took part and organized all the unheard-of crimes. He often supervised the transfer of the new arrivals at the infamous ramp of Birkenau. He directed many times the murder in the gas chambers. He ordered the guards to tear away forcibly the children from their mothers and to throw them into the chambers of death or straight to the burning fires. He was the Commandant of Auschwitz, and nothing had been done without his direct order. The guards, the prisoners were afraid of him. They simply trembled from panic and fear in his presence. Nothing could be done without his knowledge and approval. It would be very dangerous to attempt to do anything without his consent and permission.

Yet, in prison, he said on page 168 of his book, "I never maltreated any prisoner... nor have I ever tolerated maltreatment by my subordinates."

MIRACLE #7. THE KREMATORIA

How could he utter such words was beyond my comprehension.

It is my opinion that Rudolf Hoess knew that the atrocities committed by him had never been encountered in any country, throughout the annals of history. The people at large would not be able to conceive, fathom and absorb it. The world was not conditioned to it and would consider it as something out of this planet, something not real. Therefore they would accept his explanations. According to National-Socialistic doctrine, "The bigger the lie, the quicker the people will accept it." Here, again is the voice of Hoess: "From time to time, women would suddenly give out the most terrible shrieks while undressing, or tear their hair, or scream like maniacs. These were immediately led away and shot in the back of the neck with a small-calibre weapon."

And again Hoess: "During the spring of 1942, hundreds of vigorous men and women walked, all unsuspecting any danger, to their death and into the gas chambers."

Here again Hoess: "On one occasion, two small children were so absorbed in their game that they refused to let their mother tear them away. I nodded to the noncommissioned officer, who picked up the screaming children and carried them into the gas chamber, accompanied by their mother in the most heart-rending fashion."

Later the same Hoess looked through the peephole and watched the process of death itself.

The pro-German Hungarian Government helped the Germans in the extermination of Jews. Hungary sent official commisions into the camps to coordinate with the Nazis on the rate and speed of deportation.

Some of the women tried to free their little children crying, "We don't care about ourselves but let the innocent little children live!"

But the Germans were deaf and dumb to any plea. Their only desire was more killings, more atrocities. It seemed to be that they could never satiate themselves with their wickedness.

The world came to an end!

Not one of the atrocities throughout the history of man-

The black smoke emanating from the chimney of the crematorium carries the remains of millions of innocent human beings, men, women and children.

Miracle #7. The Krematoria

Crematorium I, Auschwitz.

kind, perpetrated by criminals, could compare to those committed by the Nazis. Nobody would believe it, unless he had seen it like the survivors had, with their own eyes. Even now, thirty years later, when everything has become clearly documented and known, thousands of people still won't believe it. The crimes surpassed any imagination, any contact with reality. They came directly from the purgatory, and as such were incomprehensible to the mind of an average person.

The Year 1943

* * *

January 30th, 1943, Saturday, 3rd day in Birkenau.

At 3 A.M. the gong woke us up, or shook us out from our state of deep apathy, where no death or life existed. We jumped out, instantly, from our places and ran towards the exit, because the usual harassments and beatings started. The Blockälteste

Gas chamber, where millions perished by cyclon B. In its walls remain forever immured incommensarable despair, suffering, prayers, last sights of expiration of the unfortunate victims of the Nazis.

Miracle #7. The Krematoria 233

with some of the orderlies stood already at the door, flogging everyone who passed by. Again we were assembled and aggregated in rows of ten. "MUTZEN AB" and "MUTZEN AUF" were repeated as past morning. Finally the German arrived, counted and left.

"ARBEITS KOMMANDO FORMIEREN," the kapos started to yell. On this Saturday noon, forty-eight hours after our arrival, we received our meal for the first time, which was a watery soup. In spite of the hunger, some of the inmates couldn't swallow it. Later, they put us to work. We had to carry bricks and empty the water in the yard with our food receptacles.

I met there Dr. Epstein, who had arrived with our transport.

This is Block 26 of Birkenau, where I was imprisoned with over 1000 others, on January 28, 1943. (Photo made in 1973 on my visit to Poland.)

He had contracted a severe form of typhus in the Concentration Camp Wolkowysk. When the evacuation of the camp took place, he arrived to Birkenau with high fever, reaching 40°C—104°F. I could not understand how he was able to overcome the terrible disease which decimated our camp. What made him resist the beatings, floggings, the journey in the cattle train and the selection at the ramp by the German doctor, who was ignorant of the contagious disease Dr. Epstein was afflicted with? On the contrary, the illness added a little color to his face.

Dr. Epstein was about thirty years old, of short and robust stature. I admired him for his bravery, and especially for resisting death and for clinging to life. I helped him put his numbers on his clothing and to sew them on his garments. He was very weak and his hands were trembling. "How do you feel, Dr. Epstein? I am glad to see you," I said.

"Very bad," was the answer, "I wish I were dead. I really envy Mr. Kaplinski, who was murdered yesterday. Sooner or later, they'll kill me. Why suffer?"

I didn't answer anything, but I helped as much as I could.

At 6 P.M., the working Commandoes returned, and we had to assemble for the roll call with the usual ill-treatment, abuse and molestation. Later, we were allowed to enter our barrack, which was very pleasing to us because of the freezing temperature outside and the relative rest during the next few hours.

January 31, 1943, Sunday. 4th day in Birkenau.

We did not go out to work because of Sunday, and couldn't remain in the barracks either. We had to stay outside all day in the cold weather. How I craved to go into the barrack and warm up myself a little bit! Nothing would be too expensive for this little privilege. Freedom is being taken for granted. It is like good health. We appreciate it when we lose it.

Later everyone of us had to be shaven. Six barbers were working full-power. From our transport, two barbers were working. Mr. Faitelewiez and Mr. Sulkes. The later was of my age. A handsome tall fellow. We studied together in the low grade school.

I stood near Mr. Sulkes and greeted him.

Miracle #7. The Krematoria

"How are you, my friend in sorrow?"

"I feel like anybody else in this hell. I wish I were dead."

Then he turned his head towards me and said, "Was it worthwhile, to go and study many years? To become a doctor, to help the sick? Money and years of studying were wasted and went down the drain."

I did not answer his question, and saw him again two days later. He was thin, pale, depressed, tired and was carrying bricks. Then he disappeared. I had never seen him again.

February 1st, 1943, Monday, 5th day in Birkenau.

Monday morning was already the 5th day. I was still alive. I would have never believed that I'd suffer so much in such a short time. Our transport had to go out to work this morning. We already had our rags and tatters with the numbers on the top sewn, according to regulations. Who was going to survive the first week of work? This was the question on everybody's lips.

"ARBEITS KOMMANDO FORMIEREN [formation of labor commandos]," yelled the Kapos. The prisoners started to run in all directions, everyone to his group. I didn't know which was my group. When some official started to hit me with a club over my back, I ran away, and didn't know where to escape. I felt like an animal fleeing his hunters.

Finally, I succeeded in hiding and avoided my persecutors. Many persons from our transport didn't go out to work, because no new groups were formed as yet. We remained in the camp and worked carrying bricks, stones, cement and water.

Dr. Kaplan, Dr. Gordon and myself decided to go to the clinic on Block 12 and to ask for employment. We entered the block and said, "We are medical doctors, who arrived with the last transport and would like to get some employment."

An official, a prisoner also, answered, "We have no work for doctors. It is a small hospital and clinic. All positions are taken already."

"We are ready to work as simple workers, not as doctors. Please, don't let us perish."

"Come tomorrow immediately after the roll call. We'll see what can be done."

Corpses accumulated in front of the crematorium.

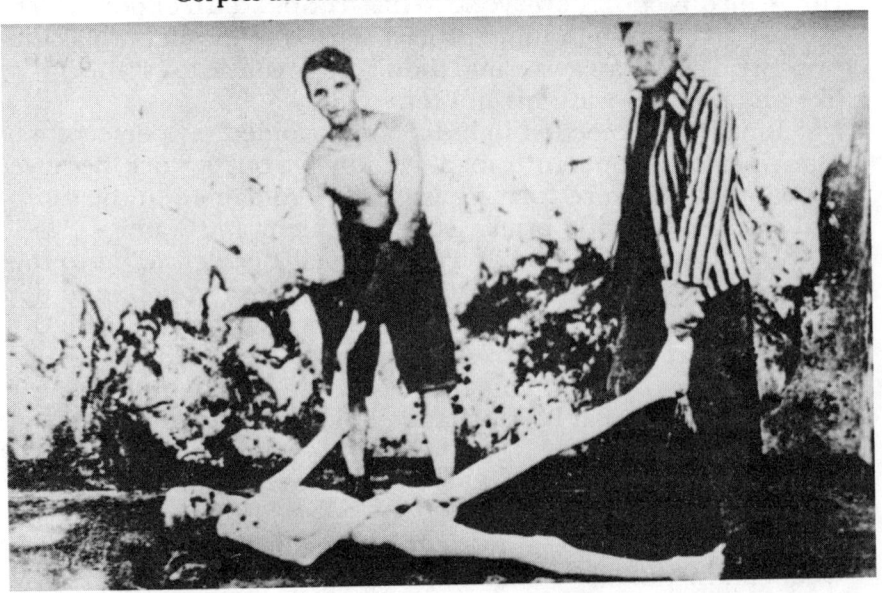
Corpses loaded on trucks and transported to the crematorium.

Miracle #7. The Krematoria

Birkenau. The pond near Crematorium V into which human ashes were thrown from Crematoria IV and V.

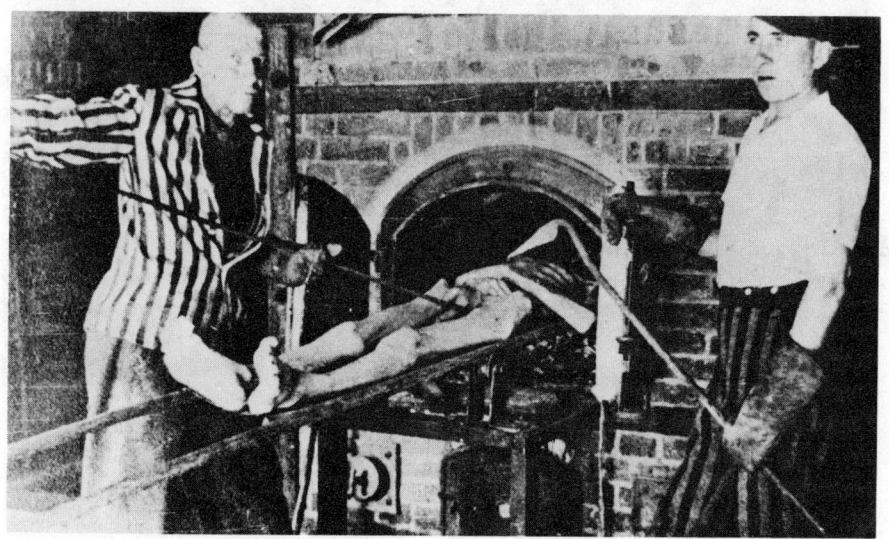

A corpse is put into the oven of the crematorium, to be cremated.

Ruins of one of the crematoria destroyed by the Germans before the evacuation of Auschwitz. They were afraid lest the Allies see the interior of the crematorium and the gas chamber.

Miracle #7. The Krematoria

We were extremely satisfied and hopeful and passed the next hours with happy prospects in view. But hope is only a dream and a delusion.

"He who lives only with hope," said the old proverb, "will die with despair."

Yet, for us, it was better to maintain hope, which lifted our spirit, than to fall in bottomless despair.

We let the other doctors know about the prospects of getting some work. Every doctor had to have the same chance. Most of the doctors from the previous transports died after one or two weeks. The transport from Grodno, a town near Wolkowysk, arrived at Birkenau three days earlier. All together from both transports there were still thirty-five doctors alive.

February 2nd, Tuesday, 6th day in Birkenau.
Next morning, immediately after the roll call, we assembled in rows of five and went to Block 12 (hospital and clinic). An official met us on the way.

"Who are you? What is the name of your commando?"

"We are going to work in the clinic and hospital of Block 12. The name of the commando is K. B. (Krankenbau)."

He let us go. We were very glad of not being beaten. But alas! We saw the "Lagerälteste" approaching us.

"Who are you?" he asked. "And where are you going?"

"We belong to K.B. and we are going to the hospital."

"There is no commando K.B." yelled the chief, and started to hit us with a truncheon.

We ran away for shelter in all directions. Soon, we assembled again and began marching in the direction of the hospital.

After a while we entered Block 12.

"What do you want here, you miserable creatures?"

"We came here to work. We were told yesterday to come."

The word "come" was hardly finished when all of us were thrown out of the building.

"Wait outside, you dummy vertebrates. wait till somebody will talk to you."

We waited outside, and observed in the meantime the different commandos marching towards the exit of the camp.

The Kapo walked in front. I saw one of the prisoners falling behind. He was very weak and not able to keep in step with the marching group. The Kapo started to beat him and left him on the ground. The commandos marched through the gate like nothing had happened.

The orchestra was playing beautiful military marches, having been formed by prisoner musicians. One from our transport, Mr. Karnawalczyk, participated in it. The orchestra played when the workers left for work and when they returned. Although the music was beautiful, I never liked to listen to it. To hear music at a time when people were being killed, when races were being exterminated, did not agree with my mood and spirit. I closed my ears.

We saw the commandos passing the "BLOCKFUHRER STUBEN" where the Germans lived. Finally, they disappeared completely from our eyes.

We were still waiting in front of the hospital in this freezing morning. One hour passed, two, three, four hours. Nobody came out to us. Finally, Dr. Gordon and myself took a chance and entered the hospital again. We were told that it was too late and nothing could be done today.

"Come tomorrow again."

We didn't know what to do, and were afraid to walk back to our block. We might be exposed to harassment and beatings because we did not join any commando. We decided to walk and mill around in the camp. There were many other prisoners, who did not go out to work for fear of being killed. Suddenly, we noticed a confusion in the camp.

What happened?

Prisoners escaping, trying to enter their own barracks, but couldn't because the doors were locked.

Orderlies with clubs, truncheons, beating the prisoners and propelling them to one particular place which was surrounded and supervised by other orderlies. We were informed that this was the end. The action was called "SPARE," as a punishment for not going to work. Trucks would soon arrive and take us to the extermination place to be killed. The prospect was a desper-

Miracle #7. The Krematoria

ate one. The Lagerälteste (senior prisoner) was running from place to place, supervising this action (Späre), which was ordered by the Germans.

In my forlornness, I approached him and said, "Herr Lageralteste, I am a medical doctor. I was returning from the hospital on my way back to my barrack, when this action started."

I took out my original diploma, which I always kept in my pocket, and showed it to him. He unfolded it, looking curiously, and saw large letters printed on a large quadrangular thick paper *DOCTOR DE MEDICINA Y CHIRURGIA* (surgery).

The diploma was written in Italian. I don't know whether it was understood by him. He was fascinated by this paper, maybe he had never seen one before.

"Good," he said. "Stay on the side. When this action is finished, you'll return to your barrack."

I was overjoyed and sad at the same time. Overjoyed, that my annihilation was postponed, and sad for the other unfortunate prisoners, who had to die. Other doctors spoke to the Lageralteste, but nobody had diplomas. I certified that they returned from the hospital together with me and they were saved also, and put on the side together with me. *This was Miracle #7.*

The life-saving was only temporary, because death had always been in ambush behind us and ready for the final leap. All the other prisoners, a few hundred in number, were loaded on trucks and perished.

We returned, very unhappy, to our bunker.

February 3rd, Wednesday, one week in Birkenau.

Next morning, immediately after the terrible roll call, we the doctors, with broken hearts but full of hope, returned to the hospital again. Dr. Gordon and myself entered the infirmary. The others waited outside, each praying to his G-d. This time we spoke to the Blockälteste of Barrack 12. He said:

"I am very sorry, but the German doctor did not come as yet. He will not come today at all. He'll come probably next morning.

I am afraid you'll have to come tomorrow."

"If we go back to our barracks, they'll kill us," said Dr. Gordon. "We told the orderlies that we were going to work at the hospital."

We explained to him that the way back to our barracks was full of danger. We described the action (Späre) of yesterday, in which we nearly perished.

The Blockälteste looked at us with mild and compassionate eyes. His face expressed sympathy and commiseration. He was of medium height, a German himself, a prisoner. He had a red triangle attached to his garment, which meant that he was a political prisoner, not a criminal. Most of the German inmates had green or black triangles (Winkel), which meant criminals or unsocials respectively. He was, apparently, of good nature and character, because he had never hit anybody and tried to help us, as far as he could. He was completely the opposite of the Polish chief doctor of the same Block #12, Dr. Zenkteller. Later he was released from the camp, and sent to fight on the front.

He looked at us again and said: "I understand your situation too well, I'll give you some work here around the block. You'll have to clean up a little bit. No hard work. Don't worry."

He took all of us to the yard and handed each one some tools to work.

"I gave you, especially, a light job, because as doctors you are not accustomed to doing heavy physical work."

We thanked him for his unusual, in Auschwitz, kindness and started to clean up the place. The job was really very light. Nobody hurried us, nobody beat us, we did as much as we could, resting most of the time.

At noon, he gave us our meal, a full dish of relatively good soup, much better than in the barracks. In the afternoon, we milled around the hospital yard and thanked the Almighty for the little good fortune, free from beatings, harassment and free from the fear of being caught and deported to the gas chambers. We were even permitted from time to time to enter the hospital barracks, and to warm up a little bit. Extraordinary good luck!

Towards the evening we heard the camp orchestra playing again. This was a sign, that the prisoners were returning to the

Miracle #7. The Krematoria

camp. We left the hospital grounds and resumed our slow motion back to the barracks.

After the evening roll call, I entered Barracks 26 and found this time an upper berth. To my surprise, I noticed a few prisoners from our transport, namely the barber Faitelewicz and Berl Amscibowski. Both of them looked very miserable and wretched. It was no wonder, they suffered plenty.

How they changed physically and spiritually in a few days. I must have looked the same because they directed their eyes towards me and observed me without talking. Berl Amscibowski had swollen legs and face. He could hardly walk. Mr. Faitelewicz said that he couldn't resist any longer and that he was going to commit suicide.

It was clear, that they were not going to survive. To suffer another few days and to be killed in the process was no way out. I never saw them again. Mr. Faitelewicz committed suicide by opening the arteries in both wrists.

Berl Amscibowski was beaten to death at work.

February 4th, Thursday, 8th day in Birkenau.

Next morning, after the roll call (Appel), we rushed again to our only place of salvation, to the hospital. The Blockälteste came to greet us.

"Today", he said, "you'll go to carry bricks. whenever you feel cold, come in and warm up yourself for 10-15 minutes." We carried the bricks, rested, and from time to time entered the hospital to warm up a little.

We worked on the hospital grounds for another day.

February 5th 1943.

The Blockälteste treated us very nicely and permitted us to enter the hospital building to warm up from time to time. On Saturday morning, 2/6/43, we didn't do anything. We just waited.

After a few hours one of the officials came out and ordered us to assemble. He selected five of us to serve as Pflegers in different barracks. The rest should return to their respective barracks and go to work, like any other prisoner, which meant death sentence to thirty young and good doctors, mostly specialists in different fields of medicine. Among the fortunate ones were: Dr. Kaplan; his brother-in-law, Dr. Alexander Rosenbaum; Dr. Gordon; myself and another doctor from the transport of Grodno. We received the necessary papers.

Final approval had to be confirmed by the German doctor, who would arrive any day. The rejected doctors left the hospital terrain, sad, and despondent. After one week all of them perished.

The five of us remained in the hospital and continued to perform various functions. Once we cleaned up the yard, another time we carried cement, bricks, garbage and so on.

An official came out and asked, "I need a medical specialist. Who is an expert in cleaning windows, doors?"

"I am", answered Dr. Kaplan.

They gave him a rag and the "DOCTOR SPECIALIST" started to clean the windows.

Suddenly we heard "ACHTUNG [Attention]!"

I looked around and saw a car stopping in front of the hospital. The German doctor arrived. He was a tall, thin man, slightly bent, with very sharp facial marks. As soon as he appeared, everything changed. Some of the prisoners were so frightened, that they trembled all over. The appearance of a German had always been a bad omen. He entered the hospital together with another German, the S.D.G. All of us were frightened. Dr. Kaplan cleaned the door with much energy and with a lot of nervous tension. After a while he came out and said, "They are talking, also, about us."

After the German left, we were called in to the hospital. An official informed us that we'd be assigned as pflegers to different barracks as follows:

Dr. Kaplan was directed to Block 27 where a transport from Czechoslovakia arrived. He was very happy about it. This Block had been recently built and was the reason for having a lot of cement and bricks on Block 26, the block of our arrival.

We have to remember that in certain weeks or months two or three transports of prisoners arrived daily at Birkenau. Each transport was composed of civilians caught on the streets or

Miracle #7. The Krematoria 245

taken from their homes in different European countries occupied by the Germans. Their number reached 1,700-2,000 men, women and children for one transport.

Dr. Gordon received Block 22. This was the barrack where the new arrivals entered, and where they were searched for gold, diamonds and other valuables. This was considered to be one of the best blocks, because the "PFLEGER" did not starve there.

Dr. Alexander Rosenbaum, the husband of Nuna Kaplan, and myself got Block 17, which was the Block of "CANADA." As we remember, the inmates of this Block used to collect all the packages, bundles, and all the belongings left on the ramp by the unfortunate people after leaving the trains. Their function was to sort out all the goods and tools brought in to Birkenau. They had plenty of food at their disposition.

"A PFLEGER" (sanitary man) attended the sick people very little. His obligation was to bring them to the clinic. The Pfleger had no medication, no bandages to treat the sick. He helped, as any other orderly in cleaning the barracks, bringing the heavy kettles of food, etc., and was the real victim of all.

Most of the orderlies, including the senior prisoner and his deputy, loved to harass the more educated prisoners. The doctor was abused by all. He had to work very hard and was beaten frequently. On Block 13, "THE PFLEGER," a doctor from Lodz, was beaten to death. The fifth doctor from Grodno was assigned to another barrack.

Everyone of us, the five selected doctors, received statements directing Block 26 to transfer us to the corresponding barracks. After the evening roll call, our numbers were called out of the standing prisoner rows and we were directed to the assigned barracks. Dr. Rosenbaum and myself were taken to Block 17. The rest of the prisoners assembled for the roll call, about one thousand in number, were standing and looking at us with envy and jealousy. To get a position, a hold on something, a support, in those circumstances of devastation and butchery, was an extraordinary feat. It was similar to one being sentenced to death and waiting for the executioner to arrive who, instead of perishing, received a position in the confinement. We also received a double portion of bread, and were, naturally, pleased for the moment. We were very tired and exhausted, hardly able to drag our feet, dressed in tatters, not shaven and dirty. *It was Saturday night 2/6/43.*

The shaving in Birkenau took place only once a week, namely on Sundays. We looked dirty, not washed, and were still wearing our overcoats smeared with cement and mud. Our appearance was very erratic and queer.

Dr. Rosenbaum and myself entered Barrack 17, dilapidated in our appearance, weak in our legs and sad in our hearts. It was a large building, kept pretty well. The inside and outside structures were the same as the other barracks, but here the prisoners slept in separate wooden beds.

On both sides of the interior of the building, were three-tier bunks. In the middle was the so-called oven to warm the interior of the barrack. The inmates slept two in a bed, at that time (February 1943). Only at the very end of 1943 and the beginning of 1944 did every one have a separate bed. Even being two in a bed, and being able to undress at night, was an extraordinary privilege for the inmates of Birkenau. We couldn't take our eyes off the beds, the prisoners, who were sitting on the top talking to each other. It was another world. One of the prisoners passing by noticed us and he asked: "What are you doing here? This is Canada."

"We came here to serve as Pflegers," I answered.

"You'll have it much better here, because in our group called Canada the food is better. But the beatings are the same."

"Do you sleep in one of these beds?" I asked.

"Two prisoners sleep in one bed, which is better then in any other barrack, where 12 prisoners sleep in one berth. We are permitted also to undress at night."

"This is unbelievable, extraordinary!" we both exclaimed in admiration.

"Is this the only good barrack?" asked Dr. Rosenbaum.

"No, there are a few other blocks which are kept like ours. For example, block 16, where the other half of our Canadian group sleeps. Block 2, where the prisoner's administration (Schreibstube) is located. Block 5, where the orchestra crew sleeps. There are a few other good blocks, but the rest of them

Miracle #7. The Krematoria

are dilapidated, dirty, with leaking roofs, and people die there like flies."

This place was a paradise in comparison with our previous Block 26. We realized that in spite of the paper given to us at the hospital we were still not accepted as Pflegers until the senior prisoner (Blockälteste) approved it. We waited a while, till he appeared in front of us. He asked, "What are you doing here?"

We showed him the paper from the hospital and said, "We were sent here from the hospital to work in the capacity of block pflegers."

He took a sidelong look at the paper and at us and said: "I'll never accept such miserable and wretched people on my block."

"We were here on Block 26 more than a week, and you know the conditions there. We are lucky to be alive. Please do not send us away, because the alternative means death."

"I don't care, you woeful, steeped-to-the-lips-in-misery, whether you live or die," he snapped at us. "Get out, you can not be here!"

This senior prisoner had green angles on his garment, which signified that he was an habitual criminal to such a degree that even the Third Reich couldn't use him. He cracked a few other not understandable words at us and left. He evidently became angry that we dared to work in his block.

Brokenhearted, despondent, dejected and downcast, we waited for the return of the Blockälteste.

One of the prisoners explained to us, "The Blockälteste went to the hospital to recall your appointment. Your situation is very bad, but wait till he comes back."

We didn't wait too long. He returned and said, "Get out from here, you are not accepted."

"Don't blame us for the tatters and rags which we are wearing. It is not our fault. We received them at our arrival. You know also that we were not permitted to wash and shave on Block 26. The work there is very hard and food very little. We slept in our tatters all the time. 12 prisoners to one berth. Please, let us stay here for one day and you'll see that we'll look differently"

"Get out you miserable beings. You'll die anyway in a few

days, and I don't give a damn about you, not about any other musulman. Get out, otherwise you'll be carried out as corpses."

We left Block 17 and didn't know what to do. After hope came a disaster, which hit us like a thunderbolt. We were afraid to return to Block 26. They might kill us. We reached the end of the rope.

My friend and myself decided to return to the hospital. This was the only path open to us. We entered the hospital and met Karol, the Polish bookeeper (Schreiber) of Block 12. We told him the story, which he probably knew already. "Please send us to another block," we entreated Karol. "Otherwise we'll perish."

"Come on Monday after the roll call."

This was, as I mentioned previously, on a Saturday night, on the tenth day after our arrival to Birkenau. We wondered that we were still alive. So many died already. We attributed our survival to miracles which occurred to us and to the fact that we didn't go out to work outside the camp.

We held on to the magic word "MONDAY," which was a very slight hope, but which kept us alive till Monday. We had to return to this dirty, murderous, wicked and devilish Block 26. On the way back, Dr. Rosenbaum said, "What kind of a block?! With the possibility of undressing at night and the better food, we might be able to live maybe another three, four months, and to survive the war. But we were not fortunate enough, we were born under an unlucky star. I can not stand it any longer. This is my end."

We entered Block 26 and told the Bookkeeper (Schreiber) everything that happened.

"To hell with you," yelled the Bookkeeper.

"I've closed the books for the day already. You already gave me a lot of headache and trouble."

"You can not blame us for what happened!" snapped my friend.

"Shut up, you stupid blockhead," yelled the bookkeeper. "Who would take in such miserable creatures?"

He wrote our names in again and ordered us to leave. Everybody was lying already in his berth, twelve prisoners to one small berth. Nobody let us in. Every berth was full to capaci-

Miracle #7. The Krematoria

ty. Finally we found a place. I got into a middle berth and my friend to a lower one. We were glad to find some shelter. At least we wouldn't be murdered on the spot.

Sunday 2/7/43 1 A.M.

After one hour, all the prisoners were waken up. The "general" bookkeepers arrived for new registration. Everyone had to come down when his number was called. If the prisoner failed to come down he would have been killed on the spot. I noticed that my number 94430 was far away from being called. Our berths became more roomy and I was able to stretch out and to lie down. I watched, also, the other prisoners. Some of them were stealing coffee prepared for next morning. It was a very dangerous enterprise. If caught, the inmate would have to pay with his life for this venture. Still some prisoners risked their lives because the thirstiness and dryness drove people to insanity.

Exhausted, I fell asleep. Suddenly I woke up, feeling restless. Maybe my number had been called and I didn't hear it. I jumped out from my berth and looked for my shoes, which the orderly had commanded us to take off and leave on the ground. I looked around, searched, and couldn't find my shoes. What is going to happen now? Without my shoes they'll murder me right during the morning roll call. In desperation I yelled, "Where are my shoes?! Did somebody see my shoes?! please help me! My shoes . . . my shoes! . . ."

Nobody answered my desperate call. I continued to scream. "Please help me find my shoes! I'll be dead in the morning! Please, my shoes, my shoes! . . ."

I felt pressure in my chest and throat. My heart was palpitating enormously, darkness engulfed me . . . I was about to faint. Suddenly I heard a voice.

"Are these your shoes? They stole mine, so I took yours."

This was Israel-Naches, of the family Yunowicz. He was a gentleman of about twenty-nine years old. I knew him practically all my life. His family lived near us in Wolkowysk, and they used to have nearby a large dairy store. If stealing shoes, why not from a friend and a neighbor?

"Israel," I said, "why did you take away my shoes? You know

what it meant to me and what the consequences would have been."

"This was the only way out," said Israel. "As a matter of fact, I didn't know that the shoes were yours. Take them back. To you, it is very important and might cause your death. I am more tough and I am accustomed to walk without shoes."

I took the shoes and thanked the invisible and supernatural forces who managed my faith.

"I'll keep my shoes with me all the time, regardless of consequences," I promised myself and returned to my berth. It became very late and the bookkeepers left. I retreated to my place and took the shoes with me.

It was very difficult to sleep because of lack of air. Unbelievable congestion! I was pondering about my fate. What will happen Monday? Is it going to be my last day? Block 17 was an ideal place, under the circumstances. What could be done to get a position there? Why didn't "THE BLOCKALTESTE" accept us in spite of the order and recommendation of the hospital?

I tried to answer all the above questions by myself. I pondered further. If I didn't get the job as a Pfleger, I'd definitely be dead within one week. I would not be able to see the end of the war, the defeat of Nazi Germany, and I wouldn't be able to tell the world what I had seen with my own eyes.

The answer to our rejection by Block 17 lay evidently in our appearance.

Tomorrow we would be shaved and cleaned, which was a certainty, but our garments looked awful, tattered and dirty.

What to do about that? How to get another garment of my size which is cleaner and more acceptable?

After contemplating for a long time, I came to the following conclusion, which was the only possible salvation and the only way out.

I'd save my bread portion and exchange it for a better garment. I'd try my luck again on Monday. I was sure that the Blockälteste would not recognize me. He saw me only once in dim light, wrapped in rags, not shaven, and dirty.

I have nothing to lose. Monday will be the deciding day. Was

Miracle #7. The Krematoria

I going to live or die? I dozed off in expectation of my last day to come.

Next morning was Sunday, a holiday for many prisoners in the world, but not for us. We had to work and to clean, carry bricks and cement. Beatings and harassments as usual. We were not permitted to enter our block and to warm up a little. After the meal, which was dirty soup with some leaves and many worms, we were ordered to go to the barbers' house where prisoners were shaven.

There were many barbers doing the job. About one thousand prisoners had to be shaven. I stood in a row waiting for my turn. I was glad to be shaven and have my face washed in the process, because it coincided with my plan. After two hours I left the block washed, cleaned and shaven. We waited outside in the freezing cold of Auschwitz. Suddenly, I noticed one prisoner wearing a nice overcoat of my size. I came near him and said:

"Give me your overcoat for tomorrow, one day only, and I'll give you my portion of bread."

The prisoner, tired and exhausted, looked at me, perplexed, and finally said, "Fine. I'll exchange my overcoat with you for one day, and you'll give me your portion of bread. For two portions of bread, I'll sell you the coat, because I am not going to live more than two or three additional days anyway."

Around 5 P.M., during the roll call, the Blockälteste called out a certain number. A thin prisoner of medium height appeared. The "BLOCKALTESTE" explained, "This man sewed his numbers on the wrong places. therefore he has to be punished, as an example to others. Bend down! quick!"

The unfortunate prisoner bent down. The "BLOCKALTESTE" started to beat his victim with a heavy club counting one, two, three.... Ten.... Twenty.... Ninety. ... At the beginning the victim yelled enormously. Later the yelling stopped, but the Blockälteste still counted 100 ... 125 ... 150. He stopped and ordered his helpers to take him away. They put him at the side of the barracks.

The "BLOCKALTESTE" continued his explanation to us as follows: "I usually do not beat. The orderlies do it. But this time I had to intervene myself."

This was not true. He was a big liar. I had seen him beating severely many prisoners, some of them fatally. He was the one who murdered the brother of Dr. Kaplinski, and now he had the audacity to tell us that he usually did not do the beating. It couldn't be otherwise. He was a son and descendent of the Super-race.

We heard the sound of a gun shot. What happened?

The German, who had to take up the evening roll call, met a prisoner on the way. He took out his revolver and shot him on the spot without any questions asked.

"MUTZEN AB!" we heard the order.

One thousand caps were taken off, but unfortunately not everybody at the same time.

"What is it?" yelled the German. "You did not train enough. Therefore you'll be punished with kneebending (Kniebeugen) for one hour."

This consisted in bending the knees for one hour. We had to fulfill the order. Later, it became impossible to endure. Many prisoners fell down and were shot on the spot. I felt my legs getting weak, darkness appeared in front of my eyes, and a little while later I felt like collapsing. I looked around and saw nobody around, so I straightened out and remained standing. Slowly I came to myself.

As soon as I saw the German approaching, I bent my knees again.

After an hour, the German returned and ordered us to straighten out, and to remain standing. He approached one prisoner of the first line, knocked him down, put his heavy boot over his head and pressed it deeper and deeper into the mud. The prisoner cried, yelled, begged. To no avail! The German laughed. Ha, Ha, Ha—and kicked the prisoner's head harder.

Finally he left and we were permitted to enter our barrack. I was getting weaker. G-d help me tomorrow morning. It was my last hope. Next morning, Monday, 2/8/43, the same German arrived and ordered "KNEEBENDING" again for a half an hour. Many heads were beaten at the occasion. Then we were glad to hear the order, "ARBEITS KOMANDO FORMIEREN."

My friend and myself went again with heart palpitation and medium hope to the hospital. Before going, we noticed that Dr. Kaplan and the other three doctors selected to be "PFLEGERS" on different blocks were not there. This was a sign that they succeeded. We were very glad for them but felt sorrow and anxiety for us.

We opened the door of the hospital and met again the Polish official "Karol," who told us to return on Monday morning for a possible job.

"We must get a job in some of the barracks, otherwise we are going to perish."

A job?" asked Karol, who evidently forgot his promise of Saturday night.

"I have no jobs for you. I can give you *a cord, (in Polish Stryczek), to hang yourselves,* get out of here."

Karol lifted a heavy club, threatening us.

We left the hospital ground in deep despair. All hope was gone. This was the end. Some orderlies started to beat us, ordering us to join a work Commando. We ran away in all directions to avoid the beatings. I was separated, in this pandemonium, from my friend.

I was running like a hunted and tormented animal, not knowing where to run and where to find shelter. I knew that my body would not be able to endure more than two or three days of Birkenau labor, where one was beaten most of the time and very often fatally.

What should I do? G-d help me!

Suddenly, I noticed the prisoner of yesterday who wanted to lend me his nice overcoat for one day, in exchange for my portion of bread.

"Please lend me your overcoat for one day. I'll return it to you in the evening. Here is my portion of bread. Take it."

The prisoner took the bread and exchanged his overcoat with me. I put on my new garment, which fitted me excellently, like it was made to order. I was also clean shaven and washed.

With new energy, born from desperation, I proceeded towards Block 17, opened the door, entered the barrack and found myself facing the Blockälteste (Senior prisoner of block 17), who rejected us on Saturday night. He was without his jacket and without his insignia and badges.

He turned towards me and asked, "What are you doing here?"

He did not recognize me. This was a good start and a good omen. He looked at me with mild eyes and did not use his truncheon, nor did he yell at me. Evidently, he was in a good mood and in a normal frame of mind.

"I am a medical doctor," I said. "and was informed that you need a pfleger in your barrack."

While talking, I took out my diploma and showed it to him. The Blockälteste looked at the paper and turned his eyes towards me.

"I can see that you are a bright fellow. But we need here a very alert pfleger, endowed with specail skills. I'll try out your personality and intelligence by asking you a question. If your answer is right, you'll be accepted. If not, then even G-d, with all his angels, would not help you. Are you ready?"

Here my life was hanging on the good will and benevolence of a criminal. I was in his hands and tried to enter into the thinking of this man.

"Please, ask your question. I am ready."

The "BLOCKALTESTE" observed me for a while and said, "Who am I? What function do I fulfill in this block?" I hesitated for a moment. It was clear that he didn't recognize me, otherwise he wouldn't have asked me this question. Secondly, it coincided with my assumption that the lawbreakers and the desperados love themselves very much and welcome any mentioning of their names. I remembered from my psychology studies that young criminals in all the prisons of the world usually request, first, after their arrest, to see those newspapers which made them out as heroes. The prospect of the electric chair or life-imprisonment seemed distant so long as they could see their faces in the newspapers. The same happened here.

I didn't answer his question immediately, it shouldn't make

the impression of an easy question. I knew also that these kind of people frequently change their minds and without any warning.

"I am not a foreseer, nor a crystal-gazer, put on your jacket and I'll see the insignia."

"This is the peculiarity of the trick," answered the Blockälteste. "This is a quiz and a test of your alertness. I repeat, if your answer is right, you'll get the job, not otherwise."

I hesitated for an instant and said, "According to your personality, behavior and deportment, I am of the opinion that you are the Blockälteste of Block 17."

He observed me for a while and said, "your answer is right. From today on, you are the pfleger of this barrack."

I was very pleased, happy and cheerful and felt like flying to the hospital administration to get the necessary papers confirming my job. I met the same official, Mr. Karol. "I was accepted as a pfleger on Block 17. Please give me the necessary papers."

"How is that," asked Karol. "You were rejected on Saturday night by the same Block 17. How was it that they accepted you now?"

I didn't tell Karol the nature of my success and said: "The Blockälteste, evidently, had a change of heart and mind and told me that I was accepted. He advised me to get the necessary papers for presentation to Block 26 for the transfer."

Karol, astonished, was wondering and couldn't understand what happened. Finally he gave me the transfer papers, which I brought over to Block 26. The bookkeeper screamed and screeched at me and warned me.

"This is your last chance. I'll give you the transfer to Block 17 for the last time. If you come to me once more, I would advise you to say your prayers and your confessions beforehand."

I was very glad to leave this murderous, brutal, bloodthirsty, satanic Block 26, and speedily moved to Block 17.

CHAPTER X

Germany's retreat.   Work in Birkenau.

THE GERMANS ARE RETREATING. WORK ON BLOCK 17. METHODS OF GERMAN ATROCITIES. DOES GERMANY CONTAIN COURAGEOUS MEN WHO WOULD THROW OFF THE NAZI YOKE? THE "PIPL." DR. ZENKTELLER'S MEDICAL EXAMINATIONS. MR. RABINOWICZ. REGISTRATION COMMANDO. "ORGANIZATION" IN BIRKENAU. BLOCK 16.

One of the orderlies was ordered to go with me to the "Bekleidungs Kammer" (clothing barracks), and to ask new clothing for me because I was the new Pfleger of the BLOCK CANADA." I received a new suit and overcoat which fitted me excellently. When I returned to Block 17, the Stubenälteste looked at me, and said: "Your appearance changed enormously. You look like a baron. This is the way I wanted my pfleger to look, sharp, majestic and distinguished."

Block 17 was one of the best barracks in Birkenau, built from wood. It contained real triple- and double-bunk beds on which prisoners slept. I also received different kinds of drugs, tablets, liquids, ointments, bandages, etc. from the inmates, who sorted out the belongings of the new arrivals. For the first time, I possessed some tools to treat the sick and the injured people. The inmates of Block 17 had to work very hard, always under tension and being constantly beaten by the SS-men. But food was enough, which gave them a better chance to resist and to survive. I had to give medical help to the inmates, to clean the barrack, to bring the kettles of food and to do all kinds of odd jobs.

At the evening roll call the inmates assembled on the yard. No beatings, no tension, because the inmates paid for everything with valuables found at the sorting of merchandise.

I heard low voices behind me.

"Who is this fellow, so nicely dressed?"

"He is our new pfleger."

"It is amazing, he looks like a real prince."

"His number is 94430. Evidently he arrived in the last few days. A real lucky fellow."

One of the foreman, a tough, violent, hardened outlaw, looked at me and without any question asked hit me in my upper abdomen. The blow was so fierce that I fell on the ground and my respiration stopped for a while. The diaphragm became apparently paralyzed for a moment because of the violent blow, and the respiration stopped.

This was the way prisoners were murdered without leaving any signs of bruises or lacerations on the body. This was, evidently, the way the brother of Dr. Kaplinski, was murdered. First came the blow over the upper abdomen, or head, causing the prisoner to fall down, in a temporary paralysis of the diaphragm. Later the abdomen of the victim was depressed more, with a board or strong feet, and the prisoner died from suffocation within minutes. Sometimes an additional board was pressed over the anterior neck, which finished up the cruel job.

When I was hit by the criminal, I heard voices.

"What did you do to our pfleger? You murderer! Leave him alone!"

I felt a little better and started to breathe again. The pain was so severe that I couldn't stand up straight. A few inmates helped me to get up from the ground and threatened the wild foreman with reprisals, in case he did it again.

After the roll call, we were permitted to return to the barrack and do whatever we liked. No forcing us to lie in our beds. As we remember, the inmates on Block 26 had to go immediately to the bunks or berths. Twelve or fifteen people to one berth, which constituted no rest at all but a continuation of the suffering.

Here, the inmates had to watch and to listen to two gongs. One, at 8:30 P.M., signified "PREPAREDNESS," and the other, at 9 P.M. when everybody had to be in bed. If a prisoner was not found in bed after the second gong, he was punished very severely. Sometimes he paid with his life for this slight overstepping.

Every barrack had a night watchman, who was responsible that nobody left the barrack and that the light was off in case of an alarm.

The Germans used to come in the middle of the night to check on the watchman. If he dozed off, even unintentionally, his fate was doomed.

My bed was the upper part of a double bunk. I could lie down and turn around at will, like in a real bed. It had a cover and an underbedding made out of straw. Naturally no pillow and no linen. No one could expect such luxury in a German concentration camp. To me it was something of a magnificence, splendor and sumptuousness.

It was the first time since Wolkowysk that I was able to undress myself. I put my clothing under my head and had the feeling of a fine pillow. When I covered myself with a real blanket, I felt well and relaxed.

Here I experienced for the first time in my life, something unusual. All the muscles in my body started to jump, contract and relax, which was unpleasant at the beginning. What happened? All the muscles in my body were kept tight by my clothes, first in the cattle train, and later in Birkenau on the berths, where we had to sit all night long pressed closely, one against the other. When the tightness suddenly disappeared, the muscles, freed from the constant pressure, started to react by contractions and expansion. It lasted for an hour and then stopped. I'll remember this muscle play as long as I live.

Next morning, after the first sound of the gong, the prisoners jumped in a jiffy from their beds and two unusual things happened. First, the prisoners were dressing themselves up, which was unusual to me. Up to this time, we had to sleep in our tatters and there was no need to dress up. Secondly, nobody was beating us.

Our breakfast consisted of a portion of bread and some coffee. One of the prisoners sat down near me and talked to me. "I recognize from your number that you arrived recently at the inferno. What part of the world did you come from?"

"I arrived from the camp of Wolkowysk, a city where I lived many years before the war. But I was born actually in the nearby town named Rozana.

"Although, I don't make any illusions about the hell we are in, I would like to ask you the following question: Since you have been working at the camp, where the new people arrived from all over the world, I would like to know whether it is true that the Germans murdered all the people who did not enter the camp, not excluding even small children."

"Yes, all the masses of people who reached the ramp of Birkenau and who do not enter the camp are being exterminated, because this camp was especially built by the German government to annihilate entire races."

"Do most of the inmates who enter the camp perish?" I asked.

"Yes," he said. "99% die from starvation, beatings, malnutrition. Many are being killed every day. The kapos or the senior prisoners must show their efficiency by killing inmates, especially the new arrivals. To expedite the killings, the Germans create special methods."

"What are the methods?" I asked.

"There are many methods, the most important are those located in Auschwitz I, on Block 11.

1. "*The standing cells* (Stehzelle).

"Each cell is divided into four cubicles. Each cubicle has an opening near the floor level, like in a kennel of a dog. Four prisoners are squeezed into one cubicle. The inmates can stand, but not sit, because the cubicles are small. There is not enough air to breath and most of the victims are choked to death. Those who are still alive in the morning are compelled to work in the day time and at night they have to return to the cubicle again, to stand and be suffocated. Most of the inmates die the first night. Some survive two or three nights, which is rather the exception. This is a terrible method of extermination, born in the minds of those who were trained for years in their cruelties.

2. "Another method," continued my friend, "is the so-called *dark windowless cells,* where fifteen to twenty prisoners are packed in. No food nor drink is given to them. In the morning they have to go to work and to return in the evening to the same cells."

Here is a description of Maximillian K. who miraculously survived the dark cell.

"I was sent to block # eleven, together with thirty-eight other prisoners, where we had to stay for three nights in the dark cells. . . . the temperature rose higher and higher, so we took off our coats and trousers. At 12:30 A.M. it was impossible to stand . . . . we tried to break the door, but it did not give in. The lack of air was insupportable. The odors emitted by gasping men were unbearable. Those physically weak collapsed, those who were stronger fought to get nearer to the door. After some time all the prisoners lost consciousness, and in the morning we had to be dragged into the corridor and were laid there. This was cell # 20."

3. *"Flogging* is administered upon a whipping block. The victim is forced to count in German. In case of a mistake in counting, the flogging begins anew. Fifty to seventy-five strokes are the rule. Most die from the wounds or are sent to the gas chambers to be finished.

4. *"Hanging from the stake.* The prisoner is tied to a stake. His body is lifted so that he could hardly touch the ground with the tips of his toes while he hung with his arms behind his back. It took place in the garret (Attic) of Block Three. If the victim lost consciousness, they poured cold water over him and the torture continued.

5. *"Executions by firing squads* on the yard of Block Eleven.

6. *"Portable gallows,* erected for the occasion in front of the kitchen. The executions take place during the evening roll calls and have to be attended by all the inmates.

7. *"S. K.* (Straf-Kompanie) penal company, which in Birkenau is block # one. Here prisoners are kept for the

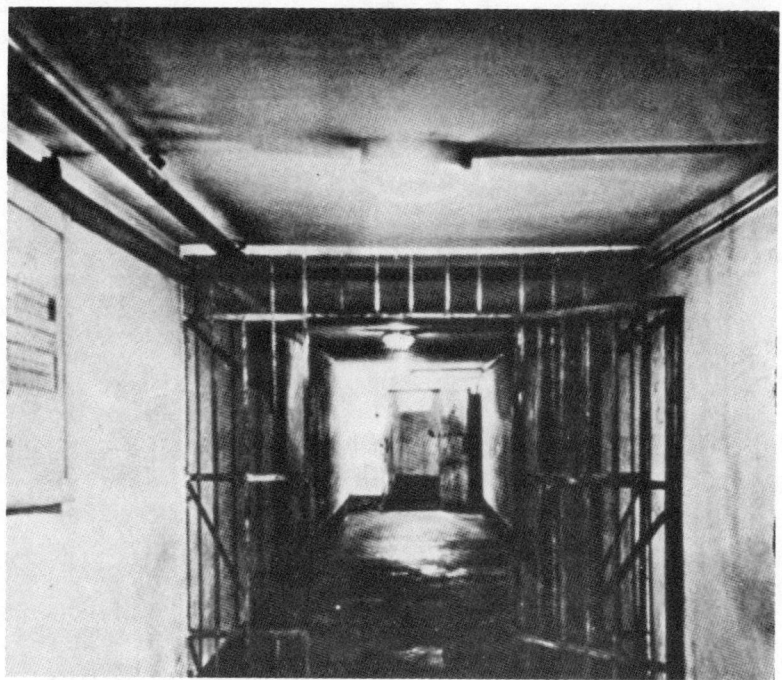

This is the underground of Block 11 (the basement) where the tools of torture were kept, such as: the standing cells, the dark cells, the room where the prisoners were flogged, the room where the prisoners were hanged from the stake, and so on.

slightest infraction. For example, for picking some apples, for smoking, for going to the latrines in the working hours, for bartering their gold teeth for bread.

"The purpose is to terrorize and weaken the prisoners. The barrack of the penal company has always been locked. Nobody is able to go in or out. The work is very hard and has to be accomplished by running. No rest is given for a minute. Most of the suicides take place in this barrack, because the suffering is enormous. During the roll call, a German asks the inmates whether some of them would like to die. Many step forward.

The entrance to Block 11, called "Block of Death." Whoever entered this block knew that in a short while he would have to part from life. This knowledge paralyzed any thinking, any ideas. . . .

They are hanged on the gallows waiting for them on the yard. In case the number of prisoners surpasses the capacity of the gallows, they are shot in the yard."

All the sad news that I heard from my new friend enhanced my despondency, in spite of the slightly improved conditions. Only a biblical miracle could help us.

We heard the second gong and we assembled for the roll call. This was 5 A.M.

I thought of the unfortunate, exhausted, hungry inmates of my previous Block 26, who had been standing already for two hours in this bitter cold.

After the roll call, I had to clean, wash, carry the garbage

Nazi victims left to die. Some were still alive; others all around them succumbed to a slow agonizing death.

A prisoner, one of many, hanged in concentration camp. The inmates were forced by the Nazis to watch the hanging.

Hanging from the stake. The prisoner was tied to a stake and his body lifted so that he could hardly touch the ground with the tips of his toes. The prisoner was hung with his arms tied behind his back.

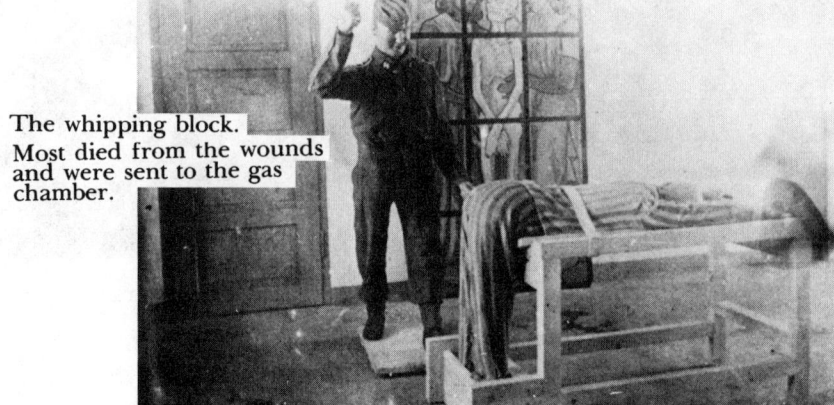

The whipping block. Most died from the wounds and were sent to the gas chamber.

and do everything on the block, like a slave. I also had to carry water to the barracks, which chores I loved most of all. I could take my time, nobody ordered me around, and mainly I was able to wash myself with real water instead of with sweat.

I pondered over my situation and over the fate of all the young men who were perishing daily in the thousands for no reason at all and by the will of a group of criminals, elected freely by a nation which was considered up to then to belong to the civilized countries of the world.

How was it possible?

I asked myself time and time again. In spite of the difficul-

A prisoner left to die. No food or water was given him until he expired.

Prisoners murdered by the Germans.

ties, hardness and ruggedness of our lives, I decided to fight with all my strength and not to fall in the usual despondency and depression, which were the first steps to the grave.

This was February, 1943. Rumors were spreading about the collapse of the German armies in southern and middle Russia, about the calamity in North Africa, about discontent in Germany, which grew directly proportional to the defeat of the German army on the battle fronts.

Under such conditions, an internal outburst could cause a revolution in Germany and free the world, as well as Germany, from the Nazi tyranny.

Did Germany contain courageous men, heroes, who would throw off the National-Socialistic yoke from the neck of the German body? The future will tell.

On my way to the water pump I had to pass the hospital, on the yard of which I met Dr. Epstein, who had arrived to Birkenau with my transport.

"How are you doctor? I am very glad to see you and for many reasons. You arrived at Berkenau still sick with typhus. You succeeded in entering the camp instead of the gas chamber. You hold yourself nicely in spite of all the obstacles. It is a remarkable achievement as far as Auschwitz is concerned."

"My dear friend," answered Dr. Epstein, "I try my best not to perish. Maybe a miracle will occur."

"Do you know, what happened to the other four doctors selected as pflegers?" I asked.

"All of them are alive. Their situation varies according to the blockälteste. Worst off, is the doctor who got Block 13, because his blockälteste is a real criminal. Dr. Rosenbaum is on Block 18. He is very sick and walks around like a shadow. His legs and face are swollen. His delicate body is too weak to sustain such atrocities. Dr. Kaplan and Dr. Gordon are holding their own."

"What happened to the other doctors who were not accepted as pflegers?"

"They are all dead. I am the only one who survived," said Dr. Epstein.

"You have a very strong constitution.

"It is remarkable and you deserve a big reward for your

stamina and being able to resist the physical and mental obstacles of our new surroundings. Are you still sick?"

"It is correct, I am still sick, but much improved in comparison with last week, when I entered Birkenau. My temperature now is about 102°F, whereas previously my temperature reached 105°-106°F. But I feel extreme weakness all over my body. Under these conditions, with very little food, I have to continue to work. otherwise they'll kill me."

"How did you get your job?" I asked.

"At the beginning, I went out to work with the work commandos. I saw with my own eyes how innocent people were murdered on the job. It was terrible. I can not understand how I could survive up to now.

"Very often, I thought in the morning that I wouldn't be able to survive the day.

"But you see, I am still alive.

"Miracles! Every minute an other miracle!

"When you were selected as pflegers, the other doctors resigned and submitted to their fate. They didn't return to the hospital any more, considering it to be useless. I realized that I was very sick and that I wouldn't be able to survive another two, three days of work in Birkenau. Therefore, I decided to return to the hospital and to ask for something to do. I was lucky. They needed someone to perform odd jobs now and then. I cleaned the walls, the windows, carried garbage, water, collected bricks and stones, broke them down and built roads."

I said goodbye to Dr. Epstein because it was getting too late. I wished him good luck and promised to see him again tomorrow.

When I returned to my barrack, I saw the orderlies preparing some food for themselves, which they were able to "ORGANIZE." *"ORGANIZATION"* meant, in Auschwitz, stealing some food or other objects. The inmates of "CANADA" had a lot of food hidden in or around their beds. One had to be always on the watch, to observe and to warn of an approaching German, in order not to be caught, which could carry very unpleasant consequences.

When the German arrived, the prisoner near the door, shouted "ATTENTION . . . N . . . N!" (Achtung).

All the prisoners present had to stand straight, hands and caps down.

One time, when the barber was shaving one of the orderlies, a German appeared.

"ACHTUNG!" yelled the inmate near the door.

The barber was at the other end of the barrack and didn't hear the word "ACHTUNG." The German came in and noticed the barber continuing his job and not standing at attention, as the rest of us did.

"COME HERE," said the German. He took his truncheon and started to beat the poor barber, who fell unconscious on the floor, spurting blood all over and around him. The German left.

I administered all kind of medical help to my friend, the barber, that was available to me. After a short while, he opened his eyes. I stopped the bleeding, bandaged his head and gave him some tablets to ease the pain.

Usually, children arriving with a transport were sent immediately to the gas chambers together with their mothers. It happened, seldom, that the inmates of "CANADA" were able to hide a child, who later joined the selected prisoners and entered the camp. Usually the Blockälteste took the child over under his supervision. From then on he was called the "PIPL," who served the Blockälteste. He cleaned his boots, prepared water for him, completed small errands, etc.

The "PIPL" was respected by everybody. He had enough food, nobody dared to molest him, and he slept usually in one room with the Blockälteste. Some of the block seniors were homosexuals and used their "PIPLS" for this purpose.

On Block 17 was a "PIPL," about ten years old, a nice boy, very active and always cheerful.

One day, he complained of headache and prostration. His temperature was elevated to 105°F. I examined him and found the characteristic typhus spots on his body. He was transferred to Block Seven, where all the sick, the weak were taken. From there, twice weekly, a truck arrived and took all the prisoners to the gas chambers. Any prisoner who developed a contagious disease had to be transferred to Block Seven. Normally the "PIPL" would have ended his life right there. But the Blockälteste was able to hide him on Block Seven, twice weekly, when the trucks arrived. He lived there for three weeks and was taken back to Block 17. His life was saved temporarily.

As we can see, the Germans had a very simple method of treatment of contagious diseases in the concentration camps, namely sending them to the gas chambers and Krematoria.

Next morning, when I went to the water pump, I met Dr. Epstein again. He was sitting on the ground, a hammer in his hands, bricks between his legs, which he crushed to small pieces. Some were pulverized. I turned to him.

"How do you do? How are you progressing, my friend?"

"Pretty well," he answered. "I am trying my best. The main thing is to exhibit a spirit of fighting, to resist to the end. Maybe we'll succeed."

The old adage of "the spirit" was very true here.

"He who lost wealth, lost much: he who lost friends, lost more: he who lost *his spirit,* lost everything."

"Nobody bothers me. I sit and do what I can. Nobody beats me. My spirit is free and my dreams are high. I am trying to get some more food, in order to increase my resistance. The main things that bother me are: the freezing cold winds, because I am outside all the time and my clothing does not protect me adequately. I am afraid of getting complications, like pneumonia, bronchitis, etc."

"Don't be afraid, you have a strong body, resistant to any disease. If you were able to overcome typhus under such dreadful conditions, unheard of in the history, you'll prevail over any other disease and you'll surmount any obstacle. Keep your spirit high. Remember that after winter comes spring, which is true not only for the four seasons of the year, but also for most of the world events. Maybe you'll get a job as a pfleger."

"I was trying to get a job. They assigned me to Block 16. But the Blockälteste rejected me because I was too short and weak in addition, unable to perform the necessary physical work on the block."

I encouraged Dr. Epstein in his effort. Most of the doctors were killed and the Germans needed some doctors for their own protection. He should not give up and continue his struggle for survival.

After a few days, I was informed that Dr. Epstein was accepted as a "PFLEGER" on Block 16. I met him outside the block collecting broken bottles, rags, paper and all kind of garbage. I observed him for a while.

"How do you feel in your new position?" I asked.

"It depends under what point of view you are looking at. Food is enough, but they harass and torment me, annoy and beat me. I am being treated worse than a dog. I have no rest, not during the day, not even during the night."

"Did you hear something about Dr. Kaplan?"

"Yes, I did. They torment and persecute him too. The block senior beats him very often. Once he wanted to kill him. He would be lucky to get out alive from there."

"Did you hear about the other doctors?"

"Yes. All day long I am outside and meet some friends from time to time. The doctor from Block 13 was killed.

"Sorry, such a nice and quiet fellow. "G-d BLESS HIS SOUL."

"Dr. Rosenbaum was very sick. He was hardly able to walk. The legs and face were very swollen, and therefore he decided to go to the hospital. Maybe they'll take him in on Block 12 and let him rest in bed for a few days. After all, he is a doctor, a functioning pfleger, and his disease is not contagious. Maybe that Dr. Zenkteller will take the above in consideration, and will not send him to Block Seven, which is equal to death."

In the afternoon, I helped to bring the heavy kettles of food. I had to rest every five minutes, and later felt weakness and heaviness in both upper extremities. The strain was substantial.

The orderlies and the Blockälteste didn't harass me, but the bookeeper who was considered as the deputy of the block senior bothered and tormented me. He was a German too and exhibited evil and jealousy at the same time. Whatever I did was no good, which he reported to the block senior.

The number of corpses increased every day. They had a special barrack where the dead were put and which had always been full. Trucks arrived every night for evacuation of the corpses. The prisoners of the adjacent barracks heard frequently the sounds of loading the dead. They were taken straight to the Krematorium.

In the afternoon a Kapo came to me, asking for medical help. He had deep lacerations over his head and his face was covered with blood. I cleaned the wounds, disinfected, bandaged his head and gave him some tablets to alleviate his pain. He told me that a German pounded him and knocked him down for no reason at all.

My obligation was, also, to bring the sick and wounded to the clinic. In spite of the fact that he was a Kapo he did not want to take a chance and go to the clinic, because he was beaten up by a German. I agreed.

Some other inmates asked me to be taken to the hospital. They were not afraid, because they belonged to the Commando "CANADA."

I took my sick prisoners and brought them to the clinic, being sure that Dr. Zenkteller was not going to molest them because they belonged to the Commando "CANADA," and he was afraid of them like hell.

We entered into the clinic where Dr. Zenkteller was supposed to administer his medical skills. It was a large room. The sick people brought in by other doctors were standing in a row, one behind the other, to be examined by Dr. Zenkteller. We were waiting for our turn. One sick young prisoner stood before Dr. Zenkteller, who asked him, "Show me your tongue."

The prisoner put out his tongue.

"Remove your trousers," ordered the doctor again.

The prisoner didn't understand the order.

Dr. Zenkteller started to beat him with his heavy fists, mainly over the head and face, and shouted, "You miserable creature, can't you hurry up?"

The unfortunate, exhausted, sick prisoner tried his best to remove the trousers, but since he was under tension, and in a hurry, the trousers didn't fall down right away.

"You worthless wretch! How long am I going to wait for you?"

And he battered him again. Finally the prisoner removed his trousers. Zenkteller shouted at him, "Turn around! bend down!"

The prisoner fulfilled immediately all the orders.

Finally came the last question.

"What are you complaining of?"

"Headache and chills,"

Zenkteller took out his pen and wrote down *Block Seven,* which was equivalent as I explained previously, to the death sentence.

"Next," yelled Dr. Zenkteller.

The succeeding prisoner received the same questions and the same treatment.

Almost all the sick people received the same Zenkteller treatment, "Block Seven."

My people, as explained above, received a few tablets and were ordered to return next morning.

Next day, when I returned with the sick prisoners, I witnessed the same scene of yesterday. In addition, I saw how Dr. Zenkteller dragged a sick person by the hair and put him on the side, like a piece of rag.

It was a terrible, unforgettable scene. A sick human being in his agony being dragged by the hair. His coat was smeared with mud, his face pale and covered with blood, his eyes bulging out. He had been beaten up at work and brought to the clinic.

Dr. Kaplan was standing near me with his sick prisoners. He turned to me and asked, "Do you know this sick person who is dying here?"

Dr. Zenkteller suddenly appeared in front of us and barked, "Don't you know it is forbidden to talk here?"

He kicked Dr. Kaplan in his abdomen. The blow was very severe, because Dr. Kaplan was crying from excruciating abdominal pains.

I received a few blows over my head.

I was waiting for my turn to present the few sick prisoners from my Block "CANADA."

A prisoner from another block came in front of Dr. Zenkteller. "What is wrong with you, and how many times did you move your bowels?"

"Six times," was the answer.

No more questions asked. "Block Seven" was the treatment.

Another prisoner came in front.

"What do you complain about?" asked Zenkteller.

"Fever and chills." Zenkteller took the stethoscope to listen to his chest.

"Breathe deeply,"

The sick prisoner started to breathe as deeply as he could. Zenkteller was not satisfied. "You nobody, contemptible rubbish, you don't know how to breathe." He hit him in his abdomen.

"Remove your trousers!" The prisoner fulfilled the order in a jiffy. The trousers were not very clean, naturally, in Birkenau.

"You good for nothing scum, you didn't tell me that you had diarrhea!"

"Doctor, I don't have diarrhea. I swear by G-d, it is the truth."

"You dare to lie to me again!" shouted Zenkteller, and he started to pound the unfortunate prisoner with his fists. After that he transferred him to Block Seven.

The behavior of Dr. Zenkteller perplexed me very highly. He was a prisoner exposed to the same danger as all of us.

Maybe he was a spy, I thought, especially since he spoke a perfect German. After a slight reflection this idea was rejected and I reached the conclusion that a spy would not be able to stand misery, be incarcerated in Birkenau and behave in such a cruel way.

In my opinion he was a psychopath, which explained all his conduct and behavior.

In the afternoon, I met Mr. Rabinowicz in the camp. I knew him from Wolkowysk. He was an old bachelor, about fifty years old, who took an active part in communal affairs of the city. He was very highly respected by all who knew him, primarily for his decency, modesty and chastity. He was a good friend of the engineer, Barash, because both of them were active in municipal affairs and both of them were known and liked for their decency. Moshe Rabinowicz had been incarcerated with all of us in the concentration camp of Wolkowysk at the end of 1942.

As we remember, every few weeks transports of inmates were taken by cattle trains to Treblinka extermination camp. Moshe Rabinowicz was not taken to any transport because his friend, Engineer Barash, who was the chief of the Judenrat in Bialystok, sent a special truck for him to take him to Bialystok, which was, at that time, an oasis in the devastating desert of occupied Poland. All of us envied him when he left for Bialystok.

When I accidentally met Mr. Rabinowicz in Birkenau, I could not believe my own eyes.

"Mr. Rabinowicz," I said, "you were supposed to be in Bialystok. Be safe there and wait till the end of the war. What happened, Moshe? Why are you here?"

Moshe Rabinowicz looked at me with sad eyes.

"Very bad! Very bad! I am a victim of bad luck! I felt safe in Bialystok, because the Germans asserted that Bialystok will never be liquidated. The city worked for the German armament, producing weapons and above all textile products, indispensable for the army."

He started to walk, back and forth, mumbling to himself.

"My G-d, My G-d, why did you forsake me?"

His desperation was deep, his forlornness and hopelessness were very grave, piercing his heart and brain. He continued. "Why did it have to happen to me? The Germans caught me, suddenly, on the street and transported me here to this inferno. How just was the righteous man of the bible, Job, who said: 'The day when I was born should perish and be covered with darkness. The life of the good person is in misery and the bad, enjoy most of the good.'

"This is my fate, my destiny! What can I do? But I am asking why? Why? There is a divinity that shapes our ends, whether we like it or not. My end is near and I have no illusions about it."

Moshe Rabinowicz was right. I didn't see him anymore. G-d bless his soul, because he was a just man and was an innocent victim of Nazi bestiality.

One afternoon, I was called to attend one of the high officials in the Bekleidungs-Kammer, which was located near our barrack. He complained of headache, chills, high fever and prostration. I examined him and ordered treatment in form of salicyl tablets and rest. After a few days he felt better.

He noticed blue spots on my face and some abrasions. He insisted I tell him the cause of these injuries. After slight hesitation, I told him that the bookkeeper, a German, had a good relationship with the Blockälteste and that he gave me a lot of trouble.

"Don't worry," he said. "Such a scoundrel. I gave him the job. When he arrived he was so depressed that he wanted to commit suicide. Now he harasses and torments the new unfortunate arrivals. I'll see what I can do."

Next morning the bookkeeper told me that he wouldn't touch me any more. He was, evidently, very much afraid of my protector.

I met Mr. Fucks, the chief of the Judenrat of Wolkowysk. "How are you Mr. Fucks? How are you progressing?" "Very bad! Our life is not worth anything. I am living from day to day, not knowing what the day has in store for us. The war is moving to an end, but this end might take another few years. We are not going to last that long. What is the use?"

"My dear Fucks," I said, "We are fortunate to be alive up to now, because we experienced many miracles. We survived the concentration camp of Wolkowysk, the cattle train, the ramp in Auschwitz and the selections, and the most miserable life in the inferno of Birkenau for more than a month. Wasn't it remarkable? For all these we have to thank the invisible forces which protect us. I heard from the new arrivals that the Germans were running away from the battle fronts. They call it *'strategic retreat.'* Kharkov was occupied by the Russians in February, 1943. All the Russian front is broken. Pretty soon they'll occupy Kiev. I met an old prisoner, who assured me that in March the war will be over. He assured me that in some place it was written that 'the snake will be decapitated in the early spring.' We must hold our heads above the water and not get drawn into the dirty mud of Nazi bestiality. courage, my friend, courage!"

Fucks left. I noticed tears running down his cheeks. The proud Fucks was crying.

Usually, spring starts in this part of the world (Auschwitz) in late March or April. This year, 1943, spring came early. At the end of February, warm winds were blowing across the fields of Auschwitz, as though they were letting us know that the snake will be decapitated pretty soon.

The earth, which normally was frozen with ice, became soft, muddy and slushy. It became difficult to pass from one barrack to the other, because the shoes stuck to the mud. During the roll calls, when we had to stand in the mud puddle for an hour or more, our legs bogged down in the wet and spongy land up to our knees, and it was very difficult to pull the legs out again.

I met Dr. Epstein, who informed me of the bad news that Dr. Rosenbaum went to the clinic, hoping that Dr. Zenkteller would accept him at the hospital of Block 12, where he could rest for a few days. But the tyrant sent him to Block Seven which was equivalent to the death sentence. In a few days he was taken to the gas chamber, where he perished.

In this way he died as a martyr and his soul returned to his creator, resting among the righteous, saints, cherubim and seraphim.

I met Nahum Olszevski. He lived in Wolkowysk near us. His brother Lipa lived in New York. His legs and face were swollen. He was hardly able to walk.

"How are you Nahum? How long have you been here? I remember, that you lived lately in 'Skidl' near 'Grodno.'"

"I am here three months already," answered Nahum.

"I survived that long, because my friend was a foreman and he helped me a lot.

"But now, I am sick and very weak. All my body is swollen. I am not going to last much longer.

"I'll go tomorrow to the clinic. Dr. Zenkteller will send me to Block Seven and my Suffering will be finished."

I didn't see Mr. Olszewski any more. This was the end of February, 1943.

Transports with men, women and children arrived daily at Auschwitz. They were fetched from all the occupied countries of Europe, but mainly from Poland and Russia. The gas chambers and the pits worked all the time during the days and nights. The pits for burning of bodies were used very often because the number of corpses increased daily.

Dr. Zenkteller continuously sent the sick prisoners to Block "SEVEN," which was the last stop before the gas chambers. The Germans opened up another block, which was to supplement "Block Seven". Dr. Zenkteller filled up this new "Block 18" with a few thousand prisoners in a few days. German trucks used to arrive twice weekly and transfer them all to the gas chambers. During the waiting period (2-3 days), they did not receive any food nor water. In this way hungry, weak, exhausted, the unfortunate Musulmans (prisoners not capable of working) were driven or carried to the trucks. These scenes were so terrible that they defy any description. Even now, thirty three years later, I remember them vividly. They can never be forgotten.

The German trucks were waiting at a distance of about one hundred fifty yards from Block Seven on account of the mud. They couldn't come nearer.

The victims had to walk to the trucks, being beaten on the way by the Germans. Some could not walk and fell in the mud.

They had to be carried and thrown into the trucks, one on the top of the other.

"Mopsik" was a poor fellow from Wolkowysk who used to make a living by selling newspapers. He could not afford a newspaper stand, so he stood at the orthodox church (Cerkva) at the corner of Kosciuszka Street and sold his papers. I used to buy newspapers from him because I liked him and because the benches surrounding the "CERKVA" were nearby and I could sit down, rest and read the paper. I saw Mopsik now, wading through the mud, swaying from side to side, being beaten by the SS men and finally falling into the mud.

Mupsik got up, made a few steps and fell again.

A German came and started to beat him again. This time Mopsik was not able to get up on his feet. He tried and fell again. He was carried to the truck and thrown in, like a sack of potatoes.

This was the end of Mopsik.

The truck was big and heavy. In front of the vehicle stood Germans with truncheons, beating every Musulman who reached it. One hundred sixty victims were packed in one truck, one on the top of the other.

The truck moved away and another one was ready to receive the next group of the Musulmans. In one day, about two or three thousand prisoners were taken to the gas chambers, where they perished.

Next morning, I met Mr. Rosenblum in Block Seven. I knew him from Wolkowysk. He had a candy store near our business. I used to buy ice cream and sodas from him. He was a young fellow, who served in the Polish army, fell in love with a young girl, and married her. He was a typical citizen from Wolkowysk who, in spite of the economic difficulties of pre-war Poland, was able to make a decent living. I asked him:

"Mr. Rosenblum, how did you come to this miserable block?" "I couldn't help it. My strength left me. I felt that one more day and I'd die at work or be beaten to death. So I decided to go to the clinic. Dr. Zenkteller sent me to Block Seven."

Always the same identical story.

He told me, also, that more than 70% of our transport was not alive any more. Some were still resisting, but they reached the end of the rope.

Next morning the Blockälteste informed all the workers of his barrack that the Germans had ordered that each day two orderlies should go to work outside in the camp. My turn was once weekly, to work at one of the ditches surrounding the camp. We had to enter the water and clean the ditches from the accumulated dirt. A foreman was standing nearby, urging me to hurry up and to work faster. But I had no strength to work at all. In the afternoon, I moved away from the foreman to the other end. Far from his watching eye, I could rest and take it easy. I returned later to my barrack, wet and exhausted. It took me a long time to dry my clothing and shoes. The Blockälteste called us again and informed us that the Germans had ordered that three workers and the Pfleger should go to outside work and therefore all of us would be transferred immediately to other barracks to join the Arbeits-Kommandos (labor groups).

Heartbroken and sad, I went to see the other Pflegers.

Almost all of them lost their jobs, including Dr. Kaplan and Dr. Epstein. All of us were transferred to Barrack Three, which was located on the left side of the main road. This was a barrack similar to Block 26. The same atrocities, indignities and mistreatments. We returned to the same condition as when we had arrived initially at Birkenau. I found myself together with Dr. Epstein in the same berth. He turned to me and said:

"I was born under a very unlucky star. I suffered so much till I got the job as a pfleger and now I am back where I started. I can not resist any longer. I have reached the very end of my sufferings."

In the morning we were awakened very early, at 3 A.M. We assembled for the roll call again.

The same beatings, shoutings as on Block 26.

"MUTZEN AB" and "MUTZEN AUF."

One of the inmates escaped. A very extraordinary courageous man. The Germans sent out specially trained dogs without any results. Therefore, we had to remain standing on the roll call square, in the mud.

The Germans still continued the search. We stood two hours, three, four, five, six hours. The escapee was not found. We felt pain and extreme weakness in the lower extremities, and in spite of the misery we prayed to the Almighty that the escapee should succeed. Finally they let us go.

I met Mr. Katzengold, whom I knew from Block 17. He worked in the receiving commando of the bookkeepers, who received and registered the newly arrived prisoners.

Mr. Katzengold asked me what happened and I told him all the story. He reflected for a while and then promised to get me some job at his commando.

"Do you know German?" He asked.

"Yes I do, I studied it in college."

"Fine", he said. "You'll have to register the names of the new arrivals and you'll file a paper on each and every new arrival. The job is easy, nobody will harass you. You'll have a roof over your head, and sit inside the barrack and write, not being exposed to snow, cold, winds and rain."

Next day I came to work in the registration commando.

While waiting for a new transport to arrive, I observed some SS men who were milling around. They didn't understand anything about our job, and the main thing they were busy with was robbing the new arrivals of their valuables.

I noticed a German entering the block. He started to search the bookkeepers for hidden valuables. He couldn't find anything.

Actually some of the inmates "ORGANIZED" money or gold rings, which served as a good exchange for bread and other kinds of food. "ORGANIZATION" in the language of Auschwitz meant stealing, robbing, etc. When we arrived to Birkenau, we heard very often the word "ORGANIZATION," but it took us a few days to comprehend the full meaning of the word.

"Where did you get the cigarettes?"
"I organized it." This was enough.
Nobody cared how he organized it.
"Where did you get the sausages?"
"I organized it."

Nobody cared how, as long as it was available. But one had to pay the price. Dollars, English pounds, gold constituted good currency.

I still slept on Block Three, and had to go to work to Block Twenty-two. On the way to my new job I met Dr. Epstein again. He told me that some of the Pflegers returned to their jobs. But he himself was not accepted back because he was short and very weak. He turned to me and said:

"I can not go out to work, because I have no strength in me and there is constant fear of being caught and sent to the gas chamber. My life has become a burden to me. My legs are starting to get swollen. I also have a slight diarrhea. I have reached the point, where I can not fight any longer."

I myself liked the work on Block Seventeen better. Therefore I went to the hospital and asked the offical Karol whether he could give me back my job on Block 17. He said that this time the paper from the hospital has to be confirmed by the Camp senior (Lagerälteste).

I left the hospital and went to look for the Camp senior. He was in his forties, of medium height. His name was Danish. His previous job was Blockälteste of S.K. (Straff Kommando), penal commando.

I found him strutting on the main road and presented to him the paper from the hospital. He looked at me and said:

"Your appearance is good. Maybe, they'll accept you. Come with me."

Instead of Block 17, he took me to Block 16, where the other half of the inmates of "CANADA" lived. The block senior was a tall fat fellow whose name was "SIVA." Before the war he was a butcher and a truck driver.

"I have for you a good-looking doctor. would you like to accept him on the block as a pfleger?"

He looked at me and said, "Yes, I'll accept him."

I went to the "ZONA" (Bathhouse) where they took away from me my beautiful suit and overcoat and received instead another suit with stripes which the "OLD TIMERS" had to wear and which fitted me just as well.

I went to Block 16 and became the official Pfleger. It was, already, the beginning of March, 1943.

The deputy of the block senior showed me around the block and my bed. He was a young fellow of about 18 years old and behaved towards me in a nice way, in spite of the bad reputation that he relished.

This barrack was maintained in a better condition than the other barracks. It had wooden beds instead of berths. The inmates of "CANADA" occupied the two barracks, # 16 and # 17. On Block Sixteen, there were two shifts. The day and night-time shifts.

I went to sleep, glad to be able to rest after the last ordeal.

In the middle of the night, I woke up because of movements, shouts and sounds of beatings.

I saw the Kapo of Canada going from bed to bed, flogging the inmates. Everybody was jumping down from their beds as fast as they could, including myself. In the meantime, I got a few blows. We were running towards the exit, in order to avoid further raps.

The bookkeeper was standing there undisturbed, and he asked me, "Where are you running? This is not for you. This is for the night shift of Canada, because a new transport of prisoners arrived at the ramp of Auschwitz. Go back to sleep."

I returned back to my place and fell immediately asleep again.

The first gong woke me up.

My function was to distribute the portions of bread and the so-called "Birkenau coffee," which was brownish colored water. Later I had to clean the barrack.

There were nice sounding inscriptions, hanging all over the place like:

"Work diligently and industriously!"

"Keep yourself always clean physically and mentally!"

"Good work makes you free."

"Inside the barrack—mutzen ab."

The slogans and the inscriptions didn't mean anything, because it was impossible to keep clean in the conditions of Birkenau, and hard labor never freed any prisoner, but made him perish faster.

After the second gong all the inmates had to assemble for the morning roll call. A German arrived, counted the number of inmates, then took out a few whose appearance he didn't like and ordered to send them over to "BLOCK SEVEN" as incapable of work.

On Block Seven, the bookkeeper was a man from Czechoslovakia. His name was Mr. Zollmann, now in Rehovoth Israel. He was a very nice and decent fellow, of about thirty years old. He looked at me and said:

"Tomorrow morning, the truck will come and will take all the prisoners from Block Seven. Take them back to your bookkeeper and tell him that Block Seven is full and does not accept any more prisoners. In this way they'll prolong their lives for another few days. Maybe the war will be over by that time and they will not perish. It is our only hope."

I looked at this man with admiration and wondered: "Such a decent man was the bookkeeper of the terrible dead Block Seven, from which the inmates were being sent twice weekly to the gas chambers. What an irony of fate! In Birkenau, Everything was possible, Unbelievable things happened DAILY."

I thanked Mr. Zollman for his good heart and advice and took the prisoners back to Block Sixteen. Mr. Zollman took out a prayer book and started to move his lips in supplication.

When I returned back with the prisoners to Block Sixteen, I was threatened with reprisal, being accused of an attempt to save the prisoners.

Our Block senior, Mr. Siva, called one of the "Musulmans" and ordered him to stretch out his neck.

"Give me a knife", ordered Siva.

When he obtained the knife, he said to the Musulman.

"This is your end. I am going to cut your throat."

The unfortunate prisoner started to beg him that he should spare his life. Some of the orderlies echoed Siva.

"Cut his throat!" they roared. "There is no place for Musulmans in Birkenau!"

Siva was a new block senior. Nobody knew what he was going to do. The unfortunate knelt in front of Siva begging him to spare his life. Siva threw away his knife and said: "I was only joking. I didn't give you life and I have no right to take it away from you. Go away! Don't be foolish and you shouldn't worry."

On Sunday afternoon, our block senior, Mr. Siva, was in a good mood. He called in a few prisoners, known as entertainers, singers and dancers before the war, and ordered them to sing and to entertain the inmates.

It became very joyful and cheerful all around, but it was not to my liking. I could not stand this gaiety in Birkenau, when thousands of innocent people were getting slaughtered. I wished that they would stop it. Fortunately the gong started to sound and the singing ceased because the prisoners had to go to sleep.

Next morning, we were informed that many inmates, including a few physicians, would be transferred to the famous concentration camp Matthausen. From the hospital I got word that Dr. Zenkteller was among the physicians to be sent to Matthausen.

We were very glad to get rid of this evil man, but were afraid that the German doctors would pull him out from the transport and leave him in his old place. Without Dr. Zenkteller, the machinery of killing people, of sending prisoners to the gas chambers, would encounter difficulties. In the meantime, the inmates of Birkenau were very pleased and thrice happy, as prisoners, as Musulmans, and as getting higher chance of survival.

Because a few doctors were sent on the transport, the hospital and clinic needed substitutes. In addition, Block Eight was converted to a real hospital and new doctors were required.

Mr. Aleks, a dental technician, an old-timer, helped to get me in as a Pfleger on Block Eight. I met Dr. Kaplan and informed him about the new hospital. He was accepted also, and got rid of his block senior, who continuously threatened his life.

The group of doctors assigned to work on "BLOCK EIGHT" were taken from the hospital to the new allotment. We had to stop on our way, because the main road was blocked by trucks being loaded with prisoners from Block Seven to be transported to the gas chamber. The pleadings and lamentations of the unfortunate people were impossible to describe.

Finally the Germans cleared the way and we were permitted to continue in our direction.

I had a small injury on my leg which didn't want to heal, in spite of careful and adequate treatment. This lack of cure and restitution and integrum was caused by poor food, almost no vitamins, prolonged standing on the feet, extreme nervous tension and complete exhaustion. Nervous tension caused many problems in Auschwitz. Many fell into deep apathy and committed suicide.

It was also interesting to note that the majority of the women, including those who had good positions and had adequate food supply, lost their menstruation during all the years of the detention in the concentration camp. The amenorrhea was caused also by the general conditions of the camp, characterized by extreme nervous tension and poor hygiene. It was, medically speaking, a self-defense of the body.

My small wound did not heal and I was afraid of the terrible consequences which followed such conditions, like being sent for annihilation. Therefore, I was very glad to be accepted on Block Eight, where I could sit down and rest whenever I wanted.

Block Eight, the new alleged hospital, was a barrack, like any other in Birkenau. It had a quadrangular hall in the middle. Its four corners lead to four corridors. The later was a passageway, which had on both sides triple berths. Each pasageway, with the triple berths was called a "STUBE" (department) and served different purposes.

Stube Number One was for the Pflegers and orderlies.

Stube Number Two contained sick prisoners with internal diseases.

Stube Number Three was for surgical cases.

Stube Number Four was for gastro-intestinal diseases complicated by diarrhea.

Drugs and equipment were almost non-existent. For example: Paper was used for bandages, etc. Simple knives for incisions, etc. This was March, 1943.

The sick people on Block Eight were not in danger of being taken to the gas chambers, and hence it was not life-threatening in contrast to Block "SEVEN," where the Musulmans were kept, and were sent once or twice weekly to the gas chambers for annihilation. After a few days or weeks on Block Eight, the prisoner returned to work. All the contagious and infectious diseases were sent to Block "SEVEN," where the procedure was not changed.

One morning, I met in our barrack Mr. Kossowski, who was a carpenter by profession. He became very ill and in desperation had gone to Block Twelve for treatment, ready to die. Luckily, Dr. Zenkteller had been taken on the transport to Matthausen and the new hospital, "Block Eight," was opened. Mr. Kossowski, instead of Block "SEVEN," was transferred to Block "EIGHT," where he slowly recuperated. They needed carpenters at that time and he was accepted as one of them. In this way he was able to save his life for the moment.

The chief doctor on "BLOCK EIGHT" was Dr. Krause. He was of medium height, in his fifties, and originated from the Polish town of Kielce. He had been in the camp a long time. The prisoners didn't like him because he was rude and mean. His deputy was a doctor from Czechoslovakia, a very fine person and opposite in character to Dr. Krause.

We had to live here on the regular ration, but were still better off than in the other barracks.

As predicted, Dr. Zenkteller returned to his old position on Block Twelve. The German doctors needed him here. He was able to fill up Block "SEVEN" in a very short time and provided fuel for the Krematoria, in shape and form of human corpses. I was glad that he returned to Block Twelve, and not to Block Eight.

The roll call on our block did not last long. The German in charge of the hospital (Blocks 7, 8, 12) was the deputy to the German physician called S.D.G., who was afraid to enter the barrack because of fear of contamination and left everything to the block seniors. We were spared the long hours of standing in front of the barracks.

I arrived at the block accompanied by three other prisoners, Dr. Alteresco from Romania and two others from Czechoslovakia. The latter received packages from home and the Red Cross. They were very frightened. At night they covered their heads with caps or simple handkerchiefs as a protection against insects and above all lice. Naturally this was no protection at all.

The Lager-Führer in Birkenau at that time, the middle of March, 1943, was a German with the name of Schwarz-Huber. He was a tall fellow who loved to drive a motorcycle. His superior was the Commandant of all Auschwitz, Rudolf Hoess. The extermination camp in Birkenau, where millions of people perished, was under strict supervision of Schwarz-Huber.

He took part in all the destructive activities of the camp, like transporting the new arrivals to the gas chambers, the Krematoria, etc. He appeared to us as a demon with a human face, who possessed extraordinary and supernatural powers. The sounds of his motorcycle and the apparition of Schwarz-Huber represented always a bad omen, portending mass murder. Wretched human beings were beaten, humiliated and driven to the gas chambers and Krematoria.

The block senior of Barrack Eight was a Polish man of short stature, about forty-five years old. We called him "TATO." He was not a degenerated fellow, and many prisoners liked him. He was adored by the Polish nationals. The perpetual smile on his face was caused by extreme nervousness coupled with fear and uncertainty. He was a good "ORGANIZER" and provided the German bosses with many valuables, carrying herewith much of their favor. He was, before the war, a small farmer and understood a lot about construction. Most of the new buildings were done under his supervision.

The sick prisoners had to lie always in their berths, which caused, after a prolonged duration, atrophy of the muscles, bones, and of different organs. I had seen many young men lying in the berths and developing, after a month of two, different mysterious diseases and just fading away.

I slept with Dr. Alteresco on one of the upper berths. We were hungry most of the time, but glad of having short roll calls and not being continuously exposed to the murderous hands of the Germans and their henchmen. I preferred starvation instead of humiliation.

I met Dr. Gordon who remained as a pfleger on Block Twenty-two, where the new arrivals were brought straight from the ramp (the railroad station). All their valuables, like gold, diamonds, money, were taken away from them right there. Since their clothing would be taken away, they tried to hide their valuables in the barrack, in the wall or in the ground, with an intention to recover it later, not knowing exactly what was in store for them.

I remember having hidden on my arrival some gold rubles deep in the ground, and I wanted now to recover them. I concealed, also, a gold dollar piece in my shoes under the heels, which I had exchanged already for food. I asked my friend, Dr. Gordon, whether I could go with him to his block, to see whether my hidden pieces were still there.

"Sure", said Dr. Gordon. "Let's go, but I doubt whether you'll find something, because the place is being searched and combed daily and every hidden piece is found."

"Tell me Dr. Gordon, you have been here almost four months. What is the secret of your surviving such a long time, when others succumbed in days?"

"It depends on the physical and spiritual qualities of an individual. I had, many times, been on the verge of despair and death, but in the last moment somebody or something came to my aid and saved my life. Not long ago, they put me in the S.K. block (Straff Kommando, penal commando), which is one of the worst places in the world. Luckily, I was there only two days. Another day, and it would have been my end."

"Who helped you to get out from the S.K.?"

"A friend of mine from the same city, who was a very influential fellow here, a big shot, who was an old-timer. In the S.K. were located the 'Standing Cells,' and I prayed to G-d that they shouldn't put me in the 'Standing Cells.' I wouldn't endure there more than one night."

"Terrible, impossible to believe", I said. "That such a machinery of extermination exists in the middle of Europe, in the twentieth century. Even in the middle ages people did not suffer so much. Never in the history of mankind were known, for example, such tools of mass extermination like gas chambers, krematoria, factories to kill and destroy millions of innocent human beings, including little children and infants."

My friend agreed. "We never heard in the past of factories being built, designed by a duly elected government of a big cultured nation, whose only purpose was to kill and annihilate human beings. The German nation was considered, up to now, to be one of the most civilized nations in the world. How was it possible that one man, Hitler, could change the mentality of a nation which gave out Goethe, Schiller, Heine, Mendelsshhn, and Einstein?"

"It is also true that the German mentality had always been to conquer new territories, to subjugate other nations."

"We still remember the philosophy of Bismark, the slogan of 'Drang Nach Osten' [Thrust Towards the East], but no one would have ever believed that the Germans would fall to such a low degree of morality as at present.

"No other nation would be able to emulate such atrocities. It happened in the past that some commander in the heat of battle permitted his soldiers to rob, even to kill for a few days. But the Germans built factories of annihilation, and mass murder became the prime policy of the government.

"The Turks for example, at the end of the first World War,

when they realized that they lost the war and ceased to be an empire, when the nation was in deep despair, allowed some disorderly elements to commit genodcide, but for a very short time, because they suspected the Armenians of treason. This, later, was condemned by the entire world.

"The Germans, however, during the second World War, committed mass murder and genocide right from the beginning of the war, when Germany was winning, and not only at the end of the war. Behind the German occupying forces followed the special commandos, the so-called 'EINSATZ KOMMANDOS,' destroying thousands of civilians, robbing and murdering even infants, little children, women and old men.

"The atrocities committed are impossible to describe. Even if all the water in the seas would turn to ink and all the trees in the forests would turn to paper, we would not be able to define and portray the mistreatment, the abuse, the persecution, oppression and harassment, the evil, awfulness, dreadfulness, atrociousness, malignancy perpetrated over humanity. No vocabulary, no encyclopedia, possesses enough words!"

My friend continued. "The atrocities lasted also for years, from 1939 till today. It assumed monstrous proportions in the year 1941 and in the following years. Not a week, not a month, but four full years of genocide, unheard of in all the annals of mankind. The victims included people who didn't know where Germany was located, and what the National Socialism stood for. Not the slightest benefit accrued to the conduct of the war. It was sheer madness. Murder for the sake of murder.

"The question still remains, and is being asked by everyone, why did the German people elect so many Nazis to the Reichstag in the year 1933?

"Why did Hindenburg nominate Hitler as chancellor?

"Where were all the decent people in Germany? The philosophers, the writers, the liberals, the humans?

"They were all silent."

"The German nation", I commented, "Did not actually understand the theory of Nazism. They believed them to be German nationalists, who worked for the benefit of Germany, trying to pull the nation out of the depression. The big industrialists like G.I. Farben industries, Krup, etc. supported the Nazis as a tool against the spread of communism."

"The Nazi activities were known in Germany and all over the world before the election of Hitler," retorted my friend. "They saw with their own eyes how the Nazis killed the crippled and mentally deficient people. They witnessed the murdering even of their own best friends, like Streicher, etc., who helped them to reach power. They experienced all the terror unleashed by the Nazis. Yet they voted for Hitler, supported him and freely elected him to the highest office. The assassination of their own friends and the terror should have given a clue to the German people of the true intentions of the Nazi regime.

"Even the old aristocrat, the old Hindenburg, opposed the nomination of Hitler as Chancellor with all his strength. But later, unfortunately, he gave in to the extraordinary pressure of the people around him."

"We have to underscore the fact," I said, "that Hitler had very few followers at the beginning, which increased later, thanks to extensive propaganda and terror. Some of the people were afraid to oppose openly the Nazis, some were pulled in by the current. Don't we have to blame at least in part the preceding German government, which was in power before Hitler, for not taking the adequate measures to stop the assassinations, the murder and the anarchy? They were too lenient to Hitler and his followers. Terror, assassination, murder should be punished to the full extent of the law. Throughout all the history we see weak governments being substituted by totalitarian regimes and vice versa.

"Hitler succeeded in murdering his opponents, openly and secretly, terrorizing hereby the people. Had the liberal democratic German government acted vigorously, Hitler would have never come to power and the tragedy which followed his nomination, the world calamity and catastrophe, would have been avoided.

"I do not believe that the individual German realized, in the year 1933, that voting for Hitler meant creation of gas chambers and Krematoria for extermination of millions innocent human beings.

"Naturally, we have to take also into consideration," I continued, "The natural proclivities of the German people to dominate other nations, toward territorial expansion 'DRANG NACH OSTEN' [thrust toward the east] and 'DEUTSCHLAND UBER ALLES' [Germany over everything]."

"I do not agree with you," said my friend. "Most of the German people knew what Nazism meant, and supported him all through the crucial years, even through the years 1939-1941 when Germany was winning. Later, when the course of the war turned around and the German army sustained calamities on all the fronts, only then discontent started to spread and dissatisfaction multiplied."

It became dark and we started to return to the barracks. We reached Barrack # 22.

"Please show me," I said, "the exact place where the valuables were taken away. Maybe I'll still find something, which would help a lot in my present struggle for survival."

"Come in," retorted my friend. "Here is the room."

Yes, I recognized the place, but searching, probing and prying did not give any results. I looked all over the hidden places, but my valuables were gone forever. I thanked my friend and returned to my barrack.

Next morning I returned to my previous Block Sixteen, to get my portion of bread which was coming to me and which would help in my present starvation.

The bookkeeper, a mean person of Polish nationality, said sarcastically, "You want your portion of bread. We'll give it to you, we'll call the deputy of the block senior."

He locked the room and left.

The deputy was a young fellow known for his toughness. In spite of his youth, he perfected many ways of exterminating people. Everybody was afraid of him. For unknown reason he liked me. The bookkeeper returned after a while and was sure that the deputy would teach me a lesson for the impertinence of asking for my portion of bread.

The deputy was very nice to me. He even apologized to me, to the astonishment of the bookkeeper, for frightening me and he ordered him to give me a double portion of bread.

I met on Block "EIGHT" three sick people from the transport of Wolkowysk. One of them was a carpenter whose name was Zapolanski. The pattern of transfer to Block Eight was similar. Working hard on the outside, being beaten and harassed all the time with very scarce nourishment, he developed a small wound on his lower extremity, which did not want to heal for reasons already mentioned elsewhere.

The wound enlarged in size and finally the leg became swollen.

He couldn't walk and was sent to the hospital.

Luckily, Dr. Zenkteller wasn't present and he was sent by another physician to Block "EIGHT" instead of "SEVEN."

After a few days, the swelling became enormous and the Czech doctor in charge of his case wanted to transfer Mr. Zapolanski to Block Seven, which meant death in the gas chamber. Zapolanski came to me crying that his number was written to be transferred to Block Seven.

"Please help me," sobbed and moaned Zapolanski.

I was myself in big danger of losing my life anytime, especially since Dr. Krause did not like the new doctors.

What should I do? How could I help him?

After a moment of vacillation, I went to the Czech doctor who registered his number for the transfer and asked him straight, "What can be done?"

The answer was, that he couldn't help him, because the lower extremity was very swollen and infected. The German doctor had to arrive tomorrow for an inspection and he'd look over all the sick prisoners.

"If the number of Zspolanski is not written," he said, "I am going to pay with my own life. Cases like that happened before and all paid with their own lives. "I am not ready," he continued, "to give my life for Zapolanski. It wouldn't help either, because he'll be taken to the gas chamber anyway."

The Czech doctor was essentially a nice and decent fellow, but he couldn't do anything under the circumstances. I hesitated for a while and said: "I see your point and agree with you completely. It is a very difficult and peculiar situation. Since I know you as a noble person, I would suggest the following: I am going to operate on his leg right now. If the swelling improves or disappears during the night, will you take a chance and erase his number?"

"Sure", answered the Czech. "Do it, if you are successful, Zapolanski will live."

I ran, immediately, to Zapolanski, who had given up any hope and considered himself already dead.

"Come on," I said. "We still have hope."

Zapolanski was so preoccupied with his thoughts that he didn't understand what I was talking about.

"Come on," I repeated. "What are you waiting for?"

With the help of a few orderlies we carried him to the last room. I sterilized a simple knife, sprayed the leg with chloralhydrate, which we had on the block, and cut the leg all through the swelling. Zapolanski held himself very quietly throughout the operation. He was completely anesthetized by the events. A lot of pus came out, which I drained, and I put inside a knot from gauze for further draining. I bandaged the leg and we carried him again to his berth. I made him comfortable and lifted slightly his leg. In the morning I rushed to see what happened to the leg. Zapolanski, smiling, told me that he felt very well, no pain, and it seemed to him that the swelling disappeared. I examined the leg and hastened to the Czech doctor with the good news that the swelling disappeared. We came both over to Zapolanski, examined his leg, and his number was taken off the transfer to Block Seven.

Later in the day, the German entered the block and everything was all right.

Zapolanski remained alive. He is now in Philadelphia, working as a carpenter.

Another sick prisoner lying on Block Eight was the engineer Goldenberg from Wolkowysk, who was born in Warsaw but lived in our town, marrying one of the prettiest and wealthiest girls. His spouse was the daughter of Chirik, who had the most important mill business in the city. His machinery crushed grain into flour, providing material to all the bakers. Mr. Goldenberg was a tall fellow with a pleasant face, and was considered very handsome. I remember him coming to our sports place in Wolkowysk where we played soccer. He was able to hit the ball magnificently.

Now, this nice fellow had developed the common illness in Birkenau, namely swelling of his face and of both lower extremities caused by malnutrition and prolonged standing on his feet. He had no wounds and the legs were not infected. An operation would not help, it would make it worse, because the reason was not an infection but lack of proteins. I couldn't help him medically, because diuretics were not available at that time in Birkenau. Even if we had them we couldn't have helped him overnight.

I went to Dr. Krause and asked him to help this nice fellow.

The doctor was deaf to any plea.

"I can not help him," he said harshly and inclemently.

I returned to my place with a broken heart, not being able to give the aid requested.

The third fellow who entered our little hospital, as a patient, was Dr. Epstein.

"What happened to you?" I asked.

"My condition deteriorated. I could not get any job as a pfleger, because I was very weak and considered to be a Musulman."

I tried to help him, as much as I could. I "ORGANIZED" for him a little more soup, coffee and sometimes a piece of bread. At that time I walked around the camp very hungry myself, but Dr. Epstein was very undernourished and I had to save him.

My friend, Dr. Alteresco, was afflicted with pleurisy. He had high fever, headache, pain in the chest which increased on respiration, and had developed difficulties in breathing. He was worrying that he might be sent to the gas chambers. I encouraged him assuring him that he'd get healthy again in a short time.

The Czech doctor was transported to another place. Later we found out that he died in Auschwitz I from typhus.

I had to work very hard because of lack of physicians. One

orderly of my "STUBE" became incapacitated because of typhus and I had to do his job as well.

Luckily a new doctor arrived. His name was Dr. Heidenfeld from Breslau. He was a very decent and fine physician, about sixty years old. In spite of emphysema, he smoked all day long. He spoke only German and helped me a lot.

The bookkeeper of "BLOCK EIGHT" was a fellow from Czechoslovakia who walked around all day long with a cane in his hand. He was a very energetic fellow and the roll calls which he supervised were done in minutes. I had the impression that he was in private life a high executive.

Dr. Krause suffered from many pimples and boils, especially over both lower extremities. He called it furunculosis on the basis of malnutrition. The boils, in spite of treatment, did not heal. I applied different ointments, but to no avail. He also consumed vitamins.

The wound on my left leg started to heal. The fact, that I did not have to stand for hours on roll calls evidently helped. I could sit down and rest at any time without any restrictions, and the inside living instead of walking all day outside aided also in the process.

I noticed a strange and unexplained phenomenon, namely that the wounds on the legs of the "MUSULMANS" who had very little to eat, certainly less than Dr. Krause, healed very fast. People exhausted and so weak that they couldn't stand on their feet, yet their wounds mended and healed. Around the wounds a certain substance was visible. I decided to investigate this phenomenon if I survived the war. This was probably a penicillin or another mold gathered around the wound, which originated from the dirty soil of Auschwitz.

The Gypsies suffered the same fate as the Jews, which meant complete extermination of their race (Gleichgestalltet). Gypsies were gathered from all the occupied territories, brought to the German concentration camps and exterminated. They had no government, no representatives to defend them. A weak disorganized mass of human beings.

The Germans loved to deal with powerless masses. They could murder them and they were sure that nobody ever would protest. Some gypsies, even German officers in uniforms, were taken off the battle front and sent directly to Auschwitz. Their only sin was being Gypsies. Some high officials, highly decorated, were dispatched also to Birkenau.

How could one explain the mass murder of innocent Gypsies including women and children? Certainly not on racial basis because the Japanese belonged to the yellow race and Hitler concluded with them a pact of friendship (Axis).

Many transports of Gypsies were brought into Birkenau. The first transport arrived in February, 1942. At the beginning they were sent directly to the gas chambers, where they perished. Men, women, and children were annihilated for no reason at all. They had nothing to do with the war. They didn't cause it, nor could they have any influence on the course of the war. Yet, the murderous hands of the Nazis reached them wherever they were. Later in the late spring of 1943, a special camp was built for them, where they were forced to live—men, women and children in the same camp. They called it the "GYPSY FAMILY CAMP," and it was located between the men's and the hospital camps.

The procedure was the same. About 15% entered the Gypsy camp and 85% were sent directly to their death. From the 15% who remained alive, many died from starvation, illness and exhaustion. The rest were liquidated on 8/2/1944.

Here is what the commandant of Auschwitz Rudolf Hoess, wrote about the liquidation of the Gypsy camp.

"Four thousand gypsies were left in Auschwitz by August 1944. . . . they did not realize what was happening to them when they were led to Crematorium V. It was not easy to drive them into the gas chambers."

According to the prosecutor of Frankfurt, Alois Frey, the Nazi commandant of Günther-Grube took an effective part in this action. I was a witness for the prosecution about the activities of the above criminal, in February, 1974, in Frankfurt, Germany. What was the verdict of the court? You'll be surprised. You'll find out later in the course of my narration.

At that time, spring 1943, many transports arrived from Greece. On the ramp of Birkenau, the famous selection took place. About 80% were sent straight to the gas chambers. The rest, the young and healthy-looking Greeks, entered the camp not to live but to work hard and to suffer and then to die from exhaustion, hard work, beatings and malnutrition. The same procedure as with all the other transports.

The Germans promised the Greeks as usual that they were only being resettled to the east. The families would live together. They'd be paid nicely for their work. Some Greeks even made contracts with the Germans to buy property in the east.

When they arrived on the ramp of Auschwitz, they soon found out the truth, but it was too late.

The Greeks, as well as the other nationalities, believed the Germans because up to this time history did not record such big lies and unheard-of atrocities. Every lie has a limit, behind which it is accepted as the truth.

After a few days, some of the Greeks were sent to Block Eight because of illness. I was the only one who was able to communicate with them, because some of the Greeks spoke Italian and almost all of them spoke Spanish. The Spanish dialect was their native language and used in their homes, mainly by the descendants of those who escaped from Spain to Greece during the Spanish Inquisition in the year 1492.

I felt compassion and pity towards those Greeks, who were so ignominiously cheated by the Germans.

The first four Greeks who were sent to "BLOCK EIGHT" were young, healthy-looking men, age 20-26. Their bodies were clean, fine, and they looked like athletes, physically strong, skillful and active. Later were admitted eight other Greeks. A total of twelve.

I couldn't understand the reason why they were sent to Block Eight, which was an alleged hospital for the sick. They told me that they went to the clinic to ask a few tablets for headache. One of the Greeks told Dr. Zenkteller, inadvertently, that many years previously he had malaria. This was enough for Dr. Zenkteller. He informed the German doctor about it. All the twelve Greeks were transferred to "BLOCK EIGHT" for observation.

We didn't suspect anything bad, nor dangerous, because the

Germany's Retreat. Work in Birkenau

Greeks were sent to "BLOCK EIGHT" and not to "BLOCK SEVEN," the extermination block.

I remember, one day, in April, 1943, an SS man, whose name was Klehr, arrived on "BLOCK EIGHT." He called in the block senior and ordered him to bring, one by one, the twelve Greeks to the small room at the end of the barrack. All the windows had to be covered, because he was going to give them injections for malaria.

It was very difficult to understand why the German came to give the injections personally. It looked very suspicious to us, but we would never be able to imagine even what was in store for these unfortunate prisoners.

After a short while, we found out the reason. One Greek entered for the injection, followed by another, till all twelve received the injections.

What happened here?

We soon discovered it. The German Klehr injected "PHENOL" straight to the heart of the victims. Death took place immediately.

It was terrible! Imagine, a young healthy Greek entered the small room. He was uncertain of himself, because he didn't speak German. He saw the German holding a syringe, who directed him with his finger to lie down on the table. He understood that he was going to get an injection against malaria or maybe a vaccination against any other contagious disease. He lay down and the German injected the drug straight into the heart. The victim died immediately.

The next victim entered unaware what happened to the first one. In a half an hour all twelve Greeks were dead, lying in front of the barrack. Here we found out the real intentions of the Germans. They had a very simple cure for any disease.

What a pity?

Senseless murder!

The Greeks looked beautiful in their death: serene and peaceful. Only their mouths were slightly open, like they were wondering and asking why their young lives were so brutally taken away from them.

300   THE YEAR 1943

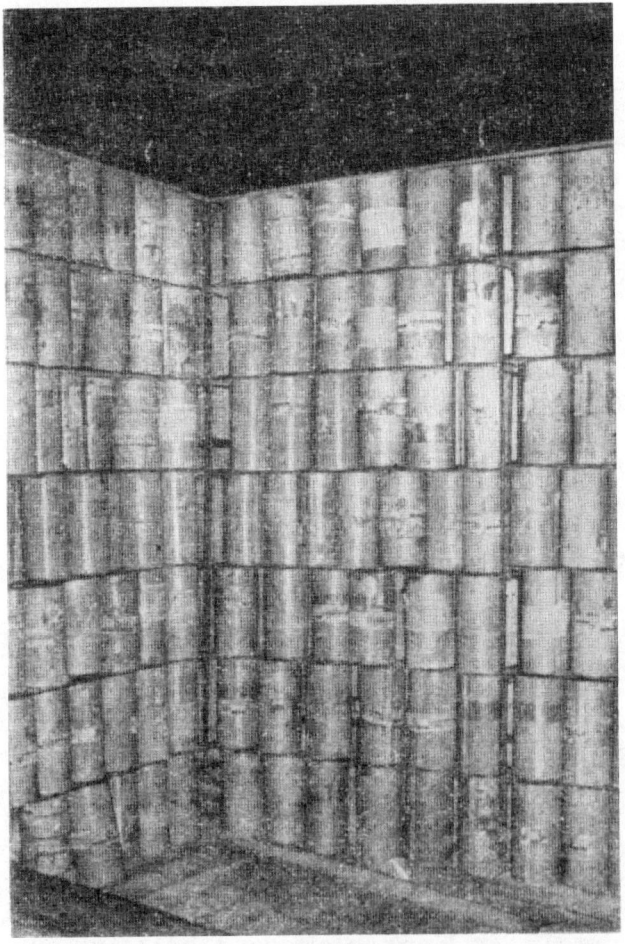

Supply of Cyclon B poison, used in Auschwitz to kill the prisoners.

Horrifying, appalling, shocking!
To what degree of low morality our world came to!
If I didn't see it with my own eyes and were told only by somebody else, I would have never believed it. Evidently, that heartlessness, ruthlessness and cruelty of human beings against

New arrivals at a concentration camp, being paraded for medical inspection. (From a photograph found on a German prisoner.)

other human beings surpass anything known in the jungle. Man is worse than the wildest animal. Compared to man, beast is an angel.

G-d, why did you permit such terrible things to happen in the world that You, Yourself created?

Why did you send Hitler and the Nazis on our earth?

We believe, that everything is being done according to your will and wishes.

Why then? ... Why? ...

Yes, it was true, the Germans lost the war. But who will return life to those Greeks and other nationals who were tortured and killed?

The way they died was a deprecation to human dignity and a disgrace to the globe that You constructed. It is very difficult for us, blood and flesh, to understand your ways. . . .

On the other hand, we have to take in consideration the eventuality of what would have happened to our world if the Nazis had won the war, which was quite possible.

Adjudge yourself! The master race dominated the world. The Jews exterminated, followed by the Slavs like the Poles, Russians, Czechs, Yugoslavs, etc. Later, other nations would have been exterminated, like the Latin countries: France, Italy and so on. The English, Scandinavian countries would follow. More gas chambers and Krematoria would be built. The smoke of the Krematoria would have continued day and night and would have been considered a part of nature.

Aren't we fortunate after all that the war ended, that Nazism lost its original power?

But for how long? How long? You'll find it out later in this book.

"BLOCK EIGHT," as I mentioned previously, was an alleged hospital where the sick people were able to rest.

Every day people died in Birkenau. In the morning they were carried to the mortuary (Leichenhalle), from which they were taken to the Krematoria.

"BLOCK EIGHT" had every morning about eight to ten corpses. But "BLOCK SEVEN" had one hundred to one hundred and twenty corpses, dispersed all over the grounds of the barrack. To pass from one place to the other, one had to step over many corpses. Inferno was a paradise in comparison with the realities of Birkenau.

The corpses were loaded on carriages or carts, one on the top of the other. Human parts were hanging on the sides.

It was a terrible sight! unbelievable!

"BLOCK SEVEN" and "BLOCK EIGHT" were separated one from the other by a large and spacious yard. I could observe what happened on the yard from a window in Block Eight.

This was what I saw with my own eyes:

Two times weekly, German trucks used to arrive in front of "BLOCK SEVEN" to take away all the sick prisoners. Usually the German doctor or his deputy used to be present. He had the numbers of all the victims who had to die. They were previously propelled and herded in one part of the barrack, usually on

Stube IV (part 4). They were lying in their berths for the most part, naked. About twenty miserable human beings in one berth, one on the top of the other. They did not receive food nor water, and as a consequence were so weak that they could hardly stand on their feet. Many couldn't stand up and were lying in or outside the berth.

When the German trucks arrived, they were not able to put up any kind of resistance although they knew that they were going to die.

Hundreds of thousands of people, of different nationalities, from all over Europe, perished in this way. They were Russians (civilians and military), Poles, Czechs, Yugoslavs, civilians from France, Holland, Belgium, Norway. All were consumed in the fire of National Socialism.

When the trucks arrived, all the prisoners destined to die were pushed and hastened out to the yard and loaded on the trucks. Those who couldn't walk were carried to the trucks and thrown in, like pieces of lumber or rubbish.

Some of the victims had open wounds on their legs. The German doctor called the orderly in charge and shouted, "Why was the wound of this prisoner not bandaged? You are a sadist, a hostile personality".

Here stood a German, who sent thousands of innocent people to their death, complaining that one of the victims was not bandaged. What a cynicism? What a sarcasm? Incredible, if I didn't see it with my own eyes.

One hundred fifty to two hundred people were packed in one truck, which left for the gas chambers, and another truck was ready for another load of human beings. Sometimes the victims had to stay in yard naked, waiting for the truck.

I remember, one young and healthy man, running naked in the yard and screaming.

"I am healthy and strong. I am able to work, please let me live."

He grabbed a shovel and started to dig the ground, to show the Germans, that he was capable to work.

"Please help me. Don't let me die. I am strong. . . . strong . . . strong. . . ."

Nothing helped. In vain were his lamentations. He was whipped with clubs and forced to get into the truck.

I looked through the window with tears in my eyes. The German doctor was counting his victims. The trucks looked like beasts driven by demons and vampires.

I couldn't look any longer. My heart was palpitating. I couldn't see any longer. Darkness in front of my eyes. I left the window and sat on the ground. Lamentations, cryings, sounds of sorrow, sobbing, bawling reached my ears. Yelling, shrieking, shouting in German, mixed with the roar of the upcoming trucks were heard. I became dizzy..., the terrible sounds didn't reach me any more....

CHAPTER XI

Warsaw Ghetto. Transports for Treblinka. The arrest and rescue of Mussolini. The conquest of Sicily. The Warsaw Ghetto uprising.

THE GHETTO IN WARSAW. THE TRANSPORTS TO TREBLINKA. THE GERMAN DECEPTIONS. THE GHETTO UPRISING. DISSOLUTION OF THE COMMUNIST INTERNATIONAL. SEVERE FIGHTING IN AND AROUND KURSK (RUSSIA). FIELD MARSHAL PAULUS IN RUSSIAN CAPTIVITY. KIROVOGRAD CONFERENCE. THE GAS CHAMBERS AND KREMATORIA STOPPED FUNCTIONING. OPERATION CITADEL. KURSK SALIENT. THE SURRENDER OF ITALY (BADOGLIO). ITALIAN PRISONERS IN AUSCHWITZ. THE RESUMPTION OF THE FUNCTIONING OF THE GAS CHAMBERS AND KREMATORIA. DR. SCHILLIST. FORCED EXERCISES. EXPERIMENTS IN AUSCHWITZ. DR. THILO.

WARSAW GHETTO UPRISING.

At the beginning of June, 1943, a few prisoners were brought from Warsaw *ruins* to Auschwitz extermination camp, Birkenau. One of them told me the following horrible story:

In Warsaw Ghetto were concentrated, as of the beginning of the year 1942, about 500,000 persons, which included all the

Jews of prewar Warsaw, plus the others brought in from the neighboring cities.

German soldiers started immediately after the surrender of Warsaw (9/27/39) to plunder homes, shoot many people to death for insignificant reasons or for no reason at all. Daytime robberies and night lootings were regular occurrences. The Warsaw shops and stores were pillaged continuously.

On 10/4/39, the Gestapo ordered chairman Adam Czerniakow to form a council of twenty-four members and twenty-four deputies, whose function was to fulfill the German orders under threat of death. The council was named *Judenrat*. The first verdict was to perform a census of the total Jewish population and of the intellectuals separately. This had to be done in ten days. In case of non-compliance, all the members of the council would be shot.

On 10/16/40, the establishment of the ghetto was ordered. All the Jews had to live within the ghetto boundaries, which were located between the Saxon Garden and the two railroad stations: the Main and Danzing station. The ghetto area was two and a half miles long and one mile wide. One hundred forty thousand Jews from other parts of Warsaw had to be squeezed into this area, which was already overcrowded previously. It had twenty-seven thousand apartments of approximately two and a half rooms each. The congestion was enormous, about ten persons to one room. Still people kept coming, asking for some place to put their tired heads down.

The first mass murder took place at Nine Nalewki Street, where fifty three people were shot. It happened in the morning of 11/16/39. Among the victims were boys of twelve years old. Above all, the Nazis tried to exterminate the intellectuals like physicians, lawyers, etc. Although the Nuremberg laws did not permit personal relations between Jews and Germans, the latter forced their way into Jewish homes, raping even young girls. It was horrible! The German excesses reached an extreme proportion of brutality.

On January 21, 1940, all the Jewish property had to be registered.

On Passover, 1940, the Germans staged a pogrom in Warsaw, which lasted eight days, during which time many Jews were killed and their shops and houses pillaged.

The ghetto was closed completely on 11/16/1940 and the Jews could not leave the enclosure under threat of death. At the moving, no cars or horses were permitted. Pushcarts were the only way of transportation. The ghetto was surrounded by a wall about three yards high covered with pieces of broken glass.

Here is a report of a German, W. Doering:

"The Jews were filthy, ragged.... Wherever we looked we saw miserable, fallen creatures. Let them be choked in their dirt. It's all right with us (Moegen sie in ihrem dreck ersticken—uns soll es recht sein—German translation)."

Death from starvation was common. Epidemic diseases were rampant. The mortality was very high.

Fisher, the Governor of Warsaw, said: "We will destroy that breed. They will disappear from hunger, disease and abuse."

In 1941, over 15% of the people died. Almost three hundred every day. Corpses were lying all over, covered with newspapers and held down by bricks.

On 7/21/1942 at 11 A.M., Germans entered the Community Center and arrested all the present members of the council, except Chairman Czerniakov. At the same time squads of German police entered different apartments in the ghetto. About one hundred upper-class Jews were shot on the spot. Later in the afternoon, the arrested members were released.

Next day, *7/22/1942*, on the eve of *"Tisha Beav,"* the day of the destruction of the temple in Jerusalem, the ghetto was surrounded by the Gestapo and their helpers. SS men entered the office of the Judenrat and told Mr. Czerniakov the following:

"All the Jews will be resettled to the East. Six thousand have to be delivered daily to the railroad station (umschlagplatz) starting from today. The Judenrat is responsible for the execution of the order. Otherwise they'll be all shot."

The Germans left.

Six thousand people were taken out from their homes or caught on the street and marched of to "umschlagplatz" at Stawki Square. From there, they were loaded on cattle trains and deported to the East.

The Germans assured them that they'd work in factories or on improvement of roads. The men would work and the women would take care of the household chores, children would go to school.

It was the first time in the history of mankind that people were sent to be murdered instead of, as promised, to work in factories. It happened before in the annals of history that people, even entire cities, were resettled during war time, but never to Krematoria and slaughter houses. The victims believed the Germans. Had they known, that instead of the East they'd be put in gas chambers and killed, they would have revolted. In this way the Germans succeeded in their lies. Hitler said:

"Tell them lies. The bigger the lie, the better they'll believe you."

Train after train loaded with innocent human beings left for the East. Nazi victims including children were resettled every day.

Then, late in July, the Gestapo came into the office of Adam Czerniakov and left only after ten minutes. What happened?

They asked him to increase the daily number of resettled people to ten thousand. Mr. Czerniakov did not fulfill the order. He did not want to be instrumental to the Nazis and committed suicide by poisoning himself with Potassium Cyanide. After his death, engineer Marek Lichtenbaum was assigned as chairman. For a few days ten thousand were deported daily, then seven thousand.

Could you imagine, dear reader, the number of six or seven thousand people, including old people and children, sent from Warsaw alone to be murdered in cold blood? It is like the entire population of a small town being sent to their death every day. I believe that a normal human being is not able to comprehend such a tragedy.

In the first week, forty-seven thousand five hundred people were sent to Treblinka extermination camp.

The people in the cattle trains did not know exactly where they were being resettled.

One day, a man working at the railroad station noticed, mentally, the numbers of a few wagons, which left in the morning and which returned to Warsaw, to his astonishment, on the same afternoon. It was a clear indication that the people were taken not deep into Russia but near Warsaw. Another checking revealed that the trains leaving in the morning returned after approximately six hours. This signified that the people were taken to a place of about three hours by train from Warsaw.

In the month of August about one hundred fifty thousand were resettled.

But where? What was the name of the place? Three hours by train from Warsaw. . . .

In order to allure volunteers to the resettlement, the Germans used the following deception.

They supervised the ghetto very closely and didn't let any food to come in. Then, they announced that anyone who was going to be resettled voluntarily would get seven pounds of bread and two pounds of marmelade. They also declared that work in the East *was guaranteed*. This offer of food to people who were dying from starvation blinded many victims, and numerous unfortunate people accepted the offer. Naturally, nobody believed that they'll be slaughtered.

"How would," they reasoned, "the murder of innocent children help the Germans in the war against Russia?"

It was a very sound question to an average mentally balanced person. But the Nazis were mentally sick. A sick breed educated in special schools of bloody murderers. Their ideals were different from those of other people. Their actions were incomprehensible to the average person. The world was in a state of shock.

The Germans continued on the same road, in accordance with the supreme tenet "the bigger the lie, the quicker people will believe it."

Here is how it worked.

The relatives of those who were sent away to Treblinka received from their resettled relatives German postcards dated weeks or months after the resettlement and postmarked from various places in Russia. The relatives were absolutely convinced that they were authentic. The handwritings were exactly from their relatives. In these postcards they wrote that they were healthy, working, eating well, and urged their relatives to join them and to get out from the dreadful Warsaw Ghetto.

Here were a few examples of those postcards as given by N.L.

"The work here is quite hard, but we eat well. Join me." Signed Moisze Katzen.

"Urge you apply for transfer to this camp. We make small airfields. Love." Signed Pearl Samson.

"We get here two hot meals a day! My back is bothering me, but I am much happier here. Come." Signed Nahum Freund.

The brother of Nahum, Mr. Hirschel Freund, said that the handwriting was from his brother and that he suffered from a painful back.

These postcards were written in Treblinka, right after the arrival and before they were forced to the gas chambers. They were later sent out by the Germans from different places in Russia weeks or months after the unfortunate prisoners died and burned in the Krematoria.

The relatives in Warsaw who received the above postcards were sure that they were written by members of their families. They had never been conditioned to such lies. They believed it and joined the transports.

Still the fate of those who were resettled had never been clear. Rumors were spreading about massacres and killings in the Eastern territories: Bialystok, Slonim, Wilno and other cities.

People couldn't move outside the wall of the Ghetto. Those found outside were shot on the spot. Traveling to another city was very risky. Many were killed for disobeying this order.

Where did the cattle trains with the deportees go?

Some very courageous young men decided to take the risk and to find out exactly what was happening to the deportees. One of those was Zygmunt (*Frydrych*). It had to be done because some of the families who received the letters reported for deportation.

One had to take into account the terrible living conditions in the ghetto. The starvation, the overcrowding, (8-10 to one room), the contagious diseases, the maltreatment, the beatings and hard labor, the daily shootings and mass dying on the streets of Warsaw. These realities of life had to be reflected in light of the postcards. No wonder that many, out of desperation, and hoping to improve their terrible situation, agreed for deportation.

Therefore, at the beginning of August, 1942, "Mr. Frydrych" left the Ghetto to find out the truth. He crossed the Vistula, picked up the railroad tracks and followed them till he reached the main railroad line junction. He saw the switches and noticed one line going in the direction of Bialystok and the other one to the north. He was able to hide himself not far away from the railroad junction and waited for the Warsaw train and the deportees. The train came slowly and it was a cattle freight train. From his place of hiding he heard cries and some prayers!

"G-d is our G-d, G-d is one."

"I believe surely, that the Messiah will come soon."

These were words of desperation.

The train approached the switch, shuddered and continued eastward in the direction of Bialystok.

He rested a while and followed the rail lines towards the east. He walked all day and evening till midnight. Then he found a place in the bushes, sat down to rest and fell asleep. In the morning, he resumed his walking along the railroad tracks. Soon he saw a cattle train approaching. "Frydrych" ran away from the tracks and heard shouts and wails from inside the trains. Now he walked briskly behind the disappearing train and found himself near a railroad station, called *Malkinia*. He noticed a side track from the station leading further into some woods.

He turned in the direction of the thicket into which the rail spur curved away from the main line, and far away he observed the camp, being afraid to come too near.

It was a very daring and courageous undertaking. He could have been caught any minute and shot. He took an enormous chance in spite of his weakened condition.

He returned to Malkinia and met an escaped prisoner from Treblinka who told him the real truth of "*Treblinka*."

It was a camp, recently constructed, which lay behind the

woods. The camp was enclosed with barbed wire and contained a few buildings, one of which had an unusual design. The later contained three rooms of two yards high. It had pipes and valves and the doors had hermetic seals. The first room had signs, "Tailors, carpenters, road—builders," etc., making the prisoners believe that they were being sorted out for particular labor further east. An SS man would get up and declare:

"All of you are going to be resettled and transferred further east, according to your vocation and specialty. First you have to wash yourselves and your clothing will be disinfected. Keep your receipts. You'll get your clothing back after the disinfection."

Everybody received a small piece of soap and his personal documents. They entered the next room and they saw the alleged water pipes and the valves. The doors soon closed hermetically, and the people died from the poisonous gas. After fifteen minutes the corpses were carried away by a special Commando and buried.

This was the story, which "Mr. Frydrych" (Zygmunt) brought back to the ghetto in Warsaw. There was no doubt any more about the true fate of the "resettled" prisoners.

The Jewish underground started to prepare then for an uprising, to fight for their lives, although they knew that the outcome would be death.

"Let's die with dignity! Let the Nazis pay for their crimes!"

It is interesting that, even then, some didn't believe or didn't want to believe that the Germans were out to kill everybody for no reason at all. "Treblinka is bloodcurdling and hair-raising, but the Germans would not dare to do with Warsaw what they did with the provincial cities," they said. Soon they found out that it didn't make any difference.

From 7/22/42 till 9/22/42, over four hundred thousand Jews were murdered. They had no ammunition. Their appeals for help to the Polish Underground were not answered. The statement of Bor-Komorowski, the Polish General, that the Underground offered arms but the Jews rejected the offer, did not correspond to the truth. It was a ludicrous and cynical statement. The Jews in front of death and Nazi bestiality would have accepted ammunition even from Hell if offered.

The Polish masses showed, at best, indifference to the fate of the ghetto. They succumbed to the German propaganda. The Jews were blamed for everything. For the political and economical conditions of prewar Poland, for the ignominous defeat of the Polish army, for the irresponsibility of their leaders, for starting of the Second World War, for the suffering of the Poles, for the starvation, diseases, calamities in Poland, etc. Desperate appeals for help fell on deaf ears.

The Polish masses, at that time, were devoted Catholics. I believe that a declaration from the Pope in Rome that any massacre of human beings is a sin and that any help rendered to the unfortunate victims is a virtue and chastity and corresponds with the teaching of Christianity would have been an enormous help and relief.

But the Vatican was silent, which was interpreted by the Polish masses as a sign of conformity and advice to follow the beaten path, the path of no-interference.

The Polish underground did not want to identify themselves with the ghetto. They didn't want to be compromised in the eyes of the Polish masses.

And so people perished from starvation, diseases, gas chambers and Krematoria. From over five hundred thousand people there remained in 1942 about fifty thousand persons. Then it became quiet, more or less, till the end of the year (1942). On January 18, 1943, right after the calamity of Stalingrad, another wave of extermination started. Hitler could not take revenge on the Russians, nor could he persecute the English or the Americans, so he decided to murder the fifty thousand Jews who still remained in Warsaw.

This time the victims were able to organize themselves. They bought arms of small calibre and some hand grenades. They put up a resistance, which confused the enemy. The defenders fought bravely and even took away some arms from the attackers. It was the first time that Germans were running for their lives in Warsaw. Some were lying dead on the streets of Warsaw. The defenders achieved a small victory over what till then had seemed Nazi invincibility. Some rifles and machine guns fell into their hands.

The fighting took the Germans by surprise, and even the Poles. The later were so enthusiastic that they delivered fifty pistols and fifty hand grenades, which was a drop in the bucket in comparison with the heavy German armaments, tanks and airplanes.

The Germans started a new tactic. They promised the defenders work, food, security. But nobody wanted to listen to their lies, which were proven time and time again. The victims knew that they'd succumb to superior force, but they wanted to die with dignity.

The defenders bought additional ammunition, regardless of price. They put out guards, day and night, to warn the defenders of the approaching enemy. They created under the ground interconnected tunnels and bunkers, and even mines were planted.

At the beginning of 1943, Himmler visited Warsaw. This was a bad omen. The Germans again promised work in the factories. To convince everybody of the truthfulness of their promises, they even brought witnesses, prisoners from Trawniki and Poniatow, who tried to persuade and reassure the victims. To no avail.

On April 19, 1943, on the eve of the Jewish Easter Holiday, the Germans attacked with full force, including tanks and airplanes. They reckoned that the fighting would last no more than three days. The newly appointed German Commander was SS General Stroop. He had under his command over two thousand men, armed to the teeth, against six hundred and fifty poorly armed defenders.

The first encounter took place in the section around Zamenhof Street, in which many Germans were killed and the others escaped. Even two tanks were knocked out.

The Germans then started to shell the ghetto with heavy artillery. There was also bombardment from the air.

In spite of the enormous German superiority in arms and heavy ammunition, the defenders did not surrender. Every house became a fortress and the Germans had many casualties.

General Stroop realized that he had no prospect to succeed and ordered flamethrowers to be used. Under artillery and tank cover, they started to set fire to all the houses. The Germans looked for revenge and broke into Czysta Hospital and shot to death all the sick people in their beds. The German bestiality was indescribable in fury and horror.

The defenders did not surrender. They preferred death rather than submission and capitulation. Many, including women and children, were seen jumping from burning buildings and flaming windows. Some threw themselves on the Germans and attacked them with their bare hands shouting, "My life should perish together with the Germans."

General Stroop did not expect such courage, sacrifice and disregard for life under these circumstances. He continued to use flame throwers, artillery, heavy bombardment of houses already burned, poison gas and all other means of the most modern warfare.

Still they did not surrender. They preferred to be burned alive rather than to fall into the hands of the Germans, where they knew that they'd be tortured and then killed.

Stroop wrote that some of the Jews were firing pistols from both hands and that only flamethrowers and fire dislodged them from their hideouts.

On 5/8/43, Mordechai Anielewicz, the commander of the ghetto, lost his life.

Later, the Germans burned the Great Jewish Synagogue as an expression of victory. But the battle was not finished as yet. Jewish heroes still lived in the hidden bunkers and tunnels, under the rubble and ruins.

Some were able to escape outside the ghetto or to hide in the cellars of a burned house. Some even reached the forests and joined the partisans.

So the battle lasted, not three days as foretold by the Germans, but more than a month. Even then, there were many people hidden in the ruins or outside the walls of the ghetto.

Most of the unfortunate people who lived outside the ghettos on Aryan Papers (not Jewish) were hunted all the time by Polish spies. When they caught them they used to rob the victims of all their valuables and then to report to the Nazis in order to collect the reward.

Poland was the only country in the world where so many victims were blackmailed, robbed and given over to the Gestapo for additional money. The magnitude of this extortion and pillaging was unique in history.

Most of the Jewish heroes were killed by starvation, diseases and malnutrition. Some perished in the gas chambers and krematoria of Treblinka and Maidanek. Some died in the cattle trains on the way to the extermination camps. Some reached Auschwitz.

I remember seeing the bodies of some of the unfortunate victims of Warsaw in Birkenau. They had hair on their heads, which was by itself an unusual sight because we prisoners in Auschwitz had no hair on our heads.

The killed people were all of them heroes unmatched in history. They knew the superiority of the enemy arms, they realized that they would not survive, and still they put up a fierce resistance.

Most of the people of any nationality, race or creed—Russians, French, English, Czechs—after falling into the hands of the Germans and seeing all the bestiality of the Nazi hell gave up any hope. They fell into an apathy which paralyzed their actions and thinking. The tendency of human beings, when they encountered a strong, formidable and wild enemy whom they couldn't fight, was to give up, to be despondent and to surrender.

Whether they realized it or not, in the subconscious, in the back of their minds, there always lay a spark of hope.

"Maybe they are not going to kill me."

"Maybe I'll remain alive."

"I have no strength to fight, and if I do I'll be killed in a minute and lie on the dirty soil like a torn rag. Let's wait. Maybe, maybe. . . ."

This is what makes the heroes of Warsaw different. They fought the enemy, knowing surely that they'd die. They fought, knowing that their bodies would be torn to pieces. They knew all that, without any shadow of a doubt. Still they didn't give up and continued to fight. In the back of their minds they hoped that somebody would remain alive and be a living witness of the unheard-off atrocities committed by the Germans on defenseless people. They fought also to show the German beasts that human life is not cheap and that there is a price for taking away innocent lives, small as the price may be in comparison with the crimes committed. They were real unmatched heroes, where no trumpets were blaring, not flags were waving, no songs were chanted, no citations, no decorations were presented.

They died simply as they lived, with courage, fearlessness, bravery and prowess, boldness and heroism rarely found in the annals of history.

Honor to their memory!

They'll never be forgotten by all the decent people of the world.

The Jews not only from Warsaw but from all the other occupied territories were murdered. This was true for Eastern Europe—especially Poland, White Russia, the Ukraine, Lithuania, Latvia and Estonia. In Eastern Europe lived the bulk of Jewry. They built most of the cities and towns. They developed the trade and enriched the countries where they lived.

They perished by the will of one person, Adolf Hitler, and by the willing actions of thousands of Germans.

Every action was made possible due to deceits and big lies, according to the motto "The bigger the lie the better they'll believe you." The lies were fantastic and so big that the average person had to believe it. After all they were uttered and promised by one of the most cultured nations of twentieth century Europe.

Who could have imagined that they'd reach the bottom of morality, the peak of evil, in a few years years under Nazi rule?

Who could have thought that the individual Germans, fathers of children, would have murdered in a cruel way children of other nationalities, even infants?

The normal, average, human mind could not have comprehended this, and in fact the Nazi's unfortunate victims did not believe it even when they were concentrated around the pits or on the roads towards the gas chambers.

Had such things happened before in the history of mankind, had the victims known the true intentions of Nazi Germany, they would have fought with all their strength. They would have escaped to the forests, to the mountains, to the fields and fought. Only the last transports realized the truth.

Testimony of a survivor of the Warsaw Ghetto, before an Israeli tribunal, in the year 1961.

Mrs. Zivia Lubetkin Zuckermann belonged to the very few who remained alive after the Warsaw uprising. She recounted how the Germans, right from the beginning of the Warsaw occupation (1939), degraded all the inhabitants of the city, but especially the Jews. They were degraded, humiliated, beaten severely and forced to perform hard labor.

In order to be recognized, as subhumans, they were forced to wear the yellow stars on their garments.

Already in 1939, the Jews were under no protection of the law and the Germans could do whatever they wanted, even murder undisturbed by the Nazi law. On the day of atonement (Yom-Kipur) of the year, 1940 (Autumn) there was an announcement over the radio that henceforth the Jews must live in separate sections of the city in the so-called "*Ghetto.*" The ghetto was guarded by the Gestapo, but simple German soldiers, not only the Gestapo, could come into the ghetto to plunder, to kill, to torture and to do whatever they liked. She told of growing hunger, of children begging for a piece of bread, walking around with swollen bellies and digging in garbage pails for potato scraps.

People did not believe at the beginning, in spite of the deepening misery, that in the twentieth century a nation would pronounce a sentence of death on an entire race, without any reason.

In July, 1942, the ghetto was informed that all those who were without a job would be transported to the East, where "Conditions would be better."

At the beginning, some believed the German promises, but later it was found that they were sent to Treblinka extermination camp.

The Jews, continued Mrs. Zuckermann, started to prepare themselves. They bought and accumulated a small armory of

The Arrest and Rescue of Mussolini

Warsaw is burning. The Germans realized that in spite of their enormous superiority in manpower and ammunition, the defenders fought to their last drop of blood and did not surrender. General Stroop ordered flame throwers to be used to set fire to all the houses. The defenders threw themselves on the Germans, attacking them with bare hands.

People jumping from the burning houses.

One of the Jewish heroes, who lived in the bunkers and tunnels under rubble and ruins, detected by the Nazi beasts.

Major-General Stroop, destroyed the Warsaw Ghetto by burning the houses. The hiding Jews, forced out of the ruins, were murdered or sent to Auschwitz.

Nazi victims in Warsaw before the execution. Civilians in Warsaw were robbed of their valuables, later packed in cattle trains and sent to concentration camps.

Ghetto fighters in Warsaw caught by the Germans. They were forced out of the ruined bunkers by poisonous and irritating gasses and by flame throwers which set fire to the houses. The people were murdered on the spot.

rifles, grenades, Molotov cocktails (gasoline-filled bottles with rags for wicks) and other home-made bombs.

The uprising, she said, began on April 18, 1943.

"We learned, at midnight, that the ghetto had been surrounded by German troops.

"Morning came. I was standing by an attic window, and suddenly I saw thousands of German soldiers enter the ghetto, as though they were going to the front against Russia."

But the fighters, who were lightly armed, were very few in comparison with the heavily armed Germans.

Those were German officers and soldiers, who were afraid to fight the Russians but preferred to fight the inhabitants of the ghetto. Real heroes of the Super-race.

Mrs. Zuckermann was part of a group of twenty men and women. She said, and I quote:

"It was strange to see these twenty Jewish men and women standing up against the great enemy, glad and merry because we knew that although they would conquer us, we would go down fighting."

Mrs. Zuckermann threw back her thin shoulders and continued.

"Many of you will not believe it, but when the Germans came up to our post, marching by, we threw on them those hand grenades and bombs and we saw German blood flowing on the streets of Warsaw, instead of the usual blood of their victims.

"It was a miracle, wonderful to see, German heroes retreating in confusion, leaving their dead and wounded behind."

The reader must understand the myth of German invincibility and the terrible fear of seeing any German in the ghetto.

It was a big surprise for the fighters as well as for the Nazi criminals.

"The Germans came back," she continued. "The fighting lasted many more days, weeks and months. We suffered enormous casualties. It was clear to everyone that we'd not be able to remain alive.

"We were fighting to avenge our brothers and it was easier to die in this way."

* * *

Enough with German atrocities and persecution of innocent defenseless people. Let's turn now to the war itself. The Germans, as we know, had lost by then North Africa, and the Allies were preparing for another assault, on the continent of Europe. The Russians achieved an enormous victory at Stalingrad and Field Marshal Paulus, the German General who surrendered, remained in Russian captivity. But the Nazis did not learn any lesson; they were preparing the summer offensive on the Russian front.

They believed that eliminating the Kursk Salient would open the way to Moskow again.

In the spring of 1943, Stalin felt very uneasy. Rumors were circulating that Hitler tried to make a separate peace agreement with England and U. S. America.

Although the Russians achieved spectacular victories, the war was not won as yet by any stretch of the imagination. This was before the battle of Kursk.

Stalin was nervous, restless, and ordered the press to praise the Allies' achievement in North Africa.

Here something extraordinary and unexpected happened, namely:

On May 22, 1943, the Presidium of the Communist International announced the dissolution of the Comintern. This was a gesture to please the Allies. Stalin wanted to show that the Soviets did not intend to interfere in the social structure of other states and that America and England should not be afraid of Communism being forcibly spread to their countries.

He relaxed also the surveillances over the churches.

Here Stalin again overdid himself, because he had sworn on Lenin's grave never to abandon the cause of world revolution.

Before starting the offensive, Hitler wanted to lull the Russians into a false sense of security and to check their self-confidence.

In June, 1943, before the planned offensive, the Germans arranged a secret conference with the Russians at *Kirovograd*, which was inside the German-occupied territory, midway between Kiev and Odessa and east of Uman.

Molotov and Ribbentrop were present. Hitler demanded all

the territory west of the Dnieper River including the Ukraine. Molotov said, and justly so, that the Germans would have to withdraw to the previous prewar 1941 border.

As I mentioned above, we have to take in consideration the fact that Stalin was not satisfied with his Allies, because the second front in the West had not materialized up to this time, and in addition he was very suspicious of England and America.

He would prefer to stay on the side and watch how Hitler fought the West.

He, Stalin, would come in at the appropriate moment with the rested and better-trained Russian armies.

Hitler, the megalomaniac, was oblivious to the fact that this was June, 1943, and not the year 1940.

Instead of taking advantage of the golden opportunity of arranging a separate peace with the Russians, Hitler pulled out another deception from his sleeves by leaking out information to the Western Powers about the conference. The Russians left the conference disgusted, and all the material of the parley and the discussions were destroyed.

One of the German Generals, who was present at the conference, told this story to the British Army historian Basil Hart. Otherwise, it would have been completely unknown to history.

In view of the preparation of the Kirovograd Conference, and the desire of Hitler and his henchmen to make a separate peace with one of the Allied forces, by deception and subterfuge, a milder wind started to blow in Auschwitz at the end of May and during June, 1943.

Very few transports arrived, and finally they ceased. The Krematoria stopped functioning. No more beatings or gassings of human beings. The black smoke of the chimneys was extinguished. "Block Seven," which was a stop-over of Nazi victims to the gas chamber, was changed to a hospital, like Block Eight.

They now needed real doctors for treatment of the sick. We did not understand the abrupt change of Nazi behavior and conduct. We were right in assuming that some kind of peace arrangements were in the offing. But they were still on the horizon. Although we didn't know anything about the Kirovograd conference, our hope was based on the desistance of the atrocities and inactivities of the Nazi factories of death.

A drastic change took place on Block Seven. They started to restore and renovate the berths, the walls, the leaking roof. Broken windows were replaced with new ones. The sick prisoners were not transferred any more to the gas chambers. The trucks of death did not arrive.

Prisoners treated and cured were sent back to the camp (MännerLager) where they returned to work. The usual beatings and harassment ceased.

Dr. Heidenfeld and myself were transferred to Block Seven to make the necessary changes and to restructure all the barrack in order to set up a hospital on the level of "Block Eight" or "Block Twelve."

Dr. Heidenfeld, as the oldest doctor among us, who came from Breslau, Germany, was designated as the chief. The barrack was divided in four departments (Stuben).

"Stube" I for the Pflegers and orderlies.

"Stube" II for Internal diseases under supervision of Dr. Gorlicki.

"Stube" III for convalescents, where I was the doctor in charge.

"Stube" IV for very sick prisoners with Dr. Knott (Poland).

I met Dr. Gorlicki, in Poland, after the liberation. He is practicing probably in France at present. Dr. Knott survived also and is practicing medicine (gynecology) in Rehovoth, Israel.

The very sick received white bread, instead of the usual black, and a better soup called "Diet soup," which was prepared on "Block Twelve" and which had to be distributed to Block Eight and the women's camp also. The later was located near our camp. A small carriage was used to bring the white bread and "Diet soup" to the women's camp.

One afternoon, I decided to participate in transporting food to the women's camp. I heard very much about the suffering of the female inmates in this section of Birkenau. Four of us had to carry the food. We were warned by our Block senior not to talk to any of the female prisoners, because it was punishable very severely. Dr. Goldstein had been punished with three months of S.K. (Straf Kommando-penal commando) for exchanging a few words with a woman. When we entered the female camp, we saw women in such miserable conditions that they defy any description. No wonder that many committed suicide.

The soup and the white bread had to be put in front of the hospital. We had no permission to enter. Female inmates took over the kettles of soup, and brought back the empty receptacles.

I was standing near a man who used to carry the food to the female camp, almost daily. I turned to him and asked him to tell me about the women's camp because I was there for the first time.

"Tell me, please, are the women being treated the same as men?"

He looked at me and said, "Exactly the same. Sometimes even worse. The Germans treat them like dirt. A small furuncle on the body causes immediate transfer to the gas chamber."

We returned to our camp and I promised myself not to visit any more the female camp, because it awoke in me a kind of depression and despondency that I had not experienced previously.

For the sake of completeness, comprehensiveness and the benefit of future historians, I'll describe here in more details the infamous Block Seven and the orderlies who worked there.

It was a delapidated barrack similar to any other one in Birkenau, and separated by a spacious yard from "Block Eight," which I described earlier.

The entry led to a small vestibule, which had a small room on each side, right and left. In the right room slept the block senior Mr. Witold, and the Russian Andrei, who supervised the goods in the camp (Warenhaus). In the left room lived the deputy of the block senior, Mr. Pepan, a Czech, who will play a role later in the separate hospital camp (Revier).

Vis a vis, on the other end of the center hall, was a small room where the three bookkeepers lived. "Mr. Zollman," whom I described previously, was a very decent person. He was a tall man, considered handsome, and came from Slovakia. He risked his life many times to save others, and was a valuable asset to the prisoners. He remained spotless in the dirty soil of Birkenau. Mr. Zollman lives at present in Rehovoth, Israel. The other bookkeeper was Mr. Gang, who did not enjoy a good reputation. People were afraid of him, although I didn't know the reason thereof. Maybe from his past activities.

The third bookkeeper was Mr. Gorin, a college graduate who spoke a few languages. He didn't live in harmony with Gang. These three bookkeepers played a particular role, caused by their special positions.

There were also a tailor and a watchmaker. Both operated for the Germans and therefore were influential in the camp.

"Gezele" was one of the orderlies, slightly deaf, about forty years old. He was an old-timer in Birkenau and therefore very influential. He regretted a lot of things done in the past and had become repentant and a reformer.

"Maier" from France was a nice decent fellow. The soup and coffee were distributed by "Felix," also a prisoner from France. There was "Ismach," a young fellow who spent most of his adolescent life under the German occupation and understood life as presented by the Germans. He was tough toward the sick prisoners and even towards his own father.

The Germans were frightened of contracting contagious diseases like typhus or dysentery, etc.

Therefore they used to order from time to time the evacuation of the hospital barracks and the pouring of lysol inside the berths and over the walls.

One day, I was informed that Mr. Fuks, the ex-senior of the Judenrat from Wolkowysk, who arrived on my transport, had been brought from work to "Block Eight" semi-unconscious. He was supposed to be in Stube III, but I couldn't find him.

Therefore I decided to call out his name loud, maybe he'd answer.

"Mr. Fuks, where are you?" I called.

Nobody answered. I called again his name. Finally I heard a very weak and low voice coming out from one of the middle berths.

"I am here. Please . . . please!"

I came near him and saw Mr. Fuks lying flat, motionless. He did not recognize me.

"Who are you?" he asked. I told him.

"I was beaten up by a German, at work. I feel very weak. I cannot breath.... My head is noisy.... My ears are ringing.... Darkness in front of my eyes.... They carried me back to the camp and put me here."

I examined his pulse and heart. He was really very weak and had, probably, internal injuries caused by the beatings.

Under the circumstances of Birkenau, nothing could be done to save him. I gave him some tablets to strengthen his heart, and analgesics for the pain.

The gong was jingling, and I had to return to my place. I asked the Pfleger-doctor near him to watch him during the night and help him as much as he could.

Mr. Fuks died in the middle of the night and perished like any other victim of Nazi bestiality. He was a nice, quite fellow, caught in the jaws of a brute. G-d bless his soul.

More and more sick prisoners were admitted on "Block Seven." I was working many hours trying to help the sick and to send them back to their respective blocks as early as possible. Dr. Zenkteller used to come very often for control, and then every sick person was in big danger. He always beat up a few weak and sick prisoners, including the doctors. Nothing could be done because he was trusted fully by the Germans.

"Gezelle" came to me and said, "You are working many hours. But you have to relax a little bit also."

He presented me with a gift, a nice pen and a silver pencil.

Dr. Zenkteller had always found faults with Dr. Heidenfeld. He considered him to be a competitor for his position because Dr. Heidenfeld was a German from Breslau, spoke a perfect German, and was a very respectable physician. Dr. Zenkteller harassed him, beat him frequently, and tried to eliminate and annihilate him.

I got recognition from the orderlies for my work and treatment of the prisoners. Even the bookkeepers were of the same opinion. They admired my drawings of the temperature charts, the working of many hours, the examining and treating of the sick and above all my ability to communicate with the Greeks in Italian or Spanish.

An orderly had found in my bed my original Italian diploma, which he could not understand. Since then, they had respected me more, not knowing exactly my position in the free world.

The Germans provoked and caused the outbreak of the Second World War by attacking Poland. They seized Austria and grabbed Czechoslovakia. Pacts and agreements were not worth the paper on which they were written. Russia was attacked disregarding any treaty and contract.

The tide of the war turned around. Instead of victories, there were defeats. After the disaster of Stalingrad came the retreat on all the fronts. North Africa was lost and had to be evacuated. The Allies prepared an assault on Europe. Frustration in Italy, disappointment in Germany.

Now the Nazi lords wanted peace.

"We must have peace. Germany never won a war fighting simultaneously on two fronts," screamed Goebels.

They tried with the West and then with the East. To no avail. Nobody trusted them. How could one have confidence in a nation which murdered millions of innocent human beings and which built factories of death, whose cruelty and crimes surpassed anything seen before?

On 7/5/1943, The Germans launched operation "*Citadel*." The salient of Kursk was attacked with so much armor that the sky was completely black from the smoke of the burning tanks alone. The Russians were prepared for this attack. They fought valiantly and repelled the Germans, inflicting many casualties in men and destroying many tanks and war materiel.

On 7/10/1943, the Allies landed in Sicily, which was occupied within one week. Hitler called off the battle of Kursk because the losses in men and ammunition had reached staggering proportions.

Since then the Germans had retreated on all fronts.

On 7/15/1943, the Russian counteroffensive began.

Orel, north of Kursk, was occupied on 8/4/43. Kharkov was taken on 8/23/43. Smolensk was recaptured on 9/25/43 and

Kiev, the capital of Ukraine, on 11/6/43. Dissatisfaction spread through Italy. On 7/25/43 Mussolini was arrested by the King and replaced by Badoglio.

Although Mussolini was rescued by the Germans, Italy surrendered on 9/8/43 and a month later, on 10/13/43, she declared war on Germany, in accordance with the wishes of the Italian people, who hated the Germans with all their hearts and minds.

Rome was still occupied by Germany. Italian soldiers and civilians were arrested and sent to German concentration camps, where they perished.

The gas chambers started to be active again and the Krematoria resumed the burning of the bodies.

Dr. Zenkteller felt like a fish in water again. The Nazis needed him and he became a very prominent figure in Birkenau. Every Greek was sent to "Block Seven" or "Block Eight" with the diagnosis of malaria. Many had never been sick, some had simple colds.

Dr. Zenkteller, unexpectantly, appeared on our block and selected fifty-six Greeks as sick on malaria, in spite of the fact that the majority of them had no fever and no malaria. How he could make a diagnosis, without the blood examination for plasmodium malaria and without being present during an attack, was behind my comprehension.

Next morning, the SS man Klehr arrived. He ordered all the fifty-six Greeks to assemble in front of "Block Eight."

One after another, the young, healthy, handsome Greeks entered the little rooms, where the German was waiting for them with the syringe. The Greeks found themselves in a strange country, without any knowledge of German or Polish, and they sincerely believed that they were getting vaccinations against contagious diseases. They voluntarily submitted to this procedure. The syringe, alas, contained, instead of vaccine, the destructive chemical Phenol. All of them died within minutes.

A completely blind young Greek was admitted to "Block Seven." His affliction was not caused by illness of the eyes but by avitaminosis and beatings over the occipital region. I felt sorry for him for being sightless in a German concentration camp. One day he called me to his berth and said:

"Doctor, I dreamed about you. We were all in Athens, the capital of Greece. Everybody invited you to his home. But you accepted my bidding and entered my house. I was very glad of having you with us."

"But, how could you have seen and recognized me, when you are blind?" I wondered.

"Although I am sightless, I know exactly how you look. I don't know how to explain it, but it is a fact."

One Sunday afternoon, the sun was shining brightly. Dr. Zenkteller ordered all the Greeks to assemble. There were a few thousand Greeks in Birkenau. All of them had to be examined by Dr. Zenkteller. The examination consisted of an abdominal palpation in order to find out a possible enlargement of the liver and spleen.

One by one had to pass quickly in front of Dr. Zenkteller, who made the examination. How he could have found enlarged livers and spleens under such conditions constitutes a mystery to me even now. Very often a hardened or contracted abdominal muscle could give the false impression of an enlarged liver. In one afternoon a few thousand Greeks were examined and the diagnosis of malaria was made on many of them. To our surprise they were not killed in Birkenau but transferred to the concentration camp of Maidanek near Lublin, allegedly for further experiments and death.

Another doctor was accepted as a pfleger on "Block Seven." He was arrested in France and brought to Birkenau in 1942. He had to help me in my work. His name was Dr. Schillist. Because of an insignificant infringement he was punished before coming to us with the usual three months of S.K. (penal company), which occupied Barrack # 1 in Birkenau.

"How was life in S.K.?" I asked.

"There was no life at all there," he said. "I must have a very strong constitution to be able to endure there for three months. The very first night I had to sleep on a floor made out of hard cement, without a cover. I shivered all night and couldn't sleep because of the cold. Next morning I had to go to work, which consisted of very hard labor. We had to toil while running. If the prisoner didn't run fast enough he was beaten severely with truncheons and clubs. We worked more than horses, undernourished and exhausted. Often we had to overexert ourselves while immersed in cold water or digging dirt and mud out of the grave-pit (Kiesgrube), where it was wet and very cold.

"I see now, that a human being is stronger than iron. No slave ever worked so hard."

"Could you rest a little bit after the roll-call?"

"No. We had to continue to work after the roll-call, and were beaten in addition for no reason at all at the same time. Many died from exhaustion, weakness and hard work. Many more committed suicide.

"Our block had always been locked, which signified that no prisoner could go out to another barrack."

"How could you endure such torture?"

"It was a miracle. They needed a doctor in the block, and fortunately they took me. Otherwise, I would have succumbed in a few days."

"What did you do as a doctor-Pfleger?"

"My job consisted in distributing some tablets of aspirin and taking the sick prisoners to the hospital. I had to help, also, to clean the barrack and do other odd jobs. The most difficult chore was to clean the so-called "standing cells" every morning at ten A.M. The later were located in barrack # 2 (Sonder Kommando). Four prisoners were compelled to stand in a very small cubicle all night long. In the morning most of the prisoners were dead. The smell of the excretion and perspiration accumulated during the night was impossible to describe. I had to enter inside the cubicle, which had insufficient air, and clean it."

There were many other punishments prepared and set for the prisoners of Birkenau. As I mentioned previously, the same sort of torture was provided, also, in Auschwitz I (Stamm Lager) on Block Eleven. Whereas the torture tools and the barracks in Birkenau were destroyed or burned after the war, in Auschwitz I they *remained intact* and preserved for all humanity to see the terrible, unbelievable tools of Nazi bestiality.

One of the sick prisoners was an old man who served in the Polish army as a general. He was over eighty years old. Every morning he used to get up and perform physical exercises. He claimed that they improved his blood circulation and prolonged his life. He had a strong desire to survive the war and see what was going to happen to the German nation which exhibited atrocities that he as an old man never dreamed possible.

Dr. Schillist and myself had to sit near a table, which was located at the end of the "Stube" (department), near a window. We used to work there many hours to prepare the case histories and to administer some treatment for the sick in the realm of possibilities which we were able to organize from the new transports, like different medications, bandages, and even Quinine tablets for malaria. The window was half-broken and a strong wind used to blow on us, which disturbed us enormously. To avoid the wind, I used to bend down over the table and let the draft or air current flow over my back. In this way we were able to continue our work.

Looking through the broken window, I noticed two old rabbis from Greece standing near the next barrack and warming themselves under the sun. I asked Dr. Schilist what was the significance of keeping these old men in Birkenau. Normally the elderly, even the middle-aged, were sent immediately from the ramp to the gas chambers. They never entered the camp.

Dr. Schillist explained.

"The reason of this unusual phenomenon is that the Germans wanted to show to the world that the publicity about the gas chambers and Krematoria was not correct. They photographed the old people, sitting quietly, taking sunbaths, and printed them in many newspapers. Sooner or later they'll perish."

After a few days I didn't see the rabbis any longer. They disappeared from the scene. The Nazis lived all the time on lies. Their structure was based on fraud, swindle and deception. These photographs were one of the misleading tricks in the chain of Nazi duplicity and treacherousness.

One of the prisoners, who worked in the Sonder Kommando (special commando or company), was Mr. Bekenstein from Wolkowysk. He had a master's degree in history from the University of Wilno. His father was a tailor in Wolkowysk and his ambition in life was to educate his children. His brother was engaged to Chasha, the pretty and energetic sister of Michle.

I met him while taking water from "Block Seven."

"How are you, my friend?" I asked him, "and where are you working?"

"I belong to the Sonder Kommando and came here to get some water."

The activities of the "Sonder Kommando" were not entirely clear to me, and therefore I asked him for explanation and description of this special group. Mr. Bekenstein explained.

"They are prisoners assigned to take out the dead people from the gas chambers and burn them in the krematoria.

"Transports after transports of young healthy people from all over the world, but mainly from different nationalities of Europe, are being hauled and delivered to Auschwitz."

"Do the people gassed by 'Cyclon B' suffer much?" I asked.

"We believe that they do undergo enormous torture," answered my friend. "Which is evident by the following facts:

"1. Heart-breaking screams, yelling and lamentations at the beginning of the gassing.

"2. Nail signs and lacerations on the bodies of the victims, who suffered pain and agonizing choking sensations, who in death struggle tucked their nails into the flesh of their nearby neighbors.

"3. The faces of the sufferers portrayed torture.

"4. Vomiting blood on the floor.

"Very often, before throwing in the Cyclon B the air from the gas chambers was removed by special machines, which caused the agonizing choking sensation, the bursting of the blood vessels and vomiting."

I was shocked hearing the cruelties and inhuman ruthlessness of the Nazis.

"Do the Germans keep always the same prisoners at work at the Sonderkommando?"

"No. Very often they murder the special Sonder Commando and choose a new commando from the new transports."

Mr. Bekenstein had a special permission to go out and bring water for the S.K. Block.

The Germans were afraid of the disclosure of the above atrocities and this was the reason that this group was locked in their barracks and never permitted to mingle with the other prisoners. They didn't want to have living witnesses of their terribleness and nefariousness.

"How many bodies are burned in twenty-four hours?"

"All the four krematoria in Birkenau are able to burn about eight to ten thousand corpses in twenty-four hours. If the number of the dead bodies exceed the capacity of the Krematoria, the Germans use in addition wood pyres and pits.

"The black smoke and frightening fires coming out of the chimneys originate from burning human beings. The pungent odor smelled miles away is produced by the scorched human flesh and bones."

During one of the Greek transports, a young boy about twelve years old was able to hide himself during the selection. When the trucks took away the people assigned to die in the gas chambers, he managed to enter the camp together with those selected. His father, fifty years old, was taken to the gas chamber, but his mother and sister entered the women's camp.

The boy was nice-looking and very affable. At first he lived in the bookkeeper's room on "Block Seven," later in "Stube One," in the same berth of Mr. Katz, who tried to get for him a regular number and make it possible for the boy to remain in the camp. Finally, he got the number engraved on his left forearm.

The boy craved to see his mother and sister. He was allowed to participate in carrying over the kettles of "Diet soup" from Block Twelve to the women's camp. From a distance, he recognized his sister. At the beginning, he was shocked and couldn't utter a word, and just looked at her. How strange she looked. Malnourished, tired and without hair on her scalp. Later he came to his senses and screamed, "Sister my sister. . . ." He wanted to run to her. The other prisoners stopped him, because it was very dangerous.

His sister heard his call, recognized him too, and with tears in her eyes ran to her mother to tell her the good news. The boy returned to our camp very satisfied and happy. He saw his sister with his own eyes.

The weak and dying, the hopeless and the very sick, were all transferred to "Stube IV," where the orderly was the young Ismach. The Germans ordered that those prisoners who were very ill and those suffering from diarrhea be put on the lower berth naked, which was pavement covered with hard cement. Most of them died after a few days.

At night, the corpses were lying outside their berths, occupying all the length of the passageway leading to the toilet. Sodom! Gomorrah! Alsation hell! Den of iniquity! All these were merely children's play compared to the torture of the victims in agony. Hell, Gehenna, Hades, was a paradise in comparison with the abyss of "Stube IV" in Birkenau.

The terror of Birkenau was, at that time, a German whose name was Schillinger. He used to beat and murder without any reason.

He loved to perform "Special Exercises" with the prisoners and in the following manner:

"Rollen!" (To roll). The prisoners had to lie down in the mud and dirt and roll about one hundred fifty yards.

"Hupfen!" (To hop). The prisoners had to put their hands behind the knees, stand on the toes and hop. The latter was very difficult to perform for a prolonged time. Whoever stopped was beaten and forced to continue. When one of the unfortunate prisoners fell on the ground, not being able to continue, he was flogged very severely and often killed.

One afternoon, Schillinger entered "Block Seven" to call the two Hungarian prisoners, who performed the tattoo (tätowieren) by engraving the numbers on the forearms of the prisoners who were selected to enter the camp. He found them both sitting idle on their berths. For this reason, all the pflegers and the orderlies of Block Seven were ordered to assemble at 7 P.M. in front of the barrack for exercises, so-called "sport."

We were thunderstruck and apprehensive of Schillinger's announcement. Some might not survive such an ordeal. The block senior went to the S.D.G. (the deputy of the German doctor) to complain, and it was settled that the "Exercises" and the so-called "sport" would be performed by the S.D.G. and not by Mr. Schillinger.

Exactly, at 7 P.M. the S.D.G. appeared and the sport started.

The S.D.G. was Mr. Klehr, the same German who injected the phenol into the hearts of the Greeks.

"Laufen!" (to run) was the first order, followed by "Rollen" and "Hupfen." The later was the worst. This time we had to hop on our toes in a semi-sitting position with our upper extremities stretched forward. It was very tiring and strenuous.

We hopped all through the length of the spacious yard and back. Many fell on the ground because they could not continue. Dr. Heindenfeld looked very pale, exhausted, and was not able to hold out. He fell on the ground motionless, and his respiration was very heavy. The German came near him and flogged the poor Dr. Heidenfeld over his back, head, and legs. Dr. Heidenfeld remained lying, he couldn't get up. He was still able to breath. Next Dr. Fastman fell, the specialist of ear, nose, and throat. Many others lay on the ground. They couldn't continue.

"Hüpfen," shouted the German. I exerted all my strength to persevere, but I felt that my capacity to endure was diminishing. I was still hopping and leaping like a frog. Finally, the block senior, who was in good terms with the S.D.G., told him, "Please stop it, because I won't have pflegers any more."

The S.D.G. heeded the pleas of the block senior, stopped the "sport" and left.

We returned to our block half-dead. During the entire next month most of us felt exhausted and had difficulties walking.

Next morning, when I was sitting as usual near the window, I heard a familiar voice.

"Dr. Harsaw, please, doctor. . . . I have a letter for you. . . . From Michle. . . . She is alive."

This was the younger Itzkowitz, who handed over a letter to me. I opened it up and read.

"Dear Doctor! I was informed today that you are alive, which pleased me very highly. All my family was murdered. You are, almost, the only relative who remained. Please answer my letter through the same messenger. How do you feel? What are you doing? I feel very depressed. I don't dare to think about the future.

Faithfully Yours,
Michle."

I looked at the letter and asked myself, Was it possible, that she was alive? She had, always, been delicate and weak. How was she able to endure all the atrocities?

I looked over the letter again, examined the handwriting. Yes, this was her script. She wrote it. I took a paper and wrote:

"Dear Michle! I received your letter and was proud of your accomplishment. I gave up, already, any hope of seeing you alive. It remains without saying that I was overjoyed. Don't be depressed! Fight with all your strength and resist the evil perpetrators with all the power of your will. I have a hunch and a premonition that you'll make it. You have to do it for the sake of your family, which perished. I am working as a pfleger and my health is, thank G-d, still good. I am going to fight hard and hope to see the lights of freedom. Write what you need.

Faithfully yours,
Dr. Harsaw."

I closed the letter and handed over to Mr. Itzkowotz, who informed me that Michle worked in the clothing company (Bekleidung Kommando) and that her group passed every day through the men's camp.

Next day, I received another letter by the same messenger.

"Dear Doctor! I am passing daily through the men's camp because I belong to the clothing commando. If you'll wait near the main road, we'll be able to see each other. Keep healthy.

Faithfully yours,
Michle."

Next evening after our short roll call, when all the workers returned to the camp, I stood near the main road and waited for the group of women passing our camp.

After a short while, I saw the female group passing on the main road. The female Kapo, in the first row, followed by the inmates. I searched with my eyes the passing group and didn't see Michle. Suddenly, I noticed Chasha from Wolkowysk, who showed me with her hand where Michle was walking. She looked very pale and weak, and had lost a lot of weight. She walked in the tenth row with a kerchief over her head.

The older Itzkowitz Moshe, who worked previously on Block Seven, was transferred to another block. He had much less to eat now. He came to me asking for a plate of soup. Every day, I organized for the two brothers Itzkowitz a few plates of soup. I had to help them so they wouldn't break down.

In a few days the older Itzkowitz told me that he was going to be transferred to the concentration camp of *Yavozna*. It was a very tough camp belonging to Auschwitz III (Buna). The work was very hard in the coal mines. I felt very sorry for him. He was going to need a lot of stamina to endure the hard work and the unusual harassment at this particular camp.

The prisoners were considered not only subhumans but guinea pigs, rats or dogs, which justified in the eyes of the Nazis the many experiments performed in the German concentration camps. Here are a few cases which I witnessed myself:

1. *Sterilization*. Mr. B. I. came to me one day with tears in his eyes, complaining that he was to appear before the German doctor for sterilization by x-ray machines. They did it with hundreds of prisoners. I advised him to put the electrode of the x-ray machine, not on the testicles, but on the thigh. In this way he would not be sterilized, but he might develop a burn or an injury of the thigh, which would heal in a short time. Mr. B. I. followed my advice. He kept the electrode over the thigh, and the testicles were not injured. He was very happy, and overjoyed to avoid the dreadful sterilization.

Mr. B.I. lives at present in U.S.A., married, and has a handsome boy. I was glad of having contributed somewhat to his happiness.

Mr. Leon was one of the two prisoners who lived on "Block Seven." He performed the tattooing of the newly arrived prisoners. The reader will remember that the two tattooists were the cause of the famous "sport" or "exercises" performed on the orderlies of "Block Seven," which nearly killed us.

Leon was a young, handsome-looking man of about twenty-five years old. Suddenly he received an order to appear in the experimentation barracks of Auschwitz. He returned after ten days telling us the dreadful story, that he was completely sterilized. Both testicles were removed.

"I would rather die than live in such a world and be a cripple all my life."

We encouraged him, saying that all of us would be killed, but he, Leon, might remain alive and be a living witness of German bestiality. Leon continued, "At the beginning, I wanted to touch the electric wires and be executed, but the desire to see the end of the war and to repay the Germans for all the atrocities committed on my friends, my family and myself kept me alive."

Sterilization was performed on prisoners, men and women, by surgery or x-rays.

Dr. Carl Clauberg was experimenting with women on "Block Ten" of Auschwitz I. Here is a letter sent by the German physician Dr. Clauberg to Himmler on 6/7/1943.

"Should the investigations conducted by myself continue as expected—and I foresee no obstacles—then in the nearest future, I hope to be able to say that a properly trained surgeon, working in a suitably equipped surgery, with perhaps ten medical assistants, will most probably be in the position to sterilize several hundred or even one thousand persons in the course of one day."

Dr. Clauberg believed that he had found a method of mass sterilization of the Slavs and other subhumans.

2. Professor Hirt, the director of the anatomical institute of Strasburg, was in charge of collecting human skulls. Here are his own words.

"We have a large collection of skulls of all races. The campaign in Russia enabled us to collect, also, many skulls of Jewish commissars.... The prisoners should be taken alive, then a series of photographs should be performed, followed by anthropological measurements.... the prisoner then should be killed, being careful that the skull is not damaged. A physician should sever the head of the commisar, put it in a tin with a special preservative."

The skulls were collected and deposited in Strasbourg.

3. Dr. Heissheyer injected children with tuberculosis and watched them dying.

4. Dr. Rasher performed experiments in Dachau concentration camp.

Thirty prisoners were put in a van, from which the air was

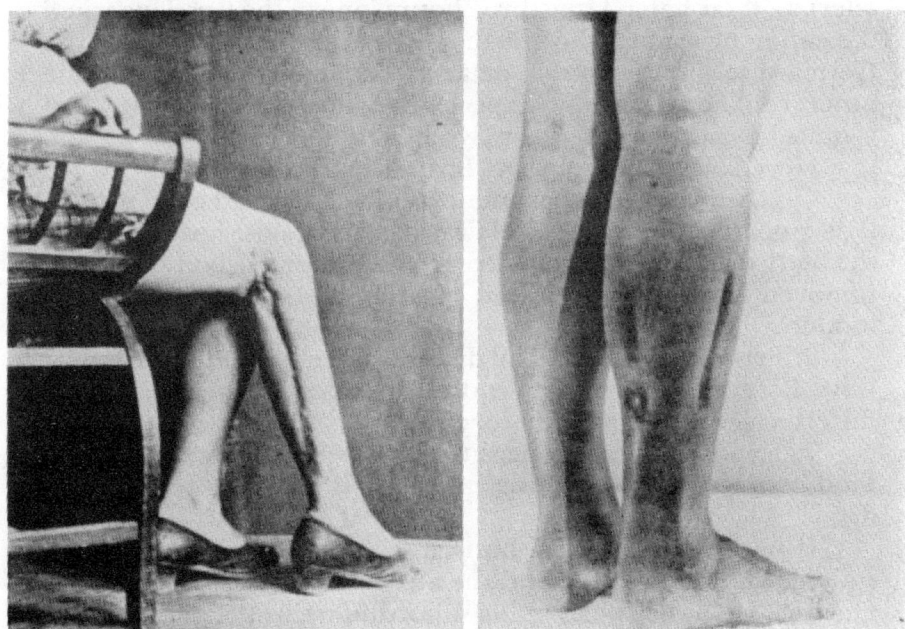
Polish women's legs disfigured by human guinea-pig operations

pumped out. Through a window he observed how they died by hemorrhages of the lungs and brain.

5. Prisoners were put in icy water. Blood was taken from the victim each time that the temperature fell by 1° degrees C, and analyzed. When the victim lost consciousness, he was taken out from the water and revived by putting him between two females.

Alfred Rosenberg, the notorious Nazi theoretician, described in his book (Memories of Alfred Rosenberg) the following episode:

"Two Russian prisoners were ordered by Dr. Rasher to

enter a tank of freezing water. Hour after hour passed and the unfortunate prisoners were still in the water. They suffered enormously. Dr. Rasher refused to give them an injection to alleviate their pain. After three hours, one of the Russians asked the other prisoner, who spoke a little German, 'Please ask the Germans to shoot us and to make an end to our sufferings.' The other replied, 'I do not expect any clemency from the Nazi tyrants.' Death arrived after five hours."

Here is a letter from Dr. Rasher to Himmler.

"In the freezing experiment conducted, it had been proven that quick heating is more efficacious than slow heating, since the body temperature still keeps sinking after the body has been removed from the cold water. Heating by female bodies takes too long."

6. Prisoners with similar diseases were treated in different ways. Later they were killed and autopsied to see the effect of the different treatments on the organs.

7. Exposure of prisoners to the burning sun rays without food or water and observing how long it took the prisoners to die.

Himmler considered himself a man of science and he rationalized the murder and the atrocities in the following way: On 10/4/1943, he spoke to his subordinates in Poland (*Posen*).

"What happens to a Russian or a Czech does not interest me in the least. . . . Whether ten thousand Russian females fall down from exhaustion while digging large anti-tank ditches interests me only insofar as the anti-tank ditch was finished."

Himmler didn't care whether ten thousand young females died or not.

About the mass extermination of women, children in the cities, Himmler explained, "Most of you know, what it means, when one hundred corpses are lying side by side, or five hundred or one thousand corpses. To have stuck it out and . . . at the same time to remain decent fellows, that is what made us hard. *This is a page of glory in our history which has never been written and is never to be written.*"

It is incomprehensible how a Nazi who murdered thousands of innocent people, including children and small infants, would remain a decent fellow.

Dr. Gebhardt, chief of Hohenlgehen Hospital in Berlin, one of the German doctors who performed cruel experiments on prisoners, causing innumerable deaths of innocent human beings and without benefit to science.

The infamous Ilse Koch from Buchenwald. Extradited to Germany. What was the verdict? Note the German newspapers of the time; shocking!

A lampshade made from the tattooed chest of a murdered prisoner; property of Ilsa Koch, wife of the commandant of Buchenwald.

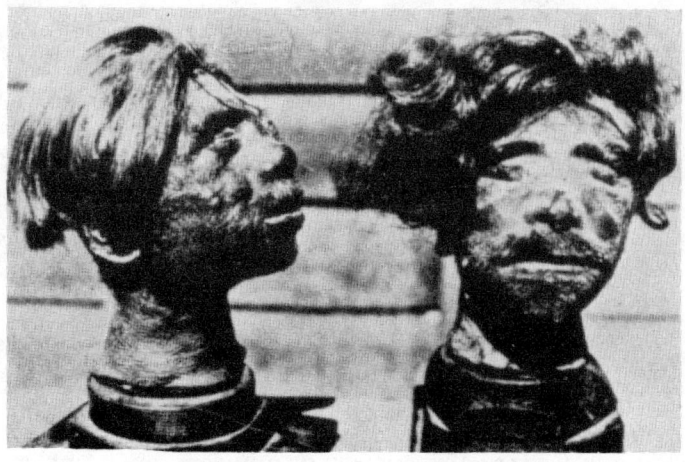

Shrunken heads of human beings, who once lived on this earth like you and me. Property of Ilsa Koch.

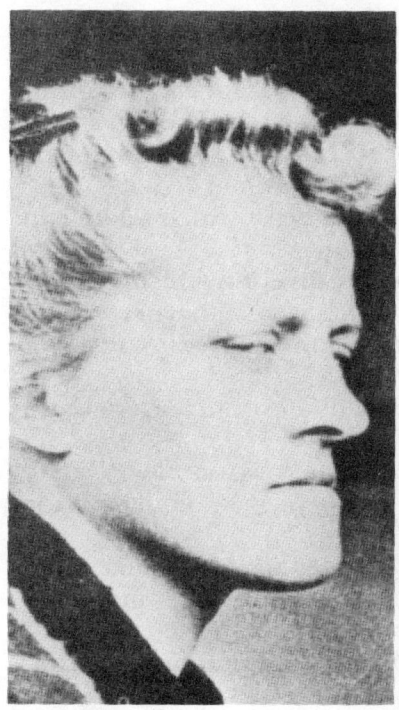 

Hilde Lobauer, a guard in a Nazi concentration camp, exceedingly cruel. German women guards in general surpassed the male guards in ruthlessness, brutality and heartlessness.

The commandant of the prison of Landsberg. Prisoners shot to death can be seen. A pile of human ashes is in sight in the background.

This was the theory and reasoning of a Nazi, the theory of a master race dealing with subhumans.

It was interesting how Himmler criticized Goering for hunting animals. He said, "Goering kills every animal he can shoot. Imagine, a poor deer is grazing peacefully, and up comes the hunter with his gun and shoots the poor animal."

This was Himmler talking, the worst beast which walked on this earth.

Even Hitler, the originator and the inventor, the organizer of all the unheard-of atrocities, on watching a film where animals were chased by the hunters, used to close his eyes in order not to see it.

Was it a deception, a masquerade, or a product of a sick and degenerated mind?

It was true that Goering, the hunter, was a bloodthirsty animal. In talking to Ciano, the son-in-law of Mussolini, he made the following remarks:

"We can not worry about the hunger of the Greeks. This year twenty or thirty million people will die of hunger in Russia. In the concentration camps, the Russian prisoners started to eat each other (cannibals). It was obvious that if humanity was condemned to die of hunger, the last to die would be our two peoples."

The number of sick prisoners admitted on "Block Seven" increased by leaps and bounds. No place was available anymore. They wanted to put the ailing sufferers on my "Stube," on the down berth (floor), where they would die like on "Stube Four."

With the help of the bookkeeper Gorin, I explained to the block senior that first, it would affect all my other patients, and secondly, it was better to have a lower mortality and to send over the sick to "Block Eight," where they had better facilities and a better chance to survive. Finally he agreed with my argument, and my department remained as before.

Mr. Gorin walked with me in the yard, to discuss certain ideas. He would like to speak Italian, it was a beautiful language. He was going to learn twenty words daily. In two months, his vocabulary would reach twelve hundred words, which would enable him to speak Italian. Could I teach him?

I told him that I would be very glad to teach him twenty words daily, but to learn a language it was not enough to know words alone. One needs to know the grammar, the pronunciation, certain sentences, and the ear should be accustomed to the sound of the Italian language.

Most of the healthy good-looking prisoners were afraid to be taken for sterilization. Now, when the hope to get out from the German concentration camps alive increased somewhat, the prisoners shuddered at the idea of sterilization.

Gorin was young, good-looking, and he was afraid also.

"Is it possible," he asked, "to inject the outer covering of the testicles and make it temporarily unhealthy-looking? The Germans operate and make experiments only on healthy testicles."

"Sure," I said. "I'll inject you with some liquid which will make the scrotum swollen. After a few days the scrotum will return to the original condition."

"This is a very good idea," said Gorin. "I'll come to you, as soon as the German order arrives."

One day the German doctor entered our block, accompanied by Dr. Zenkteller, in order to control the charts. Everything was in order.

Dr. Zenkteller got in a habit to visit, often, our block. He detested Dr. Heindenfeld and Dr. Gorlicki, and he beat them often and kicked them with his shoes.

Finally the Germans, on the suggestion of Dr. Zenkteller, nominated a new doctor, whose name was Dr. Stern, as the chief doctor of "Block Seven." Dr. Heidenfeld still remained and worked as a simple pfleger. Dr. Gorlicki lost his job, and had to do hard physical work.

Dr. Stern was born in Vienna, where he said that he practiced gynecology. Later he escaped to Greece, from which the Gestapo brought him to Auschwitz. He made a very good impression on everybody. We all liked him very much. Being from Vienna (Austria) he spoke, naturally, a perfect German.

In Birkenau there were prisoners who survived two or more years in German camps. They were considered "Prominent Prisoners" and were feared by the rest. When sick, they were admitted immediately to Block Twelve, because Dr. Zenkteller looked upon them with awe.

Dr. Goldstein belonged to the prominent prisoners, and when he was punished with S.K. he was transferred to the hospital.

The same happened to a prisoner whose name was *Edek*. He was of Polish nationality and "Tato," the block senior of "Block Eight," admitted him on his block.

Edek was a nice-looking fellow, tall, intelligent, and strong physically. He used to help somewhat on Block Eight, but his mind was occupied with better ideas.

One day he disappeared. We looked for him all over, but we couldn't find him. "Tato," the block senior of barrack eight, was very aggravated, because he carried all the responsibility. On the roll call it was declared that one prisoner was missing (Einer fehlt).

The Germans, accompanied by wild dogs, searched for him all over, even outside the camp. To no avail!

Edek vanished into thin air.

Rumors spread that Edek got in contact with civilians, who prepared for him false personal papers. He left the camp together with other civilians about 3 P.M. wearing a sweater, but without a jacket.

We were very happy that he succeeded. Most of the other escapees were caught, returned to the camp and publicly hanged.

What was going to happen to "Tato" and "Block Eight"? Would the Germans take revenge? Luckily everything ended peacefully. "Tato" had a pull with the Germans. He provided them with valuables, like golden dollars, diamonds, etc. They needed him. They did not want to destroy him. We all returned to our block without any penalty.

This was the beginning of July, 1943, when the Allies made all the preparations for the attack of Italy proper. On 7/10/43, as we mentioned previously, Sicily was invaded.

The Island became isolated, thanks to the Allied navy and air force. The landing succeeded and many towns and villages were occupied. Finally, Palermo, the capital of Sicily, was overrun.

Our hopes to come out alive increased day by day. Maybe some of us would see freedom again.

Gorin, the bookkeeper, told me that he would have agreed to come out, even as an invalid. He would like to see the end of the war, the collapse of Germany and how the world would react to the enormous, unheard-of Nazi atrocities. What would be the treatment of the Nazis and how would the victors behave toward the sainted victims of Nazi bestiality?

Gorin would have been very disappointed. The war ended, Germany surrendered unconditionally. I repeat unconditionally!

Does it mean that Germany had to repay for the atrocities and crimes committed over millions of innocent people who were choked in the gas chambers and burned in the Krematoria?

Does it mean that Germany had to reimburse all the wealth that she robbed from the occupied territories?

Does it mean that the "1000 year Reich" had to rebuild the cities that she destroyed?

Germany after the war had a prosperity unknown in all her previous history. Her currency was the strongest. The perpetrators, who committed the horrible crimes, were getting very mild sentences, if any at all, in the German courts.

No! my friend Gorin, wherever you are, alive or not, it didn't pay to come out an invalid and see what happened to the world after the war ended.

Birkenau was expanding. Many prisoners were arriving. Our camp was changed to a women's camp. The men were moved to a nearby location, the men's camp (Manner Lager) near the Gypsy camp (Zigeunerlager)

Dr. Fastman, the E.N.T. specialist, was going to the women's camp about two or three times weekly to attend those women who had ear, nose and throat afflictions. I asked him to find Michle Pomeraniec and to give her a small package of food. The most important thing was to talk with the block senior and Kapo so they would treat her in a nice way. Dr. Fastman promised to arrange it to the best of his abilities.

The Germans were very much afraid of the spread of contagious diseases, especially typhus. They ordered, for their own protection, the vaccination of all the prisoners. The doctors were ordered to perform the vaccination in all the camp. Dr. Zenkteller was in charge of the project. Each time when he arrived on any block the prisoners as well as the doctors were terrorized.

"You don't know how to give the vaccination," he screamed and hit the doctor with his shoes.

"You don't know how to stretch your arm," and he beat the prisoner.

All the inmates were transferred to the men's camp, only the hospital branches like Barracks Seven, Eight and Twelve still remained in the old camp. The doctors and the sick prisoners were the only occupants of the old murderous camp of Birkenau.

I walked all along the camp. No prisoners, no yelling. Quiet all around. The barracks were open. Papers and broken objects were lying all around. I felt free, nobody bothered me. It seemed that the war was ended, the concentration camp closed and I was milling around visiting the old camp. The only thing that brought me back to the terrible reality were the watch towers, where the German guards stood with their machine guns, ready to shoot and kill.

I visited Block Twenty-Six, where I first arrived when my transport entered Birkenau. I observed the different berths, the place where I slept and suffered. Here was the little room, where the block senior lived and where the brother of Dr. Kaplinski was murdered. I recognized the hall, the places where so many people suffered and died. Here was the famous yard, where the prisoners used to lie naked in agony.

The roll call place and the walls were the only witnesses of past atrocities. Quiet all around. No yelling, no shooting, no screams. I still seemed to hear the sighing and suspiration of the prisoners in their agony.

No sound, no lamentations, awful silence of the grave and death around.

The crimes committed here surpassed any other wrongdoings memorialized in history.

G-d almighty, why didn't you bring on the waters of the flood, as at the time of Noah? The bow in the cloud was not visible on the horizon of Birkenau. It was ashamed and not willing to appear and to remind G-d of His covenant, "Never will any flesh be destroyed by the flood."

I visited "Block Seventeen" where I was a pfleger for the first time. Death-like silence. No prisoners, no shrieks and no shouts. The same beds with straw mattresses. Here was my bed, where I was able to undress for the first time, and where I experienced the play of my muscles, the contractions and the relaxations which took place when my body became free of the constant pressure of the prisoners' clothing.

A warm and mild wind blew through the door, faintly whispering into my ears, "Bravo, Dr. Harsaw, you have survived already almost six months in Birkenau. You are a real hero to be able to sustain such brutalities. Many miracles occurred to you. Let's hope that pretty soon you'll reach the gate of freedom."

I returned to the hospital, "Blocks Seven" and "Eight." Dr. Schillist met me and said:

"Let's visit the S.K. Block Number One, where I spent a few months of my life being penalized by the Germans." We entered the dreadful Block S.K. (penal company). The yard, on which the most horrifying atrocities, unheard of in the history of mankind, were perpetrated, and where semi-living and dying prisoners were lying in droves, was soundless now, and silent.

Here thousands of inmates were hanged, flogged, shot to death. Here reigned Lucifer, Beelzebub, Mephistopheles, the Satan, all day and all night long.

Here the soil was soaked with blood, sweat, and tears of innocent human beings. The spirit of Berlin towered above.

Here the Germans called the hopeless prisoners to volunteer and to be hanged immediately. Many volunteered.

Here on the side, stood the whipping block, where the prisoners were flogged, as a result of which many died and all lost consciousness. Now, it was all quiet.

The S.K. block inside was the same as in other blocks. Triple berths and a hall at the entrance. On the walls were visible sketches made by the prisoners with pencil or charcoal depicting work at the Kiesgrube (Gravel pit), with the "Kapo" beating some prisoners, many lying motionless on the ground.

I asked Dr. Schillist:

"Did the Germans permit these sketches?"

"Yes, they did. They did not believe, and they still don't believe it now, that the world would find out what was happening in Birkenau. They still believe in final victory by using their new weapons."

"Here," continued Dr. Schillist, "is the lower berth where I spent my first night in the S.K. Another few nights, followed by hard physical work during the day, would have meant the end of my life."

Later we entered Block Two, the barrack where the Sonder-Kommando (the special commando which worked at the Krematoria) lived.

Dr. Schillist showed me the most terrible standing cells (Stehzelle), where the victim could not sit, certainly not lie down.

Four prisoners had to stand pressed one against the other, suffocating from lack of air.

Near the floor was a small opening, like a dog's kennel, the prisoner was forced to push himself into, to stay there all night.

Dr. Schillist explained:

"This was a form of torture unknown in the history of mankind. This was a product of a degenerated mind which reached the highest point of perfection."

We left the two wicked blocks to return to our hospital barrack. On the way back, we felt a severe itching, all over our bodies, caused by bugs. Dr. Schillist remarked, "These bugs were fed previously on the bodies of the inmates who lived there. Now, in the absence of the usual tenants, they attacked us."

It took us a few hours to get rid of these starved enthusiasts.

Next morning, we were informed that the hospitals would be transferred to the new location, dubbed "*F Lager*" or hospital camp (Revier).

The Gypsy camp was located between the D and F Lager

(men's and hospital camp respectively). All the camps were separated one from the other by electrically charged wires.

When we arrived at the hospital camp, we saw, on the other side of the wires, the Gypsies—men, women and children.

It was very interesting to see families living together again. We forgot already that such a device and thingumabob existed.

It was dangerous to approach the wires, but we could see them and even talk to them.

The Gypsies were treated by the Nazis exactly the same as the Jews, and were destined to die.

No pity. Complete destruction of the entire race was the goal.

What was the reason of this genocide?

Did the Gypsies harm in any way the German war effort?

Did they dislike each other, for some reason? Nothing at all.

The motive for this genocide was the weakness of the Gypsies. They could be maltreated, murdered and nobody would say anything. They had no government, no representatives to make complaints. There was no risk in massacre, in indiscriminate killing of the Gypsies.

It would help to terrorize the people of the occupied territories and keep them quiet while witnessing the massacres.

The Gypsies lived in very overcrowded and unhygienic quarters. Almost one thousand persons in one block. No wonder that contagious diseases like typhus, typhoid, dysentery spread like fire. As we know, the Germans had one treatment for all epidemic diseases, which was mass murder.

All of them were sent to the gas chambers and exterminated.

We had to carry over certain items from our old camp, which was going to be taken over by the women, to our new camp (hospital, Lager-F). We had to pass the main road where the terror of Birkenau, the Nazi Schillinger, used to stroll very often. Once he met us on the road and, without questions asked, he started to beat us with his truncheon. It was amusing to see how Zenkteller ran away pursued by the German who had in one hand a gun and in the other hand a truncheon. Zenkteller ran for his life too. He was cowardly and scared of Schillinger. He was a hero toward the weak, exhausted sick prisoners, but was frightened to death in front of any German.

From the hospital lager (F-lager-Revier) the chimneys of Krematoria II and III were clearly visible. The black smoke, caused by burning of human beings, was discernible distinctly and prominently. Even Krematoria IV and V were in sight at the end of the hospital camp, near Barrack Eleven.

Starting at the middle of July, 1943, Birkenau had the following separate camps:

Camp a.—Quarantine. The new arrivals lived there six to eight weeks.

Camp b.—Theresienstadt.

Camp c.—Hungarian camp. Prisoners from Hungary.

Camp d.—Men's camp.

Camp e.—Gypsy camp (Zigeunerlager). Family camp for Gypsies.

Camp f.—Hospital, which admitted all the sick male prisoners from men's camp and quarantine.

The women occupied two camps. One, the old women's camp. The other was our old men's camp, changed into a women's camp.

The above division of Birkenau played an enormous role in the life of the prisoners and was very important for the historians who were doing research in the field of German concentration camps and who were studying the lives of the prisoners, their sufferings and death.

I am going to describe here, in more detail, the hospital camp where I worked for many months.

The hospital, or *lager-F*, was separated, as I mentioned previously, from the Gypsy camp (E Camp) by barbed wires, electrically charged.

It contained many barracks for different diseases.

Barrack # 1—Administration (Schreibstube).

Barracks # 2,3,4,6—surgery.

Barracks # 5, 7,—Internal diseases.

Barrack # 8—Infectious diseases except typhus, mostly tuberculosis.

Barrack # 9—Gastro-intestinal. Mainly diarrhea.

Barracks # 10 and 11—for typhus and typhoid.

Barrack # 12—for the very weak (musulmans) who ended up in the gas chambers.

Barrack # 14—storeroom.

We had very little medicine to treat the prisoners. Some tablets of aspirin, charcoal, etc. The bandages were from paper. We had no quinine for treatment of cases of malaria. Therefore neo-salvarsan was used, which was the drug of choice for syphilis.

Neo-salvarsan helped symptomatically the malaria sick, but the disease recurred shortly. We had no calcium, no equipment for pneumo-thorax and pneumo-peritoneum used at that time.

We had no remedies for treatment of tuberculosis of any form, nor did we possess medicine for typhus or typhoid.

The pharmacist was a prisoner whose name was Mr. Gotlieb. He was a short fellow, about thirty-two years old. He had very few medications to dispose of and it was, therefore, very difficult to get from him the necessary drugs and medicine.

Dr. Zenkteller was in charge of the clinic of Lager-D, (men's camp) and he supervised also the clinic of the quarantine, where the block senior was Mr. Gorin and the physician was Dr. Kleinberg.

Dr. Zenkteller sent to us many Greeks with the diagnosis of malaria. Realizing by now the danger inherent in such a diagnosis, we changed it to a bronchial condition or any other non-contagious disease. The Greeks were kept for a few days and transferred back to the men's camp. In this way their lives were saved.

The German doctor at that time was Dr. Thilo. He used to arrive almost every week for selection of the sick. Those selected were put on the side, the numbers written down, and they were transferred to the gas chambers.

Dr. Thilo used to perform, also, selections in the men's camp. He was accompanied, frequently, by Dr. Zenkteller. Those selected were transferred to the gas chambers. The two German doctors, Dr. Mengele and Dr. Thilo, were also at the ramp and were in charge of the gas chambers.

Dr. Thilo ordered to present to him the most interesting cases. He could learn something from the unusual cases, especially since we had many very famous physicians from all over the world.

The German doctors considered themselves very superior to the prisoner doctors, who in their opinion were all subhumans. I'll present here one case for illustration.

On block number five, there was a world-famous specialist in neurology from France.

This physician presented to Dr. Thilo a case with a paralysis of right upper extremity. According to his experience and knowledge the paralysis was due to a tumor, which pressed on the nerve which caused the paralysis. By removing the tumor, the paralysis would be cured. The German doctor examined the patient and said in a monotonous voice, "This is a slight dislocation of the joint."

The doctors all around, were hardly able to hold off their laughter. This was a ridiculous diagnosis. The patient was transferred to the ward. It was very dangerous to contradict the Nazi doctor.

Most of the doctors from the old camp received new assignments in the new hospital camp, called "Revier," namely:

Dr. Kaplan worked in Barrack # 6 (surgery). Dr. Krause in Block # 7, Later he was transferred to Quarantine. Dr. Stern—Barrack # 9 (diarrhea). Gastro Intestinal

Myself—Barrack # 8, infectious diseases especially Malaria and Tuberculosis.

Dr. Knott—Barrack # 10, typhus.

Dr. Heidenfeld—Barrack # 12, Musulman blocks.

Dr. Epstein—Barrack # 6, together with Dr. Kaplan.

Different rumors started to spread in our camp, some favorable, some not. One of them was a hearsay that Hitler was shot and Keitel had taken over the Government. Although the mind usually follows hidden and subconscious desires, we did not believe these rumors this time for the following reasons:

The gas chambers and Krematoria did not stop functioning.

Keitel was not a revolutionary, rather he followed blindly

the "Führer," including many atrocities with disastrous consequences to his country, his own name and welfare.

Another rumor developed—that Auschwitz would become a Jewish camp, with all the other nationalities being removed to other camps. In fact, many French prisoners were transferred to other camps, followed by removal of the Czechs from Birkenau.

A pure Jewish camp in Auschwitz would be a bad omen and would mean complete destruction of all the prisoners.

Although it was very difficult, we started to make plans to escape from Birkenau.

Zollman suggested to dig a canal below the barracks, where the corpses were located. This plan was abandoned, because the guards in the towers could have noticed it.

It was a very dangerous undertaking because, if detected, all the prisoners working around the corpses would have been killed. Not every one was courageous enough to take a chance and endanger so many lives.

Another plan was to wait after the second gong, when the truck with one German only arrived to pick up the corpses. It was necessary to neutralize the German and then to put on his uniform and to drive the truck out of the camp.

This attempt was also very risky and hazardous, because the Germans would have caught us on the roads and killed hundreds of prisoners. We decided to wait for the moment when the liquidation of the camp would really start, and to get in contact with the Partisans.

During the years 1939-1942, the Germans murdered all kinds of nationalities. But starting from August 1st, 1943, only Jews were killed. Non-Jews were exterminated only in exceptional cases.

CHAPTER XII

Maidanek Concentration Camp. The Moscow Conference.

MISS QUACKERNACK. RESUMPTION OF SELECTIONS, GASSING AND KILLINGS. DR. THILO. THE ARREST AND EXECUTION OF COUNT CIANO. CYCLON B GAS. OSWALD POHL. GERMAN INDUSTRIES EXPLOITING LABOR OF THE PRISONERS. MUSULMANS. SELECTION AND EXTERMINATION OF CHILDREN. BLOCK ELEVEN. SCENES OF ARRIVING TRANSPORTS. THE DEATH OF DR. HEIDENFELD. THE MOSCOW CONFERENCE. THE DECLARATION OF ROOSEVELT, CHURCHILL AND STALIN. MR. ITZKOWITZ.

One day, in October, 1943, a transport of human beings was brought on the ramp of Birkenau. They were people of different nationalities having foreign passports.

They were told by the Germans that they'd be transferred to Switzerland, in accordance with the International Law.

When their train reached the ramp of Birkenau, they asked the prisoners around them ("Canada") where they had arrived and what was going to be their fate?

When informed that they arrived at the extermination

camp, Birkenau, and that all of them were going to die, they asked what was the reason thereof? And what did they do to deserve the death sentence? And why were they deceived?

The prisoners told them that it was Auschwitz, where millions of people were destroyed for no reason at all. It was the philosophy of National Socialism to exterminate people.

Schillinger, the Nazi, whom I described earlier, was in the gas chamber.

He urged the people with the foreign passports to undress.

"Schnell! Schnell [Quick]!" he yelled, brandishing in front of him a gun and threatening to shoot anyone who didn't undress fast enough.

Suddenly, his eyes caught a beautiful woman with the name of "*Quackernack*." He became transfixed by the beauty of the woman to such a degree that he kept looking, not being able to take off his eyes from her. Such a charming loveliness, splendor and daintiness.

An unusual scene took place. An SS man, a known killer, waving a gun with his hand, but his eyes fixed upon the woman. The murderer was grinning in a snickery way.

She noticed that. She looked at this wild destroyer of human lives.

Unexpectedly, while pulling her dress over her head as though conforming with the order, she threw abruptly her dress over the head of the German. A confusion took place. Schillinger started to shoot in all directions, but was not able to take off the dress, which blinded him. In the confusion, she grabbed his gun and shot him.

Schillinger was fatally wounded. On the way to the hospital, he lamented that he was going to die and that he didn't deserve it.

"I was a good fellow, why did such a misfortune befall me?" Schillinger blamed others for his misfortune.

"He didn't deserve it." The classical adage "The wrong-doer blaming everybody but himself."

The act of Quackernack was sheer heroism of the highest magnitude. Only a survivor of a Nazi concentration camp could appreciate such a bravery.

A person in the gas chamber, exhausted and depressed, standing before the gate of death, usually had no physical nor mental strength to attack the perpetrators.

I know it. I was in it. During my two years incarceration in Auschwitz, no such phenomenon happened.

Millions of people, of different nationalities—Russians, Polish, Jews, French, Greeks, Italians, people from Holland, Belgium, Denmark, Norway, secular and religious—perished in the gas chambers, without putting up the slightest resistance. People of different levels of education and classes, military, civilians, entered quietly the gas chambers. It was true that all of the Nazi victims were deceived by the master-race.

It was true also that all of them were brought to the ramp exhausted, tired and desperate. All of them were bullied, beaten and terrorized.

It was true furthermore that it didn't make any difference to the victims. They desired to get over the ordeal and finish their miserable lives on this earth.

Why suffer? Every one will be killed anyway. The sooner, the better.

The heroic act of this beautiful woman, whose name was Quackernack, will forever be remembered as an act of the most supreme courage and daring.

Hail to Quackernack!

In the name of the survivors, I salute you heartily and congratulate you on your extraordinary and supernatural courage.

Schillinger died next day. All the transport was massacred and burned in the Krematoria.

In the middle of the summer, 1943, as I mentioned previously, the gas chambers became active again. The black smoke of the Krematoria was visible many miles away.

The selections of the prisoners started again. The German doctor accompanied by his deputy S.D.G. and the Commandant of Birkenau, Schwarzhuber, arrived at the camp for this purpose.

The prisoners stood naked in front of the Germans in a row, waiting for the verdict to see who would live and who would die.

The slightest scratch on the body, insignificant injury, a small furuncle were causes sufficient for the death sentence.

Their numbers were written on a piece of paper and they were transferred to a separate block, where they lived for one to three days till the trucks arrived and took them away to the gas chambers.

During the few days on the "Block of Death" they were maltreated and beaten. They did not receive any food nor water. When the trucks arrived they were so weakened that they were not able to put up the slightest resistance. On the contrary, the majority was glad to die and to get rid of all the sufferings.

Those who were strong enough to stand on their own feet cried out to the Germans.

"Murderers! You are going to pay for our innocent blood!"

"Killing us is not going to give you victories!"

"Remember, the war is lost for you and the day of reckoning and judgment is approaching!"

The Germans didn't answer, but the beatings, floggings intensified.

When the trucks loaded with human flesh and blood started to move in the direction of the Krematoria, national songs mixed with prayers were heard:

"Hear O Israel, G-d is our G-d, G-d is one."

"We did not lose our hope, our old hope!"

"The hands of our brothers should be strengthened in the fight against tyranny!"

Some recited from the Bible. The trucks sped on the road of death, in the direction from which no return existed.

The selections in the hospital camp were the same.

When the Germans arrived, every one of the sick prisoners had to stand naked in front of his bed. Almost all the Jewish inmates were selected to die. It didn't make any difference whether healthy or sick.

The German doctor at that time who performed all the selections was, as I mentioned previously, *Dr. Thilo*.

He and Dr. Mengele were the ones who supervised the gassings in the chambers and the burnings in the Krematoria.

During my presence in Birkenau, I had seen during the selections only *Dr. Thilo*. He was the angel of death who had on his conscience millions of human beings.

His face was like any other human face. Looking at him, we would never be able to discern traces of crime, unheard of in the annals of history.

What made him do it? Was it a blind belief in the Nazi philosophy? Or a way of saving his own neck, by avoiding the battle fronts? May be, slowly and gradually, he was sucked in into the Nazi atrocities and was not able to free himself.

But did he try? He never did. Otherwise he would have been on the Russian or Western front.

Everybody had the possibility of resigning from his position in any Nazi concentration camp, and declaring his willingness and consent to participate actively in the war.

The trucks of death were followed by cars on the roofs and walls of which was painted the Red Cross.

What had the Red Cross in common with the gas chambers and Krematoria?

It seemed unbelievable, but it was one of the realities and truth of Auschwitz.

The Red Cross, the international symbol of pity and compassion, was perverted by the Nazis to a symbol of death, of extermination of entire races, of enormous human sufferings.

One day, a German prisoner was admitted to the hospital, to the department of malaria. His name was Schoof Henryk.

He was a short fellow, very active, age about forty, and had a green angle on his jacket, meaning a criminal.

He loved to tell us stories of crimes and how the police were running after him, over the roofs of the city of Köln.

They could not catch him. For his arrest he blamed his partners.

For a short time, he was the kapo of painters (Maler in German) and they called him the "Maler-Kapo".

He cackled loudly and his laughter was heard in the neighboring barracks and in the nearby Gypsy camp.

He used to have long conversations with the pretty Gypsy

Maidanek Concentration Camp

girls, being separated from them by barbed wires electrically charged.

One of the girls who worked in the kitchen fell in love with him. She used to provide him with additional food.

Very often, the "Maler-Kapo" used to go over to his girl friend, to the Gypsy camp. When he returned, he was fond of telling us the stories of his achievements.

The Gypsy camp was a family camp where men, women and children lived together.

One day, after a visit by Himmler, they took away the men. The women and children were taken to the gas chambers, where they perished.

When Mussolini was arrested and Badoglio took over the reins of the Government, the Germans reacted and occupied the part of Italy not taken as yet by the Allies.

Although Mussolini was "liberated" by Skorzeny, he had no power over the affairs of his country. He couldn't help even his own son-in-law, Count Ciano, who was tricked and apprehended by the Germans.

Count Ciano, the foreign minister of Italy, was imprisoned in November, 1943, in the medieval fortress of Verona, together with many old Fascists who voted against Mussolini in July.

There he wrote a book, "The Diary of Count Ciano."

This book was secretly taken out by his wife Edda, the daughter of Mussolini, and published after the war.

He depicted in his book how the Italians hated the Germans and how Mussolini, his father-in-law, the dictator of Italy, had been many times incoherent and confused because he suffered from latent syphilis, contracted probably in Switzerland, where he worked as a foreign laborer in his youth.

Count Ciano described also the arrogance and brutality of the Nazi hierarchy.

He detested especially the pompous Goering and the megalomaniac Hitler, and accurately predicted the outcome of the war.

This book, written in Italian, had a good historical value and represented true facts. I read it, after the war.

The book disappeared shortly after it was published for some mysterious reason. I didn't see any foreign translations either.

The post-war Italian Government did not like the excessive and unorthodox exposure of Italian politics during the time of the Fascist era.

I felt sorry, because the book represented the true feeling of the Italian people towards the German Alliance and the intricate politics of an era gone forever. Count Ciano was executed in the jail of Verona on 1/11/44, together with Marshall De Bono.

The German doctor (Lager-Arzt), Dr. Thilo, used to come very often to the hospital camp. Whenever he arrived the sick prisoners were horrified, because his visit had always been connected with some kind of perturbation and trouble, like selections to the gas chambers or transportation to another extermination camp.

The camp senior (Lager-Alteste) was a prisoner from Austria whose name was Schuster. He was about forty-five years old, middle height, and brought to Auschwitz for political reasons. He was a very nice fellow and spoke Italian fluently.

On 9/3/43, Allied troops landed in Calabria (southern Italy) and an armistice between Italy and the Allies was proclaimed five days later, namely on 9/8/43.

The Germans occupied the northern and central part of Italy including Rome. A few Italian divisions were disarmed and made prisoners of war.

Many Italian civilians and military men were brought to Auschwitz, where they perished in the gas chambers.

Mr. Schuster, the camp senior, told me that a special camp would be built in Birkenau for the Italians and that he, because of his knowledge of the Italian language, will be the camp senior.

Mr. Schuster was wrong, no camp was formed for the Italians. They were simply exterminated right away.

A daring escape from Birkenau took place at that time. A few orderlies, who worked in the hospital of the Gypsy camp, made all the preparations and succeeded.

At 9 P.M., when everybody was asleep, they cut a few wires, causing darkness over all the camp. They quickly cut the wires of the Gypsy camp and the hospital camp and found themselves on the outside, behind the towers of the guards.

In half an hour all the prisoners were awakened and stood on the roll call square.

The Germans searched all over the fields, but the escapees could not be found.

I remember, we were assembled in front of the administration barrack (Schreib Stube), near the exit gate.

We were standing and waiting trembling from fear and cold.

A wild SS man with a heavy club in his hand appeared and started to hit us for no reason at all.

He poured most of his fury on a Polish prisoner who was privileged, as a very exception, to wear his own hair.

He probably did not like him and took this occasion to beat him up.

Although we were not certain of our own fate, we wished the courageous and skillful prisoners success in their undertaking. Finally, after a few hours, we were permitted to return to our barracks.

Many prisoners were transferred to Maidanek Concentration Camp, especially those sick from malaria and tuberculosis.

What was Maidanek? Maidanek was the second largest concentration camp, and was located east of the city of Lublin, near the main road of Lublin-Zamosc. It was built as an extermination camp by the order of Himmler, given in 1941 to the chief of the SS Police of the Lublin area, Odilo Globocnik, and prisoners were brought as of 7/21/1941.

Later, in 1942, the same Odilo Globocnik was confirmed by Heydrich and nominated as chief executioner of the extermination policy of the district of Lublin. He built the following three extermination camps simultaneously: Belzec, Maidanek and Sobibor. In this way, the district of Lublin became one of the most important extermination nuclei for the implementation of Nazi bestiality.

The first commandant of Maidanek was Standartenfuhrer Karl Otto Koch, from July, 1941, till July, 1942. (Previously in Buchenwald.)

The second Commandant was SS Obersturmbaufuhrer Max Koegel, from July, 1942, till November, 1942.

The camp contained many fields separated one from the other by electrically charged barbed wires. Five fields were constantly in use. Each field had twenty-two barracks separated one from the other by an empty space used for the daily roll calls and for the gallows to hang prisoners.

Field # 1—Hospital. Later changed for camp of women and children.

Field # 2—Russian prisoners.

Fields # 3 and # 4—Male prisoners of different nationalities.

Field # 5—For women and children. Later changed to a hospital (Revier).

All the camp was surrounded by a double row of barbed wires charged with a high voltage of electricity.

Maidanek had seven gas chambers where thousands of people were killed by carbon monoxide and later by Cyclon B. 7711 kg. of the fatal gas Cyclon B was used during the two and a half years of the existence of the camp.

Very heart-breaking was the murdering of the infants and small children.

The SS men used force to grab the children from their mothers and throw them into the waiting trucks like pieces of wood.

On 10/20/1943, alone, three hundred children perished in this way in the gas chambers.

On 4/17/42, the entire ghetto of Lublin was transferred to Maidanek, where many perished.

11/3/43 was a catastrophic day for the inmates of Maidanek. Over 18,400 Jews from the camp itself and from other camps which had been transferred to Maidanek were shot to death in cold blood by the Germans.

It was very difficult to escape from Maidanek. Some sporadic getaways did occur.

I'll mention here one, a very daring escape.

Three prisoners, Nahumowic Efraim, Diament and Rubinstein, persuaded the guards to let them go outside to repair some

Maidanek Concentration Camp

plumbing facilities of an SS officer. They reached safely their town of Bialystok.

It is worthwhile mentioning that the guards had two hundred Alsatian dogs at their disposition in order to track down the escapees.

The procedure and methods of extermination used were the same as in the other concentration camps.

Who were the inmates of Maidanek?

People from all the German-occupied territories, men, women and children, were caught and forced to enter the cattle trains.

Some were seized on the streets and landed in the trains. 80-100 people to one wagon. No food nor water were given.

When the trains arrived on the ramp, many were dead from the ordeal. The rest were forced to leave the trains, being severely beaten and otherwise maltreated by the Germans.

On the ramp there was a selection of the new arrivals, who should die and who should remain for the time being alive. Those to die were sent immediately to the gas chambers. Those to live entered the camp, where they had to work very hard, under terrible conditions, till exhaustion. They were later sent, also, to be exterminated.

Very often, the Germans did not make any selection and all the transport was carted over immediately to the gas chambers.

The inmates in the camp suffered enormously, physically and mentally, maltreated and beaten on every step.

Food was scarce and diseases, contagious or not, were rampant.

Many had no strength to withstand and resist the ordeal and torment, the sufferings and the afflictions, the despondency, and seeing no hope, chose to commit suicide. All the above was common to all the concentration and extermination camps.

The same Germans and the same prisoners personnel, such as camp seniors, block seniors, orderlies, Kapo foremen, etc.

In Maidanek alone were exterminated 1,500,000 people. Many were murdered without being registered.

The evacuation of the camp started in March, 1944. The prisoners were sent to other camps in Germany.

The sick, weak and disabled were transferred to Auschwitz, where they perished.

The last evacuation took place on 7/7/1944, right before the arrival of the Soviet Army, and contained 1,700 prisoners, who arrived after a week at Mathausen. Many died or were killed on the way.

On 7/23/1944, the camp was taken by surprise by the Russians and one thousand unfortunate prisoners were lucky enough to see freedom again.

Many of the SS men fell in captivity.

The Field 3 of Maidanek, together with the gas chambers and Krematoria, remained intact and can be seen by any visitor, even today.

It is kept by the local authorities for the benefit of mankind, to convince the skeptics and doubters that the terrible things happened. By showing the camp to millions of visitors it was believed that those atrocities would never occur again.

I visited Maidanek twice. One time right after the liberation when I visited Lublin on my way to Wolkowysk. The second time during my latest trip to Poland, in 1973, when I visited most of the concentration camps.

One could still see the barracks, the walls which were imbued with blood and tears of thousands of people, and also the little windows in the Krematoria, where Germans were watching the choking and agony of the dying.

Silence was all around when I visited Maidanek.

The earth and the sky, the roofs and the walls, the sand and the grass were taciturn and speechless witnesses of the crimes committed, right here, not so long ago.

Let's now return to our narration of the Auschwitz concentration camp.

During the last four months of the year 1943, the gas chambers and the Krematoria were active day and night.

The black smoke coming out of the chimneys presented a terrible and agonizing scene, unnatural and unbelievable.

The smell of the burning human bodies was nauseating, offensive and repulsive.

Maidanek Concentration Camp

According to Rudolf Hoess, the commandant of Auschwitz, over four million people perished in Auschwitz.

Among the victims were Jews, Russians, Poles, Czechs, French, etc. Most of the victims were Jews.

Among those who perished were men of different social strata and professions, including priests.

Healthy and sick, young or old, all shared the same murderous fate.

The SS doctor Johan Kremer wrote in his diary the following:

"Compared with Auschwitz, Dante's Inferno seems, almost, a comedy."

In October arrived a transport of children at Birkenau. Let me quote S. Gostyuski, an eyewitness:

"The children were so pretty... so well made, that it was striking in comparison with the rags that they were covered with. The children had noticed the smoke from the chimneys, and they realized that they were being led to their death. They began running in the yard, in a dead fright, clutching their hands in despair.

"It was a heart-breaking scene, dreadful, horrid and terrible."

The gas used by the Nazis was called "Cyclon B," and was produced by the German firm "Degesh," in the form of small crystals which were discharged to the gas chambers through special vents.

Death arrived by suffocation, preceded by enormous fear, followed by vomiting.

Auschwitz used 20.000 kg. of Cyclon B during the years 1941-1944 for four million people.

After the corpses were burned, the ashes were thrown into nearby ponds and rivers.

The entire property of the new arrivals was taken away from them, stored in special barracks and sent to Germany.

The total amount of loot, robbed and plundered by the Germans, during the 2nd World War in all the occupied territories, amounted to hundreds of millions of dollars.

No wonder that the German currency, after the war, became one of the strongest in the world. The prosperity of Germany reached an all-time high and surpassed many of the Allied nations which fought the Nazi tyranny, losing the best of their young men.

Financially, Germany did not lose the war.

Oswald Pohl. He was the chief economic administrator of the concentration camps. He was a tyrant and oppressor of the first magnitude.

Almost all of the SS men who worked in the concentration camps were criminals, otherwise they wouldn't have been there. But there was a different grade of wickedness. Some found the concentration camps a good shelter, where they would be able to survive the war and not to be sent to the Russian front. Some enriched themselves by robbing the prisoners.

Others developed in the Nazi schools a sense of cruelty and a craving for atrocities unmatched in the annals of all the past history of mankind.

To the later belonged the Germans who occupied the higher positions in the Nazi hierarchy like: The Lager-Führers (the commandants of the different concentration camps), the Block-Führers (who were in charge of the individual barracks), and the top administrative officials.

I'll mention here only a few whom I had seen in Birkenau: Rudolf Hoess, Mohl, Pohl, Schwarzhuber, Dr. Thilo, Dr. Mengele, etc.

I'll quote here Oswald Pohl. It was a letter written by him at a late date, November 7, 1944, when the Germans themselves knew that the war was irrevocably lost. The letter was an answer to some guards, who complained to the administration of the senseless maltreatment of the prisoners. Here is the answer of Oswald Pohl.

"To all the commandants of the concentration camps: It is inadmissible to complain about the bad quality of clothing and to pity the 'poor fellow,' who has no footwear. The 'poor fellow' should be instead flogged."

I want to mention here that bad clothing and no footwear in the winter time, in Auschwitz, meant certain death for any prisoner who was forced to go to work and to walk on the snow, with very little food, being beaten by the Germans and Kapos all day long.

Even the Commandant of Auschwitz, Rudolf Hoess, realized that from bad experience, and he permitted the prisoners of Birkenau at the beginning of 1943, when my transport arrived, to wear their own shoes.

Hoess did it, not because of pity, compassion towards the "poor fellow," but because he realized that most of the prisoners would die in the freezing weather of Birkenau if not permitted to wear their own shoes.

Prisoners were forced to work for different German industries, whose boards of directors asked, especially, for prisoners because the labor was very hard and cheap.

They placed their request with the above mentioned Pohl.

As a matter of fact, some of the members of the board of directors had a special permission to enter the camps and select the prisoners themselves.

I. G. Farben Industrie had priority in securing manpower from the concentration camps. There was a special order from Himmler giving them the priority.

Other industrial plants who used prisoners were; Deutsche Ausrustungswerke (DAW), Deutsche Erd-und Stein Werke (DEST), and many others.

I. G. Farben Industrie built a factory at Monowice (Buna-Auschwitz III) producing synthetic rubber and petrol.

A member of this concern, Dr. Otto Ambros, said in his letter of April 12, 1944 that their cooperation with the SS had been *a blessing*.

The same concern bought the mines of Fürstengrube and Janingrube, where prisoners were forced to work under terrible conditions and where many died.

During the period of three years, thirty thousand prisoners from Auschwitz died in the *I. G. Fraben* Industrie factories alone.

The firm Degesh, which produced the Gas Cyclon B, formed part of the *I. G. Farben* Industrie.

Besides the gassing, many were killed by axes, sticks and stones.

Many died of exhaustion, malnutrition, different illnesses without adequate care and treatment.

Bodies of young innocent men, murdered by the Nazis. Allied soldiers were shocked at these scenes.

Women starved to death by the Germans.

The statement that more than four million people perished in Auschwitz alone is not an exaggeration at all.

Other German industrial concerns which forced prisoners to work were: Krupp, Siemens, Herman-Goring Werke, and others.

The prostrate, tired, malnourished exhausted, disabled prisoners were called "Musulmans," as I mentioned previously. Their bones were barely covered with skin, their eyes were glazed and vacant. They moved slowly, apathetically, and were somnolent.

The complete physical decline went together with a mental exhaustion, typified by extreme indifference to the surroundings and lack of interest in their fellow prisoners.

Ghosts, mere shadows, walked slowly at different corners of the camp until the day came when they simply ceased to exist. These shambling ghosts were a terrible sight.

Pregnant women and children arriving at Auschwitz were transferred immediately to the gas chambers, where they perished.

There were some cases of childbirths in the camp. The mother was able to hide her pregnancy because of her particular body build or adaptability to the circumstances. The result was as follows:

The mother, usually, died from infection, maltreatment, and starvation. The newborn infant was taken away by the Germans and killed.

Some children were able, unnoticed, to slide into the camp together with adults.

Therefore, selections were performed by the Germans on the children also, and in the following way:

The SS man placed a rod at the height of 1.20 meter (1 meter and 20 cm, less than 4 feet). Children who passed under the rod would be sent to the gas chambers.

Some of the children understood what was awaiting them and tried to stretch their necks out, hoping to escape death.

It was a heart-breaking scene to watch those children passing under the rod.

Luigi Ferri was twelve years old when he arrived to Auschwitz.

His grandmother was separated from him and sent to the gas chambers. The boy did not realize, at the beginning, what was going on in the camp.

One day, when the infamous SS doctor, Thilo, arrived for the usual selection of prisoners for the gas chambers, the boy asked him to take him to his grandmother.

Dr. Thilo, looked at the boy, and said to the Raportfuhrer Karpanik, who accompanied him, "Don't let me see this boy here tomorrow."

The boy understood what was meant by this order and started to cry.

The prisoners kept him hidden, in different barracks, realizing the danger.

In 1973, I visited Auschwitz. Birkenau was almost completely destroyed, including the men's camp, Gypsy camp, Theresienstadt camp, and the hospital. Only the women's camp was not destroyed.

Auschwitz I remained intact. Most of the barracks remained, including the infamous Block Eleven and "The Wall of Death" situated at the end of the yard of Block Eleven.

Block Eleven, of Auschwitz I, was called "Block of Death" because almost all the prisoners who entered there were killed.

Its yard was surrounded by a high wall. The windows of the adjacent barracks were covered with boards in order that the inmates could not look into the yard.

Under "The Wall of Death," covered now with flowers brought by the visitors and mourners, twenty thousand prisoners were shot.

The *ground floor* of Barracks Eleven contained different rooms:

One room for civilians to hear the verdict of the Gestapo Court which arrived from Katowice.

Another room for the Court, which held its sessions once a month.

The members of the court were:

This is the "Wall of Death" called also the Black Auschwitz Wall, where numerous people were shot. The wreathes of flowers against the wall were brought by relatives in memory of the slaughtered.

Yard of the Block of Death. On the right is the Block where thousands were tortured to death. They contained all kinds of tools of torment and horror. The Wall near the birch tree (center) is where prisoners were shot. The Block on the left has the windows covered with boards so the prisoners inside would not witness the shootings.

Jankiel Handelsman, one of the leaders of the uprising of the Sonderkommando. Died under torture.

Roza Robota, one of the most active members of the resistance movement. Died under torture.

Dr. Rudolf Mildner, head of the Gestapo of Katowice. Maximilian Garbner, head of the camp's political section. Lachman, Dylewski, Boger, and others.

One session lasted 2-3 hours, in which two hundred death sentences were pronounced.

The execution took place at the "Wall of Death" in the yard. Many were shot without any court sessions.

The *underground* or basement of Block Eleven had different cells, as follows:

Ordinary cells with *windows* for prisoners under interrogation.

Windowless, dark cells for prisoners already sentenced and waiting for the execution. They were not given any food, nor water, so that they died in a few days from starvation and lack of air.

Standing, flogging and hanging cells, the same as I described in Birkenau.

In Autumn 1942, there was a mutiny in the women's penal company which was subdued in a terrible blood bath. Many were killed with axes and poles. Some had their heads completely severed. Others were thrown from the windows of the upper floor and killed. Many received injections of phenol straight into the heart.

Later the investigation started, during which the female prisoners were brutally tortured. Fingernails were extracted, needles were inserted into particular sensitive parts of the body. Water was poured down the throats, causing suffocation. Many were shot or hanged.

All these atrocities were performed in the twentieth century by a so-called civilized and cultural nation.

Information about the evil mistreatment was transmitted abroad, thanks to contact with the external world.

Even the London radio broadcasted a list of Germans who were guilty of the most atrocious crimes.

In spite of this, nothing was done to alleviate the sufferings of the inmates of the German concentration camps.

It was amazing how the world stood silent, inactive in front of such unheard of atrocities, permitting them by their muteness to continue.

It was true that the Allies were busy conducting a terrible war. But a strong protest should have at least been raised, followed with a promise of leniency if the torture stopped.

I am convinced that such a declaration by the U.S. of America, England, Russia, the Pope, by the other superiors of different religions, by the heads of the so-called neutral governments like Central and South America, by the nations of Asia and Africa would have had an enormous impact, even on the Nazis.

A promise of leniency and a tacit agreement with Goering, Himmler would have had an enormous effect, even put a stop to the senseless killings.

This was true especially during the years 1943-4-5 when all

the world, including the Germans themselves, knew that the war was lost, and by stopping the crimes they could have saved their own necks.

Millions of innocent lives could have been rescued.

Wasn't it worth it?

How much was worth the life of one child, of one innocent woman and man?

It was incomprehensible how nothing had been done by the Allied leaders and by the educated and the influential forces of the world at large.

Was the world numbed?

Was humanity shocked in front of the Nazi tyranny?

Maybe so, but those who suffered, those who lost their lives in the gas chambers found the leaders of that time guilty of inaction.

Let history pronounce the just verdict.

We opine that the world should learn an adequate lesson from the past, in order to prevent similar happenings in the future, for identical conditions are developing again.

The Nazi fire, although condemned by all, did not extinguish completely.

A new conflagration might arise again. The Neo-Nazis still exist and spread their hatred all over the globe.

The so-called Nazi trials in Germany were very lenient in their tasks. Nazis who murdered many innocent people and who exhibited awful atrocities, got away with mild sentences, which seemed unbelievable even to the perpetrators themselves.

Many officials, even of the Wiedergutmachung offices, who were supposed to show compassion towards the survivors, were exhibiting hatred, and the meager survivor's pensions were taken away from them for insignificant or no reason at all.

Why should the criminals regret the atrocities and the crimes committed when everything was almost forgotten?

The wicked, the children of darkness, will explode again when the opportunity arises.

Oberscharfuhrer Mohl was one of the SS men who surpassed many others with his atrocities and savagery. He was the one who proposed to liquidate all the inmates of Auschwitz by mass bombing of all the buildings and killing of all of the prisoners. This was called "*Mohl Plan*."

He had a face of a normal human being, round and fat, but his brain was made out of some kind of a tissue worse than the wildest animal, a brain tissue unknown as yet on this planet.

His heart was made from the toughest rock, but evidently was functioning like in any other human being.

I'll bring here a few examples of the activities of Mr. Mohl:

In the year 1944, Eichmann organized many transports of human beings especially from Hungary, which arrived at Auschwitz one after another.

Few, as usual, entered the camp. The great majority, at least 80%, were sent straight from the infamous ramp to the gas chambers, where they perished.

Mohl had a habit of throwing living human beings straight into the fire of the pits, where the bodies burned.

He must have enjoyed this spectacle, like the abnormal Roman Imperator Nero, who ordered the city of Rome to burn while playing a musical instrument. Nero never ordered living human beings thrown into a fire, not even animals.

This kind of atrocity was strange even to Nero.

The pits were used when the number of victims was less than two hundred, or too numerous for the Krematoria to handle—more than eight thousand—when additional fire was necessary to burn the people.

One time, Oberscharfuhrer Mohl ordered a woman prisoner to climb on the top of a great mass of bodies, to undress naked, and to dance on the summit of the agglomeration of the corpses.

The woman did what she was ordered, hoping to save her own life. While the naked woman was dancing and singing, Mohl started to shoot the living prisoners, forcing them with the help of other Germans to jump into the fire and be consumed by it. This was a terrible scene, which Mohl's imagination created. Finally he shot the woman, too.

I had seen Mohl many times in Birkenau, and Günther Grube. He was a man of about forty years old, very fat, of medium height. His voice was heavy. He terrorized people just by yelling alone. On looking at him, one would never believe that he was able to commit such atrocities, which surpassed any other atrocity known to mankind.

It came, probably, after years of training in the SS schools, watching and participating, day in and day out, in the murdering of innocent people, including women and children. He was a born criminal, but his real bestiality, as exhibited in Auschwitz, was a congenital abnormality plus an acquired particular behavior.

It was my opinion that a man could not be born with such destructive propensities, but had to be influenced, also, by outside activities and experiences.

His field of action was all over. Most of the time, he was the one of the chiefs of the gas chambers and Krematoria.

He used to proceed as follows:

As soon, as a new transport arrived, he assembled the people in rows of four. Then he got up on a bench, making a short speech.

"Everybody has to undress and enter the bathroom to wash, then you will be sent to work."

The bathrooms were actually the gas chambers with fictitious water pipes, attached to the walls, simulating showers.

If somebody expressed any doubt, Mohl used to shoot him on the spot.

With the help of other SS men, he used to create a terrible confusion among the prisoners, who most of the time did not realize the hell they were in, and with the help of savage and vicious beatings and gun shootings, he forced the prisoners to the gas chambers, always promising work instead of death.

If a prisoner refused to enter the gas chamber, Mohl used to take him out, beat him viciously with a heavy stick. When the victim fell on the ground, Mohl trampled him with his heavy boots and threw him alive into the burning pits.

There was another Scharführer trained in the SS school. His name was SS man Frost.

At many transports he used to wait in front of the gas

chambers and search the female organs of the young and pretty girls passing near him.

At the beginning of the year 1943, some strange episode took place which called for a psychological interpretation.

The gas chamber was packed with people to be soon murdered. A young boy was trying to hide himself. An SS man noticed him and he started to beat him with a heavy stick. Blood was running from the face, neck and the rest of the body of the boy. The SS man continued to hit him with a wild fury, determined to finish him off. He stopped only when he thought that the boy was dead. All of a sudden, the boy got up on his feet and looked at the SS man, the brutal animal, who almost killed him. The SS man's eyes met the eyes of the boy, which transmitted without words the question of why he was murdering him. He didn't know the German. He didn't know his country. He had never seen him before.

A strange thing happened. The SS-man became frightened. . . . He could not stand the glance of the boy's eyes and started to laugh hysterically. Then he pulled out his gun and shot the little boy to death.

Psychologists and psychiatrists, could you explain this phenomenon?

In September 1943 a transport arrived from Przemysl. Many young men of this transport had knives hidden in their clothing.

When they were ordered to undress, they decided to attack the Germans and to die together with the evil perpetrators. Their leader was a certain doctor. The doctor made a deal with the Nazis to calm down the youngsters, being promised not to be killed but to be sent to the camp. The doctor promised his followers that they were not going to die. They had to wash themselves before being transferred to the factories for work. When the youngsters entered the washrooms, which really were the gas chambers, the Germans reneged on their promises and forced the doctor and his wife to enter the same gas chamber, where they all perished.

On September 1, 1943, a transport from the city of Tarnow

arrived. They were assured by the Germans, till the last moment, that they were going to be resettled to the east for work.

When they found out the truth, they lamented at first, then they started to pray:

"G-d, Holy Almighty G-d, look from your heights, and see the blood of the righteous, the innocent, being spilled without any reason. Make an end to this massacre, your gracious king."

"O Lord G-d, shine forth. Lift up yourself and judge the murderers, the slaughterers and the exterminators."

"How long shall the wicked triumph?"

"They boast and speak arrogantly. They slay innocent men and have no pity on innocent women. They do not spare even little children and infants. Is it possible that the Lord doesn't see? He, who planted the ear, shall not hear?"

From the Heights of Heaven, a voice replied:

"Be sure, that the Almighty sees everything and he hears all and sundry, alpha and omega, length and breadth. Everything will be taken care of, in the right time and in the near future. Judgment will be returned unto the righteousness. The Lord will stand up against the evildoers. He will stand up against the murderers. He shall cut them off, in their wickedness. The thrones of iniquity have no fellowship with the Almighty."

All the victims stopped their prayers and a strange silence engulfed everything, the barracks, the Nazis and the victims.

Suddenly a man got up and called out.

"My brothers, you should know that we were not going to die. It was impossible that the Germans would take us completely innocent people and murder without any reason and for no purpose at all. Such atrocities could not exist on our earth. It never existed! It never happened before! It was a lie, a sheer propaganda. We were going to live! All this nightmare would soon disappear!"

This talk quieted down a lot of people. They hoped. Maybe a miracle would occur.

All this happened in the gas chamber. Then the Red Cross vehicle arrived. The Germans threw in the gas Cyclon B and all perished.

At the end of the year 1943, a transport from Holland

arrived. They were brought to the gas chamber and compelled as usual to undress.

After a short while, a group of Poles were brought into the same gas chamber. This group had among them twelve women. One of the female prisoners got up and started to address the naked prisoners.

"We are not going to die now. Our spirit will live forever. The Germans are going to pay very dearly for our spilled, innocent blood. The barbarism of the Nazis will never be forgotten."

Then she turned toward the other prisoners, the orderlies, the workers who were not condemned to die as yet (the Sonderkommando), and said:

"Remember, that you or anyone else who remains alive have an obligation to tell the world what the Nazis did to us, completely innocent people. At this moment of our death, we are calling all the world to remember and never to forget."

Then all the prisoners fell on the ground praying to G-d and asking Him why He permitted such barbarism to take place.

Then, they got up and started to sing their National Hymn. While they were singing, the car with the Red Cross on the top arrived, and it carried the dangerous gas Cyclon B.

The Germans used the Red Cross car, not only to carry the deadly gas Cyclon B, but also to lead the people, on their last road, towards death itself.

The Germans closed hermetically the door of the gas chamber and threw in the gas, Cyclon B.

The unfortunate prisoners continued to sing. Soon the voices quieted down and in fifteen minutes all of them were dead. Their bodies were removed by special hooks. The gold teeth extracted. The hair of the women cut off and all the bodies were thrown into the pits. A black smoke burst out, spreading all over the neighborhood and letting the people of the surrounding villages know that the prisoners did not exist any more.

Their bodies turned to ashes. But their spirits went up towards the sky, together with the black smoke, reaching Heaven and demanding justice.

As I mentioned previously, the extermination camp Birkenau (Auschwitz II) was expanding. All the working men were transferred to D-Lager (camp for men).

The inmates living in the hospital barracks, like Blocks 7, 8, 12, were all transferred to a special section of Birkenau called F-Lager, which included many barracks and was used as a hospital (Revier in German).

I was the doctor or pfleger of barrack number eight, where they kept inmates sick of different infectious diseases, but mainly malaria and tuberculosis.

Dr. Heidenfeld, the old gentleman who was especially maltreated and beaten by Zenkteller for personal reasons, became deadly sick.

He was lying in his bed in barrack number twelve. We tried to help him, as much as we could. Good medication was almost non-existent. Dr. Heidenfeld became more weak every day. He had contracted the dreadful disease of typhus. He was old and his natural resistance was not strong enough to combat the disease.

His strength left him and he was lying in a semiconscious state. After ten days he succumbed. Dr. Heidenfeld died peacefully in his sleep.

The suffering, maltreatment, atrocities were all behind him.

Honor to his memory and shame to his persecutors.

His country, Germany, where he was born and where he worked as a physician, saving many lives and helping them in their physical and mental afflictions, betrayed him. He was sent to Auschwitz to die, not because he committed a crime, but because he was a Jew by birth.

We, his colleagues in profession and in suffering, built a special coffin for him and carried out his body in honor and respect.

It was evening. The body had to be put on the top of the other dead inmates who had succumbed during this gloomy, bleak, late autumn day. They all shared the same fate in their life and in their death.

The Russians were fighting the enemy who had invaded

Maidanek Concentration Camp

their land and forcing the Germans to a shameful retreat, called by the Nazis "Strategic and according to plan."

Kharkov was captured on 8/23/43. Novorossisk was taken on 9/16/43. The Dnieper was broken through and Kremenchug was taken by the Russians. Even Smolensk was recaptured. Kiev, the capital of Ukraine, was taken on 11/6/43.

The Moscow conference of all the three secretaries of state—Cordell Hull, Eden, Molotov—took place between 10/19/43 and 11/1/43.

The Moscow Conference published a Roosevelt-Churchill-Stalin declaration in which was said that the Germans who took part in the terrible atrocities and massacres *would be sent back to the countries in which their abominable crimes were committed*, in order that they be judged and punished by the people who suffered the atrocities.

How was this fiery declaration of justice fulfilled? Were the Nazis, who committed the atrocities, sent back to the countries where the crimes were committed? Very rarely. Most of the trials took place in Germany proper and the guilty Nazis were getting away with very mild sentences if any at all. Such a disregard for the declaration of Roosevelt, Stalin and Churchill at the Moscow Conference of 1943, in which it was clearly stated that the criminals will be brought to justice in the countries where the crimes were committed, is a flagrant violation of the above declaration and may be a cause of another holocaust.

I'll bring later in my narration an example of such a trial.

One day, while I was attending the sick people in my barrack, comforting them in their despair, I was informed that the younger Itzkowitz was taken to Block Twelve, where all the Musulmans were to be dispatched one to two days later to the gas chamber.

I rushed to Block Twelve and found Mr. Itzkowitz full of despair, pale, emaciated, weak, and debilitated.

"What happened Mr. Itzkowitz?" I asked. "Why are you here? It is a very dangerous barrack. All the sick are sent from here straight to the gas chambers."

"I know," answered Mr. Itzkowitz. "I couldn't help it. A

lesion formed on my thigh which became ulcerated. They wrote down my number and sent me here. Please help me! Save my life! I don't want to die as yet."

"My dear Itzkowitz, I'll do everything possible. I realize the seriousness of your situation. Twice weekly, the German trucks arrive here and take away all the sick people straight to the gas chambers, where they perish. It is very difficult to take you out from here before the deadly trucks arrive. Nobody wants to take chances and lose his own life in the process. I'll go to the chief of the barrack, Mr. Katz, maybe he'll help out. I know him personally. He is not a bad guy."

"Go! Go!" pleaded Itzkowitz. "Help me! Save my life!"

I found Mr. Katz standing in front of the Block.

"Please, Mr. Katz," I said. "In your barrack is a relative of mine. His name is Itzkowitz. He has a little lesion on his thigh. Otherwise, he is healthy and capable of work."

"My dear friend," said Mr. Katz, "it does not depend on me. I am in danger myself every day and every minute of the day. Mr. Itzkowitz was sent here by the Germans and his number is kept in the administration barrack (Schreib-Stube). If they don't find him here, they'll kill me. I am responsible for all the inmates here."

"I understand Mr. Katz," I retorted. "Your life should not be endangered. I understand that it is impossible to let him go out of the barrack once he was dispatched here and his number written and kept in the 'Schreib Stube.' But, if his number is cancelled and I'll bring you an order to transfer Mr. Itzkowitz to another barrack, would you comply and let him out from here?"

"Sure, my dear Dr. Harsaw," replied Mr. Katz. "I'll be glad, very glad to let him go out from here."

I left Mr. Katz with mixed feelings. What should I do? How could I save the life of Mr. Itzkowitz? How could I cancel his number and transfer him to any other barrack? I had a good friend in the Administration Barrack. I'll go there and ask him this favor.

I went to the Schreib Stube, which was located at the end of the hospital terrain, not far from the exit.

I found my friend inside.

"Please, a relative of mine, is in Block Twelve. You know the German truck has to arrive tomorrow and take away all the sick to the gas chamber. You must take a chance and save him. I know it is dangerous, very dangerous, for you and for me and for everybody else. But our lives are in danger anyway. It is very questionable if we'll come out alive. The Germans will kill us in any event. Let's tempt providence and defy danger. We sit anyway on a barrel of gunpowder."

My friend answered, "The risk is really very, very great. For your sake, I'll play with fire and I'll put my head in the lion's mouth. I am sure that we'll have to fight very hard at the end, when the Germans will try to liquidate us. I want you to promise me to stay near my side when the tragic moment arrives and to fight together. I want you to be my brother. I feel so lonely and desperate."

"I promise you, my brother in sorrow," I said.

My friend went to the table where a list of all the numbers of the unfortunate sick people was lying. He took a pen and cancelled the number of Mr. Itzkowitz. He gave me also a transfer slip for him.

I thanked my friend and left him.

On my way to the dreadful Block Twelve, I thanked the Almighty for giving me the possibility of saving for the time being the life of one human being.

I was free to transfer him to any barrack I wanted, but where?

Should I admit him to my block?

No! It was impossible! On my block, there were inmates sick on tuberculosis, malaria, and severe colitis. Mr. Itzkowitz might contract one of the contagious diseases. In addition, Dr. Zenkteller, the trustee of the Germans, came very often to the hospital barracks to check the sick ones. He'd find out, immediately, that Itzkowitz had no contagious disease and that he had instead a lesion on his thigh. He'd report it to the Germans and this would be the end of Mr. Itzkowitz, myself, and all the other orderlies of the barracks.

No! This was no solution.

I rationalized further. Would a transfer to any other barrack save the life of my relative? Yes, it would save him temporarily. He would get out from Block Twelve, but what would happen later?

The doctor of the block after a few days would send him back to the men's camp. Nobody wanted to take chances and Mr. Itzkowitz would be in danger again. I knew too well the usual procedure. What to do? How to save him?

I noticed from far away Dr. Kaplan in front of Barrack Six. As we remember, Dr. Kaplan and myself struggled many months till we got our present positions. In addition, Dr. Kaplan belonged to the same transport, which arrived at Auschwitz from Wolkowysk.

I greeted Dr. Kaplan:

"Hello! My friend, how do you feel?"

"I feel much better than in the previous men's camp," answered Dr. Kaplan.

"You know," I continued, "Mr. Itzkowitz from our transport is in Block Twelve because of a small lesion on his thigh. Your barrack treats small lesions like these and other dermatological and surgical cases. Could you admit him in your barrack and keep him there till the wound would heal completely?"

"Sure," answered Dr. Kaplan. "I'll admit him. But the problem is, how to take him out from Block Twelve and make the official transfer to my block? It is a very difficult task. It might be also dangerous for all concerned."

"Don't worry my friend," I said. "Everything is arranged." I showed him the transfer slip from the "Schreibstube." Dr. Kaplan went to consult "Tato," who was the chief of his barrack (Blockälteste). After a while, he returned with a positive answer.

I rushed to Block Twelve, took out Mr. Itzkowitz from the doomed confinement, and transferred him to Block Six. He lived there for a few months, till his lesion healed completely, helping out the other orderlies in their chores. Later, on my initiative, Mr. Itzkowitz was accepted by Mr. Katz as an orderly of Block Twelve.

In this way, a life was saved, by taking him out from the very jaws of death.

Mr. Itzkowitz survived the war. He is married, has a son and a good business in the city of New. York. It makes me feel good, and enhances my well-being, whenever I see him.

Kalman Teigman testified before the Israeli tribunal how a transport of Jewish prisoners from Grodno (not far from Wolkowysk) refused to disrobe and enter the gas chambers. The Germans started to beat them mercilessly. One prisoner then threw a hand grenade. The Germans of the watchtowers opened fire and all the prisoners were driven fully clothed into the gas chambers where all of them perished.

I continued to work on Block Eight doing my best for the fellow sufferers.

Dr. Thilo, the German doctor, used to arrive about twice weekly, to write down the numbers of all the Jews. He was accompanied, very often, by Dr. Zenkteller.

When Dr. Thilo arrived, he used to first enter the "Schreibstube" which was located right at the gate.

We immediately found it out, and fear, panic and trepidation engulfed the inhabitants of the hospital barracks. The dreadful selection would start in a few minutes. Who was going to live and who was going to die?

I entered the interior of my barrack and advised all the Jews to get outside and hide themselves on the hospital grounds.

The German doctor came into every barrack and registered the numbers of the sick Jews, regardless of their health. He made no exceptions. All the Jews registered as sick and found in the hospital barrack had to die.

When he reached my barrack I used to come out forward and declare in a loud voice:

"100 Häftlinge Im Block. Keine Juden." (One hundred prisoners in the Barrack. No Jews.) Dr. Thilo left immediately and the sick inmates slowly returned to their beds.

I succeeded many times in this maneuvering and stratagem.

Now it is necessary to bring the course of the war events into accord with the narrative.

At the end of 1943, two-thirds of the occupied Russian territory was liberated.

The Germans were running for their lives (Planmässiger Ruckzug) and their satellites, Finland, Hungary, etc., tried to get out of Hitler's chains and fetters.

THE YEAR 1944
FOURTH YEAR OF WAR.
DEFEAT OF AGGRESSION.

CHAPTER XIII

The Reasons of Germany's Defeat. Liberation of Europe.

SCENES IN FRONT OF AND INSIDE THE GAS CHAMBERS. THE DREADFUL SELECTIONS. CONTINUOUS GERMAN DEFEAT ON ALL THE BATTLE FRONTS. LIBERATION OF LENINGRAD, MINSK, WOLKOWYSK, CRIMEA. THE RIVER VISTULA WAS REACHED. MAIDANEK. REBELLION OF THE SONDERKOMMANDO. JESUS CHRIST. HITLER'S MISTAKES.

One day, at the beginning of January, 1944, three thousand young girls were concentrated in the three blocks of death, Barracks 25, 26, 27, of Birkenau (Auschwitz II) female camp. They were kept there for three days and nights, without food nor water. The girls were so weakened, exhausted that they could hardly stand on their feet.

When the trucks arrived, they were ordered to undress in the cold freezing weather of January.

Naked, they climbed the trucks, shivering from cold and exhaustion. When the trucks arrived in front of the gas chambers, they were lifted on one side, and the naked girls fell out from the trucks on the frozen ground, one on the top of the other, like the unloading of vegetables. Some were dead on arrival from exposure, beatings, exhaustion. Some were able to get up and walk into the gas chamber.

One of the girls, very young and pretty, covered her face and cried.

"I am so young. I have hardly lived as yet. Why should I die with such a terrible death? What did I do? I wish I could live a little longer."

When she finished, her eyes looked motionless in the distance, far in the emptiness.

Her friend was lying near her, shivering from cold and misery. She said, "Finally, the hour of freedom from suffering and slavery has arrived. When the heart is full with pain, aches and distress, when the barbaric world is full with the worst atrocities, evil and outrageous dreadfulness, then life becomes a burden, and death is seen as a redeemer, and as a balm to the heart and mind. How sweet is death. I am waiting for it!"

At the other end of the gas chamber, a mother and her daughter were sitting. Her arms embraced the head of her daughter, as she murmured, "Pretty soon we are going to die, you and I. My heart is full of pain on account of you. The thought of you makes me lose my mind. I lived partially in this world, but you haven't started to exist as yet, and already you must die." She took away her stiffened arms and the daughter's head fell on her knees. The daughter started to shiver all over her body and cried.

"Mother, Mother, why? . . ."

She didn't finish, what she wanted to say. Soon the door of the gas chamber closed. The gas, Cyclon B, was thrown in and in fifteen minutes they were all dead.

During the Easter Holyday (Passover) of the year 1944, a transport from Vittel arrived. Vittel was a camp in Southern France. The liquidation of the camp had started already in April, 1944. Most of the people were sent to Auschwitz. Among them was Rabbi Moshe Friedman, the Rabbi of Bayonue. He was a known authority and respected all over Europe.

As they entered the gas chambers, he advanced towards the Germans and in a loud and clear voice said:

"You, the Germans, the nation of murderers, will pay very dearly for the spilled innocent blood. Not only the Nazi regime will be destroyed, but the German nation, as a nation of bloodthirsty animals, will disappear forever from the world arena.

"Our souls and our blood will not rest, till G-d's wrath will come upon you and destroy you, your barbarism and your satanic inner nature."

He finished by praying: "Hear O Israel, G-d is our G-d, G-d is One.

"Hear our voice, O Lord our G-d, be pitiful and compassionate with us and don't turn us away empty-handed.

"Redeem us speedily, because You are a powerful and mighty redeemer. Let the wickedness be perished from the surface of the earth. Let Thy enemies be annihilated in their crimes and evildoings. The dominion of arrogance whall be uprooted and crushed, now."

All of them soon perished.

The following happened at the end of 1944. A group of Slovaks were brought to the gas chambers. They knew that they were going to die. But they were so exhausted, tired, malnourished and despondent that they wanted to die and get rid of all their sufferings. They undressed quietly.

One woman said, "Maybe a miracle will happen and we'll remain alive."

No miracle occurred. All of them soon were killed.

This was a proof that even when the people were already in the gas chambers waiting to be killed and for Cyclon B to arrive, most of them still secretly hoped for some miracle to occur.

The reason was that the people were not conditioned for such senseless murder.

Their minds, in spite of reality, could not comprehend it. Their "unconscious" was not prepared for such unnatural things. The previous generations did not know of gas chambers nor of any Krematoria built by a legal and duly elected government.

It was known in Aushcwitz and every one was talking about it. The Germans were not going to permit the existence of living witnesses to their enormous crimes. All the prisoners would have to be killed. The SS men knew it. The prisoners knew it.

The Germans would not allow the prisoners, who saw with their own eyes the senseless murdering of millions of people, to live and tell it to the world. The Germans believed that, by exterminating all the prisoners, the world would never find out about the existence of the gas chambers and the Krematoria. They had to defend themselves.

In the Bible it was written: "Head for head, life for life." This kind of repayment should be done in order that justice be fulfilled.

Could the Germans repay it according to the law of the Bible? No, they couldn't.

Even if the repayment would be made not with the lives of the evil perpetrators but with their work, they would never be able to atone.

Even if all the German nation would work, twenty-four hours a day, they would never be able to compensate a small part for the evil that they brought to mankind.

The Nazis knew it as well as the prisoners. The best thing would be to exterminate all the eyewitnesses to the Nazi crimes. Mohl, as we know, proposed mass bombing for this purpose.

Preparations were made beforehand to annihilate all the prisoners, to destroy all the buildings, all the gas chambers and Krematoria. Nothing should remain. No living witnesses.

The greatest murderers in all the history of the world, including the Huhns, the Barbars, were a small play in comparison with the Nazi atrocities manifested and exhibited by the creation of special factories which had the only purpose to destroy human beings.

The prisoners were aware of all that. There was no hope left. Still they wanted to live for one reason only, that the world should find out all the happenings in the German concentration camps and that the Nazis should not be able to hide their crimes.

The prisoners tried their best not to despair. Maybe somewhere someone would remain alive and tell the world what he saw with his own eyes in Auschwitz.

The Nazi victims believed that the world at large did not know the full truth about the Nazi concentration camps. How could it be otherwise?

The Reasons of Germany's Defeat

Had the leaders of the world like Roosevelt, Churchill, etc. known the truth, they would have done everything possible to stop it. Many things could have been accomplished to save the lives of the victims of Nazi tyranny.

This kind of thinking encouraged many prisoners to try the impossible, to revolt, to rebel and even to try to escape from Auschwitz.

They realized that all of them would be killed at any attempt, but maybe someone would survive. In that case, the sacrifice was justified.

The victims of Nazi tyranny would be shocked to learn that the world leaders knew, partially, what was going on and didn't do anything to halt it.

In those gruesome years of the Second World War, the press was describing many atrocities. The people, the readers, didn't believe it. It was impossible, they thought. It was only war propaganda. It was inconceivable that human beings, with human faces and human hearts, could commit such enormous crimes on other human beings. It was unbelievable!

It was clear that it couldn't penetrate the brains of civilized nations.

People never heard of that. They were not conditioned. The Nazi reality could never be comprehended.

The information that they received through the press and radio did not stick to their brains. It glided off like ice from a smooth surface, melted away and disappeared in the daily strategy and plans of conducting the war.

On the first fire were the Sonderkommando. They were the prisoners who knew most of the Nazi wickedness because they worked at the gas chambers and the Krematoria. They had to be destroyed first.

The prisoners knew what was going to happen and they rebelled.

On October 7, 1944, a revolt broke out which ended with the destruction of Krematorium IV, and partial demolition of Krematorium II. The mutiny was not successful because it was started earlier than intended.

All the prisoners of the Sonderkommando were killed, including Dr. Bekenstein from Wolkowysk, whom I described earlier.

The women who supplied the explosives and ammunition were first held in the terrible cellars of Block Eleven of Auschwitz I.

In spite of the torture they did not betray anyone, and finally, after long weeks of interrogation and torment, they were hanged on January 6, 1945.

Their names were:

Ella Gartner, Roza Robota, Tosska, and Regina.

These women should always be remembered, in the annals of history, as the most courageous women, who fought the Nazi tyranny and sacrificed their lives on the altar of courage, not betraying anyone.

The complete liquidation of the Gypsy camp took place on 8/2/1944. They were driven by the SS men to the gas chambers and exterminated.

One of the SS men was the infamous Alois Frey, who later, for his good Nazi work, was elevated to the rank of the Lager-Führer of Günther-Grube, one of the mines belonging to Auschwitz III. I lived in this camp for one year and saw with my own eyes the atrocities committed by this Nazi. I was a witness for the prosecution at the Nazi trial in Frankfurt, Germany against Alois Frey, the ex-Lager Führer of Günther Grube.

What was the verdict of the court in Frankfort/Main (Germany) regarding this criminal? You'll learn later all the proceedings of the German court, in Frankfort, which was an example and a pattern for all the other German courts trying the Nazi criminals.

Why did the Germans exterminate the Gypsies? Because they had no country of their own and because they were weak and defenseless. The murder of the Gypsies was no help to the war effort and there was no question of an inferior race. The yellow race was very highly respected, because they had a strong Government behind them.

I was firmly convinced that the Nazis would have never dared to annihilate the Jews had the Jews at that time had their independent State of Israel!

Had this state shown strength and vigor, as we witness today, the Germans would have reacted completely differently. But, unfortunately, the independent Jewish State did not exist then.

Many took advantage of the Jews, who were abused and maltreated for centuries.

Pogroms were performed in different countries with the active help of the existing governments.

Jews were killed in the thousands throughout the millennium of history. Nobody defended them.

To murder them, to rob them, to rape their women, was an accepted occurrence. Read through the pages of history and you'll find out of pogroms, robberies, destruction of Jewish property for no reason at all.

It started with the ancient Romans, who destroyed their temple, murdered many of their inhabitants—and the rest were taken to Rome for slaves.

The Circus (Amphitheater in center of Rome today) was soaked with Jewish blood as well as with the blood of the first Christians.

Later, the inquisition of Spain, the Crusaders, Chmielnicki, the pogroms in Russia and other countries.

Very few lifted their finger or raised their voices against such injustices.

Did any Government try to defend the helpless and the defenseless victims of historical falsification?

No! Thousand times no!

If a crisis broke out in any part of Europe, the Jews were to be blamed.

If a contagious disease spread over Europe in the Middle Ages, like cholera or pests, the Jews had to be blamed.

If the Russian economy was bad, if the peasants suffered under the Tzar, the Jews were guilty.

"Let's exterminate the Jews!"

"Beat the Jews and save Russia!"

These were the slogans.

"The Jews killed our G-d!" was an other proclamation.

The people who said this, did not realize that Jesus Christ

himself and all the Apostles were Jews by birth, life, and death. They belonged to a very pious sect of Judaism called Essenes (Asiim), who conducted an ascetic life, were very religious and believed in the kingdom of heaven and the Messiah.

Jesus Christ was crucified as a Jew.

When the Roman procurator Pontius Pilate asked whether he was King of the Judeans, he answered, "Thou has said it."

When Jesus Christ walked on the Via Dolorosa, for the crucifixtion, he carried a crown of thorns on his head and the Roman soldiers scoffed at him and called him "The King of the Jews."

They put an inscription on the cross, "Jesus of Nazareth, King of the Judeans."

The last words of Jesus were: "Eli, Eli, Lamah Shebaktani." which means, "O G-d, my G-d, why hast Thou forsaken me?"

After the crucifixion, the Romans permitted to take down the body for burial.

The Jews took his body from the gallows, washed it according to the Jewish custom and buried him.

Jesus Christ lived and died as a Jew.

It had been documented and it is visible right now, at the Golgotha, in the Sepulchre Church of Jerusalem.

There is still present the board on which the body of Jesus Christ was washed according to the Jewish custom.

All the proof is there and everybody can see it.

The dark masses, before, during and after the Middle Ages, did not know all about this truth. They were not told what really happened.

They never thought of Jesus Christ as a Jew.

The hatred against the Jews was and continues to be an injustice to the real facts of history.

The late saint, Pope John XXIII, tried to correct this injustice and iniquity. He ordered all the places of hatred erased as historically wrong.

The Ecumenical Council was created in Rome to legalize the above corrections and to make the people of the world know and understand the truth.

* * *

The Reasons of Germany's Defeat

What is the reason that Russia was attacked and that Germany lost the war?

At the beginning of the Second World War, Germany was winning because she was armed to the teeth. They had a vast superiority of planes, tanks and heavy armaments. The Allies were not armed. France was preoccupied, at that time, with social reforms. To shorten the working days of the week, to five days, to four days, at a time when the German factories worked day and night to produce more and more of the most modern armor.

England and America were not armed either.

No wonder that the Germans were able to overrun almost all of Europe.

Poland succumbed to a terrible and disgraceful defeat in the year 1939.

France was occupied in a very short time in 1940. Belgium, Holland, Denmark, Norway, Greece, Yugoslavia were conquered. Italy was fighting on the side of Germany, and so were Hungary and Romania.

Spain in the West and Turkey in the East were friends, ready to jump for the final kill.

A friendly, nonaggression pact was signed with Russia. The African campaign started out well. Rommel's army was at the outskirts of Alexandria (Egypt).

The Arabs, with the Mufti, were waiting for the Germans to arrive. The English were desperate.

Had the Germans, instead of creating a new front against Russia, attacked the Middle East, like Palestine, Syria, Iraq, Iran, and joined hands with the Japanese through India, they would have, undoubtedly, conquered North Africa.

The loss of Africa and Asia including India would have meant a terrible disaster for the Allied forces.

England, deprived of the badly needed raw material, would have to surrender and to conclude a separate peace. Then Germany could have attacked Russia, having only one front to reckon with, and the Nazis would have emerged as the masters of the world, with all the consequences for mankind as we know it now.

But the Almighty, did not want the earth and its inhabitants, which He so carefully created, to be destroyed.

Therefore He confused the mind of Hitler. He hardened his heart and let him believe that he was a genius. He made him do just the opposite of what his military advisers told him.

Instead of attacking the Middle East and thereby creating two fronts for the British, he attacked Russia creating two fronts for himself.

Stalin, as we know, was terribly afraid of Hitler. He gave him everything he desired: grain, meat, oil, vegetables, etc. Stalin wanted, by all means, to avoid the onslaught of the German Army, which was considered at that time, June, 1941, invincible.

The Russian Army in the West was ordered not to answer militarily to any German attack.

Hitler said to his followers, "I don't want anything, I want war!"

The Nazis wished to exterminate the Communists, to rob the Russian people of all their wealth and to starve them to death. The rest of the subhumans would become slaves to the master race. It was very characteristic for dictators to behave in such a way.

When the French were in the year 1940 on the verge of defeat, Mussolini attacked France in the south. The Government of France, in desperation, sent messengers to Mussolini offering him everything, including colonies, even Corsica.

What did Mussolini say?

Did he accept the offer?

Mussolini's answer was: "I don't want anything. I want war."

War he received.

Hitler answered the same to Stalin. "I want war, only war," he said.

War he received.

The Germans considered the Russians as a big elephant standing on feet of straw. One strong push and the elephant would collapse.

The Slavs were subhumans anyway. It was proven in the war against Finland. The Russian Army could not defeat the small

Finland. It took them almost a half a year to conclude peace with the Finns.

The truth was that the Russian soldier did not want to fight Finland.

The Germans thought, and they were convinced, that the Russian campaign would not last more than six weeks.

At the beginning it looked this way.

The Russians were defeated on all the length of the front. Almost no resistance.

In less than one week, Minsk, the capital of White Russia, was conquered. The Russians were running for their lives. As I described earlier during the first week of fighting, when I walked on foot from Wolkowysk to Rozana, a distance of about 35 Miles in White Russia, I saw lying on the ground thousands over thousands of Russian soldiers killed in action. There were also enormous amounts of broken ammunition, numerous destroyed tanks, artillery pieces and guns.

I figured that if all the battle front, from the Baltic states in the North to the Ukraine in the south, sustained similar losses, then the Russians were defeated right then.

After a few months, the German army overran Smolensk and reached the outskirts of Moscow.

The Russian soldier, just as in Finland, did not want to fight. The Russian people as a whole hated Stalin. He murdered the bulk of his officers. He caused the death of millions of peasants. Millions of civilians suffered in terrible labor camps. There was hardly a family which did not sustain losses caused by Stalin and his regime.

No wonder then that when the Germans set foot on Russian territory, the population welcomed them, glad to be able to get rid of Stalin.

The Ukrainians, the White Russians, the Lithuanians met them with bread and salt, promising full collaboration.

What did the Germans do?

Did they accept their friendliness?

Did they promise them justice?

No! The Germans exhibited hatred and arrogance towards

the inhabitants of the occupied Russian territories. They committed heinous crimes on defenseless people for no reason at all.

The Nazis were blind and deaf to the pleadings of the natives. Hitler's mind was to terrorize the people when terror was not necessary.

"Frighten the subhumans, let them know who is the master race. Let them tremble from fear when they see the master before their eyes."

In many towns and villages of occupied Russia, people were murdered. The best and most respectable men were hanged in the center of the town, for no reason at all.

At first, the Russians were perplexed and shocked by such behavior. They couldn't comprehend it.

Later, they realized that the Nazis were much worse than Stalin. They looked with apprehension upon the murdering of thousands of children and women, the destroying of entire cities.

They could not comprehend the German special commandos (Einsatzgruppen), who followed the army and whose task was not to fight the enemy, but to murder the civilian population in cold blood and for no reason at all.

Then they put up a terrific resistance. The war started really at that time for the Russian people. Every house, every village, every river and bridge, was defended to the utmost.

The Russian soldier, who did not want to fight at the beginning, became the best soldier in the world.

The Germans killed every Communist, every commissar, on sight.

There were at that time about three million Jews in Russia. Most of them occupied positions in the army, administration and other vital departments.

They also did not like Stalin. Like the rest of the people, they would have liked to see the overthrow of the hated regime. But they realized the danger of the Nazis, and that Hitler was one thousand times worse than Stalin. The Nazis would not let them live at all. They were informed about the Nazi atrocities and crimes committed by the Germans in Poland, Greece, France, Yugoslavia and all the other occupied territories.

The Reasons of Germany's Defeat

In order to live, they had to fight Hitler, as hard as possible, using all their strength to the point of sacrifice. There was no other alternative. They understood that there was no choice but to undertake a terrific struggle for life and subsistence.

It became clear to the Russians that the Germans were out to exterminate them for no reason, but for the sake of terror.

The entire nation stood up for the holy fight in order to save their own lives and the lives of their families.

The Russian soldier was admired by the entire world for his gallantry and courage.

This was the same soldier who could not conquer Finland, the same soldier who did not want to fight at the beginning of the war, June, 1941, surrendering territories and fortified cities.

It was clear from the above description that the Nazis unleashed a war with all the chances and conditions to sustain a victory.

Hitler lost the war because he committed many mistakes, which any normal person with average abilities would have avoided.

Here were the mistakes which, in my opinion, turned the tide of events.

I. Germany attacked Russia, creating a second front. The attack for military and economic reasons should have been directed against the Middle East, like Syria, Iraq, Palestine, with the purpose of joining hands with the Japanese through India.

The British would have to fight on two fronts in North Africa, with most of the supplies and raw materials cut off.

The English were not in a position, at that time, to sustain the full onslaught of the German and Italian armies on two fronts. They would have to surrender, after getting very favorable terms and to conclude a separate peace treaty.

American help would be hampered and not very decisive, especially since they had to fight the Japanese in the Pacific.

II. The enormous atrocities committed on completely innocent men, women and children.

Hitler did not take advantage of the hatred that most of the Russian people felt against Stalin. Instead of being friendly to the natives and promising them freedom, and happiness, the

Germans started to terrorize the people by shooting and hanging the most prominent citizens.

Hitler did not comprehend what friendliness and amicability meant. Those words did not exist in his vocabulary. Atrocities, abuses, killings, molestations, destructions, terror, those were the essentials by which he lived.

III. The senseless, illogical and purposeless murdering of the Jews. The ghettoes, Einsatz Kommandos, the gas vans, the gas chambers, the Krematoria, all the factories of death—will remain forever in the minds of mankind. They'll never be forgotten. It is and will forever remain a tragedy for the history of the German nation.

One could easily imagine and predict the effect on the direction and the solution of the war had the three million Jews, together with the other enemies of Stalin, instead of fighting the Germans, helped them. The Russian campaign would have been victoriously finished in six weeks, as universaly predicted.

Those were the three cardinal mistakes committed by evil and sick minds which caused the defeat of Germany in the Second World War.

The Third Reich, which had to endure a thousand years, was destroyed for the benefit and salvation of mankind.

Postwar Germany, with the help of America, became one of the wealthiest countries in the world. They enjoyed a prosperity that they never dreamed of.

The National Socialists would have never been able to create such well-being, such a high standard of living and thriving economical conditions as they exist today.

In January, 1944, Leningrad, the city which was besieged for thirty months, and where the inhabitants suffered enormously from German bombardment, diseases and starvation, was finally liberated. Six hundred thousand people still remained alive in the city.

Finland was completely defeated in the middle of the year 1944. Crimea was liberated entirely. The rivers Bug, Dniestr and Pruth were bridged.

White Russia was conquered. Minsk was reoccupied and my city Wolkowysk was overjoyed when the Russian troops reentered the town. Unfortunately, the city was almost completely destroyed and most of the people killed. From the thousands of Jews who lived there not one remained in the city. Almost all men, women and children perished in the German concentration camps.

The Russians continued their offensive and reached the Vistula.

The Ukraine was reconquered. Lemberg, the capital of West Ukraine, was liberated. The southern part of the main Polish river, the Vistula, was crossed over to reach the old capital of Poland, Krakov. By September, almost all the countries of the German satelites, like Hungary, Romania, etc., were occupied.

As more Russian or Polish territory became liberated, horrible, wicked, devilish, demoniacal, hellish scenes were revealed before the eyes of the Russian soldiers.

In White Russia, Poland, the Ukraine, hundreds of towns and villages were destroyed.

The people, including women and children, were mur-

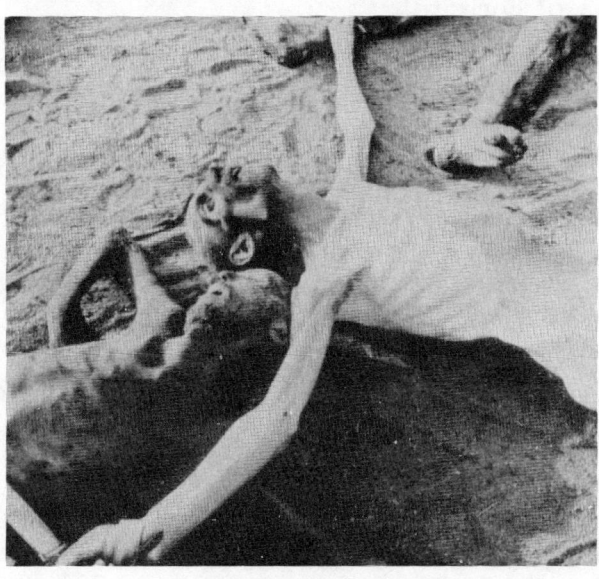

Some of the victims in the camp

dered in cold blood in the outskirts of the cities, in the ravines or forests.

Many were transported to the German concentration camps, where they perished.

Ghost towns, with devastation, desolation, destruction and ruin, dominated.

Here and there some queer, disoriented, unbalanced, debilitated, human beings left their hiding places and told the story of unbelievable atrocities and crimes perpetrated by Germans over the defenseless civilians. Almost no children were visible. The soldiers were shocked at the beginning, then they started to shed tears over the murder of their children and women, old parents and relatives.

Why? . . . Why? . . . murmured the soldiers. Illogical, foolish and insane! . . .

They left for the front with their hearts full of sorrow and despair. The fighting was going on mercilessly and with more vigor.

Forward! Forward!

New territory must be liberated!

Troops cleared camp area with bulldozers

The Reasons of Germany's Defeat

The more swiftly, rapidly, the better.

Maybe an innocent soul, a life will be saved. Maybe a child will be found alive.

In July 1944, as the Russians advanced and as more and more atrocities and killings were revealed, Maidanek, one of the death factories of the vast Nazi empire, was occupied almost intact (7/23/44).

The Russians had seen with their own eyes many criminal acts committed by the Germans. But what they saw in Maidanek was unbelievable.

Scattered skeletons of human beings all over the camp. Fragments of bones and ashes near the Krematoria and the gas chambers.

Pounds of the deadly gas Cyclon B.

Thousands of shoes, clothings, children toys, valises and all kinds of luggage.

Some had the names and addresses of the owners attached. It was inconceivable, incredible, beyond belief, to such a degree that the newspapers in the west *refused* to print the stories from their correspondents. The radios *declined* to broadcast the dispatches and reports as unreal, impossible, and assumed that the unbelievable reports were part of a Russian propaganda.

Only when Buchenwald, Dachau, Mathausen were discovered, did the news media of the west change their minds and print the stories. The world became convinced that the stories of Maidanek, Treblinka, Auschwitz were not products of sick minds looking for revenge, but genuine stories.

Dr. Joseph Mengele, the angel of death in Auschwitz. He made selections on the ramp of Birkenau, determining the fate of everyone.

The Year 1944

A group of Nazis. In the first row, right, is Rudolph Höss, Commandant of Auschwitz; left, Himmler.

Globoenik, Chief of the SS and Police of the District of Lublin. He was in charge of the extermination camps of Majdanek, Treblinka, Sobibor and others. One of the most bloodthirsty men, which only Nazism was able to produce.

H. Müller, SS General of the Police. One of the Gestapo Chiefs who disappeared and was never found.

Alois Brunner, Eichman's deputy in Vienna.

Rudolph Günter, one of Eichman's helpers.

Some of the Nazi Criminals
Top Row, l. to r.:
Martin Borman, nearest adviser and Hitler's helper.
Adolph Hitler.
Herman Goering, Hitler's deputy and chief of the German Air Force. He created the Gestapo originally and the concentration camps.
Center row, l. to r.:
Reinhard Heydrich, SS Lieutenant General chief of the Reich's main security office (RSHA), responsible for most of the crimes.
Heinrich Himmler, Chief of the Gestapo. He organized the concentration camps. After Hitler, he was the most responsible for the deaths of millions of innocent people.
Ernst Kaltenbrunner, an Austrian, chief of Himmler's Security department, including the SS, SD, etc. Yet, in Nurenberg he testified that he didn't know of anything; he blamed others.
Bottom line, l. to r.:
Theodor Eicke, inspector of the concentration camps. Under his guidance the prisoners were treated brutally.
Adolph Eichman, head of the Jewish Section IV B 4.
Rudolph Höss, Commandant of Auschwitz.

Goebels, Joseph Paul (1897–1945) German Nazi propagandist.

CHAPTER XIV

Gunthergrube Concentration Camp. Assassination of Hitler. Miracle # 8

THE SLANDEROUS, SCANDALOUS AND MALICIOUS REPORT OF DR. ZENKTELLER. ALOIS FREY THE CHIEF OF GUNTHER GRUBE (LENDZIN). DR. FISCHER. THE HANGING OF PRISONERS. THE ATTEMPT ON THE LIFE OF HITLER, BY VON STAUFENBERG, ON JULY 20, 1944. THE PRISONER WEINBERG. YANOWSKA CAMP. MY LIFE WAS SAVED AGAIN.

I continued my work on Block Eight of the Hospital. As soon as Dr. Thilo, the German doctor, entered the administration building, I immediately sent out all the Jewish sick inmates and told them to hide in some places outside the barrack. As I mentioned before, at the end of 1943, only Jewish sick, without exception, were sent to the gas chambers.

One day, Dr. Zenkteller came to my barrack and saw many Jewish sick inmates lying in their beds.

"You told Dr. Thilo yesterday that you had no Jews in your barrack." He kicked me with his shoes and left.

Next morning, I was called by the German doctor, Dr. Thilo, to the "Schreibstube."

"I was informed by Dr. Zenkteller," he said, "that you sent out the Jewish inmates from your barrack before the selections. You forgot, evidently, that you are in Auschwitz. I'll remind you of it."

He took a piece of paper and wrote down an order to transfer me to Block Eleven of Auschwitz I and to shoot me in the yard in front of the famous "Wall of Death."

"This paper," he said, "is an order for you to be shot (erschossen zu werden)."

He lifted his head and looked at me. I stood straight, did not complain, did not beg for mercy. I directed my eyes towards him and didn't say a word.

The German became wild:

"You don't care to die, ha! To be shot is too good for you!"

He tore the paper to pieces.

"I'll send you to the coal mines, where you are going to work very hard, half immersed in water, being constantly beaten by the kapos and our guards. We Germans need the coal and you are going to work hard and waste away till you'll die (schwer arbeiten, um langsam zu Krepieren)."

I had to leave the hospital grounds immediately, and was transfered to the men's camp (Männer Lager).

I received a place in one of the delapidated barracks and had to sleep in an upper berth under a broken roof which was leaking. I had to lie constantly only on one side in order to avoid the dripping water.

This was the beginning of January, 1944. I had been in the camp for one year already. Everybody knew me as an old veteran of Birkenau. I had to wait till a transport was sent to the mines.

In the "Schreibstube" (Accounting and administration barrack), many other veterans of Auschwitz worked, prisoners who arrived a year or more ago.

They were all concerned about my fate. They hated Dr. Zenkteller almost as much as they hated the Germans. To perish after enduring a year in Birkenau was a calamity and a catastrophe which touched their own safety. They tried to help me with better food. The orderlies were directed not to bother me.

I looked at the electrically charged barbed wires and decided to attack at least one Nazi and to run to the wires. I waited for the transfer.

"O G-d!" I prayed, "strengthen my soul only this time, and let me avenge my life and the lives of those who are perishing every day! Let me die together with the Nazis!"

At the selections, which regularly took place in the men's camp, I was told to hide and not expose myself, because Dr. Thilo might put down my number at one of the selections and my fate would be sealed.

Many transports left for different mines, where a prisoner could not endure more than one to two weeks, and I wondered why I was left in my barrack and not sent away with the transports.

Finally, the day arrived when I was informed that a group of newly arrived prisoners was being formed, and that I would have to go with them.

The group consisted of prisoners from Sosnowice, Bendzin, or other parts of Silesia, and about fifty from Belgium and Holland. Old veterans (Numbers), orderlies were dispatched with this group, namely: Two Kapos, two Chiefs of Blocks (Blockälteste) and one accountant (Schreiber).

The location was a mine in Silesia called Lendzin (Günthergrube). I was told not to worry because we were going, at first, not to the mines, but to build a new camp, which was going to be ready not less than another six months later. The work for me would be not too difficult. The war might be ended by then. The accompanying orderlies were informed about my misfortune and asked not to make any difficulties for me.

Next morning, after the roll call, our group assembled in front of the gate and was dispatched to the washing room, which was not far away from the gas chambers and Krematoria.

The washroom was a large hall. Inmates were running all around completely naked. Germans were keeping their guns directed on the inmates. We were told to enter inside. We washed ourselves and were waiting among other hundreds of prisoners for our clothing.

Suddenly, I noticed the German doctor Thilo walking in

our direction and looking for something. He came, watched us for a while and observed the faces of the prisoners near him.

I tried to stay far away from him and take care he should not recognize me. Such a beast could change his mind and send me to the gas chamber, which was nearby.

Luckily he left soon.

We were glad to get some clothing and waited till the working commandoes returned to the camp.

It was a beautiful sunset on this winter day, one of the last days of January, 1944.

The orchestra was playing, as usual, in front of the gate as thousands of unfortunate prisoners returned from a hard day of work.

Some were carrying the dead bodies of their neighbors, who were killed at work.

Some were supported and helped by friends, because they were too weak to walk by themselves.

The orchestra continued to play and the prisoners were marching.

We entered the men's camp again. Our group was packed into one of the barracks for the night. Next morning, before noon, we were ordered to enter into a few trucks waiting for us near the gate. Nearby stood SS men with truncheons beating us severely while we pushed ourselves into the trucks.

It was a cold winter day as we were sitting on the floor of the truck thinking about our new situation.

What kind of a camp was it going to be?

How many of us were going to survive?

Actually, we contemplated it would not make a big difference one way or the other.

We reached the end of the rope.

I was able to save my medical diploma again. I concealed it in a dark corner of the washroom. Nobody noticed it. As soon as we received our clothing, I recovered it and put it in my pocket.

I asked myself many times: Why did I need the diploma? Would I ever be able to use my medical profession?

We would never come out alive anyway.

Still, I didn't want to be separated from it. I felt safer touching it and feeling it in my pocket.

The road was rough and bumpy. SS men were sitting at all the four corners of the truck with their guns directed at us.

We finally reached our destination.

It was Lendzin (in Polish) or Günthergrube (in German), in Silesia. It belonged to Buna (Auschwitz III). This was the end of January, 1944.

The gates of the new camp opened and we marched inside. There were two large buildings for the prisoners, one building for the so-called kitchen. A small room served as a "Bekleidung Kamer" where old tattered clothing was kept.

A large yard separated the above buildings from the other structures, where the SS guards lived and which were located outside the barbed wires.

We stood, shivering from cold, in the middle of the huge yard, waiting for the Germans to arrive.

In the meantime, we observed the camp. After a while, we saw two Germans emerging from the SS building with guns and truncheons in their hands. One was a fat robust fellow with a mean expression on his face.

I recognized him immediately. This was the infamous Mohl, whom I had seen many times in Birkenau and whom I described earlier in my narration. The other one, was a little shorter, of dark complexion, about thirty years old.

Later we found out that his name was Alois Frey and that he was appointed by the Nazi hierarchy, after years of training in the Nazi spirit, to be the Lager-Führer (Director) of our camp.

What was our first meeting with our new boss and master going to be like?

Was he going to talk to us, to make some explanation about our new life? After all, two hundred prisoners were waiting for him to make the first acquaintence.

Alois Frey, our new master, came nearer. As soon as he reached us, he started to beat us with his heavy truncheon, brandishing a gun with his other hand. At the same time, he was yelling, howling, and roaring like a wild beast from the jungle.

It was amazing that Mohl, who was known in Birkenau for his atrocities, stood grinning sardonically, but didn't beat us.

Our new master continued to pummel and hammer us, shrieking at the same time.

"You miserable, wretched, good-for-nothing subhumans, you are going to work hard here. Otherwise you'll be shot or hanged. No mercy will be shown to this despicable rubbish."

This was our first encounter, as a result of which many received swollen heads, lacerations, contusions, abrasions and even hematomas.

They left.

We entered our new homes. Barrack Number One, where the chief prisoner was Zepl, and Barrack Number Two, where the chief was Yirmeyau. Each barrack had one hundred prisoners. I belonged to Barrack Number One.

Broken hearted, sadness inside us with bitterness in our heart, we entered into our new abode. It was already dark, the very beginning of a winter night in Polish Silesia.

Although protected by the walls of the barrack, we felt very cold, freezing.

I remembered our first days in Birkenau and I organized two circles of prisoners, one inside the other, with the backs touching each other. The circles were separated from each other by a yard. Then we returned walking backwards, touching each other's back and rubbing one back against the other. It was a very good system of warming up when other means were not available. I recommend it to the unfortunate souls of the far cold steppes and vast spaces of exile, and in the prisons.

We arrived at Günthergrube with our own shoes.

Birkenau, the worst extermination camp, already permitted the prisoners to wear their own shoes in January, 1943. They were able to find out by bad experience that shoes were indispensable for the inmates of Auschwitz in the cold Polish winters. The prisoners simply could not work without shoes. They couldn't even walk in the freezing snow. The so-called "Hollanderki" were pieces of wood which resembled shoes and had a hole inside in which the prisoners put their feet.

They were no substitute for shoes. They fell off the feet, did not protect from cold and often inflicted injuries to the feet, caused by friction, which turned, under the conditions of Auschwitz, gangrenous.

The Germans needed workers. The inmates in the concentration camps were ideal workers in the spirit of National Socialism. The feeding was very minimal, the work was very strenuous with long hours. Wages—nil. Since the supply was already limited in 1942, the Nazis were ordered to murder only old men, women, and children and to keep temporarily the young, strong men and women alive, till they succumb.

It was necessary to create for them minimal conditions of existence in order to get maximum production with minimum of expenses. To let them wear their own shoes was a necessary and an essential requirement for continuation of their miserable existence.

Only when the inmates lost their strength and became debilitated were they sent to the gas chambers.

Like Eichmann, who overdid himself by sending thousands of Hungarians and others to their death in the last months of the Second World War, so was our new master, Alois Frey. He was more Nazi than his Nazi superiors and teachers.

It was very clear to us that a German Lager-Führer, a director of a concentration camp, had to be a German who by his past activities and services gained the full confidence of his superiors, which meant extreme cruelty to the subhumans, including murder and annihilation of entire races and nations.

A nice decent fellow, even a person with an average, normal character, could have never belonged to the Nazi party, not to talk about the Chief Nazis who supervised the terrible concentration camps. All of them had to be tough criminals, and show their toughness by the activities of the daily routine in the camps.

Alois Frey exceeded any expectations of his superiors by his thoughness, vulgarity and rudeness, to such a degree that he was entrusted by the Nazi hierarchy to be an independent Lager-Führer, i.e. to direct the activities of a small concentration camp *all by himself*.

Yes! Alois Frey became the unconditional master of Günthergrube, our boss of life and death. Not every Nazi could be awarded and entrusted with such a position and post.

Aloid Frey craved to show his superiors like Rudolf Hoess or Pohl that he was worthy of their trust and commission.

Therefore, like Eichmann, he overdid himself.

His first order of the day was to take away our shoes and to force us to walk in Hollanderki, which was the cause of many fatalities and sufferings.

Many froze their feet and developed gangrenous lesions. They were selected by Alois Frey for the gas chambers. Still others lost their wooden shoes on the road to work and had to walk in the snow in their bare feet.

The daily food consisted of a small piece of bread, colored water in the morning and a cabbage soup in the evening. The soup contained very often white worms of 1-2 inches long. It was very difficult to swallow it, even when one was starving. I just couldn't eat it, my esophagus contracted and refused to let it pass down to the stomach.

Some prisoners, desperate, hungry, debilitated, gulped it down. The more educated explained that the worms contained aminoacids, protein necessary for survival. I spoke to the inmates who worked in the kitchen, and mainly those who sorted the vegetables and potatoes. They told me that all the vegetables were rotten. It was impossible to clean the worms out because they were numerous and inside the vegetables. Alois Frey told them to use it as it was, and no other food would be given.

The medical doctor who was in charge of Auschwitz III (Buna) was Dr. Fisher. He used to travel from mine to mine like Yavozna, Günthergrube, etc. and depart. His function was similar to Dr. Thilo in Birkenau. He used to give instructions on what to do with the weak and sick prisoners. Every two or three weeks, trucks used to appear and transfer the miserable sick prisoners to the gas chambers. In the little hospital of Günthergrube worked a dentist, Dr. Kovacs, in the capacity of a medical doctor, because no doctor was available for our little camp. New inmates used to arrive at our camp to substitute for those who were taken away.

I used to go out with all the other prisoners every morning and perform very strenuous physical work. The outside temperature in February, 1944, dropped often to 0° F which, combined with cold winds, made one feel like −5° F. Taking into consideration our poor clothing and the scarce and bad quality of food, I felt that I would not be able to continue for a long time.

What should I do? How could I spare and save myself? I had endured the ordeal of Auschwitz by now for more than a year. There was a better chance to survive now than ever before. The Germans were losing the war and retreating on all fronts.

From where would come my salvation? This was a moot question for which I couldn't find any answer. Suddenly, an idea passed through my head and I grasped the meaning and the enormous significance of it.

Dr. Fisher was coming to visit our camp. Since we had no real physician in the hospital, I would present myself to him and ask him for a job. He was in charge of Auschwitz III and the small mines and had nothing to do with Birkenau. He probably never heard about me and didn't know the reason why I was transferred to Günthergrube.

After a few days, I saw Dr. Fisher arriving at our camp. I came over to him and said:

"Herr Doctor! I am a physician and would like to ask whether I could be employed in my profession."

I knew that there was a scarcity of physicians in all Auschwitz, because the Germans at the beginning murdered almost all of them.

Dr. Fisher, a tall German, looked at me, observed the number on my jacket and trousers.

"What is it?" he asked. "Your number is 94430, which is an old number. You have been in the camp more than a year. I was wondering why you were not employed up to this time. We don't have enough physicians and we need them very badly. An epidemic of contagious diseases is spreading over Auschwitz, which might also reach the German barracks.

"Tell me, what was the reason that you were not employed as a physician up to now? Have you ever worked previously as a doctor in the camp?"

I didn't answer, because I saw that our talk took the wrong direction.

Dr. Fisher continued:

"Now I remember, Dr. Thilo told me about a doctor prisoner who had the audacity to save sick inmates from the selections to the gas chamber, and that he sent him as a punishment to the mines for hard work.

"Now I remember clearly. What is your name? Quick! Answer!"

"My name is Dr. Harsaw."

"That is it. I recall now exactly what happened. You had done something terrible, unheard of in a German concentration camp. Dr. Thilo was right in not shooting you. You have to work hard till you perish. We Germans are very efficient in taking out all the strength of the enemies of the Third Reich, by hard work and maximum production, till they die gradually, peacefully. . . ."

My plan failed. I had to return again to my previous hard job. I had to dig all day long with a heavy pickax and to try to break the frozen ground.

The ground in February was so frozen and hard like a cover of iron and steel. The pickax couldn't penetrate.

Cold, hungry, exhausted from hard work, exposed to the winds and freezing weather all day long. This was my fate at that time.

All the other inmates suffered the same way. Many died on the job, many returned with frozen feet. They couldn't work any more and were transferred to Birkenau, to perish in the gas chambers.

The same process of annihilation was going on in all the other mines which belonged to Auschwitz III (Buna), where thousands of desperate human beings starved and were compelled to work for the German industrialists, who especially asked for prisoners of the concentration camp because of the cheap labor.

The directors saw with their own eyes how the Nazis treated the unfortunate, exhausted and dying prisoners and evidently liked it; otherwise, they wouldn't have asked for more prisoners. Not one word of protest, not one voice of objection to the terrible conditions of their own workers, was uttered. The German directors accepted this new way of production. They didn't care about the extreme misery of the prisoners and nothing was done to alleviate the lives of the workers. Let the subhumans die and be consumed by the fires of the Krematoria! Other prisoners, other human beings will be supplied by the Nazis to take the place of those who perished. This was the ultimate rationale of the German directors.

The work in our camp was organized and supervised by an architect sent from Berlin. He was "The Master" of our labor.

The guards stood all around our labor place and watched the inmates, compelling them to work hard with the last strength of their sinews. From time to time Alois Frey used to come and give additional instructions to the guards.

Dr. Kovacs, the dentist, as I described previously, was the chief in the clinic. He didn't like the idea of my asking the German doctor for a job in the clinic. After all, he was not a physician. He was afraid of being substituted for by a real doctor of medicine. Although Dr. Kovacs would have still remained a dentist, he felt threatened. I had asked him many times to let me work at the clinic and the little hospital. I assured him that under no circumstances would I be the chief of the clinic. All that I wanted was to have a little job in order not to go outside in the freezing cold and be exposed to the fury of the Nazis.

Nothing helped. My expressed desire met deaf ears. My call, plea and appeal remained unanswered. Dr. Kovacs was in a very good relationship with the German Lager-Führer, Alois Frey. Once or twice weekly, especially on Sundays, he used to go to the living quarters of Alois Frey, allegedly for repair of his teeth. What he did there, besides the repairing of teeth, had never been known. Everybody was curious to find out the reason the Germans knew everything that was going on in the camp. It was clear that the Germans had informers, stool pigeons.

One day, while I was working at loading coal, I saw unexpectedly the helper of Dr. Kovacs, Mr. Shmulik, standing near me. I asked him the reason for his working there and not at the clinic.

"I wanted to go out for fresh air," he answered.

I did not accept his answer as a reasonable reply, because he had enough air in the camp and hospital grounds.

Next Sunday, which was the last week of February, 1944, Alois Frey entered our barrack and announced that Dr. Harsaw, number 94430, would remain in the camp and would not go out to the usual outside work.

Dr. Kovacs came into the barrack and congratulated me for remaining in the camp.

"You'll be accepted pretty soon in the hospital. You'll be one of us," he said and handed me an additional plate of soup.

I couldn't understand all the happenings. Many questions entered my mind which demanded an explanation.

First of all, why was the announcement of Alois Frey so harsh-sounding?

Secondly, why did the German Lager-Führer find it necessary to state it personally. It was very unusual. He could have given an order to employ me at the hospital, and hand over the order to Dr. Kovacs, who attended him the same Sunday in the morning.

Thirdly, how could Alois Frey overrule the German doctor, Dr. Thilo, who directed not to employ me at the clinic, but to compel me to work very hard and to give me the toughest assignments?

I was told, also, that Dr. Thilo sent a special letter to Alois Frey in this regard. The latter even did not consult Dr. Fischer. All this made me very apprehensive.

Next morning, I was informed by the French prisoner Mr. Pastell, who worked in the administration and who wrote all the letters and managed all the correspondence for Alois Frey, the real reason thereof.

"I feel my obligation," he said, "to tell you the truth and to reveal to you the real cause of not letting you outside the camp. A stool pigeon informed Alois Frey that you were trying to escape. Still more, you were in contact with a woman civilian engineer while working outside, who was making all the preparations for your escape. This is the reason why they keep you inside and they don't let you out. The German Lager Führer dictated a letter to the Gestapo in Katovice informing them about your plans and ordered me to dispatch the letter immediately. I wanted you to know all about it. The situation is very serious and very dangerous. Try to do something if you can."

What could I do? I was watched at every step. Any wrong movement would spell death and annihilation. I would wait. I could attack a German at the last moment and fulfill my promise to die with the Nazis.

I kept repeating to myself, "Remember, even when a sharp sword is touching your neck, you should not despair."

I had been many times in similar conditions and had, always, been able to come out intact. I would wait! The war was approaching its end anyway. But who was the informer? Terrible!

We had in the camp only about two hundred inmates. Who could be the stool pigeon?

It was superfluous to say that all the story about my escape was fabricated from the beginning till the end. I had never seen, nor had I ever been in contact with any civilian. It was strictly forbidden to talk to any civilian under penalty of death.

Who could have fabricated such a lie?

Maybe Alois Frey wanted to advance himself in the Nazi hierarchy and reported to his superiors about his ability to unmask a plot. Everything was possible. I heard of such tricks in the past.

I remained in the camp, not knowing what my fate was going to be.

Dr. Kovacs used to bring me an extra plate of soup from the hospital kettle. Was it compassion or remorse and pangs of conscience?

I was waiting for the worst, but nothing happened. One week passed, a month. . . . Nothing, no reply from Katovice!

"No news is good news," I said to myself and continued to hope.

On the seventh night of Passover of the year 1944, which was the fourteenth of April, Friday night, about 11 P.M., we were awakened by the guards. The gong started to sound very loudly and we were ordered to assemble on the yard, in front of the barracks for an "Appel" (roll call).

It was very unusual to make an "Appel" at this time of the night. Something extraordinary happened.

Since the Germans were sustaining at that time enormous defeats on the Russian as well as on the Western fronts, some of us thought that the Nazis were going to murder us as a form of revenge, which was the usual Nazi reaction to calamities. In any event, they would not permit us to live and to be living witnesses to their crimes.

Some inmates, awakened in the middle of the sleep and pushed out in the darkness of the night, were trembling from fear.

"This is the end," I heard voices all around me.

I myself was perturbed and agitated. I thought of the letter which Alois Frey sent out to his superiors in Katovice and Auschwitz about my allegedly contacting the civilian engineer in order to escape.

I saw a truck entering the camp's grounds and surmised that some prisoner would be taken to the infamous Block Eleven of Auschwitz I for investigation.

Some inmates fearing the same, like Zev and his brother, were hiding and couldn't be found. Finally they were found out and brought to the yard.

After a short while, Alois Frey, the supreme lord, came out and read the names of the following five prisoners:

Idl Potok, Heniek Ehrenfield, Firstenfield, Buchweitz and Bakalash.

All of them stepped out in front and entered the waiting truck, accompanied by wild shouts of Frey.

The truck left, the camp gates closed again and we were told to return to our barracks. Nobody knew what was happening.

Why were the above five inmates taken away? What was the reason?

Even the other Buchweitz, the brother of the one who was taken away, didn't understand the reason. They were very close to each other and one knew all the intimate thinking of the other. Yet he couldn't solve the problem.

"Maybe they were transferred to another camp, to occupy leading positions," suggested one of the inmates. This was a possibility, because all five prisoners were the strongest and most intelligent prisoners. Idl Potok was a Kapo, the others were all foremen, working in Commando Number One. It was a mystery and an enigma to all of us. Pretty soon everything was forgotten.

In retrospect, I couldn't understand why I wasn't taken away together with the above-mentioned five prisoners?

My alleged conspiracy was punishable very severely. Although it wasn't true, the letter with my intention to escape was sent out by Alois Frey. In looking back, I think that the paper dispatched by Frey was lost on the way, or maybe some decent fellow at the desk destroyed it, knowing exactly well the Nazi plots fabricated in order to advance themselves.

Maybe my life was spared and protected by Providence in order to tell the story to mankind and to warn humanity of the consequences of Nazi brutality.

I believe that G-d took a look at the gas chambers, Krematoria and promised that such evil, badness and dreadfulness should not recur.

I was still imprisoned inside the camp and was not permitted to return to work. Being in the camp, I saw from time to time a truck arriving from Birkenau. The sick prisoners were herded and forced to enter the truck. They had always been taken by Alois Frey and Dr. Kovacs. The sick prisoners never returned. They were sent straight to the gas chambers and consumed by the fires of the Krematoria.

One day, a new doctor arrived at our camp. Although he was an old man, the German doctors sent him to work in the clinic and the little hospital attached to it. They knew that our camp had no physician but a dentist only. As I explained earlier, I was not allowed to work in my profession, because of the order of Dr. Thilo.

Dr. Kovacs did not like the idea. He was afraid of being substituted for by the old physician.

One day, the nice respectful physician was unexpectedly,

without any reason, put on the truck and sent to Birkenau with all the other sick people.

Honor, tribute and glorification to his memory.

At the end of May, I was ordered to return to work with Commando Two. I was glad to go outside to work. The sword which was hanging over my head was removed for the time being.

The foundation of the newly formed barracks were already formed.

We called the German architect "The Master." He was about forty years old, of medium stature, and he didn't abuse the inmates. Under the circumstances he was considered to be a nice fellow. He had suffered on a gastro-intestinal ulcer for many years. Very often, abdominal pains kept him in deep distress. The attacks were intensified during the spring and autumn.

One day, the "Master" was stricken by severe abdominal pains, accompanied by nausea and vomiting. No doctor was available at our working place, nor was any doctor to be found in the nearby villages. The pangs of pain intensified. The "Master" became pale, weak, caused probably by internal bleeding. The inmates nearby told him that there was in the camp a doctor who might help him. In desperation, he sent over a messenger to call me.

When I arrived, I saw a thin short man lying on a bench complaining of severe epigastric pains. I tried to help him as much as I could by administering different medications which I found in his room. They consisted of Belladonna preparations, antiacids and some protectans like bismut subcarbonate, etc.

Above all I tried to quiet him down, because his face expressed anxiety. He told me that he had been suffering a long time, and had been hospitalized many times. But the treatment had always been the same. It consisted of a strict diet and the medications which I found already in his medical chest.

We spoke for many hours. For the first time, I spent a full day in a warm, cozy room, sipping tea and talking with a German who seemed to me to be a little different than the others.

I told him that in my private practice, before my arrest, I

used to treat similar patients with new injections, named "Larostidin," made by "Roche Laboratories."

"How was it possible," said the "Master," "that an injection should help the lesion in my stomach and duodenum?"

"The medication injected," I explained, "reached the stomach and duodenum, by way of the blood stream. It provided the necessary elements to heal the affected area. Something was missing in your blood which, together with inadequate diet, wrong food, and stress of daily living in a susceptible person, caused the formation of the ulcer. Now, by supplying the element which was missing with the help of Larostidin, we reversed the vicious circle. In addition, by adjusting the mental outlook of the patient and removing his anxiety, and by providing the adequate diet to avoid local irritation of the intestine, the ulcer might be completely healed. The cure of the lesion can be accomplished only by removing the causes."

"You mean that I still have a chance to be cured?" asked the "Master." "I'll still be able to live like any other human being? To enjoy life and not to be on this detestable ulcer diet?"

"Yes," I replied. "I had many cases in which the ulcer was cured completely."

"Please, doctor, give me a prescription for this wonderful medication and I'll get it in Krakow or Katovice."

"I don't have here my prescription blanks, but I can write it down on a piece of paper and the local pharmacist will honor it. Don't forget to bring a syringe and needles. Remember one very important thing, I am a prisoner of Auschwitz and it is strictly forbidden for me to treat civilians. If the Nazis find it out, they'll kill me and you together. Please be careful."

"Don't worry, nobody will ever find it out. Secondly, I have many good friends among the Nazis of Silesia, and if necessary also in Berlin."

He continued to talk about the treacherous Russians and unfaithful English. "According to our newspapers," he said, "the Führer did everything possible to avoid a war, and even now he would like to conclude a peace agreement, but the allies refused it."

I didn't answer the Master because I didn't want to contradict him. To tell the "Master" that his Führer is a bloodthirsty animal, who murdered millions of children and for no reason at all, did not make sense at all. He would not understand it.

In the evening, I returned to the camp, together with all the other prisoners. I was glad of having had a nice rest during the day and was hoping for the future.

Next morning, as soon as we arrived at our working place, I was called again by the "Master." He opened a box full of ampules of "Larostidin." There were, also, a new syringe and needles.

"Sit down," he said, "and I'll explain to you what happened. I went to the local pharmacist and showed him your prescription. The pharmacist said that this was a very expensive new medication and that he didn't know the name of the doctor. I answered that I received the prescription from my family doctor, who lived in Hamburg. The pharmacist said that it was very difficult to get the injections, but since this was intended to be used for an important German, he was going to oblige. I received the injections and here they are.

"Don't be afraid," continued the Master. "All the influential Nazis are my friends. I want you yourself to administer the injections. Naturally, you can not go and work outside, because your hands must be clean. Otherwise, I might get infected when you inject me. Therefore, as soon as you arrive in the morning, you'll come straight to my room. I'll be waiting for you. You'll sterilize the syringe and give me the injection. You'll be my personal doctor. My health is worth more to me than all the constructions here. You'll make tea for yourself and me and help me in the paper work. You'll sit in my room till the evening."

I administered the first injection and prescribed additional oral medication. Next morning when I entered the Master's room, I was met with excitement, gratitude and appreciation.

"You know" he started, "the medication works. I have never felt so good in all my life. It is a definite improvement. I am overjoyed and thankful to you. I even tried to eat some fruit and it didn't harm me. When are you going to give me the next injection?"

"Tomorrow," I said.

All day long I was sitting in the Masters room, resting, sipping tea and talking, reading and helping in the paper work.

A few weeks passed, and the Master's health continued to improve. The abdominal pains subsided entirely. He gained weight and started to eat, gradually, food which was considered previously to be taboo and strictly forbidden.

The intestinal ulcer of the Master was probably caused by a disorder of histamine, and by providing Larostidin the main cause of the ulcer formation was eliminated.

"I don't understand," complained the Master, "why nobody suggested this medication to me before."

"Larostidin is a new medication on the market," I answered.

Day after day, and week after week, I was sitting in the Master's room, doing nothing and spared from the outside violence and hard labor.

One day the Master told me, "I don't understand the Führer. He is a very important and capable man. He achieved a lot of victories, in Poland, France, Holland, Belgium, Balkans, etc. I am sure that miraculous weapons will be found which will give us the final victory. But I don't understand one thing. He keeps you, a decent human being and a highly skilled physician, in the concentration camp. I know that there are thousands of similar imprisoned men like you. Why doesn't the Führer send you and the others to the front to help our injured soldiers. They need you there. Thousands of German soldiers are dying because of lack of physicians. I was told previously that the prisoners are criminals, enemies of our 'Reich.' I see now, after observing you for quite a long time, that you are no criminal, but a decent fellow. I believe that the Führer is wrong in keeping you in the concentration camp for no reason at all."

The Master brought me bread, butter and even fruit. One day he put on the table a bottle of "Vodka" and said, "Let's celebrate our friendship. You saved me a lot of suffering and I am grateful to you."

"Thank you very much," I said. "I accepted your bread, butter, because I don't want to succumb to malnutrition. I want to sustain my health. I see that you are different from the Nazi guards and would love to celebrate our acquaintance. But I can not accept any alcohol as long as I am imprisoned in a concentration camp, and while so many human beings are being killed, maimed and destroyed. Let's postpone it till after the liberation."

The Master looked at me.

He understood.

One day on July 21, 1944, he brought me, for the first time, a German newspaper to read. It was forbidden under penalty of death to do it. Yet he risked his life and, handing over the newspaper, he said, "Take a look. The Führer was assassinated, yesterday, *July 20*. Maybe he is dead. Read it."

I took the paper and I started to read.

"Colonel von Staufenberg attempted to assassinate Hitler. He was not successful. Several officers were killed. Hitler was wounded but remained alive."

I couldn't believe my own eyes. Was it possible? An attempt on Hitler. Maybe he was dead by now.

I left the room and went outside to tell the prisoners the wonderful news. It was necessary to be very careful, lest the suspicions of the guards be aroused. I looked all around and observed the exhausted hard-working prisoners, full of despair, exerting their last strength not to collapse. Some were mixing cement, some were putting up bricks. The barracks were already half-ready. I approached one of the prisoners and said, "An attempt on the life of Adolf Hitler. It is true. But please, be careful! Tell the other prisoners! Don't reveal the source of the information."

The prisoner lifted his tired eyes towards me. He couldn't comprehend at first. He was very tired and depressed. I repeated what I said. Soon all the inmates were informed about the assassination. A prisoner near me was reciting a prayer.

"It is written that G-d will avenge the blood of the innocent victims and will make an atonement for them and His people....

"Let it be known, among nations, that innocent blood will be revenged and that the evil perpetrators will pay dearly for their crimes. The cry of the humble will not be forgotten."

This was the best day of my incarcerated life. Humanity would get rid of the devil with a human face. The gas chambers would stop killing. The Kramatoria would stop burning. The subhumans would become humans again and the slaves would be free once more.

During the following days we found out that Hitler was still alive.

Many high-ranking officers were arrested and shamefully murdered. The wrath of His Satanic Majesty poured over hundreds of men. Some of them were completely innocent. Almost all were tortured.

Field Marshal von Witzleben was hanged and affixed on a meathook. Seven others were hanged together with him, like cattle. The hanging was filmed and sent to Hitler. It was so gruesome that even Goebbels couldn't look at the film. The film was shown also to the high officers of the army, navy and air force. They refused to watch it.

From seventeen field marshals, ten were dismissed during the war, three died, three were murdered as a result of the Hitler plot and one remained alive. From thirty-six generals, eighteen were dismissed during the war, five murdered, ten died and three survived.

By showing this film to the military men, Hitler meant to frighten them in to submission. Here again were used the old tactics. Evidently, criminals are not capable of changing their behavior and not intelligent enough to understand the consequences.

The prisoners continued to work and build the new camp. I used to sit in the Master's room, helping him out with the paper work. I became a specialist in warming up the iron stove and preparing tea. I also cleaned and kept everything in order.

The Master felt excellent. No attacks of pain. He returned to a normal diet and even gained weight and strength. He was very satisfied.

The Master had many friends among the high Nazi hierarchy and the German administration.

Experiencing the welcome and gratifying improvement of his health, the Master recommended me highly to his friends.

He used to arrive with one of his friends and close us up in one of the unfinished barracks. I examined the patient, prescribed the necessary medication, and warned the official not to reveal to anyone who was his doctor.

The Master assured me that his friends in the administration occupied very high positions.

"It is nothing to worry about," he repeated. "The patients I am bringing you conduct all the work in Silesia."

One day he arrived with the director of the railway station of Katovice. He locked us up in a room and left. The director undressed and I started with the medical examination. Suddenly we heard knocking at the door.

"Open up. This is the guard." Soon the door was broken and two SS men entered, and found the director undressed and me writing a prescription.

"Don't you know," the Nazi said, "that it is forbidden under penalty of death to contact civilians. Medical treatment of a German by a Jewish doctor is unlawful and against the spirit of national socialism. We'll report it to the Lager-führer and the fate of both of you is sealed." They left.

"Don't worry," said the director. "The threats don't mean anything. They have the same value as the barking of dogs. The commanding officer of all the district is one of my best friends. What is wrong here anyway? I am sick for a few weeks already and I need medical treatment. There is a scarcity of doctors in war time. Leave it to me."

I ran to the Master and told him the story. He called up Katovice in my presence, and spoke over the phone for a short time. Evidently satisfied he turned to me and said, "Alois Frey wouldn't dare to start anything. If he did, he'd lose his head. You don't know what kind of a coward the Lager Führer is. He trembles from fear when he talks to a superior. Return to the inmates, nothing is going to happen. After all, I and the director are involved here too."

In the evening, I returned as usual with all the other prisoners to the camp. We assembled for the usual "Appel." Alois Frey called out my number.

"Number 94430, step out."

I didn't know what was going to happen to me, in spite of the assurances made by the director and the Master. A dreadful silence engulfed the camp. Everybody was standing at attention and waiting. Finally Frey spoke.

"Where do you think you are? It is Auschwitz! You are not permitted to treat civilians. Do you think that you have a private medical practice here?"

The eyes of all the prisoners were directed towards the German, as they were concerned about my fate. They waited to see what was going to happen.

"Poor Dr. Harsaw, he'll be killed," they murmured and mumbled.

Alois Frey continued.

"It is strictly forbidden to treat or to be in any contact with civilians. Remember it in the future. Dismissed."

As soon as he left the roll call grounds, I was surrounded by the prisoners, who congratulated me for the unusual Nazi behavior in my case.

"You are lucky," said one, "that it happened in 1944 and that Alois Frey was frightened by the telephone call."

In the camp was a prisoner by the name of Weinberg. He was of medium size, about thirty years old, a very active and intelligent fellow. His nose was flat, due, as he said, to boxing in his youth. He had keen and sharp eyes, but his manners were mild. He claimed to know everything, and even gave English lessons to some inmates as a preparation for freedom. He claimed to be one of the best massagists in the camp and he competed with me in massaging the Polish Kapo. He told the "Master" that he was a certified public accountant and he could do all the accounting for him. The "schreibstube," which was managed by Polish inmates, was convinced by him that he was a very important personality on the outside. He managed to escape a few times from the murderous hands of the Gestapo.

It was also true that he jumped out of a running train right under the noses of the Nazis. After the liberation we met each other again in Lublin. He occupied a high position in the administration of Silesia after it was reoccupied by the Russians.

Instead of continuing on my way to my city, Wolkowysk, I consented to his dialectics and rationalization and went with him

GÜNTHERGRUBE CONCENTRATION CAMP

to Katowice, where I became one of the chief doctors of Silesia and helped in restoration of the medical facilities, which were destroyed during the war.

In the concentration camp, Günthergrube, we became very good friends, sleeping in the same barrack and working at the same commando outside.

Every morning, on the first sound of the gong, Mr. Weinberg was the first to get up and to call out loudly, "Get up, you unfortunate prisoners, the time of hard labor is commencing."

"Please stop it," I said. "It makes me nervous and worrying before I really wake up."

All our conversations were turning around ways and means of escaping.

"You know," he said, "the best way to break loose is to dig a tunnel under the barracks during the night which would reach outside the barbed wires. The sand could be hidden in different parts of the camp grounds."

"This is very difficult," I said, "because the camp is very small in comparison with other camps and fresh dug-out sand could be detected by the Germans. In addition, we might have some spies on our block. It is very dangerous. If discovered, all of us would pay with our lives. . . ."

"You are right, we'll have to think about some other way."

One day, he whispered into my ears a top-secret new plan.

"The Lagerälteste (the chief of the prisoners) is planning to take over the camp and to escape to the nearby mountains or forests."

"How is he going to accomplish all that?" I asked. "Please give me all the particulars."

"The Lagerälteste, together with a group of inmates, will attack suddenly, in the middle of the night, the building where Alois Frey and his deputy are sleeping. I, myself, with another group of inmates, will cut all the telephone connections with the outside world. You, Dr. Harsaw, will get with you the toughest prisoners and attack the building where the guards are sleeping and take away all their guns and ammunition. Than we'll escape armed and form a partisan group."

"This is already a better plan, but we have to work out all the details. We have to get in contact with the outside world, especially with other partisan groups, and to prepare a good hiding-place right after our escape."

"That is right," said Weinberg. "We must escape. I realize that it is very dangerous. Many of us are going to be killed in the process. I am not afraid to die. But I am terrified when I think about the camp '*Yanowska*,' where I was incarcerated previously. I am fear-striken and haunted by the memory of this dreadful camp. I am afraid that they'll apply the same methods here."

"I never heard of this camp. What kind of a camp was it?"

"Yanowska camp," explained Mr. Weinberg, "was called also 'Lemberg camp,' because it was located on the outskirt of the city of Lemberg, the capital of western Ukraine. The camp was situated on the street of Yanowska, from which the name was derived. It was a camp for training SS men in atrocities and bestialities. There were many camps, like this one, dispersed all over Poland.

"Nobody heard of them because nobody survived those camps. I think that I am almost the only one who survived one of those SS training centers," continued Mr. Weinberg.

"Please unfold the story of the camp."

I'll tell it to you," said Weinberg, "for two reasons: First, because everything you'll hear represents the truth. Second, if anyone of us will survive by accident or good fortune, he should reveal it to the world.

"Camp Yanowska was surrounded by barbed wire and guarded by heavily armed SS men. The building in the middle had two large rooms, in which five thousand civilian prisoners were kept at one time. The place was too small for such a number. Therefore the prisoners had to stand all night long on their feet. There was no room to lie down. Many did not survive the night. In the morning numerous bodies were carried outside and put in the front of the building.

"The roll call started in the early morning and lasted a few hours. Hundreds of people were murdered during those hours. Those who survived a few days in this camp lost their identity. They changed to half-animal and half-ghost. Near the gates were standing the tools of torture. One of the worst was the pole put in operation by Hauptsturmführer Frank Warzok, to which two prisoners were fastened with thin cords, which cut into the flesh and the bodies were covered with blood. The prisoners remained hanging on the poles till they died. But death did not come very quickly and the prisoners begged their tormentors to shoot them. The criminals instead poured water on their victims to keep them alive longer. I am asking you, Dr. Harsaw, and am asking all the people of the world, could such atrocities be forgiven? Could such animals with human faces be forgotten? Our world must take action and make sure that those crimes should never be repeated.

"The commandant of the camp was the SS man, Untersturmführer *Gustav Willhausen*. Every morning, he waited near the exit to select those prisoners who appeared weak in his eyes. A small scratch or furuncle was enough. The selected prisoners had to remain in camp and peel potatoes or carry water or do any other physical work. In the evening, they were all shot and buried in one grave. Willhausen loved to shoot prisoners from the balcony of his office. He ordered infants and very small children thrown in the air and shot them high up above the ground. His daughter loved it. "Bravo Papa!" she exclaimed with delight. "Do it again!" His wife, Otilie, loved it and did the same.

"The work inside and outside the camp was very hard labor. Everything had to be performed while running. If one wasn't quick enough, he was shot on the spot.

"The German *Fritz Gebauer* was a specialist in choking people to death. This beast, who came from a location not far from Poznan, used to grab his victims by the neck and murder them. This happened many times and it included little children. Gebauer loved to put prisoners whose hands and feet were tied into cold water and let them freeze to death.

"The evening roll call lasted a few hours. Hundreds of prisoners were shot or beaten to death. The master was the SS man Untersturmführer *Rokita* from upper Silesia, who was a musician by profession. He formed an orchestra and people were murdered while the band was playing.

"Rokita used to shoot hundreds of people every day. He gave short orders, 'Dreh sich um' which means 'turn around,' and shot the victim.

"It was amazing how people obeyed his order. Were they in a state of shock or hypnotized? They lost their own identity. They became merely automatons fulfilling any order. Rokita perfected himself in tearing and opening the victims' bodies.

"All those atrocities were performed by many SS men who were trained in this camp, which served as a school for the Nazis, where they learned the real spirit of national socialism. From here and other similar camps, they were sent after 'graduation' to the big extermination camps like Auschwitz, Maidanek, Treblinka, Buchenwald, Matthausen, etc.

"How fast and easy human beings turn into beasts! Our world is a world of animals with human faces. If humans were superior and their nature different than animals, then no school would be able to change so rapidly their mind and behavior and turn them into brutes.

"The fact that so many Germans were able to 'graduate' from the SS schools and turn into something worse than beasts in a very short time speaks for itself," concluded Mr. Weinberg.

"You can not condemn all humanity for the atrocities committed by the Germans," I objected. "As a matter of fact, humanity never heard of such crimes in all its existence. This is completely new on our planet."

"That is right," agreed Mr. Weinberg. "By telling the true story of Camp Yanowska, I mean the perpetrators, the SS men, the Gestapo, the SD men and no others.

"Let me tell you a few other methods of mass extermination in this camp, which I myself witnessed and saw with my own eyes.

"In view of the above living conditions, the camp was infested with lice. The barracks, the clothings were full of these parasites. The German Rokita, whom I mentioned previously, decided to get rid of the insects. In the process, a half of the inmates perished.

"Here is the way it was done.

"Everybody had to leave his barrack, to undress and to remain completely naked. While the barrack was cleaned and the clothing disinfected, the prisoners had to remain outside. Five days and five nights lasted the above cleaning. It was very cold, especially at night.

"Many died in the first night. Later, more and more died. There was no way to escape the freezing temperature. The fifth and last night was slightly better, because the survivors covered themselves with the dead bodies. The corpses were not removed.

"After a few days, the odor of the rotten human flesh spread all over. There was no place to run away. A half of the prisoners perished and the German Rokita was able to make the following report to his superior, SS-General Katzman: 'Die entlausung mit erfolg durchgefuhrt (The delousing successfully performed).'

"While all the torture and dying was going on, the SS guards in their towers, holding their machine guns, were laughing heartily and enjoying themselves over the spectacle. They were passing the Nazi school successfully.

"All the inmates, a few thousand of them (the dead had always been substituted for by new arrivals), had to go to the baths, which were located vis-a-vis of the infamous prison of the city of Lemberg, called Brigidek. There was place inside for only fifty prisoners. The rest, a few thousand, had to wait outside, being constantly shot upon by the guards.

"Hundreds were killed. The floor of the bathing place was covered with the bodies of the shot inmates.

"The prisoners were glad that the bathing took place only once a week, being sure that they would not survive another 'bath.' It was a very difficult, almost impossible, to last an entire week in the Yanowska camp.

"Typhus and other contagious diseases spread in the camp like fire. The German treatment was, as usual, unique in history of mankind, namely—mass shooting of the sick.

"The dead, the sick, had always been substituted for by other human beings, mainly from the city of Lemberg and its surroundings.

"There was in the camp an SS man called 'crooked head.' His habit was to bring up and feed pigs. His perverted mind dictated to him that the best food for pigs was human meat taken from the abdomen.

"He handed a young prisoner his knife and ordered him to cut out a piece of the abdomen of one of the corpses lying on the ground. The prisoner took the knife, tried to cut out a piece of the human flesh, but couldn't. He fainted while trying to do it.

"The German took the knife, cut out himself a part of a dead man's addomen, and gave it to his pigs. The pigs couldn't eat it. They ran away.

"The German fell then on a better idea. The pigs didn't like dead rotten human meat. He'd try fresh meat from a living man.

"He called the young man again. Ordered him to undress and to lie down on the ground. He took the same knife and cut out a piece of the abdomen of the living man. The pigs didn't like this food either and ran away.

"The German became very angry that the experiment was not successful and started to shoot at the masses of the gathered prisoners.

"Everything which I told you is the truth, nothing but the truth, guaranteed to be the truth, so help me G-d, no matter how unbelievable it seems to be.

"In November of the year 1943, a rebellion, out of desperation, broke out in Camp Yanowska. Ten Nazis were killed and about two hundred prisoners escaped. The others were shot to death.

"Now you see, Dr. Harsaw, how important it is to escape."

"Yes," I agreed. "We must do it, no matter how dangerous it is."

About the camp *Yanowska* near Lemberg Dr. L.W.Wells testified also before the Israeli tribunal. Dr. Wells was the only one of a family of seventy-six who remained alive. All the others were murdered by the Nazis.

He belonged to a "death brigade" of prisoners, whose task was to wipe out evidence of mass slaughter by the Nazis. This brigade exhumed about twenty thousand bodies from mass graves and was compelled to burn them on huge pyres. The ashes were sifted for gold and platinum and then thrown to the winds. The residue of the bones was put in a grinding machine, which reduced the bones to dust.

Each morning when the brigade moved out of the camp to dig out the bodies it was led, on the order of the Germans, by a prisoner who was dressed as Satan, in crimson rags brandishing a pitchfork. An orchestra was playing lively music when the brigade left or returned to the camp.

As the war was approaching its end, the Germans were in a hurry to kill the prisoners and to burn them immediately. Therefore, groups of 20-40 prisoners were brought in front of the pyres, machinegunned and thrown immediately into the flames by means of special hooks.

Dr. Wells described horrible scenes—when a father had to burn his own two daughters, who were shot in front of the pyres.

People were forced to dig their own graves, then they were shot and thrown into the graves.

Once, while digging his own grave, an SS officer ordered him to go back to the concentration camp in order to bring a corpse who was shot. On the way back to the pyres, while dragging the body, he was able to slip away and escape.

He escaped the camp late in 1943, was hidden till the Soviets occupied the terrain of Eastern Poland.

We continued to talk about the small details, which were indispensible for a successful escape. The formation of groups, the sudden attack in the middle of the night, what group were going to attack and whom, even what individual prisoner would attack a given SS man. The only thing which remained unsolved was to get in contact with the partisans and prepare in advance a place where to escape to.

This later part was very difficult to achieve because very few partisans were in this part of Silesia.

In the middle of June, 1944, the Nazis started to erect gallows on the camp grounds, between Barrack Number One and the Clothing Barrack. We did not understand the meaning of this construction. In the light of multiple and important recent happenings and worryings about our approaching fate, the five prisoners who were taken away in April were completely forgotten. All of us were absorbed with the latest occurrences and events on the Russian front and the nervousness of Alois Frey. Mohl used to come in and hold secret meetings with him.

After a few days, the gallows were ready, but for whom? Inmates were dying, anyway, without the gallows.

One day, an order arrived from Alois Frey to stop working and to return to the camp. It was a nice, sunny June afternoon. When we arrived in the camp we were informed by the brothers Goldowsky, who were working inside the camp as potato peelers, that four of the prisoners out of the five had been brought back into the camp. They were allowed to walk free, giving an impression that the complaints against them were dropped and that they simply returned to their previous camp. Later, they were locked up again.

The names of the prisoners were:
1. Idl Potok.
2. Heniek Ehrenfield
3. Firstenfield.
4. Buchweitz.

The fifth prisoner, Mr. Bakalash, tried to escape on the way. He realized that he was taken to be killed. When they passed through a city, he dashed towards the mass of people, trying to hide himself and counting on the generosity of the onlookers and bystanders. It was an act of desperation. He was caught and murdered in cold blood.

We were not permitted, as usual, to enter our barracks and had to assemble outside in front of the gallows.

Soon, we saw the four innocent victims entering the camp. They were directed toward the gallows and were led by a few armed SS men, followed by Alois Frey, our Lager-Führer, the master of death and life in our camp, who concocted all the present criminal action.

Present was, also, Dr. Fischer, the Nazi physician of Auschwitz III (Buna). The victims were forced to step upwards in order to reach the ropes.

All the prisoners had to look and watch the hanging. On the

German Field Marshal Ritter von Greim, succeeded Goering after the latter was dismissed by Hitler April 24, 1945.

extreme right of us stood Heniek Ehrenfield. On the extreme left was Firstenfield. In the middle were standing Buchweitz and Idl Potok.

Alois Frey unfolded a paper and started to read. "By the order of and in the name of the SS-Reichsführer, Heinrich Himmler, the four prisoners are sentenced to die by hanging. It is proven that they *wanted* to escape by finding civilian clothes near the place where they worked in Kommando I. We were informed, also, that they were in contact with a third party, to facilitate their escape."

The rope was put over the head of the prisoners and the noose tightened. Henick Ehrenfield called out in clear and loud voice:

"I am completely innocent! It is a falsification, performed by Alois Frey in order to advance himself. You, Frey, will pay severely for this crime. The hour is approaching. You will have to give an account before the judges of heaven and earth for our innocent young lives, which you took away. We will not rest in our graves till justice is done."

Then he turned to us.

"Don't forget our innocent blood. Bring him to justice... tell all the world. . . ."

Alois Frey started to roar like a lion.

"You miserable creature," he screamed and hit Heniek

Ehrenfield many times with a heavy club, which he held in his hands.

Imagine, an innocent person, standing on the gallows with a noose on his neck, being beaten by a brute.

Soon the structure beneath their legs was pushed away, and all four victims of Nazi bestiality remained hanging in the air.

Alois Frey was satisfied. He succeeded in his intrigue. He'd surely advance in the Nazi hierarchy.

According to the official paper, read by Alois Frey before the execution, the four inmates were not caught in the act of escaping, nor were they found hiding and returned to camp. They were accused of only "*wanting to escape*," which wasn't proven either.

Every prisoner was dreaming and thinking of escaping, for which nobody in the history of mankind had ever been punished, unless he was caught in the act of escaping. To sentence a human being to die because he "wanted" to escape is by itself a criminal act of justice.

I personally, as all the other prisoners, didn't believe the accusations for the following reasons:

1. Buchweitz had a brother in the camp. If he really wanted to escape and made preparations for it, he would have never left his own brother whom he loved and who remained alone from a large family to be left behind in the camp to die. He would have definitely added his brother to his plan. His brother did not know anything.

2. It was a very small camp and it was almost impossible that not one of the prisoners became aware of it. Nobody knew anything.

3. All the five inmates were exceptionally strong and intelligent and had a better life in comparison with the average prisoner. They understood that nothing could be done under these circumstances and escaping would not succeed.

4. There was no place to hide, because there were almost no partisans in the neighborhood. It would be a desperate attempt without any chance of succeeding. They knew it. Why not wait

till the Russian front got nearer and then try something better with greater chances to succeed?

5. A guard shot to death, a few weeks previously, a prisoner who accidentally walked behind the permitted limits of the working place. The guard received a reward and advanced in his rank, and Alois Frey became jealous.

6. It was an accustomed and usual practice of the guards to report alleged escaping of prisoners in order to advance themselves.

Alois Frey saw it and he craved to advance also. The life of the subhumans were not worth anything, anyway. And so five young lives were cut off in the middle of their prime, for no reason at all. Their tortured faces stands vividly before my eyes, even now more than thirty years later. Alois Frey was the only one responsible for their death. He caused the death of other prisoners also. He was just as guilty as Rudolph Hoess for the crimes committed in Auschwitz. On the contrary, Günthergrube was a small camp, and Alois Frey had more freedom of action than Rudolph Hoess in Auschwitz, who was under strict supervision of Himmler.

Had Alois Frey had a human heart and a little bit of conscience in him, many prisoners would have been alive today, including those five who were hanged. But no! Alois Frey had a heart of iron and a brain of a beast.

Alois Frey was brought to justice after the war and I was a witness for the prosecution. What were the proceedings of the court? How did the prosecutor behave and what crimes was he accused of? What was the verdict of the court? I'll answer these important questions later in my narration, when I'll describe, in detail, everything that happened during my testimony in Frankfort/Main, Germany, in the year 1974. Alois Frey was definitely not less guilty than Dr. Fisher, who was present at the hanging and who was brought to justice in East Germany and sentenced to death.

The five young men who died on the altar and sacrificed themselves were saints. Honor and respect to their memory.

To this day, I could not understand why the Nazis did not

kill me, as they did the five prisoners. My crime was the same. An alleged conspiracy to escape. The motive was the same, namely, the desire of Alois Frey to advance. It was true that they did not find me in the act of escaping. It was only an assumption made by Alois Frey that I wanted to escape, based on hearsay which, allegedly, somebody informed him of. It was no evidence.

But five innocent prisoners were executed for the same reasons and on the same evidence.

It was *MIRACLE #8*.

I'll never find out the real cause. I assume that some secretary at the desk in Katowice or Auschwitz I tore up the letter of Alois Frey, knowing well from the past the subterfuges, tricks and gimmicks of the individual Nazis. I thank Providence for performing this miracle and saving my life again, and making it possible for me to tell posterity the true story of Auschwitz, the story of what happened in the German concentration camps, which shook the conscience of the world.

Just as during the flood, at the time of the Biblical Noah, G-d looked now at the unheard-of massacre of innocent little children, at the gas chambers, at the Krematoria, at the factories of death, which appeared for the first time on this planet, and said:

"Behold, I establish my covenant with you. Never shall there be any death factories to destroy humanity, and never will any flesh be destroyed by the gas chambers and Krematoria. It is for perpetual generations. The bow in the cloud will forever remind me of the everlasting covenant."

I am here to tell you and to repeat over and over again the enormous crimes perpetrated by the Nazis, and by doing this to help the realization of G-d's promise and the establishment of His covenant. For, by reminding humanity of the past, by not letting it be forgotten, we'll make it impossible for future Nazis to repeat the same crimes. They'll never occur again. The fight against crime should begin already in the lower schools. Only then will our future generations be able to absorb it and make it impossible for future Nazis to arise.

CHAPTER XV

D-Day. Polish Warsaw Uprising

LIBERATION OF ROME. THE LANDING IN NORMANDY (FRANCE). D-DAY—OPERATION OVERLORD. OPERATION ANVIL-DRAGOON. FIERCE FIGHTING IN THE EAST. RIVERS NIEMEN AND VISTULA BRIDGED. THE KATYUSHA MORTARS. REEMPLOYMENT AT THE HOSPITAL (GUNTHERGRUBE). MR. SZERESZEWSKI. LIQUIDATION OF BIALYSTOK. RUSSIAN GIRLS. *MIRACLE # 9*. POLISH WARSAW UPRISING. GENERAL BOR KOMOROWSKI. STALIN'S ORDER TO STOP THE RUSSIAN OFFENSIVE IN THE WEST. THE COLLAPSE OF THE UPRISING. GERMAN REVENGE. COULD THE COLLAPSE BE PREVENTED?

The fighting in Italy was going on in full force. "Monte Casino" was finally conquered and Rome was liberated on 6/4/44. On this day our Commando was working as usual, guarded by the Nazis.

In the evening, the prisoners assembled, surrounded by the guards, in order to return to our camp. I wasn't there. They forgot about me. I left the room, where I was working on the papers, and saw all the prisoners already assembled and ready for the marching. I wanted to return to my room, but unfortunately the Polish Kapo, Karl, noticed me and called me to join the prisoners. He even lifted his arm to hit me, but stopped in the middle. I returned to the camp as though nothing would have happened. If not for the Kapo, I would have escaped. Whether I would have succeeded or not, that was another story. Luckily, Alois Frey was not told about the incident.

On 6/6/44, two days after Rome was retaken, the Allies landed in Normandy (France), which carried the name operation *"Overlord."*

In the middle of August 1944, the Allies launched also operation "Anvil-Dragoon" and landed in Southern France, advancing to the North. The German forces were attacked from two sides. One from Normandy and the other from the south of France. They were retreating all along the front leaving fifty thousand prisoners behind them. On September 11, 1944, "Dragoon" and "Overlord" met each other at Sombernon (France).

In the meantime, on the East, the Russians advanced in full force. First Finland was attacked on the North. Although the Manneheim Line was very much strengthened, the Russians broke through and captured "Vibory" on 6/21/44. The reason was that the Russian soldiers knew this time exactly what they were fighting for, namely to destroy the snake which was out to annihilate all the world, including the Russians. It was a far cry from the soldier who invaded Finland in 1940. At that time, they did not want to fight. There was no reason to fight for Stalin and to destroy the Finns. The Russians attacked also all along the other front lines. Minsk, the capital of White Russia, was recaptured on July 6, 1944, one month after D-Day (the Normandy invasion). About thirty German divisions were trapped right there.

At the end of July, the Niemen was bridged, Kovno, the capital of Lithuania, was occupied, reaching the borders of East Prussia. Pushing further to the East, they liberated hundreds of towns and villages, being greeted by the local people with enthusiasm. They crossed the "Vistula" near Sandomierz, and established a bridgehead on the West Bank of the main Polish river. On 8/23/44, King Michael took over the reins of the Government in Romania by a master stroke, causing a radical change. The Germans were forced to leave. Moldavia and Romania were overrun.

Günthergrube, where we suffered, was not very far away from the Russian bridgehead of the Western Shore of the Vistula, near Sandomierz.

We heard the sounds of the Russian artillery, which was balm to our ears. At night we were able to see from far away some illuminations and lighted signals over the horizon. We watched it with real ardor and passion. Was it possible? Another small attack by the Russians in the direction southwest and we would be liberated. Free human beings again after so many years of enormous sufferings. Our hearts were full of hope. We didn't allow ourselves, though, to watch the pleasant signals too much, the foreruners of our salvation, just as a young mother doesn't allow herself to watch her firstborn child too much for fear that something undesirable might happen.

The new camp, which we built for many months, was ready. We left the old camp and moved into the newly-built one at the end of the summer of 1944. There were more buildings and new prisoners were brought in.

Another supernatural and astonishing event happened. The clinic and little hospital of our new camp was expanded but still had no real physician. The old doctor from Czechoslovakia, as you know from my previous narration, was dispatched by Frey to the gas chambers. Dr. Kovacs was a dentist who didn't know how to handle problems of medicine and surgery. He used to call me in to help him in those problems. One day a German doctor arrived for investigation. When he saw me working at the clinic, he was amazed, and asked Dr. Kovacs for explanation.

"I was informed," said the German, "that there was no doctor here. What happened?"

"I call him, sometimes, to help me in my work. Not very often, though," apologized Dr. Kovacs.

"This camp needs a real physician. We have no doctors to spare. Employ him temporarily till further notice."

So I was accepted again to work in my profession. True, it was only a temporary job, but better than nothing. Secondly, the Russians were so near. My hope to come out alive increased. I received a better bed and more nourishing food.

Near our camp was located a small factory which produced some necessary products for the war effort. One afternoon we heard some strange sounds, and saw Russian planes flying and attacking the factory, which was soon turned into rubbish, trash and debris. For the first time I saw with my own eyes the Katyusha mortars, the new Russian weapon. They seemed to me like red comets, flying in the air, causing blinding and numerous explosions simultaneously.

The results were superb, magnificent. The Germans were lost, they didn't know how to handle it. They were enormously scared and terror-stricken.

Many of the inmates even were so frightened that they looked for any shelter to hide, like behind the closets and even under the beds, in order to have some sort of protection. To die under a friendly mortar was no pleasure either.

In the middle of the summer a new transport of prisoners arrived at our camp. Among them was a man from Wolkowysk, who escaped to Bialystok in December, 1942. His name was Mr. Szereszevski. He told me the following story:

At the end of August, 1943, the ghetto in Bialystok was surrounded by Germans. Many were shot right on the spot and still more were sent to concentration camps. His transport took him to Maidanek, the German extermination camp near Lublin. They were lying on the bare grounds of the camp, encircled by barbed wires. People were dying for lack of food and water. It was a hot sultry day. The prisoners were in agony. The Nazis intended to murder all the people. Therefore no nourishment, nor water, was given. For one glass of water, the victims would give away all their earthly possessions.

Near him was groaning and agonizing an engineer, Weiner, the elegant son of the famous Dr. Weiner of Wolkowysk. How he looked now! The once handsome man looked wretched and miserable.

Suddenly, in his anguish and torture he noticed Mr.

D-Day. The Polish Warsaw Uprising

Yanowitz Berl, the butcher's son from Wolkowysk. He was dressed well in expensive boots and informed Mr. Szereszevski that Maidanek was one of the worst extermination camps in the world.

"The thousands of people lying on the grounds," he said, "will be murdered in a few days. As a Kapo, I was able to find out that the Germans need mechanics to be sent to another camp. Tell them that you are a mechanic. In this way you'll get out from this terrible camp. What will be later I don't know, but get out of here. I wish that I could be transferred, but it is impossible. I'll have to perish here."

Szereszewski, on the advice of his friend, was transferred to Blizin camp, where he worked as a mechanic, repairing sewing machines.

The life in Blizin camp was relatively good. In comparison with the other camps, it was a paradise. It was a real labor camp and not a concentration camp. It was under supervision and management of a better German, who did not want to destroy his prisoners, but keep them alive. The camp existed till the middle of the year 1944.

Mr. Szereszewski was transferred to Auschwitz and from there to the mines of Buna (Auschwitz III). Later he arrived with other prisoners at my camp, Günthergrube (Lendzin). He was very glad to meet me here and was very fortunate to land here, because I was able to help him in many ways. Although I had no official position as yet, when he arrived I enjoyed a certain respect by all the prisoners. The Polish Kapos, the officials in the "Schreibstube," the German prisoners, all foremen kept me in high esteem because I was the doctor of the German "Master" of the constructions.

They saw me sitting in his room, not doing anything, which created by itself a certain grade of esteem and consideration.

I provided Mr. Szereszewski with additional food and my portion of soup. Although the later was full of worms, caused by the very bad quality of the vegetables and inadequate cooking, the prisoners ate it in order to sustain life. After all, the worms were proteins (aminoacids) too, and they were better than nothing.

Mr. Szereszewski used to come to me every day for the additional bread and soup. One day, after taking the additional food, Mr. Szereszewski turned to me and said, "I am working very hard at the lorries. I have to load and unload them all day long. In addition I have to push them uphill without any rest. It is very difficult for me to continue to do it. I feel that my strength is leaving me. I'll collapse any day now. Could you help me to get an easier job?"

I had compassion for my countryman and asked him, "What kind of a job would you like to have?"

"I was informed that the electricians have a very easy and leisurely job. They lie all day long on the beams under the roof of the barracks, resting and not doing anything. As soon as the guards or Alois Frey walks in, they start to work, hammering, pulling and shouting, creating an appearance of installing electrical gadgets."

"I'll go to the administration department [Schreibstube] and ask them to do me a personal favor and transport you to the Commando of the electricians."

Soon Mr. Szereszewski was transferred to the electricians. He didn't do anything, resting comfortably on the beams all day long.

One afternoon, while I was sitting and talking with my friends in the "Schreibstube," the foreman of the electricians walked in complaining bitterly.

"Why did you send me an additional man? We don't need him. We have very little to do and have too many workers as it is."

The foreman, evidently, did not know the reason for Mr. Szereszewski's joining his group. I stood up and jokingly said, "Listen, if it is true that you have too many men in your group, then you may leave."

The foreman, amazed at the turn of events, said, "I don't mind having an additional man. It doesn't make any difference. Let him stay on."

"Now you talk, like a reasonable person. Go with peace," I said. The foreman left, glad to return to his group and not be fired.

One day Mr. Szereszewski came to me and said, "It is true, that I am resting all day long. I feel much better. The lorries would have killed me. But I don't have enough food. A piece of bread and soup full of worms are not enough. I would like to get some better food, like meat, butter, cheese, fruit, etc."

"I would like to get it too," I said, "But how? We are in the terrible German extermination camp."

"I was informed," continued Mr. Szereszewski, "that the prisoners who work outside, in the coal mines, were in contact with civilians there and were able to trade in some clothing, shoes, shirts for better food. The Kapos don't do anything. All day long, they talk with the civilians. If I were a Kapo, I would be able to 'organize' better food. I don't want to be a simple worker. I want to be a Kapo."

"You remind me," I said, "of the fisherman who caught the golden fish, which was a miracle fish, and was able to fulfill all the wishes of the fisherman. But since you are my countryman and deep in trouble like all of us in the concentration camp, whose survival is very questionable, I'll try to do my best. But under one condition, that you'll be a good Kapo having compassion for your fellow prisoners. If I'll hear one complaint about you, that you hit one of the prisoners, you'll return back to the lorries like the old fisherman."

I went to Kazik, the Polish official of the "Schreibstube," and explained:

"Mr. Szereszewski served in the Polish army. He is a trained soldier. He would, definitely, be able to salute in a military way while leaving and returning to the camp. He promised me, also, not to touch or abuse any of the prisoners. The end is approaching anyway. Please give him a chance."

"O.K.," said Kazik. "Starting from tomorrow he'll be the Kapo of one of the mine groups."

All the inmates in the camp were very much amazed when Mr. Szereszewski became the new Kapo. He was a newly arrived prisoner. How could he become a Kapo in such a short time? There were other prisoners in the camp much more capable, older numbers. Very few knew the real reason of his success.

Mr. Szereszewski continued in his new position as a Kapo,

organizing better food for himself. The "Schreibstube" received many complaints about him, especially from the foremen. But I usually intervened and protected him.

One day, Kazik called me in, and said, "I can not keep him any longer as a Kapo. Alois Frey blamed the new Kapo for laxity in his group and he didn't like the way he saluted him. I'll make him a foreman, which will be almost the same."

I came to Szereszewski and told him that Alois Frey, the big German boss, didn't like him as a Kapo, and therefore he'd continue in the same group as a foreman.

"It doesn't make any difference" said my countryman, "as long as I am not going to do the dirty work and will be able to 'organize' good food just as before."

I was informed that Szereszewski had different kinds of food, even fruits and meat, in his box, which was very unusual under the circumstances. The box was standing near his bed and I was wondering, why he never offered me, his benefactor, anything from the organized food.

I laughed to myself and didn't mind this behavior at all. For me whatever I had was enough. I was glad of helping him and not getting anything in return.

When Mr. Szereszewski noticed me in the camp, he used to turn his head on the other side, making the false appearance of not seeing me and walking away. It was very funny and odd, and I enjoyed it. But on the other hand, I learned something about human deportment, even in a German concentration camp.

At the place where we worked Russian female prisoners used to arrive from time to time.

They wore tattered rags, but they were young and pretty. Mr. Weinberg used to hide himself behind a building and start a conversation.

"Good morning, pretty girls, I am glad to see you, because all of you are very lovely. I wish I could have a cup of tea with you."

One of the girls, the most courageous one, answered:

"We would gladly accept your invitation, because we like you too. But it is very dangerous. The mere talking is forbidden. They might kill us only for this."

"I'll take a chance," said Weinberg. "I love all of you. Your movements, your shapes, your faces, especially your eyes and smiles, fill my heart with unexplained joy. Tell me please, where is your camp and when are you coming back?"

The Russian girl started to cry.

"Thank you for talking to me in this way. The Germans treat us like dirt, like animals. I thought that I was not a human being any more but a subhuman. Thank you for returning to me my self-respect. I'll never forget it. I believe now that we'll survive and will regain our identity again. Our camp is not far away and is not being guarded. We are free to leave the camp, but we don't know the language. The German and Polish languages are strange to us. We don't know the roads here and we don't have the necessary courage to escape. The Germans will catch us and murder us." She turned her head and saw Germans coming. She cried out: "Attention, please. I see that the guards are looking in our direction. Goodbye, my lover, we'll talk again."

Weinberg came to me very excited, his face was flushing.

"I spoke now to the Russian girls. They are so lovely. They told me that their camp was located not far away. Listen, I have a new idea how to escape. We'll get old women's dresses, tattered shirts, put some kerchiefs over our heads and get out of the camp together with the girls. They'll never recognize us. It is a very good idea. We'll escape together."

We started to prepare old women's cloth, tried it on ourselves, and we looked really like Russian girls.

"Let me take another look at you," said Weinberg, "if you were walking among the Russian girls, I would never be able to discern you from the other girls."

Suddenly, Weinberg became very concerned. He took off in a jiffy his women's cloth, looked outside and cried out, "Hide yourself, the German guards are coming."

He escaped right away and left me alone.

I felt that I had no time to take off my new apparel and rushed to hide myself under beams and other construction material which were piled up in the barrack. The guards came in, looked around, didn't find anything suspicious and left.

This was *M I R A C L E # 9*.

Had the Germans found me dressed in women's clothing, it would have been enough evidence to condemn me for an intention to escape.

The Russian girls did not return any more and we had to abandon our plan.

In July, 1944, the Russians achieved spectacular victories all along the front. The Germans were retreating to the West. Many divisions were destroyed or annihilated. The enormous terror of Hitler and the Nazis kept the Germans from surrendering and saving herewith millions of human lives.

All of White Russia was reconquered, and a large part of Eastern Poland was liberated, including the cities of my childhood and boyhood, like Rozana, Wolkowysk and Lyskovo.

The Vistula river was bridged in the following three places. Sandomierz, Pulawa, Magnuszew. The Russian army found itself about 10-20 miles east of Warsaw (capital of Poland). It was expected that Warsaw would be taken in the next few days, namely at the beginning of August 1944.

On 7/22/44, the Poles intercepted wireless orders from the German forces to abandon the east shore and to retreat west of the river Vistula. They gave up any hope of holding it. Russian tanks had broken into German defenses east of the city. Russian planes attacked the German strongholds of Warsaw. The Germans were running away.

At this time, General Bor-Komorowski, the chief of the Polish underground of Warsaw, was under the command of the Polish Government in London. They were Poles who adhered to the principles and policies of prewar Poland. The Russians did not trust them and created another Polish Government in liberated Poland, declaring that the administration of all liberated territories of Poland would be entrusted to the so-called "Lublin Poles." In this way there were two Polish Governments. One, "*London Poles*," which kept the policies of pre-war Poland, which did not love the Russians and mistreated the minorities, especially the Jews. The other was the so-called "*Lublin Poles*," who wanted to live in peace and friendship with the Russians. Their

D-Day. The Polish Warsaw Uprising

policies reflected the Poles of the year 1920-21, when Poland was resurrected after world war I. They believed in democracy, freedom and justice for all. They did not oppress the minorities. Naturally Stalin supported the later.

On 8/1/44, Bor-Komorowski, with consent of the "London Poles," ordered an uprising in the city of Warsaw for 5 P.M., without letting the Russians know about their plan. They counted on the general confusion and retreat of the German Army, on the help of the Western Allies, England and U.S.A., and above all on the support of the Soviets.

The reasons of the uprising were

1. To liberate Warsaw, their capital, by their own hands.
2. To force the policy of the "London Poles."
3. To be completely independent from the Soviets.
4. To prevent the "Lublin Poles" from establishing themselves in liberated Warsaw.

The insurrection took place, as I said before, without the knowledge of the Russians, without any contact and without any coordination.

The Soviets halted their advance immediately. They even retreated, claiming they were pushed back by the Germans.

The latter seeing the Red Army did not advance, brought in reinforcements. They attacked the Poles with heavy armaments, tanks and air planes.

The Poles soon found themselves in a very bad situation. They had not sufficient ammunition, no artillery, no tanks and no planes.

They were helped by the people of Warsaw, who craved to be liberated and to rid themselves of the German snake. But the military preparedness and the tactics of the insurgents were completely inadequate. They did not, for example, capture the railroad stations, nor the bridges over the River Vistula, enabling herewith the German forces to return and to attack the rebels. It was very wrong from General Bor-Komorowski not to foresee the above military strategy and to let the Germans bring reinforcements so easily, and not to let the Soviets know in advance of the insurrection.

Two days later, starting from August 3rd, the Russian activities on the Warsaw section of the war stopped entirely. No fighting, no Soviet planes in the air. Silence.

On August 4, the Germans attacked with five hastily concentrated and brought in divisions. The result was disasterous for the insurgents. The Germans killed many Poles and broke up the Polish districts. Many houses were destroyed and burned. It was, in a way, the same kind of destruction which took place in the Warsaw Ghetto in the year 1943. At that time, the Jewish fighters begged for help from the Polish underground. Poles walking on the streets saw human beings falling from the roofs of the burning houses in the ghetto. No help arrived and the Germans murdered over five hundred thousand Jews at that time. Now, the A.K. (the fighting force of the Polish Underground) sent desperate calls for help to London, New York, Moscow and the Vatican. The Allies wanted to help.

They sent aircraft from Italy full of ammunition and food with the purpose of dropping it over the beleaguered besieged city. But it was very difficult, because of the distance, four hundred miles from Italy, and because the Soviets did not permit the Allied planes to land on their territory, which would have facilitated their task.

Stalin said that he must dissociate himself from the Warsaw adventure, directly or indirectly, and therefore no permission would be given for aircraft to land on Soviet territory. Rokossowski, the Russian commander of the forces near Warsaw, explained it this way:

The Russians were not consulted and therefore no coordination existed. The military situation east of the Vistula was a very difficult one and the mingling around of British and American planes was not desirable from the Red Army's point of view. The insurgents held few isolated spots and most of the aircraft drops would fall into German hands.

In the meantime no news was coming from the Russian forces. Complete blackout.

Churchill wondered.

"It is certainly very curious, that at the moment, when the underground army has revolted, the Russian armies should have halted their offensive against Warsaw."

Frantic cries for help arrived from Warsaw saying, "Without immediate support, consisting of drops of arms and ammunition, bombing of objectives held by the enemy, our fight will collapse in a few days."

Six weeks after the uprising, on September 10, 1944, the Russians resumed the fighting and five days later, on 9/15/44, they entered Praga suburb, reaching the proper Vistula shores. But they stopped again, and did not pass the river and left Warsaw and its inhabitants to the wild fury of the Nazis.

Three hundred thousand Poles were destroyed, annihilated or deported from Warsaw by the German General Boch-Zalewski.

On 10/2/44, the Poles surrendered, two months after the rebellion. Their fate was exactly the same as the fate of the heroes of the Warsaw Ghetto. Misery, horror, terror and agony dominated the Warsaw sky. Their lot was doomed and their destiny ended in the gas chambers and Krematoria.

Could have the Soviets occupied Warsaw at the time of the insurrection, on 8/1/44?

Yes, without any shadow of a doubt.

The Russians were already very near the city. They had formed bridges over the western side of the Vistula. The Germans were defeated and running for their lives. They ordered the evacuation of all the stongholds east of the Vistula. When they saw that the Russians stopped and didn't advance, they returned to the city. Hitler, seemingly, understood the Soviets well at this point, and ordered Warsaw erased from the ground. Stalin, as the world knows now, was a very tough-minded man. He considered the underground army and the "London Poles" his enemies and he did not have any scruples in letting the Nazis do the job for him. It was very cruel indeed and not everybody would be able to do it. I am sure that Churchill and Roosevelt did their best to help. It was a terrible war, and from the political view of Stalin it was the right and sound decision. Again Stalin did the opposite of what was expected.

Did the premature Polish uprising in Warsaw and the counteraction of Stalin cause a prolongation of our suffering in Auschwitz? Yes, it did.

The Russians bridged the River Vistula at Sandomierz, as we know, and were prepared to take Warsaw. The Germans had escaped already from Warsaw, and Praga (outskirts of Warsaw) was abandoned.

Russian newspapers declared openly that Warsaw would be taken in a few days in order to advance in the direction of Berlin.

The Germans concentrated most of their forces to defend Germany proper, like East Prussia and the road to Berlin. The German troops south of Sandomierz were also defeated and did not contain enough forces to resist the victorious army of the Russian Marshal Koniev.

If Warsaw had been taken in August, then the southern front line would have to be taken also, in order to straighten out the battle line. Krakov, Katovice and Auschwitz would have to be conquered.

It happened this way, exactly in January, 1945, when the Russian army occupied Warsaw and at the same time Koniev's army moved forwards occupying Auschwitz.

I firmly believe that had the Warsaw uprising not occurred, we in Auschwitz would have been liberated in August, 1944, and not in January, 1945. During this five and a half months' delay, thousands of prisoners died from starvation, malnutrition, beatings, shootings, hangings and in the gas chambers. It was quite possible that, had a sudden Russian attack on Auschwitz taken place in August, 1944, it would have paralyzed the Germans to such a degree that they wouldn't even have had time to evacuate the prisoners—as it happened in Maidanek concentration camp, saving still more lives.

But fate wanted something else. The Poles rebelled on 8/1/44 and the Russian attack ceased entirely on 8/3/44. The Germans returned to Warsaw to supress the uprising, Koniev's army in the South became silent and didn't advance, and we, the unfortunate victims of Nazi bestiality, had to remain in Auschwitz.

This was our fate, destiny, and the lives of thousands of victims were doomed. As Shakespeare said, "A divinity that shapes our ends, rough-hew them how we will."

In the meantime, we in Günthergrube continued to suffer.

Many died from starvation, exposure to cold, humidity and malnutrition. Many more were transferred by Alois Frey to the gas chambers of Birkenau. The infamous trucks used to arrive regularly.

When the Russian front stopped, the Nazis had time to prepare plans for eventual evacuation of Auschwitz.

In order to lull us into a false sense of security, the Nazis organized plays, theatrical performances in Günthergrube. The same kind of plays occurred also in all the other camps of Auschwitz, Maidanek, Treblinka, etc.

I remember when all the prisoners had to assemble and watch the performaces. At that time we didn't understand, exactly, the meaning of all these unusual happenings.

The year 1944 was approaching its end. The days and nights were very cold. Freezing winds were blowing from the east and north. They penetrated our bones and flesh and made us shiver during the appeals. Alois Frey was running around, shouting and roaring like crazy. He was probably thinking of the moment when he'd be caught by the Russians and put on trial for all the crimes that he committed. According to the Moscow conference, the Nazi criminals, as we described earlier, had to stand trial in the countries where the crimes were committed and not in German courts. Instead of repenting, Alois Frey continued on his usual road of crime.

I tried to avoid him as much as possible and not to come to his attention.

Once, I noticed him watching me and looking at the hair on my head. We had to cut our hair every 1-2 weeks. I didn't like his staring at me and ran away immediately to our barber and asked him to cut or shave my hair because Alois Frey was contemplating something bad. It took a few minutes and my head was shaven.

A short while later, the limping deputy of the Lager-Fuhrer, came in, asking for me. He was crippled on one leg and he used to arrive in the middle of the night to examine the ears, feet etc. The prisoners who had something on their bodies were mercilessly beaten up. Some even died after this ordeal. Naturally, everything was done on the orders of Alois Frey.

He examined my head and he couldn't believe his own eyes. A few minutes earlier, Alois Frey told him that I had too much hair, and now—no hair at all.

He held in his hand, already, a heavy trancheon to finish me up. He left, and I thanked the Almighty for giving me the wisdom and foresight to avoid additional torture.

Another deputy arrived, fresh from the Nazi schools. Whenever he saw a prisoner, he used to beat him up. Once, when I was on my way to the Master's office, he picked up a heavy stone, threw it in my direction and *hit me straight in the back*. When the Master saw it, he became very agitated, came to me and said:

"Such a mean scoundrel, why did he hit you? He didn't even know you."

"This is Auschwitz," I replied. "One is glad to be alive."

The "Master" started to walk in one and the opposite direction. He was very disturbed and distressed. He came to Günthergrube as an architect, not knowing anything. When he saw what was happening, he couldn't stand it any longer and decided to leave this terrible place, especially now that the new camp was almost completed.

New Year arrived in Günthergrube cold, as usual, on the outside and a very bitter feeling inside. On the first day of the year 1945, I walked in the camp thinking about our fate and destiny. What was going to happen? The day of decision would soon arrive. Were we going to live or die? This was the eternal question.

While I was walking many prisoners, feeling the approaching end of our sufferings, greeted me cheerfully on the occasion of the new year, wishing me swift and early liberation. I wondered why they were smiling and in good spirits. Evidently they realized that the end of their miserable lives was imminent. One way or the other.

Whatever the outcome, it was still better than the terrible life of Auschwitz. Maybe in the back of their minds there was a spark of hope, a possibility of survival.

They were right, *we started to see the end of the dark tunnel* and many survived.

*THE YEAR 1945
FIFTH YEAR OF WAR.*

*ALLIED COMPLETE VICTORY.
GERMAN UNCONDITIONAL SURRENDER.
PROCLAMATION OF PEACE.
END OF SECOND WORLD WAR.*

CHAPTER XVI

My successful escape to freedom. Miracle # 10 and 11. Fierce fighting in Germany proper. Germany's unconditional surrender.

RUSSIAN OFFENSIVE STARTED AGAIN (JANUARY 12, 1945). EVACUATION OF AUSCHWITZ (JANUARY 18, 1945). THE MARCH. MANY PRISONERS SHOT ON THE ROAD. THE TOWN OF GLEIWITZ. THE COMPULSORY RETURN TO THE CAMP, UNDER GUARD, TO COLLECT THE DEAD BODIES. THE SHOOTING OF A YOUNG MAN. THE TRAIN. THE LOAF OF BREAD STOLEN. JANUARY 22, 1945 (8 SHEVAT TASHA). MONDAY. ESCAPE TO THE FOREST. MIRACLE # 10. PAWEL. HIDING IN A STABLE. GRYLKA. THE RUSSIANS ENTERED OUR VILLAGE. MIRACLE # 11. MY OFFER TO VOLUNTEER FOR THE FIRST LINE OF FIGHTING WAS REJECTED. WE LEFT OUR VILLAGE (STEIN). VICTORY DAY CELEBRATION IN THE WEST (5/8/45) AND IN THE EAST (5/9/45).

On January 12, 1945, the Russians started the long-awaited offensive which brought them into Germany proper. It started from Sandomierz, which was not far form Auschwitz. Two days later, Zhukov struck from the bridgeheads west of the Vistula and south of Warsaw, which fell on 1/17/45. The Germans were surprised by the direction of the Russian attack. They expected that the Soviets would clean up first the German forces trapped in Kurland (30 divisions) and advance toward Hungary.

Here are a few important dates of Russian conquests in 1945. Warsaw, as I said, was taken on 1/17/45. Krakov on 1/19/45; Torun on 2/1/45; Budapest on 2/13/45; Poznan on 2/23/45; Gdynia on 3/28/45; Danzig (Gdansk in Polish) on 3/30/45. On 3/29/45 the Russians entered Austria; Bratislava the capital of Slovakia was taken on 4/4/45; Konigsberg on 4/9/45; Vienna on 4/13/45. The offensive on Berlin started on 4/16/45 from the bridgehead which the Russians had on the Oder, and the city surrendered on 5/2/45.

The American and Russian armies shook hands on 4/27/45 at Torgan (on the Elbe).

The Germans capitulated on 5/7/45. It was signed by Jodl in Reims. Next day, on 5/8/45, Keitel signed it in Berlin. The end of the War in Europe was given over the radio on *5/8/45* at 4 P.M. by Churchill.

The Russians celebrated their victory over the Germans on *5/9/45*.

As we see, there was a difference in the victory day celebration of the West (5/8/45) and of the Russians (5/9/45).

The German losses in men and materiel was very heavy. In January 1945 alone, about 300,000 men were killed in action, 3,000 tanks and about 600 planes were lost in fighting.

Evacuation of Auschwitz.

One day after the conquest of Warsaw (1/17) and one day before the Krakow surrender (1/19), Auschwitz was evacuated by the Nazis. This was 1/18/45.

It was a simple early afternoon when we in Günthergrube were ordered to assemble and be ready for marching out of the camp. Every prisoner received bread. I got a loaf of bread, which I was able to hide in my pocket. This was the first time in my two years in Auschwitz that I had an entire loaf of bread. We stood in the yard waiting for further orders.

Dr. Kovacs was called to the office of Alois Frey. After a few minutes he came out telling us that the sick prisoners would remain in the camp. Then he turned to me and said, "Maybe you want to stay with the sick as their doctor?"

I knew that after the prisoners and their guards leave the camp some Nazis with machine guns would return and murder all those who remained in the camp. They didn't want to leave any witnesses to their enormous crimes. This was a policy eagerly adopted and applied by all the Nazis.

Naturally, I refused to stay in the camp and preferred to join all the other inmates, regardless of the consequences and what the future had in store for us.

We marched out late at night surrounded by the guards. The Nazis forced us to carry their bundles and packages. The fat, robust, rested members of the "Ehrenrasse" had no strength to carry their own luggage. We, the weak, emaciated, had to do it.

Many were shot on the road because they were not able to carry the heavy loads on their feeble shoulders. Some were so weak that after a few hours of marching they couldn't walk any longer. They were lying powerless on the roads and were shot by the guards.

I myself developed an abrasion on the back of my right heel which impaired my ability to walk, caused by friction of the heel and the shoe. Luckily, I found a piece of smooth plastic, which I wrapped around my heel. This was a big help, because the smooth surface of the plastic, which separated my heel from the shoe, did not cause any friction or pain on walking. This was a simple device which might have saved my life on the road.

We walked all night long. The Nazis became tired and ordered a stop. We entered into a big cold delapidated barn. The ground was wet and the unfortunate prisoners lay down in spite of the cold and humidity. I tried to rest on the floor, but soon realized that I might get sick there. I preferred to stand up and rest in this way. The guards surrounded the barn from all sides. After a few hours we were ordered to march again. Those who had no strength to continue remained in the barn in spite of the fact that they knew that Nazis would come later and murder them. We continued to drag on and on, exhausted, tired and prostrated. Some collapsed on the way and were shot. Another group of prisoners joined us and our number increased. We were driven and supervised by additional wild guards whom we had never seen before.

More beatings and more shootings accompanied our column. Finally, on Saturday morning, January 20, we reached *Gleiwitz*. There was a large prisoner camp, and all of us were brought into the camp. There were already present thousands of other prisoners brought in, from other camps belonging to Auschwitz, like from the various mines, which were part of Buna (Auschwitz III). Inmates from Auschwitz I and from Birkenau (Auschwitz II) were there also. I met there my good friend from Wolkowysk, Dr. Marek Kaplan. I was very glad to see him alive, and vice-versa. Dr. Kaplan remembered the time when I was taken out from the hospital camp of Birkenau and sent to the mines for very hard physical labor, accompanied by a letter from the German doctor Thilo in order to make sure that I should not survive.

"It is unbelievable," he said. "I thought that you were not alive anymore. It is a real miracle. Tell me what happened to you? How did you survive?"

I informed him how I was able to remain alive by telling him the story of the "Master" whom I treated for a peptic ulcer. Dr. Kaplan listened very attentively and said, "You are indestructible, I firmly believe that you'll come out alive from the barbarous tentacles and clutches of the Nazis. I'll be sticking near you."

"I'll be very glad to have you near me," I said.

Around noon, we were ordered to march again. Thousands of prisoners from all Auschwitz started to move toward an unknown direction.

Alas! The Germans were informed that our road and trajectory was blocked by the Russian forces.

Therefore they took us back to the camp of *Gleiwitz* awaiting further orders. We were watched by armed Nazis whom we had never seen before. Among them was the infamous Mohl.

Escape to Freedom. Miracles #10 and #11

I didn't see Alois Frey. He was probably among the Nazis, but I couldn't find him.

Gleiwitz is a town in Silesia which became famous at the outbreak of the Second World War.

Hitler needed a justification, before the world and the German nation, for the unprovoked and sudden attack on Poland. For this reason he ordered an attack staged on the radio station of Gleiwitz.

This was accomplished by the SS man Neujack, with the help of other SS men dressed in Polish uniforms. Inmates from concentration camps were also dressed in Polish uniforms. Then they were killed and left on the ground to show that they had been shot while fighting on German territory (Gleiwitz).

The SS men dressed in Polish uniforms occupied the radio of Gleiwitz, which was located on the border of Poland. A Polish-speaking German made a broadcast in Polish saying that the time had come to fight the Germans.

Neujack made the above declaration in Nuremberg in an affidavit dated 11/20/1945.

In this way the Second World War started. A faked attack by Nazis dressed in Polish uniforms over the radio station of Gleiwitz justified the German counterattack, according to the Nazis.

The war broke out on 9/1/39. On this day Hitler declared in the Reichstag that "Polish regular soldiers fired on our territory [meaning Gleiwitz] and we have been returning the fire."

The German Foreign Office declared before the world that Germany fought Poland in defense against Polish attacks. Naturally, the above statements were lies and cynical.

Who would have believed, at that time, that the seizing of the German radio in Gleiwitz and the speech in Polish over the same radio was a lie, a complete fake, one of many fabricated by the "Ehrenvolk."

We the prisoners of the camp Gleiwitz, taken from all the camps of Auschwitz and others, tried in this pandemonium to perform some vital services.

The physicians tried to render first-aid medical care to those mostly needed. The potato peelers opened up the kitchen and tried to cook some kind of a soup for the starving inmates.

Thousands of prisoners were milling around aimlessly in the camp, not knowing what the next few days would bring. Some tried to find a place in one of the many buildings in order to rest and to spend the night.

In the morning, the camp was surrounded by Nazis armed with machine guns aimed at us. The infamous Mohl started to shoot. Many prisoners were killed right then.

In front of me, one prisoner was shot by Mohl. What a tragedy! On the eve of the liberation. We started to retreat towards the barracks.

Finally, an order was given to assemble and to leave the camp. We walked through the city of Gleiwitz in the direction of the railroad station. Cattle trains were waiting at the station for the purpose of taking us into Germany.

In the last minute, a few prisoners were taken out from the crowd and sent back to the camp of Gleiwitz to collect the corpses and to bring them to our trains. The Nazis were afraid that the Russians would see the many dead bodies scattered all over the camp, those who died during Saturday night or were shot on Sunday morning.

All of a sudden, I saw Alois Frey approaching our group of prisoners. He helped to select a few of us to return to the camp. I was one of those selected.

"Take him," he said stretching his hand towards me. We returned to the camp, being guarded by heavily armed SS men. We took a few pushcarts and started to load it with dead bodies forming a pyramid of corpses.

In the meantime, some of the guards started to look in the barracks and in the basements, searching for inmates who didn't leave the camp when ordered and were hiding. All those found were immediately shot. I remember one young man of about twenty years old, who was found hiding in a dark hole. The guards pushed him towards one of the pushcarts and ordered him to climb on the top of the corpses.

"Go on!" they said. "Sit on the top of the corpses. You are too weak to walk."

They started to beat the young man, commanding him to climb on the top of the dead bodies.

"Go on! Climb to the top, if you want to live."

Finally, the young man obeyed and mounted the dead bodies.

The SS man approached the young man from behind and shot him in the back of his head. The young man fell on the top of the corpses, blood oozing from his head down.

Although I had seen hundreds of dead people during my internation in Auschwitz, this cold-blooded killing of the prisoner left a lasting impression on me. I still can see this young, active man: with a round, healthy, smiling face, ascending the pushcart and being shot from behind suddenly and unexpectedly by a Nazi.

This is one of the scenes, which stands vividly and forever before my eyes.

Notwithstanding the usual and customary Nazi terror, which we witnessed during the years, one's inner feeling and mind gets shaken up and deeply perturbed at another sight of German bestiality.

We returned to the railroad station carrying with us many dead bodies.

Almost all of the prisoners were already loaded on the open wagons. SS men were running wild with their guns directed at us and ordering us to pile up the corpses into the last wagon. Some were shot by the eager Nazis.

One of the guards, his gun directed towards me, shouted, "Faster, faster!"

I was in big danger. What does this German want from me? He was going to shoot me, I thought. What should I do? How to save myself? Then, he started to run after another prisoner, cursing and shrieking.

"I have nothing to lose," I thought. "I must save myself." At this moment I reminded myself of the old proverbial saying again.

"If a sharp sword is touching your neck, you should not be despondent."

I ran to one of the wagons, climbed the wall, and in a second I found myself inside among the other prisoners. All of us had to stand. There was no space to sit down. I looked down and saw the wild Germans screaming, roaring and barking.

I was safe for the moment.

Accidentally, I found Mr. Weinberg among the prisoners in the same wagon, who urged me to escape as soon as the train will start moving.

"We must escape now," he asserted. "Now is the best occasion, and the last possibility. I did it already previously, when I jumped from a train. They are going to kill us all. Mark my words."

The train started to move in the direction of the West, towards Germany proper. It was dark. The train moved all night long, but very slowly. Many prisoners jumped from the train. Some were shot. I remember one who was crushed between the wagons while trying to jump to freedom. Weinberg left us too. I didn't know what happened to him. I still had my loaf of bread in my pocket. I touched it with loving care. The congestion was very big so that I couldn't move. One hour passed, two hours, and our train was still moving. I touched my pocket where my bread was supposed to be and didn't find it. What happened? My bread was missing. Somebody cut under my coat and stole the bread. It was done evidently in a very professional way because I didn't feel anything while my coat was cut. It was an amazingly expert job. I felt sorry for my bread, which was missing now.

In the early morning of January 22, 1945, 8 Shevat Tasha, Monday, at dawn, the train stopped.

Dr. Kovacs passed near our wagon and he told us that he was going to Alois Frey, who must know something about what was happening. Different rumors were spreading. Some claimed that our train was not able to move and that it needed repairs. Others stated that we were surrounded by the Russian forces and that the Nazis were trapped. After waiting a few hours, we found out the truth, which was that the German soldiers escaping from the Russians needed the train for themselves. They wanted to run away as fast as possible. We the prisoners should walk on foot.

Around noon, an order was given to get off the train and to march towards a forest. We passed a village with the name of "Stein," in Polish "*Kamien*." This was a small village in Silesia. At the windows and near the houses stood many civilians, mostly women and children, watching us. We were informed that the Nazis were taking us to the nearby forests in order to kill us.

Dr. Kaplan was walking near me. I turned towards him and said, "Now is the time to escape. As you see, the Germans are going to kill us. We are living witnesses to their atrocities."

Dr. Kaplan didn't or couldn't escape.

"I am too weak," he said. "I am not able to run fast enough. They might shoot me." He pondered a while and said, "I am going to consult a friend of mine, a physician, wait and I'll tell you our decision."

He returned after a few minutes, informing me that they were not in a condition to escape.

In the meantime, we were beaten on the way and many were shot. We passed the village and entered the forests. Many prisoners started to escape. The Nazis opened up a hail of bullets. All of those who started to escape were shot to death. The guards turned over with their bayonets the bodies of those who were lying on the ground in order to make sure that they were dead and then sent additional bullets and hand grenades into the pile of corpses.

The march continued in the forest path. Another group escaped. Shootings, hand grenades, explosions. Many prisoners were killed, but this time some succeeded in escaping into the forest.

I noticed that those prisoners who were running first succeeded more than those who followed them.

I decided to take a chance. Nearby, Mr. Szereszewski from Wolkowysk was walking. I turned to him and said, "Moshe! I am going to take a chance and try to escape. Don't you see where the Germans were taking us?"

"I'll go with you," responded Szereszewski without hesitation.

"Good. Keep near me."

I tried to walk near a Nazi who was old and was hardly able to hold his gun. He was shaking from the cold and long marching. Then I noticed that the old Nazi put his gun on his shoulder, took out tobacco and started to make himself a cigarette.

Then it happened. I dashed out into the forest and started to run with all my strength still left in me. To facilitate my escape, I threw away my hat and overcoat in spite of the freezing cold. I raced ahead in a burst of speed, and heard shootings, explosions, bullets all around and in the back of me. The abrasions on my foot started to vex me again and to give me a lot of pain.

It was getting dark, on this afternoon of January 22, 1945. Was I going to live free as a human being, or was I going to get killed?

The next hour would be decisive.

Suddenly I heard steps behind me. Were those Nazis following me? I turned my head and saw Mr. Szereszewski.

"Run! Run!" he yelled. "As fast as possible!"

We were already deep in the forest, and heard shots from far away, mingled with sounds of barking, howling and roaring.

Was it possible that the Germans were searching the forest accompanied by dogs? Maybe they were trailing our paths. The ground was covered with fresh snow and we left marks on the ground, imprints from our steps. In that case, we were in big danger. It would be a disgrace to be killed now in a forest, after years of suffering in German concentration camps and after a successful escape.

What should we do?

Logs of firewood, cut in blocks, were piled up on the ground. The upper logs of wood were covered with snow. We pulled out some logs from below one of the piles, covered up the ground inside with forest trash, twigs and branches. The upper part of the pile of the cut blocks of wood was left intact with the snow on the top. We thought that the Nazis, seeing the snow on the top of many piles of wooden logs, would not suspect that one of these piles contained a shelter in which prisoners were hiding.

We crawled into our shelter and covered the entrance with

additional planks of wood, making sure that the snow on the top was not removed.

Explosions and gun shots were heard from very far away. Additional snow was falling down, covering our hiding place. It was getting dark early in the afternoon, as on any other winter day in Silesia. We felt free again.

For the moment we were free from danger. Unbelievable! Free men again!!!! True, we were deep in a forest, cold, wet, freezing, hungry. But free!!! No Nazis, no hanging, no gas chambers, no Krematoria. *This was Miracle # 10!*

We were overjoyed and rubbed our faces, one against the other, to make sure that this was not a dream but a reality.

The average man does not appreciate the meaning of freedom. He takes it for granted. The real significance and value of freedom can be appraised, gauged and measured only by those who have lost freedom. We certainly understood and appreciated its value at this moment.

A half hour passed and we were still lying, silently, in our shelter. Quiet all around. Very dark; then the freezing weather and wetness started to penetrate our bones.

We must go out, otherwise we'd get frozen. If we stayed longer, we'd surely get sick. Pneumonia, pleurisy or any other diseases were strong possibilities.

We pushed the planks away from the entrance and crept out on our knees and hands. We looked all around and noticed a man watching us. Who was he? A German? Maybe there were other Germans around? But no! He was not dressed in a German uniform. He wore civilian cloth, which was smeared with red paint.

"Hey, who are you?" I called out.

"I was a prisoner and escaped right now," we heard him answering.

"Do you know of any other prisoners who escaped?"

"No. I am the only one."

I was not afraid. We were two against one. I came near him and asked.

"What is your name?"

"I am a Russian soldier, who was fighting in Crimea where the Germans caught me and brought me with many other Russian soldiers into Auschwitz. Most of us died or were killed by the Germans. I saw you escaping and followed you. My name is Piotr."

"Where were you all the time? Why didn't you get deeper into the forest?"

"I climbed up a tree and was hiding among the top branches. I saw the building of your shelter and I liked it. I decided therefore to join you."

It seemed to us that he was telling the truth. He looked like a Russian and spoke a perfect Russian. But we have to be very careful. He looked strong, not emaciated. Maybe he belonged to Vlasov's army.

Vlasov was a Russian General who surrendered to the Germans in 1942 and organized a strong fighting force, composed of Russian prisoners, and was fighting on the side of the Germans. Vlasov was captured by the Americans, handed over to the Russians and hanged.

I must make sure of it, before accepting him to our group. At this juncture, we were not going to take any chances.

In a swift move, I tore off the lapel from his coat, removed his shirt, in order to see whether he had the Auschwitz number, engraved on his chest. I knew, that all the Russian prisoners had numbers on their chests.

"Where is your number? I would like to see it," I asked with a loud voice.

"Here is the number," Piotr answered, glad to show it to us. I examined the number and saw that Piotr was telling the truth.

"O.K. Piotr. We accept you in our group. Our fate is your fate."

It was about 8 P.M., and it seemed, at the moment, that we were the only group in the forest. We decided to walk in the direction of the front. Piotr, as a trained Russian soldier, advised us not to walk in a straight line but in circles forming a number 8. In this way, the Germans, who certainly were going to search for us in the morning, would not be able to trace us.

We followed his advice and walked in large circles all night long. We passed on our way valleys and hills, railroad lines and highways. While hiding in the bushes, we saw on the highways German officers escaping in their cars.

We were not afraid of them. It was dark and they couldn't see us. But we had to be careful not to fall into their hands. They were armed and numerous. While passing the railroad lines, we made sure that nobody was watching us. We waited a while and then one of us used to pass over the tracks. If everything was in order, the others followed.

At dawn, we were still walking but we were very tired. The temperature was below 0° C. We decided to find a place where we could hide from the cold and rest.

To walk in the forest in the daytime was very dangerous. Somebody could have noticed us and reported to the Germans. We looked for an old stable, where we could hide unnoticed.

Piotr did not like the idea.

"After risking so much", he said, "I am not going to take additional chances. I'll climb on a tree and remain there till nightfall."

"It is very cold, Piotr, you are going to freeze to death."

"It is better to freeze than to fall into the hands of the Germans."

"O.K. Piotr. Do what you consider to be right," I said. "We must find a place to hide and to protect ourselves from the freezing cold. At night we'll come back for you and we'll continue our journey towards the front. A whistle of a bird will be the password and countersign."

We separated. Piotr went to look for a tree and we left the forest in search of a hiding place.

We approached some scattered houses nearby, which were located near the forest. When dogs started to bark, we ran away. Some Germans might wake up. After all, we were emaciated, weak and not armed. Finally, we came near a house separated from all the other houses. No barking. It was a very cold early Silesian morning. A stable was near the house. We tried to get in, but couldn't. It was locked.

Szereszewski was very skilled in opening locks. He was some

sort of a mechanic. After a little manipulation, he was able to open the door. Inside was a horse and a goat, which were busy eating and enjoying life.

We closed carefully and silently the door behind us and looked around. There was a stepladder leading upstairs to an attic, a kind of a loft which was full with hay. We climbed quickly up the ladder and found a hideout place in the hay. We felt warmer, being protected from the wind and the outside freezing weather. This was Tuesday morning, and we had nothing to eat or drink since Sunday. We rested in the hay and fell asleep. In the middle of the day, noises were heard. People were talking downstairs in Polish, which was a sign that we were in Polish territory, which was better for us than German land. Some also spoke German and we didn't know whether they were military or civilians.

We were lying deep in the hay, worrying and hoping not to be discovered. Since my bread was stolen on the train, we shared the bread of Szereszewski to quiet down slightly the hunger. We still left a piece for later, in spite of the enormous hunger, because we didn't know what the future had in store for us. We decided to hide at different places. In case one hideout was discovered, the other one would have a chance to climb on the roof and to escape.

Later in the day, an old man came up the ladder and looked around. We were holding our breath in order not to be discovered. The old man took a bundle of hay and left.

Did the man see us? If yes, was he going to report us? This was the question that we were contemplating at this juncture. Maybe we'd have to run out in an emergency. We waited one hour, two hours. People were talking outside, but nobody came up to investigate. The man, probably, did not see us, otherwise he would have let us hear from him.

We were lying quietly, thinking carefully about our next step. A small little mistake on our side would cost us our lives. It started to get dark, and all around us became still and silent.

We decided to spend another night in the attic because we were very weak and the cold outside reached a new low temperature. It didn't make any sense to get out and collapse on the road, especially since our clothing was the same as was worn by us in Auschwitz. Somebody might see us and report to the Nazis, who were searching for us. It became also clear to us that the Germans were retreating, and in an other day or two they might evacuate our village and the Russians would come in. But what about Piotr, the Russian soldier? He didn't know where we were hiding. He was going to freeze to death. What to do?

It would be advisable to go down, late at night, when everybody was sleeping, and to look for Piotr, using the password previously arranged, and to take him to our hiding place. Szereszewski thought that it was better to go out now, because it was very quiet on the outside. The people, probably, were sitting in their homes because of the severe cold and winds outside. I was against it, preferring to go out a little later for security reasons.

I argued with Mr. Szereszewski, explaining that he might be caught when getting out or coming back. Why take unnecessary risks? It was about 5 P.M., the beginning of a long winter night. People were not sleeping as yet and someone somewhere might notice him through a window or might, even, meet him on the path to the forest. Why not wait another few hours, when most of the people would be in their beds? To no avail. All my arguments were of no help. Szereszewski did not want to change his mind.

I tried to argue again and advised him to reconsider his decision in view of the enormous risk. All my arguments were ineffectual and useless. He left and I remained all by myself, hidden deep in the hay. I was lying and thinking and analyzing our situation. We were so near to freedom, but still something might happen and we might lose our lives. Our fate hinged on very small objects. We were not in a condition to permit the smallest mistake to occur. Here, I was lying in a loft hidden in hay and the smallest mishap might spell disaster, by being discovered by the Germans.

The Russians were very near our hiding place. I heard all day long explosions, artillery bombardment, sounds of flying aircrafts, later even simple gun shots. The Germans were running for their lives. But still, our situation was very dangerous. To be shot, now, at the gate of freedom, after so much suffering, would constitute a terrible injustice to all our concepts of righteousness.

No! This was impossible. Providence wanted me to remain alive and to be a living witness to Nazi bestiality unheard of in all the annals of history on our planet. I was sure that G-d Himself, in His infinite wisdom, did not expect such atrocities to occur again on the earth which He created.

The fact that it never happened before was a vivid illustration of this reasoning.

Szereszewski probably succeeded in passing unnoticed. One hour passed, two hours, and I didn't hear anything suspicious. I hoped and prayed for a fortunate outcome. I was exhausted and dozed off in a soft gentle sleep. A noise outside and loud voices woke me up. I recognized Polish and German words and heard distinctly Szereszewski's voice.

My G-d! They caught him. No doubt about it. What should I do?

I started to look for an opening in the roof in order to escape. Because of the darkness, it was a very difficult task, especially in view of the severe cold outside, inadequate clothing and lack of nutrition.

I climbed on the top of the stacks and heaps of hay and groped like a blind man all around the walls and the roof in order to find some opening to facilitate my escape. Here! Right here, was an opening! I saw light passing through.

I reached with all my strength to the projecting light which could be my salvation, and saw two people standing and talking vividly. I could even distinguish certain words.

"The German officials were escaping."

"The Russians will soon enter our village."

Not a word about Szereszewski. I was sure that he wouldn't reveal my hiding place. I'd wait then, and try to escape later, at night. Suddenly, I heard a voice.

"Dr. Harsaw! Dr. Harsaw! Where are you?"

I didn't answer and held my breath.

"Come down, we know that you are lying in the hay. Come down, as quickly as possible!"

I didn't answer.

It was clear that Szereszewski told them where I was hiding.

How did the old man otherwise know my name? Everything was lost now.

Out of the stacks of hay, I was able to recognize the same old man whom we saw at noon, taking hay to feed his horse. But why didn't the Germans come up. Why only the old man?

I was lying quietly and did not answer. The old man called a few times more.

"Dr. Harsaw! Dr. Harsaw!"

Not receiving any reply, he left.

"He is going now to call the Germans" passed my mind.

I had nothing to lose and dashed to the opening in the roof.

I was already half outside, when I heard the voice of Szereszewski.

"Dr. Harsaw! Don't be afraid. There were no Germans left in the village. They all escaped. Come down."

I didn't answer. Maybe they tortured him and forced him to talk like this.

Szereszewski continued to call on me.

"Dr. Harsaw! Come down, it is nothing to worry about anymore. We are safe. Inside, the house is warm and pleasant. I ate and drank and feel excellent. Come down!"

I started to rationalize. His voice sounded cheerful and it didn't seem to come from somebody who was forced to do it. He sounded not only cheerful, but happy. Maybe he was right. I looked down and saw him standing downstairs. His face radiated pleasantness and gaiety. He was all alone. Nobody was watching him.

Maybe he was right, and I decided to leave the attic and to come down.

We entered the house of the old man. It was a typical Silesian home with old furniture like any other home in the village. Inside was his daughter, whose husband was mobilized by the Germans and served on the Russian front. She didn't know whether he was alive or not. She had not received any notice from him in the last few months.

The room I entered was the living room. It was warm inside and very pleasant. In comparison with the forest and the stable, where I spent all day, it was a real paradise.

I found there Piotr, the Russian soldier who came down from the tree upon which he was hiding all day long.

"Hello, Piotr! How was it on the tree? Did you feel well there?" I asked.

"Oh, no, it was very cold there. I felt very miserable. Another few hours on the tree and I would have been frozen to death."

Szereszewski intervened.

"When I came to the forest, I looked for the location where we left Piotr in the morning. I looked all around and could not find him. Everything was white, covered with snow. At first I started to whistle like a bird, which was the password between us, but nobody answered. I continued to whistle. After a while, I heard somebody sighing way up on one of the trees and I heard a weak voice.

" 'I am coming down, wait for me.'

"Snow flurries started to fall down from the tree, on the top of which I saw Piotr, covered with snow, almost frozen. It took him quite a while till he was able to move and slide down to the ground. Piotr was dizzy, cold like ice, his eyes glassy."

" 'Oh, take me, wherever you are, I can not stand it any longer.' "

Szereszewski told us how he helped Piotr to walk, who in a way was almost paralyzed. As they progressed, the walking improved, but it was still not good enough. Szereszewski blamed Piotr and his feet dragging for being caught on his return.

"Don't worry," I said. "It was a blessing in disguise. Otherwise, we would still be in the barn, cold, hungry and miserable."

I found there another young prisoner, whose name was Jacob and who had succeeded in escaping. He told us that he suffered enormously from the cold and decided to enter the house, whatever the consequences would be, and to ask for shelter. The owner of the house received him very nicely and offered him food and a place to rest.

"You know," said Jacob, "the people here were 'Volksdeutsche,' which meant that they declared themselves to be 'Germans' during the *German* occupation, and 'Poles' *now* at the approaching collapse of Germany. The territory belonged, previously, to Poland and was located near the border of Germany. The people usually were able to speak both languages, Polish and German."

Jacob continued. "The people here collaborated with the Germans. Their men were mobilized into the German army.

"Now, when the Germans run away and the village is evacuated, they fear for their lives, and expect Russian reprisals and retributions. They look for an alibi, an excuse to show the Russians that they did not collaborate with the Germans and that they sheltered prisoners from concentration camps.

"They need us more than we needed them, at present. We are their possible salvation. Most of the villagers escaped together with the Germans. Their conscience, evidently, was not completely clean."

The old man returned in the meantime with the latest news.

"The Germans evacuated the village completely. They ran for their lives. The Russians were at their heels.

"You are safe now, almost secure," continued the old man. "But earlier in the morning, it was still, very dangerous. The Germans searched the village for escaped prisoners. They scrutinized almost every house in the village. They didn't come here to my house, because we are located at the very periphery of the village, completely separated from the other houses. They even found a few prisoners and shot them on the spot."

"What a tragedy!" I exclaimed. "To lose your life, when you are already on the threshold and portico of freedom."

What an irony of fate!

I still remember the saying of "Bulwer": "Fate is not the ruler, but the servant of providence."

But why, why? After so much suffering. . . . It is incomprehensible. . . .

The daughter, whose name was Grylka, prepared for me a large receptacle of water to refresh myself. In those villages and at that time they didn't have the modern bathtubs. Everything was done in the living-room. I received soap and a large towel. The water was warm. I washed myself and felt fortified and invigorated.

Grylka then served hot tea only for me. The others had their drinks and food earlier. The tea was very refreshing and stimulating. I was very dry and needed fluid in my system. I drank and drank. . . . Maybe twenty cups. I revived and came to myself. Then supper was served and I felt happy. . . .

Later, Grylka took us to a separate room and said, "This is the guestroom and you may sleep here. Don't worry, you are completely safe."

Jacob looked at Grylka with eyes full of excitement. She sheltered him, gave him food and tried to please him in every way. He was delighted and thankful. His eyes expressed infinite love.

"Please, Grylka, stay a little longer with us. Your presence makes me full of joy. It is not too late. Please sit down."

Grylka was a woman of about thirty years old and of medium size. Her features were delicate and her movements were gracious. She sat down and said, "I am all alone. Who knows where my husband is? So much misery, so many soldiers killed."

"Don't worry," said Jacob. "I'll help you. You'll permit me to take care of you till you find out more about your husband. The war will be finished soon. Till then, I'll protect you with all my strength. You'll need someone to guard you and to watch over you. It is wartime and the Russians are not angels."

"Thank you, Jacob, from the bottom of my heart. It is very nice of you."

Jacob's eyes were full with love. They radiated happiness. He moved his chair nearer to Grylka, took her hand into his hands, brought it to his lips and whispered, "I love you, Grylka, you are the most wonderful woman I ever met."

They embraced each other and cried from happiness.

We turned our heads to the side, not wanting to disturb them. Later Grylka left.

There was one bed in the room. Jacob became very mysterious. He said that he didn't want to sleep. He'd sit on the chair and that'd be all right with him.

While talking, he looked at the door of Grylka's bedroom, which remained slightly ajar. Why did she leave the door partially open? I looked at Jacob. His face expressed confidence and secretiveness.

Szereszewski and Piotr said that they preferred to sleep on the floor. The bed remained all for myself. I undressed, lay down, and it felt so good to be in a real bed. It had two pillows, a beautiful and warm blanket and fresh linen. What a stroke of luck! Warm, pleasant, real paradise. I touched the pillows, the blanket, rubbed my eyes. Was it real or only a dream?

Szereszewski and Piotr were resting on the floor, evidently sleeping. Jacob was fully awake, constantly looking at the door of Grylka's bedroom.

It was dark in the room and I saw Jacob getting up from his chair and very quietly entering the next bedroom where Grylka was sleeping.

Silence all around. I heard only the quiet steps of Jacob. Then some sounds in Grylka's room, whispering and soft muffled, smothered and subdued voices.

I dozed off.... I dreamed of being still in concentration camp.... The Germans were preparing the evacuation of the camp. Before leaving, they forced us to one end of the camp, where machine guns were ready and directed toward us....

"Shoot," I heard an order of the commandant. I looked at his face. It was Alois Frey, the Nazi chief of our old camp "Günthergrube." What was he doing here? The Germans started to shoot.... Bullets were flying all around me. People were falling. My G-d, I was hit.... I was sinking to the ground....

I woke up frightened, covered with perspiration. Thank G-d. It was only a bad dream. I touched the pillow again and rubbed my eyes. Yes, it was only a dream. Soon I fell asleep again.

When I woke up, Jacob was still not in his room. Where was he such a long time? What happened to him? The door opened and Jacob walked in.

"What happened to you, Jacob? Where were you? It seemed to me that you came from the outside."

"Oh, nothing," answered Jacob. "I was outside listening to the explosions and the bombardments. The Germans were getting it. Fire all around our village. I love to watch it."

In the early morning we got up rested, refreshed, and our spirits were high.

Grylka prepared for us breakfast. A potato soup, which was very tasty. She had to feed four hungry men. It was too much for her budget and she advised us to visit the grocery store which was packed with food and which was located in the center of the village. We followed her advice and went out to find the grocery store.

It was a very large store, full of all kinds of food. Sacks of flower, vegetables, sugar, grains. There were also fish, meat, bread, marmalade, etc.

A few people were inside, getting what was necessary. We were dressed, except Piotr, in prisoners' striped clothing from Auschwitz. As soon as the owner saw us entering the store, he offered us food.

"You are certainly hungry, come in."

He took us to a neighboring room, where a huge table and chairs were standing.

"Please sit down, you'll be served right away."

Jacob said quietly, "He is looking for an alibi. He wants to be able to tell the Russians that he gave us food."

We didn't care. Let him suit himself. We were starved. We wanted bread. His wife came in and brought a huge loaf of bread, sliced it and put it on the table. She put also cheese, butter and fish. In a few seconds, the plate where the bread was located became empty. The woman smiled and brought another loaf of bread. This was emptied in a few minutes also. She brought us a third portion and told us to return next morning.

We left the grocery store and walked around the village. Many houses were deserted by their owners.

The Russians had not come as yet, but no Germans were there either. We returned to our temporary home and decided to build a shelter. The Germans might come back like in Warsaw. One could never tell what was going to happen.

We dug an excavation in the ground of the garret and carried the sand outside. We tried to make space for all of us. Grylka and her father would not betray us.

Next morning, we returned to the grocery for another

breakfast. After it was finished, we roamed around the village. People were watching us with curiosity and fear, because we still were wearing our prisoners' clothing.

On the way we found a cow abandoned by the owner, who probably ran away. We brought the cow to Grylka, who was very pleased. In the evening, everyone of us was served a plate of meat especially prepared by the owner.

Finally the Russian forces entered our village. Piotr was the first one to notice them. He was constantly looking through the window. It was on Sunday afternoon, when Piotr with joy exclaimed,

"Here, they are coming, my brothers. How beautiful they look!"

We all dashed to the window. Piotr ran out to meet his brothers. We saw Piotr running towards the first Russian soldier with open arms. When he reached him, they embraced and kissed each other. The soldiers were walking one after another with their guns stretched forward, always ready.

Piotr returned to the house. He knew that a lot of investigation and hardship was waiting for him. But they were no Nazis. Only an investigation and maybe some penalty for letting himself fall into the hands of the Germans. Naturally, he would have to clear himself and show that he did not belong to the army of Vlasov, the army which betrayed their own country and which fought on the side of Hitler.

Russian soldiers entered our house asking whether there were hidden Germans or ammunition. They did not search, rob nor molested any one.

When a Russian officer entered our house, I stepped forward and informed him who we were. I spoke in Russian, explaining that we were prisoners from Auschwitz. I continued.

"I don't know what plans my friends have. As for myself, I would like to volunteer to fight the Germans. They murdered all my family in White Russia, all my friends were annihilated and entire cities were destroyed. I am a medical doctor and would be happy to be sent to the first line of fighting." The officer took my name and promised me to present my request to the general staff. He'd let me know tomorrow.

Later in the evening, another group of soldiers came in. They were not as nice as the previous groups. They pushed the old man, and came near to Grylka, who was trembling from fear.

Where was Jacob? I found him in one of the rooms. He told me that he didn't know Russian and asked me to intervene.

"Excuse me," I said to the soldier who approached Grylka. "We have no Germans here. Here were only Poles."

"Who are you?" asked the soldier, who was in his forties, heavy, dirty and rough.

"I was a prisoner of Auschwitz, the infamous German concentration camp. On the way, during the evacuation, I succeeded in escaping. I volunteered to fight the Germans."

The soldier was a very violent, tough person from Siberia. He pulled out his gun and said, "Come outside. You'll learn something. I don't like this kind of talk."

What was that? A Russian soldier to behave like that. It was wartime. Some of the soldiers became very hardened, tough and not reasonable.

Luckily another Russian soldier pulled him for his sleeve and said,

"What are you doing? He is not a German. Don't you see his prisoner's clothing? He suffered more than you. Stop it, you stupid gorilla."

The ruffian put back his gun and turned away.

This was *M I R A C L E # 11*

The officer from the General Staff returned and told me that my offer to volunteer was not accepted.

"Why?" I asked. "You wouldn't get a better and more devoted soldier."

The officer explained that my application was considered by the entire staff. They took in consideration the Number 94430, which was engraved by the Nazis on my left forearm. The staff was of the opinion that my life was very important and that I might lose it very easily on the first battle line.

"You are," he said, "one of an entire family and maybe one of an entire city who remained alive. We can not and are not permitted to risk your life. In addition you are one of the few witnesses of the Nazi super-atrocities. Stay alive and write your true story for all mankind to read and study, which could help in making impossible a repetition of similar Nazi crimes."

I don't know whether the above explanation was the only reason. Maybe there were other reasons also. The war was almost at the end and no new recruits were required. It was quite possible, also, that the Russians didn't trust strangers to be incorporated into the Red Army.

I was very disappointed, because I desired to pay my share in the fortunes of the war and to contribute something in cutting down the enormous Nazi arrogance.

Next day, a Russian major was billeted in our house. A few other soldiers accompanied him. We were very glad to meet each other. We told him the story of Auschwitz, the gas chambers, the Krematoria, the unnecessary and enormous destruction of cities, the genocide as practiced by the Germans.

He related to us the difficulties at the beginning of the war and the later changes in the war fortunes, thanks to the heroism and discipline of the Red Army, and above all thanks to the German atrocities which made all the world to turn against them.

They cooked on the yard and offered us participation in the meals, which we gladly accepted.

I presented my bed to the major, but he didn't accept it, saying that he was accustomed to sleep on the floor and that he had forgotten already how to sleep in a bed. The other soldiers and Piotr shared his view. So I continued to use my bed. But this time Szereszewski was my partner, because there was no room on the floor.

The fighting on the fronts continued. Our village was located actually on the first battle line. The Germans resistance increased.

The major approved of my original assumption, that at the beginning of the war the Red Army, composed of individual Russian soldiers, did not want to fight. This was one of the reasons why the Germans were able to occupy vast Russian territories, without the adequate and stubborn resistance exhibited by the Red Army in the later fightings.

Naturally there were other reasons too: Stalin's trust in the

Russian-German pact signed as recently as 1939, Moscow's order not to respond to the German first attack for fear of provoking Germany, Hitler's atrocities over the civilian population, and so on. Only later, when the Russians saw the Nazi atrocities, the mass exterminations and the hanging of innocent civilians, and came face to face with German bestialities, only then did they realize the danger to the Russian people and to the world at large and started to fight the agressor with all the ways and means at their disposal, which reversed the course of the war and brought the Red Army to the gates of Berlin.

A few days passed and we became very friendly with the major.

"You and your few friends," he said, "are very valuable to us, because you are living witnesses of what really happened. We can not endanger your lives, because you constitute real jewels in preventing humanity, by your narration and presence, from a repetition of the unheard-of genocide."

One day, when the fighting around our village took on a severe form, he said, "I advise you to move out from here. The Germans might reoccupy the village for a day or two. Why should you endanger your lives?"

We took the advice of the major and left the village. Grylka gave us winter overcoats and food packages containing meat, bread, cake, etc.

CHAPTER XVII

Miracle # 12. The death of President Roosevelt. Zeilsheim.

THE POLISH OFFICIAL AND HIS MURDEROUS TENDENCIES. THE CITY OF KRAKOW. THE RETENTION OF OUR FRIEND PAWEL BY THE RUSSIANS. THE CITY OF LUBLIN AND THE NEARBY CONCENTRATION CAMP MAIDANEK. DR. AMSCIBOWSKI. THE TRAVEL TO KATOVICE VIA WARSAW. THE TERROR OF THE POLISH A.K. FASCISTIC GROUPS. THE REASONS FOR LEAVING POLAND. THE SHOCK OF PRESIDENT ROOSEVELT'S SUDDEN DEATH IN WARM SPRINGS (4/12/45). THE DEATH OF HITLER AND HIS DOG. GOEBBELS EMULATES HIS MASTER. THE CITY OF BERLIN. THE TEMPORARY SHELTER IN CAMP OF ZEILSHEIM NEAR FRANKFURT/MAIN. WHY DID HITLER COMMIT SUCH ENORMOUS CRIMES? COULD ANOTHER HITLER ARISE IN ANY OTHER COUNTRY?

Szereszewski, Piotr and myself started to walk in the northeastern direction towards White Russia. Piotr to Crimea, and Szereszewski and myself towards Wolkowysk.

Who knows? Maybe we'd find there some of our friends, maybe someone of our families remained alive. After a few hours, we rested in one of the abandoned houses. Later, the shooting and the bombardment intensified. It was impossible to leave the house for fear of being killed on the road. Before dawn, in the early morning, the explosions stopped for a while, probably in preparation of more intensified fighting. We left the house in a hurry, and started to run away from the place. Later, it was revealed that our village was reoccupied again by the Germans for a half a day.

We partially walked and partially hitchiked, being stopped on the way by Russian soldiers, who took away from us the meat and the cake. They left us the bread. We continued on our way. Trucks were running in all directions. Often we succeeded in mounting some trucks which brought us nearer and nearer to our destination.

Our bread soon finished and we became very hungry. When passing a large village, we stopped at the City Hall, called "Magistrate" in Polish, and asked for some food, explaining that we escaped from the hands of the Germans, and that we hadn't have any food for three days.

To our big surprise, the main official declared that he was not going to give us any food. We couldn't understand such a brutal attitude from a Polish official of the Magistrate. I turned to him and said, "Wielmozny Panie!" Which means "very respectful citizen!" "You know, that we suffered enormously under the Germans. We remained one of a family and one of a town. Your country Poland is being liberated by sweat and blood of other nations. As a matter of fact, as you know, the cause of the outbreak of World War II was the invasion of Poland by the Germans and the fulfillment of the Allies promise to protect your country. How could you deny us, victims of Nazi atrocities, some food? We haven't eaten for three days, and we might collapse on the road. As an official of liberated Poland your obligation is to help us."

The official became very angry and shouted.

"My opinion is different than yours. Sorry that the Nazis didn't exterminate all of you. Get out of here, you miserable creatures!"

We left City Hall and couldn't understand the behavior of the official. I asked myself, "Is it possible, that the Polish official was a hidden Nazi?"

MIRACLE #12. ZEILSHEIM

I could see from his fat face and clothing that he colaborated with the Nazis. Maybe he belonged to the famous Polish "A.K." or the fascist "Endekes," who killed Russian soldiers and civilians and who were famous for their anti-semitism? I was more inclined towards the second assumption. But, how could he be so heartless as to deny a morsel of bread to us who suffered so much? It was not easy to answer this question.

We left the City Hall very disappointed, discouraged and bitter. We were contemplating other ways to get some food lest we collapse on the road from hunger. Suddenly, we heard heavy steps behind us and a voice.

"Stój [Hold]." When we turned our heads, we saw an official with a gun ordering us to go back to the City Hall. Naturally we refused. A thought passed through my head. "They want to kill us."

The official with the gun threatened to shoot us if we didn't return voluntarily. He kept his gun directed at us, ready to shoot any minute. We were in big danger. Suddenly, like an angel from heaven, a Russian captain appeared. I turned to him and spoke Russian.

"Gospodin Kapitan [Mr. Captain], They want to force us to enter into the house for unknown reasons. Please help us."

"Who wants to force you?" asked the captain. We turned our head and the Polish official wasn't there. He simply disappeared.

This was *MIRACLE # 12.*

The Russian provided us with some food. We continued on our road and reached the old city of Krakow. We milled around in the city, which was destroyed very little.

It was already late in the afternoon, soon would be dark. We had no place to spend the night. It was too cold to remain outside. A Russian officer noticed us because we were still dressed in our clothings from the Auschwitz concentration camp.

"Who are you?" he asked politely. "Why don't you go to your home? Everybody has to be inside at night. It is still wartime."

We explained to the Russian that we escaped from Auschwitz and that we were on our way to return to our old town and were passing the city of Krakow at present, and that we had no place to sleep. The Russian took us to one of the nicest hotels of the city and ordered the clerk to give us a room to spend a few nights. We were very glad. At least we had a roof over our heads, for the time being. We spent the night in our room. Every one of us had a separate bed with a beautiful mattress, fresh linen, pillows and covers. In the morning, we went out to see what was going on in the city. There were places where food and some money were distributed to the victims of Nazi tyranny.

In the evening, the city was engulfed in darkness, because the war was still going on and no city illumination was permitted.

We returned to our hotel and spent another night in our room. Who could have been compared with us? We slept in a nice bed. Had enough food and even some money in our pockets. In the morning, we got up very refreshed and rested and washed ourselves with soap and water and used fresh towels. It was wonderful!

We visited the market place with the arcades, the Wawel Castle, the crooked narrow streets, the parks, etc.

Krakow was the old capital of Poland and also the capital of the General Government during the German occupation. The Nazi chief, Frank, ruled in Wawel.

We soon left Krakow, on our way to our destination, walking part of the time and being taken in, very often, by passing vehicles.

It was February 1945.

One year later, when I was preparing myself to immigrate to the U.S. of America, I was shaken by the news which arrived from Krakow. On April 21, 1946 (Easter Sunday), in the afternoon, five Jews were murdered by the Polish fascist groups. It occured in broad daylight. The victims were survivors of the German concentration camps. This was *not* the only occurrence of crime committed by the A.K. and the Endekes.

Now I understood well the action of the Polish official, who wanted to force us to return to City Hall. A small insignificant thing could spell disaster for us.

On one of the roads, the Russian military police stopped us.

Miracle #12. Zeilsheim

"Where are you going? Who are you?"

We showed them the documents received in the village "Stein" which certified that we were imprisoned by the Germans in Auschwitz.

"What nationality are you? And what is your destination?" Piotr was the first to answer.

"I am a Russian, taken prisoner by the Germans in the fighting of Crimea, and my destination is my birth place in Russia."

"Oh yes," said the officer. "Come! We'll have to detain you right here in the camp. We were ordered to do so with all the Russian prisoners."

Piotr had no chance to reply when he was pushed into the camp, where thousands of Russian prisoners were, already detained. We thought that there were numerous Russian soldiers, so-called "Vlasovcy," who fought on the German side. Naturally, they had to investigate and to detain all the passing Russians without adequate documents and permissions. In this way, we lost our friend Piotr. We never saw him again. While the officer was talking with Piotr and seeing what happened to our friend, I decided to tell them that we were Poles, and not Russians.

The officer turned to us and asked, "What is your nationality and what is your destination?" I answered immediately in Polish—Jesteśmy Polacy.

"We are Poles and our destination is Warsaw."

"O.K.", said the officer. "You may continue on your way."

Later we found out that Wolkowysk belonged to Russia and normally we would have had to be retained. But after all, Wolkowysk was a part of Poland before the war.

After many days of travel and walking and hitchhiking, we reached Lublin. When Lublin was occupied by the Germans, it was destined to serve as a reservation for the Jews. Thousands of people were brought over to this district.

Lublin was reoccupied by the Red Army on July 23, 1944. All the Nazi atrocities were suddenly detected and laid open before the eyes of the world. It was unbelievable, never seen during all the history of our planet.

Gas chambers, Krematoria, ashes. Hundred of thousands

of shoes, including tiny baby shoes. Corpses of killed men and women still in their clothings, handbags lay scattered on the ground, killed babies with toys in their hands, teddy bears. . . . It was unbelievable at *that* time, till one saw it with his own eyes. It is still unbelievable *now* to those who heard it but didn't see it. Many have forgotten it, which makes a repetition of the same crimes a possibility. The world has no right to forget it, and the recurrence of the same atrocities have no justification in the eyes of men and G-d.

This book was written with only one purpose, not to let mankind forget it.

When we reached Lublin, we saw people milling around sad and heartbroken. Thousands of Russian soldiers and civilians visited Maidanek, which was a suburb of Lublin. People were asking each other, "How was it possible? Why did the Almighty permit it to happen? Was it a surprise even to G-d himself? . . ."

I walked through the streets and, although liberated thanks to many miracles, I still felt the suffering and the desperate cries of thousands of people who perished in this inferno.

We met by chance and luck a good friend from Wolkowysk, Dr. Amscibowski, who survived the war hidden in the forests. He invited us to his place, where we received some food and a bed to sleep. The doctor was a boarder himself and he shared his food with us. The bed was made from iron and was offered to us by the landlady to spend the night. She was very poor and we got only the iron bed without any cover, bedding, or any protection at all. It was very difficult to sleep on this hard, iron bed which I shared with Mr. Szereszewski. In addition, the bed contained some iron protuberances, bumps and bulges. It remains without saying that we were not able to close our eyes all night long. In the morning we felt very tired and many parts of our body were aching. I still remember that night. Was it possible that the landlady had absolutely nothing to offer us, even a torn rug to cover the bumps of the bed? Maybe, living under the Nazis for many years and seeing so many atrocities and brutalities, she became indifferent to human distress and discomfort. I guess I'll never be able to find out the truth. But it was very characteristic of that time. The doctor couldn't help it. He was unfortunate

MIRACLE #12. ZEILSHEIM

himself. We were thankful for the courtesy that he showed us and for the food that he shared with us.

The same day, we met there Mr. Weinberg, who on the night of January 21 jumped off the train and disappeared in the darkness. I was very glad to see him alive. He told me that he lived in Katovice and that he was one of the committee members who tried to bring a little order in Silesia. He urged me to join him, because they badly needed a physician who would be able to organize medical help in this section. He was afraid of epidemics of contagious diseases there. I accepted his offer and left by train for Katowice via Warsaw, where we stopped for a few days.

The capital of Poland was completely destroyed at that time. A pile of bricks and mortar.

We walked around the deserted city and couldn't find a place to spend the night. The bridge over the Vistula was not completely destroyed and we were able to cross over it and enter Praga, the suburb of Warsaw, which was located on the other side of the city and where people still lived in their houses. We found there a few other escapees and refugees. Evidently we were not the only ones who succeeded. In one of the houses we met two sisters, who invited us to stay with them for a few days. Their chaperon was a Russian soldier, a very excitable fellow, who carried a gun and threatened to shoot us if the girls were touched.

"They belong to me, and only to me," he said, brandishing his gun.

In the morning we went to Warsaw again. While crossing the Vistula bridge, I was thinking of the time when the Red Army was waiting in front of the river while the massacre of the Polish people by the Germans was taking place, which was caused by the insurrection of the Polish Underground. Imagine, thousands of men, women and children being murdered in cold blood and many more being forcefully transported to the gas chambers, and the victorious Red Army was standing and waiting for new orders from Moscow.

Still, they were in a better position than the Jewish fighters in the same city, one year earlier.

The Allies tried to send help to the Poles. They dropped

food, ammunition from planes. Churchil and Roosevelt sent fiery letters to Stalin, urging him to bring relief to the Polish rebels.

The Jewish fighters were all by themselves. No dropping of food and ammunition. No fiery speeches by the leaders of the world. Even no help from the Poles, who were in a position to assist and to send succor and relief to the unfortunate heroes of the Ghetto.

Warsaw was, as I mentioned earlier, almost completely destroyed. There were rubble, trash, debris, bricks, broken pieces of lumber and glass as far as the eyes could reach. People were digging in the heaps and piles of rubbish in order to recover something that could be used. Only a few scattered houses were visible. On one of the houses was written in large letters, "Registration place."

We entered the place and found a few people inside. They gave us a list of people who survived. I looked over the list, in search of some member of my family. I couldn't find any name which would remind me of my people. We registered our names, our prewar addresses and our present destination, which was Katovice.

My cousin Gorfajn, who returned from Russia with his wife, Anna and son, Marian, found my name later in the register. He tried to get in contact with me, which was very difficult in wartime. Finally, he traveled to Katovice to see me, but I wasn't there. I had left Poland already, and went to the occupied German territories and from there to the U. S. of America.

A few days later, after milling around the ruins of Warsaw, we traveled by train on the road towards the city of Katovice. I remembered this road well. It was the same road where two years earlier we had been packed in by the Nazis in cattle trains and brought to the ramp of Auschwitz. It was different now. We traveled in a normal passenger wagon, not hungry, not thirsty, free men, and of our own free will. Still the memory and vicinity of Auschwitz pressed on us all through the journey. We were not able to talk to each other. Our minds were occupied with the past. We were thinking of our families, our friends, of the

Miracle #12. Zeilsheim

terrible tragedy, of the horrible injustice meted us by the forces which managed our fates.

We received a nice apartment in Katowice, on Mickiewicza Street. My task was to organize some medical aid in the city of Katowice and the adjacent towns and villages, which were in a complete chaos and confusion at that time.

I traveled from town to town, from village to village, to organize some medical aid for the people. I put in all my strength and energy to accomplish the above task. No stone was left unturned and no avenue remained unexplored. I gave freely and cheerfully everything that I possessed to achieve my goal for the benefit of the civilians, who suffered so much.

Almost all of Poland was reoccupied. The Red Army reached the gates of Berlin. Gleiwitz and Bytom, Breslau and many other towns in Silesia were occupied and handed over to the Polish Government. A new Poland was born. The borders were different from her previous prewar frontiers. She had to expand in the West at the cost of Germany and contract in the East for the benefit of Russia.

White Russia, where the population was 80% Russian, had to be relinquished to the Russians. My towns, where I lived during my childhood and young manhood, were abandoned for the benefit of the victors. Rozana, Wolkowysk, Grodno, Slonim, Baranowiecze were taken over by the Russian administration. Western Ukraine, including Lemberg, was added to the Russians. Silesia with the coal mines and industry, including Breslau, which belonged to Germany before the war, was annexed to Poland.

The Poles liked the above exchanges because White Russia constituted a poor agricultural land. Most of the inhabitants of Western Ukraine were not Poles but Ukrainians who desired an independent country. Silesia was a rich land with a very highly developed industry. The coal mines were abundant and numerous and produced a lot of coal, which could be exported abroad.

A shift of the population took place. The few Poles left the Eastern territories and many Germans were evacuated to Germany proper.

I had to organize medical facilities also in the part of Silesia which was annexed to Poland.

The remaining Germans did not want to cooperate. I remember, when I arrived in Bytom, the local Germans put obstacles. They preferred chaos instead of order. I did not insist. After all it was for their benefit only.

I thought of the difference in treatment of the local population by the Germans and the Allies.

The Governor of Silesia was General Zawadzki, the ex-sergeant of the prewar Polish army. He advanced very highly in the ranks of the Lublin Pro-Russian, Polish Government. Stalin evidently trusted him, because he became later President of the Polish Republic.

Fate wanted that his girl friend from pre-war Poland be the owner of the apartment given to us by Mr. Weinberg. She collaborated with the Germans, and the local Polish investigative authorities received many complaints about her from the local civilians, who witnessed her fraternizing and cooperation with the Germans. Many compromising pictures of her and Germans were found. She had been arrested many times, and soon released without any explanation. Nobody knew the real reason of her multiple releases in spite of the heavy charges against her.

Once she came to our apartment and told me that she was well acquainted with a very high Polish official. Therefore she'd be released each time, no matter what the charges were against her and how serious her German collaboration was in the past.

"To my friend," she boasted, "I am more important than any treason or cooperation with the Germans."

She confided to me a deep secret by saying, "My friend is a playboy. He doesn't give a damn about Russia, Poland and communism. But Stalin for unknown reasons trusts him."

I didn't want to believe her story. To me it was incomprehensible that a high Polish Official, trusted by the government, should be a playboy. We believed at that time in Russian superiority and the intelligence of her leaders. Her gallant fight against German agression was second to none. Even leaders like Churchill, Eden, Roosevelt, General Marshall, Roosevelt thought very highly of Stalin and his government. How was it

MIRACLE #12. ZEILSHEIM

possible, that a high Polish official, trusted by the Russians and the Lublin government, should behave in such a degraded way?

Later, we found out that the high official was not other than General Zadadzki, Governor (Wojewoda in Polish) of all Silesia.

Later we were expelled from our apartment on orders of General Zawadzki. The apartment was returned to his girl friend. To him was more important a German collaborator than victims of Nazi tyranny.

We then woke up from our dreams of a new just Poland since justice, fraternity, equality were no more than a balloon, which was going to burst any minute.

Then, we heard about pogroms in different cities of Poland, like Kielce, Radom, etc.

Ex-prisoners of German concentration camps, who were saved by miracles from the bloody hands of the Nazis, and who remained alive one in a family, were shot to death by the Polish fascist groups, like "A.K." and others. They were shot in cold blood by perpetrators and criminals for no reason at all. The survivors were all saints and their killers were hiding behind houses or trees. They never dared to come out in the open.

What a tragedy it was for the history of Poland!

I started to think of leaving Poland, where so much innocent blood was spilled and where most of the famous gas chambers and Krematoria were built.

This was not the country where I wanted to live nor could I live here in peace and safety. This was not the land where I should put all my energy to rebuild.

Then something happened which jostled me out of my doubts and indecision and confirmed my final decision to leave Poland forever.

The war was still going on. The end was swiftly approaching for the Nazi murder machine.

In Katovice, where we lived, as well as in all the other cities of Poland, there existed martial law. The civilian population had to remain in their houses as of 7 P.M.

In my apartment lived a few ex-inmates of the concentration camps. They were young, vigorous, strong men, ready to defend their lives with arms if necessary. They prepared themselves for any eventuality, especially after the rumors of the criminal actions of the A.K.

One night, about 8 P.M., one hour after martial law, five young Poles entered my apartment. They were armed with knives, sticks and clubs. They were brutal right from the beginning, ordering me to leave the apartment and to go out on the street.

"We belong to the A.K.," they said. "We don't need you here. Too many of you remained alive."

"Sure," I said. "An order is an order."

I clapped my hands, which was a prearranged signal for my tenants to come out. They appeared at every door, fully armed, and surrounded the Poles.

"Well," I said. "Here we are. Do you wish to go out?"

"Oh no, doctor, we made a mistake. Please, forgive us. Let us go."

The boys wanted to teach them a lesson, but I restrained them from doing so because it would incite the people against us, the survivors, and would serve as an excuse to murder. I had always believed that violence does not pay.

The perpetrators were taken away by the police, and as usual released afterwards.

The above episode reinforced my decision to leave Poland. Another physician took over my place. He was murdered by a similar group after a few months.

My decision to leave Poland was right.

The war was going on in full force. The Germans tried to create dissension among the Allies. They sent representatives to Switzerland with an offer to surrender to the English and American forces only. They would continue to fight the Russians in order not to let the Communists spread all over the world. The above negotiations came to nothing, because Roosevelt and Churchill demanded unconditional surrender to all the three Allied Governments. Secondly, nobody wanted to have any deals with the SS chieftains Himmler and Hitler, who committed unheard-of crimes by murdering innocent people, including children, by building gas chambers and Krematoria,

Miracle #12. Zeilsheim

etc. In the meantime, the Allies advanced to *the Po river*, crossed it and moved northwards.

Bologna, where I spent many years studying medicine and where I graduated, was occupied on April 21, 1945. Finally, on 4/29/45, the German forces capitulated in Italy and surrendered unconditionally to all the three Allied powers.

Mussolini tried to escape via Como into Switzerland. He was caught by Italian partisans on 4/27/45, and two days later he was shot to death together with his mistress, Clara Petacci (4/29/45). Their bodies were brought to Milano, where they were hanged from lampposts. On May 1st, the bodies were buried in the cemetery "Maggiore" of Milan (in the paupers plot).

Hitler had arrived in Berlin on 1/16/45, where he remained till his death.

In view of the catastrophic defeats of the German Army on all fronts, the end of the war was visible already in 1943, and was clearly manifested without any shadow of a doubt in the succeeding year, 1944. Yet the Nazis continued to transport innocent men, women and children to their factories of death, where they were brutally murdered. As a matter of fact most of the crimes took place in those two years. The minds of the Nazis could never be understood and analyzed by an average human being.

It is interesting that these thugs, ruffians and evildoers believed in some miracle to occur. G-d would sent his angels to save them. Hitler compared himself to Friedrich the Great, who was saved in the last minute by the death of the Czarina. Together with his henchmen, he believed the astrologers who predicted his salvation in April 1945.

Roosevelt died suddenly on 4/12/45, at Warm Springs, Georgia. He had been sick already for many months previously, and he died at the moment when the war was coming to a successful end. It came as a shock and surprise to all the people of the world. The Germans received the news in ecstasy and jubilation. The Nazis failed to understand that a U.S. President was not a Czarina and that a democracy was not an absolute monarchy. The change of an American President could not change anything in the war against the Nazis.

The rejoicing lasted a very short time. The vise of justice was closing in. The front was disintegrating rapidly.

On 4/20/45, Hitler's birthday was celebrated in his bunker in Berlin. Most of his old cronies were present. Goering, Goebbels, Himmler, Bormann, etc. They urged him to leave Berlin and to organize a last stand in the Alp mountains. Hitler could not make up his mind. Finally, he came to the following decision: If Berlin will be able to defend itself like Leningrad or Moscow or Stalingrad, then he'd retreat to the mountains in order to continue the fight. Maybe a miracle would happen. Therefore, on 4/21/45, he ordered SS General Steiner to counterattack. But nobody knew where General Steiner was, nor where his army was located. Troops were withdrawn from north of Berlin to support Steiner. This withdrawal weakened the front to such a degree that the Russians broke through the essential and vital defenses of Berlin and were able to surround the city on 4/25/45. Hitler flew into a violent rage and decided to remain in Berlin. It didn't make sense to run away. The hand of justice would reach him anyway, wherever he was.

The souls of millions of murdered children would follow him and wouldn't rest as long as he walked on the surface of the earth.

In the bunker of the Wilhelmstrasse Chancellary of Berlin chaos and pandemonium dominated. Many preferred death than to fall into the hands of the Russians.

The hopelessness of the situation and the mental state of Hitler's henchmen in the bunker, at the end of April, 1945, was beyond description and could be compared only to the despondency and heartbreaking despair of the Nazi victims who were waiting for the Gestapo and the Einsatzgrupen to expel them from their homes and drive them to the pits. The fates of Hitler, Goebbels and the rest of their tagtails were, exactly, the same as those of the civilians of the German-occupied territories, who were terrorized and forced by the Nazis to commit suicide. Depression, despondency, downheartedness, oppression and sinking spirits governed all their minds. Many received vials of poison to accelerate their demise. On 4/30/45, about 3:30 P.M., Hitler shot himself after poisoning his dog; his mistress, Eva

Miracle #12. Zeilsheim

Braun, took in poison. The bodies were later burned with gasoline. His fate was the same as his victims whom he tortured and who were killed in the gas chambers, their bodies later burned in the Krematoria. The sufferings which he caused others returned to himself. The remains of Hitler had not been definitely identified. Therefore, a long time after the war many doubted of his death. Rumors spread that he escaped to Spain and then to South America. Even Stalin maintained that Hitler was not dead.

Further investigations and accounts of eyewitnesses confirmed his death. According to Kempka, Hitler's chauffeur, his bones were not found because they were scattered by the intensive Russian artillery.

The death of Goebbels was also very characteristic of what the fate prepared for him. All his six children, ages 3-12, were poisoned by their own father. On his order they received lethal injections of a poison (it reminded me of the phenol, lethal injections given to the young Greek boys in Birkenau) by the same doctor who poisoned Hitler's dogs.

About 9 P.M., on 5/1/45, one day after Hitler's suicide, Goebbels ordered an SS man to shoot him and his wife in the back of their heads. Their bodies were burned, but not enough to be indiscernible. He too suffered the same fate as thousands of people who were killed in the pits by the Germans on his instigation and his approval, through shots in the back of their heads, whose bodies were later burned.

The Nazi victims were innocent. Some of them didn't know even where Germany was located, and didn't understand the reason for their death.

Hitler and his henchmen knew the enormous crimes which they brought on mankind. They got cold feet and weak knees, as all tyrants and cowards do, when the moment of truth arrived. Some of the criminals succeeded in escaping to South America and avoiding in this way the trials of the international courts. They feared they wouldn't be able to answer all the accusations of the enormous wickedness and heinousness committed on innocent people.

Himmler, the chief of the Gestapo, who organized the concentration camps, and who created the factories of death, was caught by the British, but he escaped the justice of the world by biting with his teeth a vial of potassium cyanide, which caused his death in a few minutes. He used the same poison which his victims used to rid themselves of the torture and pain which he, Himmler, inflicted upon them. Here, again, he met the same end as millions of others who cursed his name when they were murdered by him. Those who thought to destroy the world were themselves destroyed.

The Nazis wanted to assure happiness for themselves by committing crimes on others. Heaven, as we have seen it, would never permit it. The thousands of SS men who murdered their victims in cold blood and who robbed their belongings, thought that their crimes would never be detected. By murdering all the survivors, there would be no eyewitnesses. But they were dead wrong. There were witnesses all over. People in the surrounding villages of Auschwitz, Maidanek, and others saw the flames bursting out from the chimneys of the Krematoria, visible especially at night. The smoke of the burned bodies irritated their eyes and clogged up their respiratory tracts. Many survivors succeeded even in escaping, and became the conscience of the world, crying for justice and demanding a stop to genocide.

I left Poland, where most of the concentration camps were built and where most of the people were murdered.

One autumn morning, I found myself at the railroad station of Katowice waiting for a train which would take me to the West. I wanted to get away from that bloody land. The people, the buildings, the sidewalks, the stones depressed me. The air I was breathing was no air but smoke, which choked my interior. Away from this unclean air, away from the contaminated humanity! The further away, the better.

The train arrived at the station full to capacity. People were sitting on the ground between the benches and on the platforms of the wagons. Still, I was able to push myself into one of the wagons. The congestion was enormous. I had to stand on my feet all day long. We passed many villages, scattered houses, fields, trees. As we moved further to the West, the air became more clean and the surroundings not so depressing. The train stopped at the station of Poznan, the largest city of west Poland. Many disembarked, and I was able to find a place on one of the benches and to sit down.

I was glad to be able to rest a little. We continued in the western direction on the way towards Berlin. The train stopped at many stations, where other people came in and joined us.

At one of the stops, many Russian soldiers entered our wagon. They had to stand on their feet, because all the benches were occupied. Some of the soldiers were tough, pushed the civilians on the side and occupied their sitting places. One of the soldiers came to me and said, "You Amerikanski Burzuj [American capitalist], get up and let me sit down."

Betty, who was with me in the wagon answered the soldier.

He is not an American and certainly not a capitalist. He is a survivor of a Nazi concentration camp, rich in spirit but poor in money."

"It doesn't make any difference. I want the seat," replied the soldier.

I was glad to get up, and in spite of my tiredness I expressed my willingness to offer my place to the soldier. Betty couldn't get over the words uttered by the Russian.

"It is a prophecy," she said. "You are going to be an American and a capitalist."

The first prediction came true, but the other part escaped me up to now.

After a few days we reached Berlin, the capital of Germany. Here were the headquarters of Goebbels and most of the other Nazi chieftains and potentates. Here were contemplated the most horrible crimes. Here were fabricated most of the lies in the Nazi factories. Here, the Nazis burned the Reichstag and blamed the Communists and Von der Lubbe for it. Here they worked out all the details to provoke the outburst of the Second World War. Hitler was afraid of one thing, "that a pig should not appear and prevent the war."

This was the end of November 1945.

The center of Berlin around "Leipzigstrasse" was almost completely destroyed. All around there were burned-out buildings and accumulation of rubble. "Under the Lindern," the broad avenue, the pride of Germany, was piled with broken bricks, wood, and garbage. Hitler's Chancellery, where he finished his own life, was in ruins. Goebbels' propaganda ministry, from which all the lies spread, was destroyed. The "Brandenburg Gate" and the "Siegessaule" were still standing, "Alexander Platz" belonged to the Russian sector. Most of the black market transactions took place there. Germans were milling around, offering some goods for food. Many of them had Russian gold rubles and golden objects with Russian, French inscriptions on it. They were probably robbed in the occupied territories and offered now for sale. The Germans were worrying what was going to happen to them.

I heard the following conversations.

"We committed so many crimes in Europe," one whispered to another German.

"Wars happened throughout history. But the building of gas chambers and Krematoria, where millions of human beings perished, were unknown up to date. We exterminated even little children. We had no pity on anyone. We extracted golden teeth from corpses. We used human fat for manufacturing of soap. We made mattresses from hair of beautiful women. We used it and enjoyed it. Most of us knew what was going on. We heard stories from thousands of Nazis who participitated in the atrocities. Soldiers, returning from the front, told us of the murdering of thousands of civilians by the 'Einsatzkommandoes.' We saw with our own eyes the piles of civilian clothings, baby shoes, linen, bed covers, pillows, arriving from the occupied territories. Yet we tolerated it and even jubilated and rejoiced in it as long as we were winning on the battle fronts."

The Germans in Berlin were worrying what the future had in store for them. They didn't worry about the victims, but what was going to happen to them.

I left "Alexander Platz" and was thinking of the statement made by Mr. Becker, who was himself a German, but an anti-Nazi.

"The German women regret the loss of their flats and the destruction of their furniture, more than the loss of their men killed in the war. They regretted the loss of the war but not

MIRACLE #12. ZEILSHEIM 511

the crimes. Has anyone found some notes, written clandestinely by a German, during the war? No. They all agreed with him."

I walked over to "The Brandenburg Gate," where Germans were standing in groups talking. One of them said, "I was in England and in America before the war. We are not going to pay for the crimes committed. In a democracy, human life is important. The worst that might happen to us is that we'll have to rebuild the cities which we destroyed. This is a small price to pay for the atrocities and the lives of the innocent people whom we destroyed."

"Don't worry," I heard another saying. "We won't have to repay even that. There is a discord and a disagreement among the Allies. Every one of the big powers wants us on their side. The Soviets wish we become Communists. The Americans are trying to maintain our private enterprises. It is nothing to worry about. Everything will be forgotten in a very short time."

I was thinking of the declaration of the Allied leaders, at the conference of the Foreign Secretaires in Moscow at the end of 1942, that every criminal would be brought to justice in the countries where the crimes were committed. Was it possible that this declaration would be forgotten also? I was sure that nobody wanted a repetition of the same crimes.

After a few weeks, I left Berlin and traveled to Zeilsheim, near Frankfurt/Main, which became a temporary shelter for the survivors.

I worked there in the hospital and medical clinic. So much misery, broken lives. Indescribable pain, distress and sadness. Finally, I succeeded in getting a visa for immigration to the U.S. of America.

Here ends the true and tragic narration of Dr. Harsaw, who was saved by Superior Forces, in order to tell to posterity the real happenings of Nazi crimes during the Second World War. He'll appear again, twenty-eight years later, at the time of his testimony in a German court against the chief Nazi of the camp where he was incarcerated.

He expressed his feelings with the following phrases:

"These events I do remember.
I pour my soul out for the martyrs.
Through all the years of German terror
Hatred and ignorance devoured the sufferers.
The Nazis were brutal and savage in their power
Trying to destroy what G-d had cherished.
Subdued and crushed I begged my savior
To stop the genocide and the senseless bloodshed."

The Nazi tyranny has to be viewed as a Bubonic Plague, a pestilence which destroyed millions of human lives, regardless of age, sex, religion and color.

The scientists found a cure and eradicated the disease, by establishing its cause, its etiology.

In order to combat future Nazism and future atrocities, we must find, like the scientists, the cause of Nazism.

Therefore, I'll try to analyze and answer a few very prominent questions.

WHY DID HITLER COMMIT SUCH ENORMOUS CRIMES AGAINST HUMANITY?

Hitler was surrounded by people who were able to reason with him. He was capable of conversing with his friends, to argue, to answer questions. He received representatives from foreign countries with whom he argued and presented his point of view.

What was the sensibleness and logic in murdering millions of children and infants, without benefit to the conduct of the war?

It is true that he possessed certain psychotic traits, murderous tendencies and desires to kill his opponents, but after all he was not completely psychotic and removed entirely from reality.

Didn't he understand that murdering innocent people in the occupied territories would harden the resistance of the people and increase the spirit and intensity of opposition and counter action?

I'll try to answer the above questions as follows:

1. Hitler learned early in life, which he confirmed, also, by

Miracle #12. Zeilsheim

facts throughout all of his later existence, that murdering people and removing his opponents from the scene were the right tools in achieving his goals. An opponent killed and eliminated would never rise again.

What was the reaction of the German people?

The German people knew early during the Nazi movement about the vans, which exterminated the mentally deficient. Even children pointed with their fingers on the passing vans screaming, "Here are the vans."

The people knew of the assassinations of Hitler's political opponents, the chaos, the blood-shedding. Yet they accepted him, as long as he was making progress and achieving victories.

The German generals, the industrialists could have had removed him easily from the office and terminated the atrocities in the bud, up to the demise of Hindenburg.

Let's review the facts. Hitler never enjoyed a majority at the polls of the national elections.

On 3/13/32, he received 30% of the votes.

On 4/10/32 he pooled 36% of the votes.

During the elections to the Reichstag, on 7/31/32, the Nazis unleashed the S.A. troops on the streets of Germany, creating confusion and anarchy. Assassinations, disappearance of political opponents were daily occurrences. In spite of all this terror, the Nazis won 230 seats (37%) in the Reichstag out of a total of 608 seats. President Hindenburg called in Hitler after the elections and told him that the Nazi party contained numerous wild elements, citing the violence on the streets and the racial discriminations.

The question is, why did President Hindenburg permit the Nazi party to continue, when it became clear, that the party "had wild elements" and that violence including murder took place on the streets? The removal of such criminals from the horizon of Germany would not constitute any problem, especially if the generals, the industrialists, the educated people would help. But the truth remains that the Germans did not care about the atrocities, crimes, assassinations as long as that was in their interests. They simply tolerated it. On the contrary, when the elected members of the Reichstag convened on 8/30/32, the Center joined the Nazis, electing Goering as President of the Reichstag.

On 11/6/32, new elections to the Reichstag took place. This time the Nazis lost 34 seats, winning only 196 seats, instead of the previous 230 seats.

The chaos and confusion continued. The assassinations and terror intensified. Finally on 1/30/1933, President Hindenburg, pressed by his friends and son, nominated Hitler to the Chancellorship.

Instead of stopping crime, it became now the official policy of the new government. Hitler, Goering, Himmler and Goebbels were able and free to intensify their terror. The infamous concentration camps were enlarged and increased in number. Their rivals and competitors had to be removed. It didn't make any difference whether those rivals helped Hitler in his struggle and enabled him to achieve his goal. His best friends, General Schleicher, Roem, Strasser and many others, were murdered in cold blood in 1934. The post war trial in Munich of 1957 mentioned 1,000 members of the S.A. troops who were previously the pillars of Hitler's might and instrumental in reaching the Chancellorship were brutally eliminated.

Even at this late date, President Hindenburg, with the help of the generals, could have removed the Nazis, if they really wanted it.

Hindenburg died on 8/2/34. A letter was sent to Hitler signed by Hindenburg in which he recommended the restoration of the monarchy. The letter was suppressed by Hitler and a plebiscite was called for.

Oskar, the son of the late President, broadcast on the eve of the plebiscite, calling on all the Germans and letting them know that his father intended to hand over the presidency to Hitler. Of course, he did not tell the truth.

On 8/19/34, 80% of the voters (38 million) voted the approval of Hitler as the new President of Germany. Only a courageous four and a half million people voted *NO*. and so Hitler became President and Chancellor of the Third Reich. He

Miracle #12. Zeilsheim

was finally elected *voluntarily* by the majority of the German people to his office.

The army was bound to him by an oath of loyalty and obedience. Later, in the coming years, the military defended themselves from the accusations of crimes committed in line with the oath of loyalty sworn to the "Fuhrer." It is very doubtful whether one is bound by an oath given to a murderer and a criminal.

Whether the oath was a shield for the military men and for the individuals who occupied high positions in the government to submit to Hitler, whom they cherished and admired, before and during the war, *or* whether cowardness, weakness and fear were the real reasons for lack of resistance to the Hitler regime, will remain forever a mystery.

Hitler was free now to act without any hindrances. The recalcitrants and his competitors were brutally killed. Hitler was then forty-five years old, and free to act the way he wanted. He became the supreme Lord of Germany. His orders were above the law and above the constitution. Whoever had guts to utter the slightest protest was carted away to the concentration camps, where he perished. The majority of the German people supported him with genuine enthusiasm.

Who cared about the liberties taken away from them?

Who cared about the barbarism, the Gestapo, concentration camps?

An evil force was unleashed long buried inside the nation.

Heil Hitler, give us victories!

Let the subhumans perish!

Priests were arrested on trumped up charges.

On 9/15/35, the Nuremberg laws were proclaimed, which deprived the Jews from German citizenship.

The enormous crimes committed and the persecution of innocent civilians and religious people did not arouse the majority of the German people. They liked Hitler because he was moving at that time from triumph to triumph.

On 7/25/34, the Austrian Chancellor Dollfuss was assassinated by SS men dressed in Austrian uniforms.

Hitler's mind and those of his cronies were occupied mainly with plans of preparations for the unleashing of another World War. In 1937, Hitler called his top military men to a conference in the Reich Chancellory of Berlin in which he made the following statements:

1. The German question can be solved only by force.
2. Germany can not wait longer than 1943-45. Should social tension intensify in France, or should France be tied up by a war against another state, Germany would take advantage and act immediately against Czechoslovakia and Austria at the same time.
3. War was a possibility by the summer of 1938.
4. England and France were their most hateful enemies.

As we know, events took another turn. Austria and Czechoslovakia were handed over to Hitler, without any war. The West believed that, in appeasing Hitler, a war would be avoided. The Nazis thought differently. They believed that appeasement was a sign of weakness and they continued to make plans for a general war.

Three months before the outbreak of Second World War, Hitler assembled his generals again and informed them of the following:

1. Poland would be attacked. His pact with Poland was only to stall time.
2. Danzig (Gdansk) was not the issue.
3. England was their enemy and a struggle for life and death would ensue.
4. Holland and Belgium must be occupied.
5. There was *no question of justice and injustice*. Victory was all what it counts.

As we can see from the above, war was planned and decided upon before its outbreak and provoked by the evildoers of our century. It was irrevocable. Treaties, contracts had less value than the paper on which they were written. Hitler addressed his generals again one week before the onslaught.

1. I am Germany. There will never be in Germany a man like me.

Miracle #12. Zeilsheim

2. Our enemies are little worms. I saw them in Munich.

3. *Our strength is our brutality.* I have ordered to destroy without pity all men, women and children of Polish race.

4. Be hard. Be without mercy. Western Europe has to tremble in fear. If we win, conception of right or wrong will not matter.

5. The same brutality will occur later in Russia.

The reader has to be reminded that the above words were uttered by Hitler at the end of August of 1939, at the very time when the German-Russian friendship pact was concluded.

6. I am only afraid that some Swine-dog (Schweinehund) will come and make new proposals. I'll throw him down all the stairs, even if I have to kick him in front of all the photographers.

And so, the Second World War started on 9/1/39, by attacking Poland. Two days later, on 9/3/39, England and France fullfilled their guarantee and declared war on Germany.

Poland collapsed in a few weeks. Germany occupied Western and Central Poland. Russia overran Eastern Poland, which was mainly Western White Russia and the Ukraine.

After the victory over Poland, Hitler informed his generals secretly:

1. The sword is the only solution.

2. My own person is Irreplaceable. I am convinced of the powers of my intelligence. (He repeated again his previous assertions.)

3. France and England will be attacked.

4. The neutrality of Holland and Belgium will be broken.

In the spring, Denmark and Norway, through Skagerrak and Kattegat, were attacked and occupied. The seizure of Holland, Belgium, France followed.

Skagerrak is an arm of the North European sea, between Norway and Denmark. It is 150 miles long and 70-90 miles wide.

Kattegat is a strait between South Western Sweden and Denmark. It is about 150 miles long.

Finland was fighting on the side of Germany. Only Sweden was not occupied and remained free.

Why wasn't Sweden occupied by the Nazis? Here are the reasons:

1. Sweden gave to Germany all the materiel that she was able to and could afford. Why then a military attack? Sweden was also too small a fry to make any difference on the ego of Hitler.

2. Goering's wife was Swedish. He, also, had many influential friends in Sweden who fully collaborated with the Nazis.

3. Sweden could serve when necessary as a mediator between Germany and the Allies and help to conclude a separate peace.

Later, when the Germans started to feel the pangs of the approaching defeat, many attempts were made in this direction. Even in the last months of the war, Himmler and Goering sought Swedish intercession and good offices in mediation for new peace offerings.

The generals, the industrialists, the educated, the most important persons of Germany heard from the Führer wild, *irresponsible, barbaric words*, phrases, utterances, expressing openly a desire and craving to commit crime, such as:

1. Be hard. Be without mercy. Be brutal.
2. Destroy without pity children and women and entire races.
3. Pacts, agreements of friendship and nonaggression, have *no meaning*.
4. Conceptions of right and wrong have no value.
5. A mediator to avoid the war and bloodshed will be kicked by the Führer in front of all the photographers.

Were the above utterances and verbalism divulged by Hitler compatible with the honor of Germany? Compatible with the integrity, honesty and glorification of the army? Compatible with the tradition of the German generals? Could the leaders of Germany be bound by an oath of loyalty to a criminal and justify herewith atrocities and crimes unheard of on our planet up to date?

Would the military and the politicians of any other state or nation obey their chief of state to transgress any decency, to step over any respectable standard of suitability and to perpetrate all kinds of evil and abominations? The answer is—NO.

When Stalin mentioned jokingly that in order to weaken the

"Wehrmacht" a certain number of high-ranking German military officers would have to be annihilated, Churchill got up and declared with a rage that he'd never be a party to such senseless statements.

Churchill was aroused, and justly so, by a mere talk of annihilation of military personnel. Wouldn't any man in England, France, Italy, and any part of the world revolt against murdering of millions of innocent women and children? Wouldn't they rebel against creating factories of death, gas chambers and Krematoria, where millions of innocent human beings perished? Wouldn't they be right in assuming that commitment of crime by the supreme commander absolves them from any oath of loyalty?

It is really amazing and incomprehensible that Hitler could reveal his barbaric plans to the Generals of the Army, Navy and the Airforce, to the highest-ranking politicians, educators, scientists of Germany and get away with that. No voice of protest was heard. He was accepted as long as Germany was winning.

We still remember how the German masses applauded their leaders, knowing that they constituted evil to the rest of the world. They tossed flowers on the SS men, Gestapo knowing that thousands of innocent people were being tortured in the prisons and dying in the concentration camps. It is an unfortunate fact and a sad episode in the history of Germany that not a single general, not a single intellectual in the first winning years of Hitler had the courage to protest and try to stop him.

To summarize the above, in finding out the reasons of Hitler's crimes, we must assume the following:

1. Hitler had a special trait of evil in his personality, which caused him to destroy and to teach his followers to be brutal. This trait was intensified throughout the years, until it assumed a form of mass extermination of human beings including children.

2. He realized, also, that frightening people caused their submission and complete cooperation. He murdered his best friends, who helped him to climb the ladder of success. His opponents were annihilated in the concentration camps. He noticed the astonishing facts that fear was directly proportional

to submission. The more fear the more acceptance. Therefore, he did not try to hide the murder of his opponents. On the contrary he sent the ashes of his victims to their relatives. The same system of frightening people was applied towards the citizens of the occupied territories who greeted him at first with open arms. It became a part of his identity. He ordered the unnecessary shootings and hangings in Poland and Russia, just to frighten people to submission. He was not ashamed of his atrocities. On the contrary he exposed them. When the special commandos (Einsatzgrupen) in the East forced the people into the pits and murdered them in cold blood, they did not conceal their crimes. They wanted the native people to know it and to tremble from fear.

His mottoes were: Be brutal! Kill! Torture! Destroy Leningrad! Warsaw should never rise again!

Here he committed a cardinal mistake, by failing to realize the difference in the behavior, mental attitude, character, between the people of the occupied territories and the people of Germany. The oppressed would never submit to atrocities. The higher the crimes, the stronger the resistance. The German generals on the other hand, in Germany proper, and on the East and the West battle fronts of Europe, accepted every abominable order, including the murder of innocent children.

This is a stain on the history of Germany that will never be erased.

Hitler boasted that the Third Reich would last 1000 years. The atrocities committed by the Third Reich would last more than 1000 years. They'll never be forgotten. The Nazis incensed a fire in the hearts of those who saw their wicked acts with their own eyes and who experienced it on their own bodies. A fire which burned brightly for decades and will never be extinguished.

3. Hitler loved to torture the weak nations and the weak individuals, being sure that nobody would defend them. He exterminated the Gypsies because they were weak and not because of racial reasons. He knew that nobody would defend them. They had no governments and nobody would stick out his neck long enough to protect them. The racial theory was only a

Miracle #12. Zeilsheim

shield to justify crime. He respected the yellow race (Japanese) because they were strong militarily. Rosenberg, the theoretician, formulated National Socialism according to Hitler's wishes. They knew that purity of Nordic blood is an utopia only. Such a purity was impossible and unhealthy. It explained the atrocities.

The above method of brutality coincided perfectly with his theory of "fear." He believed that the other nationalities would be frightened to complete submission.

4. Hitler believed truly that the English and American Jews and the Jews from all over the world possessed enormous influence over their respective governments. He believed that by murdering the entire race, including women and children, the free democratic governments would be disturbed and concerned, and would ask him to stop the massacre. They might even, agree to certain Nazi demands. Sorry that he didn't know the truth of how little the leaders of the world were willing to sacrifice to save the Nazi victims.

Walter Chellenberg, chief of Himmler's security service, acknowledged that the Germans provoked hatred abroad. He cited a few examples of atrocities, including the attitude toward Christianity and the mass extermination of the Jews, which he considered to be a very stupid policy because "We had in our hands only 1/3 of the world Jewry and 2/3 were outside of our power to reach."

He did not regret the extermination of over six million human beings, but only not being able to exterminate all. This was a very characteristic, frank opinion of a prominent German.

National Socialism was not national and not socialism. The word *Nationalism* stood for destroying other nationals, because they did not recognize the master-race. The word *Socialism* stood for enslaving other people.

Hitler in his political statement said, "The seed has been sown that will grow one day in the history of Germany to the glorious rebirth of the National Socialist movement."

I believe that mankind should be on the alert and not neglect this time his warning, as they neglected it in the years before the war.

* * *

Could another Hitler arise in any other country except Germany?
I believe it is impossible.
Here are the facts.

1. In all the history of mankind, we never heard of such atrocities organized, perpetrated and executed by a legally elected government which lasted more than ten years (1933-1945).

From 1/3/1933, the day Hitler assumed the Chancellorship, till 9/1/1939, the day when the Second World War broke out, the world heard of many unusual, terrible acts of murder, assassinations, concentration camps, terror and persecution being done in Germany.

But during the years of the Second World War (1939-1945), those acts assumed such a hugeness, vastness and tremendousness that the world was shocked, at first, and couldn't believe in the veracity of the reports.

2. The crimes of the Nazis have no parallel in history. The annals of history tell us of wicked acts perpetrated by soldiers during the heat of the battle, but they had always been negated by their respective governments. They usually lasted a very short time, which could be counted in days or weeks.

Even the Barbars, the Huns, Genghis Khans did not build gas chambers nor Krematoria.

3. The extermination of the Armenians by the Turks lasted also a very short time and was not a premeditated, deliberate act of the Turkish Government, as it was by the Nazis, but rather a result of the unexpected defeat during the First World War. The Armenians were blamed for the defeat, just as all the other weak minorities, including the Jews, had always been blamed for mistakes of the governments. It was rather a release of anger and frustration of some of the military chiefs.

The atrocities perpetrated by the Nazis, as narrated in the true eyewitnessed stories of this book and others, were unheard off, previously, on this earth. Therefore people were not conditioned to meet them when the real German attacks took place. This fact confirms the assumption that no nation on earth would be able to commit such crimes.

Miracle #12. Zeilsheim

4. See the previously mentioned reaction of Churchill and Roosevelt to the suggestions of Stalin, to annihilate high-ranking German military officers.

The leaders of the First World War were to be blamed in part for the genocide which occurred during the Second World War. No adequate steps were taken to prevent it. The responsible Turkish leaders received mild sentences, just as the present Second World War criminals. The murdering of a million Armenians was not publicized for a long time and was not promoted throughout the masses.

Everything was soon forgotten. Very few people of Europe and the world knew about it and still fewer remembered it.

In his secret speech to his generals dated 8/22/1939, Hitler said, "Be brutal! Murder! Nothing will be remembered. Who talks nowadays of the extermination of the Armenians?"

Had the world talked and warned the evil perpetrators during the twenty years' interval between the First and Second World Wars not to commit genocide, Hitler and his cronies would not have dared to do what they did. They would simply be afraid of the day of reckoning, the day of justice.

Therefore, the murdering of millions of innocent civilians the building of gas chambers and Krematoria were the direct result of the carelessness and negligence of the world leaders after the Armenian Genocide.

The SS chieftains never thought of a time when they'd have to pay for their crimes. Ask them, dear reader, now and they'll tell you the truth, that they never paid any attention to such an eventuality. Many are still alive, roaming the streets of Germany, free and not regretting what they had done in the past. Read the biography of Rudolph Hoess, the infamous chief of Auschwitz, and you'll convince yourself of the above truth.

Just as the leniency of the perpetrators of the Armenian massacre and the lack of publicity thereof brought on the genocide of the Nazis, so will the present leniency in the German courts towards the Nazi criminals bring a terrible and much worse calamity on mankind.

World leaders, awake! Now is still time to make impossible a repetition of the Nazi crimes.

Don't wait too long, because signs of darkness are appearing already.

If not now, when?

The fact that this form of Nazi atrocities and the creation of death factories for the destruction of millions of human beings is completely new on our planet speaks for itself. It is the "*Corpus Delicti.*" No other nation, throughout history, brought on or conducted such dreadful acts for a prolonged period of time.

The people would not permit it.

Take a look at the events of Great Britain at the end of World War II.

Churchill took over the reins of the Government when England was on the verge of collapse. No other English politician wanted to be prime minister. They simply refused to preside over the disintegration of the British Empire. Churchill, by his courage, gathered all the forces of the nation, declaring, "We'll fight them on land, we'll fight them in the air, we'll fight them over the seas, till the Nazi evil will disappear from this earth."

When Hitler attacked Russia, he said, "If Hitler will attack Hell, we'll give Hell all help in our possession."

The British under Churchill's leadership, defeated the Germans. They came out from the jaws of death and from the mouth of the bottomless pit of inferno.

Yet, at this very time, he lost the elections. The British considered him to be an excellent leader during the war duration, but not during peace time.

This fact showed a maturity of a nation!

Here lies the answer to the question whether a Hitler was possible in England. The English would have never given him dictatorial powers. They would have revolted right from the very beginning of terror.

The same was true for all the other nations. As I explained in the previous chapters, Hitler could have been removed by the Generals without any undue difficulties, up to the demise of Hindenburg.

Therefore, I believe that a new Hitler might appear again

on the horizon of Germany. We can see already the approaching danger. The mild sentences in the German courts meted out to the Nazi criminals are eloquent testimony of what the future has in store for us and constitute new evidence of the gathering storm of another world calamity.

Could another dictator create the same or similar crimes? The answer is *NO*. I don't know of any dictator, king or absolute monarch who built gas chambers, vans of death, Krematoria, and used them for over ten years, annihilating millions of innocent people.

I don't know of any human being who grabbed thousands of children from the arms of their mothers and threw them into blazing fires, to be devoured by the terrible flames.

I don't know of any mattresses made from beautiful women's hair. I don't know of any soaps being produced from human fat.

I don't know of any gold teeth, extracted from hundreds of thousands of corpses to be dispatched to the national treasury.

All these atrocities appeared on our planet for the first time, and I hope the last time, provided the leaders of the world will undertake the necessary means to counteract evil in its bud.

Lets take another contemporary dictator, the dictator of the Proletariat, the Supreme Lord of the Soviets during the Second World War, Joseph Stalin.

1. Stalin arrested people, who were suspicious of being against his regime or did not fulfill and sometimes sabotaged his orders.

It was true that the slightest suspicion or a mere slip of the tongue could cause their arrest and sentencing. But he did not arrest people knowing, like Hitler did, that they were completely innocent.

2. Stalin did not build gas chambers, moving death vans, Krematoria, etc.

3. Stalin did not murder children and infants.

4. Stalin did not make soap from human fat.

5. Stalin did not enrich his coffers with gold teeth extracted from corpses.

I don't want, and it is not my purpose, to defend Stalin. He has been in the past and is being judged now by his own countrymen.

Solzhenitsyn should understand the difference and the reason why Russian collaborators were not brought to trial in the same number as the Germans. Solzhenitsyn should be informed also about the very mild sentences meted out to the Nazi perpetrators by the German courts. These courts assumed in the main form, not an arm of justice, but a theatrical performance. They went through all the procedures of a trial. Judges, prosecutors, witnesses, criminals. Stories of enormous crimes were heard in the halls of justice. But the sentences, which should make impossible a repetition of similar crimes in the future, were very mild. The storms created by the preparations of the trials gave birth to little mice, which shortly disappeared and were forgotten.

I'll bring later, in this book, the full details of procedures of one trial in which I participated as a witness.

CHAPTER XVIII

The mild sentences in the German courts

NAZI LEADERS AFTER THE WAR. THE NAZI TRIALS. WHY DID THE NAZIS OFFER TO EXCHANGE 10,000 TRUCKS FOR ONE MILLION JEWS? STATEMENTS MADE BY NAZI LEADERS AFTER THE WAR.

Let's hear now, certain statements expressed by some of the top Nazi leaders who brought Hitler to power and who supported his policy of lies and atrocities before and during the war, in contrast to the statements made by the same men after the war was lost. I hope that the reader will find it very interesting and it will also be a big help in understanding the war.

Herman Goering, Reichsmarshall, chief of the Air Force, the second man in Germany after Hitler. He formed the first concentration camps, which he later in 1934 gave over to Himmler. He ordered Heydrich in 1941, on behalf of Hitler, to prepare the final solution of the Jewish question, which meant complete annihilation of an entire race.

Here is a letter from Goering to Heydrich dated 7/31/41.

"On the order of the Führer I hereby charge you to carry out preparations for the final solution of the Jewish question in all the territories of Europe under German occupation."

After the war, in Nüremberg prison, he declared that he

had never heard of any atrocities, he had never known about the existence of gas chambers, of murdering millions of human beings.

"Some of the generals," he said, "might have known all about it, How could they reconcile that with their own conscience? I can not understand it."

But he, Goering, the second man in the Third Reich, never knew about anything. He was completely innocent. He was on trial because Germany lost the war.

"The victor will always be the judge."

About *Himmler*, he said, "I'll never understand how he could have done all those things and gotten away with it."

About *Hitler*, he said, "When the German people will learn of everything that was revealed in the Nuremberg trial, they'll condemn him. In fact, Hitler condemned himself by his atrocities." He didn't justify the murder committed by Hitler.

About *Schacht*. "He giggles like an innocent girl who is getting it for the first time."

About *Ribbentrop*. "He was cocky and stupid. During the signing of the Axis powers, Ribbentrop wanted me, the second man in the Reich, to stand behind him. What a nerve?"

Regarding the German people he said, "They cheered and praised us when things were going well. But now they are condemning us. The Germans are nationalistic even now. They cannot change overnight. The German youth don't give a damn about atrocities. But the German people will be forever condemned by these brutalities."

Goering was asked why he didn't break openly with Hitler. The reason was, according to him, that the German people were all for Hitler. If he had started something before the war, they would have considered him insane. After the victory over France, he could have gathered maybe one hundred people. In spite of the war and the atrocities, the Germans, Goering rationalized, loved and cheered Hitler. It was true that when the Russian campaign went bad, thousands would have joined him, but he, Goering, did not want to divide the nation.

It is a fact that *most of the Germans knew about the atrocities*. Even the wife of Goering said that she knew about the

The Mild Sentences in the German Courts

Dr. Hans Frank was Governor General of Occupied Poland, the land where most of the extermination camps were built. He said "Hitler had a mask of a human face but behind the mask a devil, death itself . . ." and "don't let anybody tell you that the Germans didn't know it. They knew it."

atrocities, because she received many letters. About Hitler, she said that he was insane.

Therefore it is amusing and tragic to hear Goering say that he didn't know anything about the atrocities.

When he was arrested, he carried with him two suitcases of Narcotics, mainly Paracodeine. Later, the doctors cured him of this habit by gradually diminishing the doses of the narcotic.

Hans Frank. Hitler's lawyer. Governor General of occupied Poland.

In his diary, he wrote that the people of the occupied territories would be slaves.

"If a German is shot, up to one hundred Poles will be shot."

"The Jews will be annihilated. 1,200,000 will die from hunger."

During the years 1939-42, I lived in Poland where Hans Frank was Governor-General. I still remember his name, when the local people blamed him for all the atrocities. I remember when the people of entire cities, including infants and children, were taken out by the "Einstzkommandos" (special commandoes), driven to the pits outside the cities, and shot in cold blood.

Auschwitz, Maidanek, Treblinka, Sobibor and others were in Poland under his jurisdiction.

Hans Frank, as the Governor, knew everything, abetted it and approved it.

In prison, the same Frank declared, "In centuries to come, people will tear their hair and say, 'My G-d, how did such murder come about? . . .' You can not call it just a crime. Crime is a too small word for it. Stealing is a crime, killing one man is a crime. But this is beyond human imagination. Murder of mass production! Ten thousand a day! Gold teeth extracted from corpses and sent to the Reichsbank, women's hair packed in mattresses. G-d Almighty! And all that was ordered by one devil who appeared in human form. . . . Did G-d ordained all this? If yes, it makes one despair of divine justice."

Be assured, Mr. Frank, that G-d was outraged, as all humanity was. It was the work, not of G-d, but of the devil!

Frank further continued:

"Don't let anybody tell you that the Germans had no idea of all this. Everybody knew it.

"A thousand years will pass and the guilt of Germany will not be erased. Our system was evil. Hitler gave orders to annihilate millions of human beings. Hitler wore a mask of a human face, but actually behind the mask was a devil, death itself. . . . Now his face is unmasked and everyone can see it. A death's head! A skeleton!"

About Himmler, he said that he would have never dared to carry out his program of mass exterminations if Hitler did not order it.

These statements were completely true. We know, that Hitler had secret meetings with Himmler very often in which they discussed all ways and means of destruction, of mass murder, of concentration camps and of all the details of the atrocities. Himmler actually was a simpleton. Hitler ordered and he fulfilled and executed it.

Ernst Kaltenbrunner (an Austrian). He was chief of Himmler's security department, which included the SS, SD, Gestapo, gas chambers, annihilation of civilians. He knew exactly what was going on in the cellars of the Gestapo, how the transportation of people to the gas chambers and their annihilation occurred. We have eyewitnesses who saw him entering the gas chambers to watch the murdering of people in action. Alois Hoelriegel, a guard of Matthausen concentration camp saw

The Mild Sentences in the German Courts 531

Kaltenbrunner in the gas chamber as early as 1942, during the process of gassing and exterminating people.

Yet, in Nüremberg, he testified that he didn't know anything. He blamed everything on Himmler, Heydrich, Müller, Pohl, and other SS men.

Maurice Lampe, a French prisoner in Matthausen concentration camp, which was under supervision of Kaltenbrunner, described the special treatment of Allied flyers who fell into the hands of the Germans as late as September 1944.

"Forty-seven Allied flyers were led barefooted to the quarry. Heavy stones were loaded on the back of these poor men. Whenever the prisoners sunk under their burden, they were kicked and hit brutally with bludgeons. . . . At the end of the day, twenty-one bodies were strewn along the road. . . . the other twenty-six died during the night. These flyers were Americans, British and Dutch."

In January, 1945, so late in the war, fifteen Americans in uniforms parachuted into Slovakia. They were caught and executed in Matthausen Concentration Camp, on direct orders of Kaltenbrunner. Yet he testified that he didn't know anything about it.

This vulgar denial constituted an offense to the intelligence of the courts and to any person who heard it. It was unbelievable! Even the Nazis wondered about such a stupid defense.

This was a typical Nazi who blamed others but not himself. He denied even his own signature when confronted with compromising documents.

Baldur Von Schirach, Hitler's youth leader, denounced Hitler as a millionfold murderer. The crimes committed by him constituted the darkest blot in German history.

He continued: "If on the basis of racial politics and anti-semitism an Auschwitz was possible, then Auschwitz must become the end of racial politics and anti-semitism."

Keitel. Chief of staff of the high command of the Wehrmacht. He ordered the killing of one hundred Communists for one German killed. He said that paragraph 47 of their military law specified that it was a crime to execute orders which were given with criminal motivation. But he, Keitel, merely *transmit-*

ted the criminal orders, he did not execute them. Secondly, Hitler was above the law.

The question remains, why did so many military men murder so many innocent people, including women and children?

Why didn't they use the paragraph 47 of their own military code, especially since not one was punished for disobeying orders to kill?

For example: *Griese* refused to execute Jews and nothing happened to him. *Palmer* refused to kill prisoners in Sacksenhausen, nothing happened to him.

In my camp, Günthergrube, which belonged to Auschwitz III, as I explained earlier, there was a guard who refused to work in concentration camp and submitted his resignation. He was sent to the front.

In murdering 23,000 Jews in the city of Bialystok, some refused to shoot. The result was that they were all sent to the front.

Dr. Hans Gunther Scraphia of Gottingen testified that he didn't know of a single case of punishment for an SS man who refused to murder. They simply sent him to the front. Sometimes not even that.

Why, then, did thousands of military men participate in the mass murder? It is a moot question and open to discussion. I am leaving it to the intelligence of the reader, who by discussion and debate will arrive at the right answer on the basis of the facts of this narration.

Rudolf Franz Ferdinand Hoess, Commandant of Auschwitz Concentration Camp, from May 1940 till December 1943.

He said that two and a half million people were murdered in Auschwitz while he was the Commandant. It started in 1941.

There were two big gas chambers which could exterminate two thousand people each in half an hour and four smaller gas chambers which exterminated one thousand five hundred people each. Totally ten thousand people could be killed in half an hour. Most of the people went voluntarily to the gas chambers, which were equipped with water pipes like in a real bath house. The people believed the German promises that they were getting showers after which they'd be transferred to the East. But instead of water, the Nazis put in poisonous gas.

He said, "It didn't occur to me, that I'll be held responsible."

Here was a vivid illustration and confirmation of the fact that the mild sentences in the genocide of the Armenians and insufficient publicity of the crimes committed were the main factors in making possible *another genocide* perpetrated and executed by the Nazis which was much bigger in dimensions and number of people killed.

Therefore, I believe that the mild sentences in the *present* German Nazi trials will make possible a repetition of the same crimes again. It was a big mistake of Allied occupying powers not to enforce the declaration of the three leaders in Moscow of October, 1943, which stated *that the Nazi criminals should be brought to trial in the countries where the crimes were committed.*

Giving over the jurisdiction to the German courts sowed the seed of a new genocide, the dissemination which we are witnessing today.

It is still not difficult to stem it in its budding, and this is the main purpose of this book.

The Moscow declaration of 10/30/43 of the Allied leaders was confirmed by the London Agreement of 8/8/45 and incorporated in Article IV of Law No. 10 of the Allied Control Council issued on 12/20/45.

So the extradition was an obligation to the German courts. But the extraditions were never honored on the grounds of minor technicalities, or were simply deferred without any explanation.

Since 1949, not a single Nazi has been extradited to Poland, where most of the crimes were committed.

Nazi criminals walk scot-free on the streets of Germany today. Those apprehended are released on their own recognizance. Only the very notorious criminals are kept in custody and most of them released soon after the trials.

I'll give here a few examples:

1. *Herman Kramey*, the infamous Nazi who helped Eichmann to transfer more than three hundred thousand Hungarian Jews to the Auschwitz death camp in 1944, was sentenced in

Frankfort on 2/3/65 to only five years of prison. Soon after the verdict *he was released* because he had been detained five years before the trial took place.

2. *Erick Ehrlinger*, who murdered at least sixty thousand people, was sentenced by the German court to twelve years of prison. But, taking in consideration good behavior, he was released many years ago.

3. *Jacob Fries* (the death angel of Auschwitz) was arrested in 1961 for murdering *one hundred thousand* people including Russian war prisoners, Poles, Hungarians, Jews, etc. But alas, in 1963 the proceedings against him were dropped.

4. *Kurt Uhlenbrook* ordered in August 1942 the killing of eighty thousand people in Birkenau, where a typhus epidemic had broken out. For unknown reasons, the charges against him were dropped.

5. The Nazis *Heckenholt, Wirth, Pfannestiel* were responsible for gassing two hundred thousand Jews in Belzen, in 1942. They are free now.

It has been calculated that the average sentence for a Nazi murderer has been *ten minutes* of prison per one human being killed.

The statute of limitation for Nazi criminals was December 1969. At present, they may be convicted only under Paragraph *211* of the criminal code, which defines a murderer as one who killed because of blood lust and for other low motives.

The above definition fits in, as we know, with most of the Nazi criminals, but it is subject to the judges' interpretation.

Lets see how the interpretation of the judges has been working in the German courts?

A Nazi criminal who murdered thousands of people is according to the German courts an *accomplice* to murder and is punishable by only a few years' imprisonment, whereas those who murdered one person received life sentences.

Even the Ex-President of Germany, Theodor Heuss, stated that the Nazi criminals are being treated differently than other murder cases and that the West German Courts do not evaluate the injustices committed by the Nazis.

According to this interpretation, Himmler, Eichmann, Kal-

The Mild Sentences in the German Courts 535

tenbrunner, Rudolf Hoess, etc. were only accomplices to murder, because they fulfilled the order of Hitler to commit mass extermination. They in turn ordered "others" to do the killing and the "others" fulfilled only the order of their superiors. In light of this interpretation, it can be assumed that Goering and all the other Nazis of the Nüremberg trial would have gotten mild sentences in the German courts and soon been released.

This was valid also for Himmler, Goebels and Ley. They wouldn't have had to commit suicide. The German courts would have taken care of them and freed them. In this way a murderer ceased to be a murderer.

There were millions of brutally killed people, but not a single culprit.

This is the logic of the present German courts. For example: Burmeister and twelve other Naxis were accused of murdering one hundred fifty-two thousand Jews in Chelmno. Six were acquitted and six were found to be only accomplices to murder.

Nazi criminals are usually considered by the German courts only as *accessories* to murder (84% of cases); therefore the sentences are very mild.

Goebbels and Himmler and other SS men preferred to commit suicide because their crimes were so enormous that they themselves thought that no court in the world, no matter how mild, would refrain from sentencing them to death. It was according to them the only sentence possible. Eichmann said, "I should perhaps hang myself in public." Yet the German courts would not have sentenced them to die because of two reasons.

1. The Germans abolished the death penalty in 1949, as soon as they took over the jurisdiction from the Allied occupation powers, in order to save them from the gallows.

2. The Nazi criminals received the orders from Hitler and therefore they were only accomplices or accessories to murder, punishable only by a few years of prison.

I believe that the present German Nazi trials were created primarily for the purpose of inducing mild sentences and as such do not take off the shame from the German history. They are acting also for the possibility of a repetition of the same crimes. There were also being taken in consideration *mitigating circumstances* in sentencing the Nazis, like the time which had elapsed since the crime was committed.

This explains why the German prosecutors were dragging their feet in bringing the Nazi criminals to justice.

For example: It took me twenty years to bring Alois Frey, the ex-Nazi Lagerführer, to justice. The murderers of Maidanek concentration camp are being brought to justice only now, more than thirty years after the crimes were committed. The German prosecutors desire mitigating circumstances.

This constitutes a mockery of justice. It is also unlawful, because the punishment of the Nazi criminals was formed under the international law, in which there was no limit on prosecuting, and was binding on all state authorities and on all individuals. Therefore, the statute of limitation is unlawful and it is also unlawful to refuse to extradit the criminals to the countries where the crimes were committed.

There is a justified public indignation over Nazi criminals walking freely in Germany and scoffing at this kind of justice. Why shouldn't they or their descendants repeat the same crimes which satisfied their animal instincts and brought some of them enormous wealth?

The passing of the horrible crimes of genocide into oblivion outrages the sense of justice of every decent man and woman.

The mild sentences of the contemporary German courts illuminated clearly the links between the present Germans and those of the Third Reich.

Never in the history of mankind have so many criminals escaped punishment and left the door open to a repetition of the same crimes.

There is an old saying, that everybody can make a mistake one time, but only a fool repeats the same mistake twice. Where are the World Leaders?

It had been estimated that during the Nazi Regime over fifteen million civilians were murdered. At least one hundred fifty thousand Germans were actively and *voluntarily* occupied by this process. As I explained earlier, every Nazi volunteer had the right to leave his criminal activities freely without being unduly punished.

The Mild Sentences in the German Courts

In 1944, Winston Churchill wrote to Eden: "This is the most terrible crime ever committed in the whole history of the world. This crime is being done by scientific machinery and by nominally civilized men. . . ."

All concerned in this crime . . . should be put to death, if their association with the murders has been proven."

The *Times of London* wrote, "The punishment should fit the crimes and serve as a future deterrent to others."

Goering, after he was captured, stretched out his hand to the Allied Commander as a gesture of greeting of one soldier to another.

"You won," he said with a smile. His hand remained hanging in the air.

The Allied Commander refused to hold the hand, which was soaked with blood of millions of innocent people. Goering forgot, or simulated to forget, all the enormous crimes that he and his cronies brought to mankind.

The Germans now say: "Let all bygones be bygones," forgetting that by their actions they achieved the peak of barbarity and made a recurrence of the same crimes almost inevitable and unavoidable.

It is impossible to describe the disappointment and pain felt by the few survivors who came to Germany to testify to what they had seen with their own eyes, hoping that justice would be done and the criminals would pay for their crimes. How could it be otherwise? Mankind cannot afford another worse genocide!

When they saw the leniency of the German courts, they regretted deeply playing a part in this tragicomedy. They were cheated again by the Germans just as their past friends and families were cheated by the Nazis, when they were transported to the concentration camps and murdered.

These unfortunate victims returned to their respective countries heartbroken, with the eternal question on their lips, "Didn't the world learn anything from the past atrocities? How can we protect our children from similar occurrences?"

The truth is that the world had forgotten and the Germans didn't care.

Karl Adolf Eichmann. He was an SS-Obersturmbannführer,

and directed the Jewish section (Amt IV B4 of the RSHA). The chief of RSHA was first Heydrich and later Kaltenbrunner.

Eichmann made sure that every order of mass destruction was confirmed and approved and often signed by his superior Heydrich, later Kaltenbrunner. To accomplish his tasks of annihilation, he had a staff of members. Each one was assigned to another country, where they gathered all the necessary information for transporting human beings to their death.

For example:
Krumey was assigned to Lodz, later Vienna.
Brunner—France.
Dicter Visliceny—Slovakia.
Dannecker—Bulgaria.
Abromeit—Croatia.
Dr. Seidl—Thesenstadt.
Burger—Theresenstadt, later Athens.
Franz Novak—in charge of all transportation.
Hertenberger—specialist in individual cases.

Eichmann ordered in March, 1943, the transfer to Auschwitz extermination center of 24 transports of 2,300 persons each from Salonika (Greece) and two transports of 2,500 each from Athens, which made a total of over sixty thousand people. Other transports had to follow later. Visliceny and Bruner had to do it. Itzhak Nehame, a Jew from Salonika, testified that he was transferred to Auschwitz with a transport of 2,300 Jews. Only *ten* survived.

This was the time when the Germans were evacuating Greece. The Nazis were afraid that they wouldn't have sufficient time for evacuation, therefore the death transports had priority over other transports, including the military. The Germans cared more about the destruction of Jews than about saving their own soldiers.

Visliceny declared in Nuremberg that Eichmann told him in February, 1945, the following:

"I'll laugh when I'll jump into my grave because of the feeling that I have killed five million Jews, which gives me great satisfaction and gratification."

THE MILD SENTENCES IN THE GERMAN COURTS 539

There were three periods in dealing with Jews.
1. *1937-1940.* Persecution of Jews, in order to accelerate their emigration.
2. *1940-1941.* Concentration of Jews into ghettos and concentration camps and preparing them for the solution of the Jewish problem (emigration or annihilation).
3. *1941-1945.* Annihilation by murder.

The Jews were killed, not because of their religion or their political belief, but because they were born Jews, without a country.

In Auschwitz, more than four million people perished. Most of the victims did not enter the camp. The latter had a constant flow of people from the outside world. The unfortunate victims were forced straight to the gas chambers.

The highest number of prisoners in Auschwitz concentration camp proper (I, II, III), men and women combined, was 140,000 at one time.

The Auschwitz I camp was three kilometers away from the city of Auschwitz (Oswiencim in Polish). Auschwitz II, or Birkenau, was two and a half kilometers from Auschwitz I.

Each transport was received by sixty armed SS men. The transports used to arrive irregularly, about two per day. Each transport contained about two thousand people.

Auschwitz will, always, be remembered in the annals of history as a symbol of horror and infamy. The method used surpassed any cruelty known to mankind.

According to Hoess, who knew Eichmann well, and I am quoting:

"He was possessed . . . and convinced that the extermination of the Jews was necessary. He even opposed the selection of healthy people who were fit to work at the ramp, because some people would survive and the world would find out what really happened in the concentration camps and in the territories occupied by Germany."

By "Final Solution" he meant "complete destruction without any exceptions."

After his arrest Eichmann said, "I, Eichmann, cannot claim any mercy because I do not deserve it. Perhaps, I should hang myself in public so all the anti-semites in the world can see the terrible nature of their acts."

Here is an interesting episode.

Heinz Roetke sent a letter to Eichmann regarding a French Jew, Abraham Weiss, who was a prisoner in Drancy. Mr. Weiss invented an electric bulb which could be used in blackouts. Roetke asked in his letter whether Mr. Weiss could remain in Drancy and not to be sent to Bergen-Belsen concentration camp.

The reply of Eichman was:

"As this invention has been sent for registration, already, to the patent office of the Reich, there is no more interest in this man. Have him sent on the next deportation."

In Buenos Aires, Argentina, Eichmann made the following statement to a journalist in 1957.

"The Jews through thousands of years of learning and development had become superior to us, Germans.... The Jews have been writing history over six thousand years by now. Therefore, they constitute a people of first magnitude, for the law givers have always been great. The Jewish people were law givers."

It is amusing and tragic at the same time to hear such words uttered by a first-rank Nazi who organized the annihilation of millions of innocent human beings and who considered the Jews to be subhumans.

Why did the Nazis offer to exchange 10,000 trucks for one million Jews?

Eichman was ordered by Himmler, on the suggestion of the high Nazi hierarchy, to propose the above exchange, assuring that the trucks would be used *only* in the East, against the Russians. This offer, according to my opinion, although genuine, was intended to plant seeds of distrust and to create a new discord in the Allied camp.

Here are the reasons and evidence.

1. When the events of the war turned around, and the world saw the approach of the German calamity, the Germans tried to bring a discord among the Allies.

2. They almost succeeded in the Kirovograd conference, where Molotov and Ribbentrop took part. Stalin was afraid that

THE MILD SENTENCES IN THE GERMAN COURTS   541

England and America would conclude a separate peace agreement with Germany. The lack of the formation of the second front in France and the Hess case served as proof to the above line of reasoning. The Nazis pulled here one of their tricks of cheating and caused the minutes of the Kirovograd conference to leak outside, in order to bring discord among the Allies. What Hitler really wanted was a separate peace with England and America *for the time being*.

3. The Nazis tried numerous other times to bring discord among the Allies. Different messengers were dispatched to the neutral countries and many meetings were convened, but they did not succeed.

4. The Nazis realized in 1944, when the proposal of the exchange was put forward, that the war was definitely lost. No new weapons, like V1, V2, and no new sacrifices in human lives were able to avoid the final German defeat.

For the first time, they started to worry about the enormous crimes that they committed, for which they'd be tried in international courts.

5. They still believed in 1944 that the world Jewry possessed an enormous power and could influence the Allied governments towards their directions and intentions, and that the Jews of the West would do everything possible to save one million Jews from a certain death.

6. They hoped, also, that Stalin would be outraged, by the giving over of 10,000 trucks, which were considered necessary war materiel, to the Germans on the Eastern front. Stalin would consider it as a breech of the agreement, and would offer them something also, in return. In this way the differences would widen.

The Germans pulled a very mean and cheap trick out of their sleeves. It showed how little they understood the morality, behavior and thinking of the Allied leaders. The Germans were too simpleminded and too dumb to comprehend it.

The proposal flopped. The English understood and conceived the meaning of the deception.

Eden sympathized, but stressed that *the Russians* and *the Americans* should in the first place, before anything, *agree to it*.

Joel Brandt, the Hungarian Jewish leader, who was dispatched by Eichmann in May, 1944, with the proposal of the exchange, was arrested on the Turkish-Syrian frontier and refused permission to return to Budapest.

The British Parliament rejected it, as a new German trick.

The Jewish leaders could not accomplish anything to help the victims, in spite of all their efforts.

1. They explained that in the middle and end of the year 1944, the delivery of 10,000 trucks, as an exchange for one million human lives, *would not make any difference* to the outcome and end result of the war.

2. Naturally, any exchange should have been by *full agreement* between the Russians and the Americans, in order to avoid any discrepancy of opinion. They further tried to clarify that arrangements could have been done in a gradual way.

For example: 100 trucks for the first ten thousand people delivered to a neutral country. It would have taken more than a year till all the 10,000 trucks would have been delivered, and by then the war would have been finished and millions of human lives would have been saved.

It is true that nobody trusted the Nazi promises, but it could have been tried on a small scale.

It showed clearly what influence the Jewish leaders had over the Allied camps. . . .

On July 6, 1944, Dr. Weizman pleaded with the British Foreign Secretary to do something to alleviate the Nazi slaughter. (*Found in the archives of the late President.*) He proposed the following:

1. The Hungarian officials, who participated in the deportations and the exterminations, should be warned that they'd be tried as war criminals if they didn't stop immediately. The above warnings should be given by all the three Allied leaders, Churchill, Roosevelt and Stalin.

2. The Allies should declare their readiness to admit refugees of any nationality, race and creed.

The so-called neutral countries, like Switzerland, Sweden, etc., should declare their willingness to give temporary shelter to the refugees.

3. To drop hundreds of Israelis by parachutes into Hungary in order to form a nucleus of resistance movement in the cities, forests and mountains.

4. To bomb the railway from Budapest to Auschwitz.

5. To bomb Auschwitz and other concentration camps, especially since the German armaments concerns like Krupp and Siemens had their factories there.

It would have been beneficial for the war conduct itself.

1. It would have achieved a far-reaching and many-sided moral effect.

2. The bombing of the gas chambers and Krematoria would definitely give a temporary reprieve to those prisoners who were doomed to die and also to those who were still alive in Hungary.

3. It would, also, mean that the Allies waged direct war on the Nazi methods of extermination, oppression, and mass murder perpetrated by the Germans during their retreat and eventual collapse.

4. It would also prove the lie of the constant assertion of some of the Nazis that the Allies didn't really care about the German atrocities.

5. It would also convince the German circles which were hopeful of Allied magnanimity of the seriousness and genuineness of Allied condemnation of mass murder.

All the pleadings were to no avail.

In the meantime, the Allied air raids tore up the Budapest-Vienna railroad tracks, but not the lines which led to Auschwitz and not the armaments concerns situated in Auschwitz proper.

Eichmann ordered a forced march of the Hungarian Jews from Budapest to the Reich's border. Many victims died of starvation, exhaustion and beatings. Many committed suicide on the way. Eichmann drank a "Schnaps," called "Mare's milk," to celebrate the occasion of the forced march of the doomed.

The Russians at that time were approaching Budapest, the capital of Hungary, which was defended by the German General Zehender. He told Eichmann that the artillery shells were on the other side of Budapest, because they couldn't be transferred to the defense lines on account of the quick Russian advances. The distance was 6-8 km., and it was very dangerous to bring the shells over.

Eichmann found a remedy right away. He made a living chain of Jewish prisoners to carry the shells where it was necessary.

This was a typical Nazi solution to a problem, to send prisoners to dangerous locations where the Master-race was afraid and didn't dare to go.

Many eyewitness survivors of the holocaust appeared in Nüremberg and in the German courts and in courts all over the world.

I'll bring in here only a few:

Severina Shmaglevskaya, a Russian woman prisoner from Auschwitz, testified as follows:

Babies born in camp were taken away immediately and never seen again. She asked: "In the name of all the women of Europe who became mothers in German concentration camps, I would like to ask the German mothers, *where are our children?!*"

She went on to describe how Jewish children were thrown alive into the Krematorium furnaces during the rush season of 1944.

Dr. Aharon Perez from Kovno (Lithuania) testified before the Israeli tribunal.

He described the *operation children* (Kinders-action) in which German soldiers seized all the children that they could find. Watching through a window of his flat, he saw children herded into trucks and thrown inside. Mothers were running to the Germans begging for mercy. To no avail! The Germans hearts were made out of steel and their brains were those of beasts.

In two days, 1,300 children were grabbed from one city and sent to the concentration camps, where they perished.

Dr. Perez related how he was able to inject sedatives into some of the children so that they shouldn't cry and reveal their hiding place.

Even when the Red Army was approaching Kovno, the Germans took time to blow up dugouts and cellars of the ghettos where people were hiding. Two thousand Jews were killed on the spot and many others were transferred to extermination camps.

Mr. Abba Kovner, resistance leader, described how Itzhak Wittenberg, leader of the Jewish resistance in the ghetto of Vilna, voluntarily surrendered to the Gestapo when the Germans threatened to massacre all the Jews of Wilno. He was tortured and murdered.

"History will judge us," he continued, "and it is my opinion that Wittenberg's surrendering to the Gestapo was one of the greatest acts of heroism."

"I saw also through an opening of a stairway," he further testified, "how two German soldiers dragged a woman by her hair. She was holding a baby in her arms. One of the soldiers grabbed the baby by the legs and smashed the head against the wall, while the woman clung to the soldier's boots begging for mercy."

Dr. Aharon Beilin testified how trainloads of Gypsies arrived

The Nazi leaders at the Nuremberg trial. Front row, left to right: Goering, Hess, Ribbentrop, Keitel, Kaltenbruner, Rosenberg, Frank, Friek, Streicher, Funk, Schacht. 2nd row, left to right: Doenitz, Roeder, Von Schirach, Sauckel, Godl, Van Papen, Seyss-Luquart, Speer, Von Neurath, Fritzsehe.

in September 1943 at Auschwitz. Dr. Mengele selected 600 Gypsies of one transport, and the rest were taken to the gas chambers right away. Some of the young men wore the uniforms of the "Hitler youth movement" or even of the German Army. They were very bitter and disappointed. "We were very loyal to Germany," they said, "and look what they had done to us. Why? . . . Why? . . ."

Some still greeted each other with "Heil Hitler." Some Gypsy girls refused to be examined by the Jewish doctors in the camp.

Here again, the Nazis destroyed thousands of Gypsies. Some of them were even taken away from the Russian front line, where they fought for Germany, and sent to Auschwitz to be destroyed. They had no country, no government of their own, nobody to protect them.

Hitler felt that nobody would seriously protest the destroying of the Gypsies. He felt that the others would be frightened to death. This desire to frighten people dominated Hitler throughout his campaign and was intensified during the war.

The Nazis explained it with racial theories, but the real reasons were different.

Mr. Hoter Yishai described moving scenes when the Allied brigades entered Theresenstadt.

"The prisoners did not look like human beings. They had an appearance of miserable, undernourished, sick creatures. They fought among themselves with all their feeble strength to reach the trucks of their liberators and to touch with their own hands the shoulder patches of the brigade groups. They kissed the flag painted on the fender of the trucks and crawled on their stomach to hug the feet of the soldiers and to kiss their boots, which carried the liberators who freed them from Nazi Hell."

CHAPTER XIX

One example of a Nazi trial. The true story of one survivor

ALOIS FREY, THE COMMANDANT OF GUNTHUER-GRUBE (AUSCHWITZ III), WAS PUT ON TRIAL IN FRANKFURT FOR *PREMEDITATED MURDER.* MY TRAVELING TO GERMANY. MY TESTIMONY IN FRANKFURT. THE TERRIBLE DISAPPOINTMENT IN THE NAZI TRIALS. A SURVIVOR TELLS HIS TRUE STORY. THE OFFICIALS OF THE "WIEDERGUTMACHUNG" OFFICES OF TRIER (GERMANY), AND THEIR CONTINUOUS PERSECUTION OF THE SURVIVORS. WHO WOULD GIVE ME WINGS? THE RATIO OF THE SURVIVORS TO THE BIBLICAL "JOB." I BELIEVE.

Let's now examine a Nazi trial in action in present-day Germany, in which I appeared personally as a witness.

The defendant was *Alois Frey*, the chief (Lager-Führer), the real potentate and sovereign, the ruler of life and death over a few hundred prisoners incarcerated in concentration camp Günther-Grube, which was a part of and belonged to Auschwitz III.

In spite of the heavy charges against him, the survivors had a very difficult time in bringing him and other criminals to justice. The Germans, in accordance with their policy toward many other Nazi criminals, simply were reluctant to put them on trial.

In spite of the accusations against Alois Frey, I received a letter from Henry Ormond, Attorney of Law at the Court of Frankfurt, Germany, dated July 27, 1965, in which he wrote, "The proceedings against Alois Frey were already terminated long ago, in January, 1964." This meant, that the Nazi Alois Frey, the murderer of so many human beings, was freed before the trial even started.

This was the way the Germans investigated the Nazi criminals, which by itself constituted an offense to the memory of those who were killed and a tragedy for future German history.

One year and seven months later, on March 6, 1967, I received a letter from the German Minister of Justice, in which he wrote, and I am quoting: "You mentioned the name of the accused as 'Freed,' instead of 'Frey.' This was allegedly the reason the proceedings were delayed."

In my writing to the authorities in Germany, I had always accused the Nazi chief of the concentration camp Günthergrube. There was only one chief in Günthergrube and it didn't make any difference whether his name was Freed or Frey. The Germans knew certainly who the Nazi chief was. It shows clearly the procrastination and the unwillingness of the German authorities to put the Nazi criminals on trial.

The accusations against Alois Frey were as follows:

1. Hanging of four prisoners in the camp Günthergrube in the summer of the year 1944, with the other inmates forced to watch the hangings.

The names of the victims were:
Heniek Ehrenfield,
Idle Potok,
Firstenfield,
Buchweitz.

One prisoner with the name of Bakalash was shot to death on the way back to the camp.

2. Alois Frey created conditions in the camp which caused

many prisoners to die from starvation, hard labor, diseases and exhaustion.

3. Alois Frey made selections in the hospital, whereby the victims were transferred to the gas chambers of Birkenau, where they perished. Not one of the selected returned back to Günthergrube.

4. Alois Frey, like the other chiefs of the Nazi concentration camps, was entrusted with his high destructive and criminal position thanks to his past Nazi spirit and qualifications. He was nominated by the Nazi hierarchy to be the only independent chief of Günthergrube (Auschwitz III).

Alois Frey overdid his superiors by his zeal and ardor.

On December 17, 1969, I was informed by Prosecutor, Mr. Klein, from Frankfurt as follows:

"*Wir ende 1970 mit dem process gegen Alois Frey rechnen können.*"

In English it means that the trial of Alois Frey will start at the end of 1970.

Although the court authorities in Germany had the findings of the committed crimes already in their possession for more than ten years, I was glad that finally the date of the trial had been established. Therefore, I was very much shocked and dismayed by the inaction of the German courts when the year 1970 passed and the expected trial did not take place.

On July 9, 1971, I was informed by the same German Prosecutor Klein that:

"*Wir rechnen damit, dass der prozess anfang 1972 beginnen wird.*" *Signed: Prosecutor Klein.*

In English translation it means that the trial will start at the beginning of 1972.

The trial did not take place in 1972. Instead, Prosecutor Klein arrived in New York and visited my office in the summer of 1972.

Prosecutor Klein was a middle-aged man, of medium height, heavy-set, with a round smooth face.

It was in the late afternoon when Mr. Klein entered my medical office in New York City.

"Please sit down, Mr. Klein," I said. "I am glad to see you in New York."

"Thank you," responded Mr. Klein, while taking out from his pocket many photographs of middle-aged men.

"Do you recognize Alois Frey, among these photographs?"

I looked carefully at all the photos and could not identify any one of them as being Alois Frey.

Prosecutor Klein took out one of the pictures, handed it over to me, and said, "This is Alois Frey."

I looked at the picture, which did not resemble the ex-Nazi leader whom I knew from the camp. The picture was of a man without hair, completely bald with a thin emaciated face. Mr. Frey had a round face and was not bald.

This is not the photo of Alois Frey, I said to myself, it is of another man. Why then did he show it to me?

"Maybe he changed during the years," I thought. This was the year 1972. I had seen Alois Frey for the last time in January, 1945, more than twenty-seven years back. He certainly changed a lot.

Mr. Klein continued, "Alois Frey changed a lot. I wanted you to see his picture because the court in Frankfurt will ask you to identify him in the hall of justice. Now you'll have a better idea how he looks."

"Thank you, Prosecutor Klein, for your foresight," I said.

We spoke for a while about New York, the U.S.A. and how magnanimous and generous were the Americans towards the German people.

"Thanks to your countrymen," he said, "we have a prosperity in Germany that we never dreamed of."

"You certainly did not deserve it," I interrupted, "after all the cheers Hitler and the Nazis received from you and your countrymen when they were winning."

"You are right," said Mr. Klein. "We never expected it. Maybe the cause lies in the antagonism between the Americans and the Soviets."

Then, Mr. Klein started to talk again about Alois Frey.

"You know," he said, "Mr. Frey has a very soft, German dialect and he speaks in a very pleasant voice that is enjoyable to

One Example of a Nazi Trial

the ear. His face is round, mild, and it is very difficult to recognize in him a criminal. Therefore, *it will be difficult to indict him."*

I could not understand such plain and candid talking by the German prosecutor.

What does it mean, "A pleasant voice and a round face"? And "It will be difficult to indict him"?

"Mr. Klein," I said, "many criminals have round, even baby faces, and speak softly. Himmler, the greatest criminal seen on this planet from the beginning of time, had a round face and he probably spoke in a soft German dialect. Most criminals look like average human beings. Why then would it be difficult to indict him in court?"

Mr. Klein realized that he had a slip of the tongue and that he made a mistake in talking this way. He tried to amend.

"I have eyewitnesses who saw Mr. Frey committing many crimes and shooting five people in the Gypsy camp. He'll never be acquitted."

On this note, Mr. Klein left my office. I thought a long time about the statements of Mr. Klein. At that time, I didn't know about the mild sentences in the German courts, and the endeavor of the German authorities to look for mitigating circumstances in sentencing the Nazis.

Mr. Klein disqualified himself right here, in my office, as a prosecutor by saying that "It will be difficult to indict him."

In light of the facts, which I know now, and which I saw myself when I appeared in Germany at the trial, it was quite natural for Mr. Klein to talk this way. It is quite understandable. It was the policy of the postwar German government.

Finally, I received a letter from the district attorney (public prosecutor) of Frankfurt, Germany, in which I was informed that the criminal proceedings against Alois Frey had started and that I'd have to appear in court on February 4, 1974, as a witness for the prosecution.

SUMMONS TO APPEAR IN COURT.

Business Number:

- 4 Ks 2/73 -

It is requested that you bring this summons with you to the trial. In the criminal proceedings versus the German national

Alois Frey for *premeditated murder*, you are to be heard as a witness before the "Assizes," at the Regional Court, in Frankfurt/Main.

You are therefore summoned to appear at the trial, on *Monday, February 4, 1974, 9.15 hours,* before the Court of Assizes, at the Regional Court, in Frankfurt/Main. Konrad-Adenauer-Strasse 20, Building C, 1st floor, room 165.

Signed: Public Prosecutor Hess.

I immediately left by plane for Germany in order to tell the court what I had seen with my own eyes in the concentration camp Günthergrube.

On 2/4/74, I entered the exact place at the exact time. It was a large room, at the end of which were sitting the judges and the jurors. Three judges and three supplementary judges. Six regular jurors and four additional jurors. So it appeared to me. On both sides of the room were sitting different people, because the court proceedings were open to the public.

I looked all around, because I wanted to see where Alois Frey was sitting. Not one of the people in the room resembled the picture which Prosecutor Klein showed me in my office. I looked all over, at every chair, every bench and every corner and examined the faces of every one present in the courtroom.

Finally, I noticed on the left side of the room, in the front bench, two persons sitting. One was thin with a face of a real criminal. The other one seemed to be a little older with a round face, and he had the features of Alois Frey. The same eyes, the same movements. But this man had a full head of hair.

When prosecutor Klein showed me the picture of Alois Frey in my office the man was completely bald.

How was it possible?

I continued to look at the man and concluded that he was really Alois Frey.

I watched him and tried to assay and analyze him. The more I gazed at him and sized him up, the more he appeared to be the Nazi I knew.

I observed that the man carefully looked at me too, talked with his neighbor and pointed his hand in my direction.

ONE EXAMPLE OF A NAZI TRIAL

He moved his head up and down while talking, like he had known me also.

Yes, this was Alois Frey! He had changed a little but not too much. He looked much older than before, and the movements were more slow. But, again, this man was not bald. He had a full head of hair. . . .

I started to analyze further. Was it possible that the German prosecutor wanted deliberately to mislead me when he showed me the picture? How could one explain it otherwise? If yes, why was he his prosecutor and not his defense lawyer?

Contradictory thoughts passed through my mind. I wanted to talk it over with my wife, Judith, who was sitting near me.

Then, I was ordered to stand up and to come to the small table with a chair which was standing in the middle of the room. Then I was instructed to swear that I'd tell the truth and only the truth. I swore in accordance with the regulations of the court.

Here I want to make the following explanation.

The exact words or sentences of the questions and answers at my testimony in Frankfort, Germany, on 2/4/74 can naturally not be relayed exactly. I had no recording machine nor was I permitted to make a record of the court proceedings. The dialogue between me and the court, as narrated in the following pages, represents nonetheless the true meaning, essence, gist and substance of my testimony.

"Please be seated," said the judge who was sitting in front of me, in the middle of the dais.

"What is your name?" asked the judge, "and where do you live?"

I answered.

"Do you recognize Alois Frey among the people who are sitting here all around?"

At the beginning, I was hesitating. The man at my left was Alois Frey, but he was not bald.

The judges were waiting. Everybody was looking eagerly in my direction.

"Many years passed since you last saw, Mr. Frey. It is difficult, evidently, to recognize him now," said the judge.

"This is Alois Frey! This is the man!" I called out, pointing my hand in the direction of the man with the round face, who was sitting to my left.

"That is right," confirmed the judge.

Prosecutor Klein was sitting at the very right end of the dais.

"Why did he show me the picture of a man who had no hair on his scalp?" I pondered and asked myself.

He almost succeeded in misleading me.

The recognition of the defendant in court evidently had some merit in the eyes of the judges as to assessment and evaluation of the intelligence and ability of the witness on the stand.

"Please, tell us about the time *after* the evacuation of Auschwitz. What happened on the road in relation to the defendant? Did the defendant commit crimes on the road?" asked the judge.

"Your honor! There were thousands of prisoners on the road. They were driven from all Auschwitz, which means from Auschwitz I, Auschwitz II (Birkenau), Auschwitz III (Buna), with all the numerous small extermination camps.

"They were surrounded by hundreds of armed SS men. I hardly saw the defendant on the road. We were driven like animals. There was a confusion, pandemonium, bedlam broke loose, the tower of Babel.

"Your honor! I came here all the way from the U.S. of America, regardless of hardship and expenses, to tell the court about the crimes comcommitted by the defendant which I had seen with my own eyes. It doesn't make any difference where the atrocities took place."

The judge turned his head to the other judges and jurors and said:

"We are primarily interested in the crimes committed by the defendant at the time after the evacuation of Auschwitz, on the roads."

"Your honor!" I insisted. "It is very difficult, almost impossible, to try the SS men only at the time after the evacuation of Auschwitz. Most of the horrible acts occurred in the extermination camps, in Auschwitz, Maidanek, Treblinka, where the gas chambers and Krematoria were functioning. I came here to testify about the crimes that the defendant committed in Günthergrube because I was hardly able to distinguish the defendant among the hundreds of the SS-guards on the roads."

"Well," acquiesced the judge, "you are free to proceed with your story however you wish, but we are interested with the events and occurrences on the roads."

"Thank you, your honor," I said, not knowing whether I should proceed at all. Maybe I should return back to New York?

"Tell us what kind of a camp was Günthergrube?" asked the judge reluctantly.

"Günthergrube was a small camp belonging to Auschwitz III. It counted only a few hundred prisoners at one time."

"Who was the Lager-Führer [director of the camp] and when did you arrive there?"

"The Lager-Führer was Alois Frey. He was the real boss of life and death over the prisoners because the camp was completely isolated from all the others. The communication with Auschwitz proper was by telephone, or by mail. Sometimes, high-ranking SS officers used to visit our camp. I saw Dr. Fischer, Pohl, Mohl, Müller, Eichmann and others appearing on the terrain of the camp.

"The defendant was completely trusted by the Nazi Hierarchy. Otherwise they wouldn't give him such independence of action."

"What was the conduct and behavior of the defendant towards the prisoners?"

"As soon as we arrived, he started to yell like a maniac, and beat us with the truncheon that he held in his hand. Many of us received contusions, lacerations, abrasions right from the beginning."

"Did he try to abuse you, torture you or make your life difficult in the camp?"

"Yes, he certainly did. As soon as we had to leave the camp for work, he ordered our shoes taken away and Holenderki given us instead, which made our lives very miserable and caused many injuries to our feet."

"What are the Holenderki?"

"They were made out of wood, in the form of half-shoes, the

middle of which was hollow. We had to put our feet into the cavity of the wood and walk. The wood was hard and caused wounds by friction which often turned gangrenous. Many lost the Holenderki on the way to work and had to walk barefoot on the ice and snow."

"What time of the year was it?"

"It was the beginning of February of 1944. The winter was particularly severe at that time of the year. Many returned back to the camp with frozen limbs."

"The taking away of the shoes and the substituting of Holenderki was practiced in all the other concentration camps?"

"No. Even in the infamous extermination camp Birkenau (Auschwitz II), where I was incarcerated one year (1943), the prisoners were permitted to wear their own shoes. The guards realized that the shoes were indispensable to the prisoner, without which no work of any kind could be performed. Alois Frey overdid his own superiors."

"How was the food in the camp?"

"Very bad. This was also one of the factors why so many prisoners died. A small piece of bread and margarine in the morning and a little soup in the afternoon. The soup contained small pieces of rotten cabbage or potato mixed with a lot of worms. I mean numerous worms, which were not completely killed because of insufficient cooking."

"Were selections performed in the camp?"

"Yes. I had seen Alois Frey entering the hospital from time to time and selecting sick people. He and Dr. Kovacs used to bring the victims to the waiting trucks which took them to the gas chambers and Krematoria of Birkenau."

"Did any of the prisoners, who were taken away in the trucks, ever return back to Günthergrube?"

"No, never."

"Do you remember of any particular event which occurred in the camp?"

"Yes, I remember how one of the prisoners, who couldn't stand it any longer, walked behind the limit which was allowed for walking at work. He was shot immediately by one of the guards. The guard advanced in rank as a reward, and Mr. Frey became jealous."

"Do you remember of any other atrocities in the camp?"

"The guards on orders of Alois Frey used to form two long rows of armed SS men and the prisoners had to run in the middle between the lines. We were beaten with truncheons, clubs and gunbutts."

"Were all the guards brutal?"

"There were some guards who didn't like it. They were sent to the front. No other punishment. I particularly remember one from Yugoslavia. He told me that he couldn't stand the atrocities. He was sent to the Russian front."

"Do you remember any particular atrocities and crimes committed by Alois Frey, the commandant of your camp?"

"Yes, I remember distinctly one night when we were awakened and ordered to assemble on the appeal place in the middle of the camp. The gates of the camp opened and a truck with SS men entered the camp. The names of five prisoners were called and they were ordered to enter the truck, which took them to an unknown destination."

"Do you remember the day when it happened?"

"Yes, it was Friday night, on the 14th of April of the year 1944."

"How do you remember exactly the date?"

"Because, it happened exactly on the 7th night of passover."

"Did you know or did any one of the prisoners know what were the reasons the above prisoners were taken away?"

"No. Nobody knew the real reasons. Even the brother of one of the prisoners didn't know either."

"Do you remember the names of the five prisoners who were taken away?"

"Yes, I do. Idel Potok, Heniek Ehrenfield, Firstenberg, Buchweiz and Bakalash."

"What happened to them? Had you ever heard of them again?"

"Yes. In June of the same year, four prisoners were brought back to the camp. The fifth one, Mr. Bakalash, realizing that they'd be hanged in the camp, tried on the returning road to escape. He was caught and murdered on the spot."

"What happened to the other four prisoners? Please tell us in detail."

"Gallows were erected. The prisoners had to step upwards in order to reach the hanging ropes. On the right side of the gallows stood Heniek Ehrenfield."

"Do you remember the names of some of the SS men who were present at that time?"

"Yes. I remember Dr. Fischer, the SS doctor from Buna, Alois Frey, our commandant, and some other SS men, whose names I don't remember at the moment."

"What happened further?"

"Alois Frey unfolded a piece of paper and started to read. 'In the name of the SS-Reichsfuhrer, Heinrich Himmler, the four prisoners are sentenced to die by hanging. They *wanted* to escape from the camp, because we found civilian cloth at the place where they were working.'

"As the nooses were tightened over the necks of the unfortunate prisoners, Heniek Ehrenfield called out loud and clear, and everybody was able to hear it.

" 'We are completely innocent. Everything was fabricated and made up by Alois Frey. You will pay for our innocent lives, taken away from us. The hour of reckoning is approaching. You will have to give an account before the judges of heaven and earth. We will not rest in heaven, till justice will be done.'

"Alois Frey roared like a lion. He ran to Heniek Ehrenfield and started to beat him with a heavy club over the chest, legs and other parts of his body.

"Honorable Judges! Ladies and gentlemen of the jury! Imagine a man standing with a rope over his head, being severely beaten by a brute with a face of a human being. Alois Frey has a heart of iron and a brain of a beast.

"The structure beneath the legs of the prisoners was soon pushed away and the victims remained hanging in the air."

I noticed many in the public were wiping away their tears.

"Do you have any idea, why the defendant did it?"

"The defendant desired to advance in his profession in the service of the SS and the administration of the concentration camps. As I mentioned previously, he was jealous of the guard who was rewarded."

At 12 o'clock, midnoon, the court recessed and an intermission was declared.

Prosecutor Klein walked around the hall, evidently disturbed. The proceedings were not running according to his wishes. He hoped that the occurrences would deal mostly with the Auschwitz evacuation, on the roads, where Alois Frey was hardly visible in all the pandemonium.

I observed him while he passed near me. He had become more fat. He rolled around like a barrel.

"Mr. Prosecutor," I started, "I would like to ask you something, if it is at all possible."

He stopped in front of me and said, "Go ahead. Ask."

"Mr. Prosecutor! Why did you show me a picture which you said was taken recently of Alois Frey? I saw him today, sitting at my left during the court proceedings. I, as you know, was able to recognize him. The picture which you had shown me in my office was not his. Why did you do it?"

Mr. Klein looked at me, giggled and left.

After the recess, I returned to the witness stand. Prosecutor Klein started the cross-examination.

"You testified that according to your opinion the defendant committed the crimes, because he wanted to advance. Mr. Frey said that civilian cloths were found near the place where the prisoners worked. How do you explain it?"

"At the same place where the prisoners worked there were a few civilians working. Maybe some of them left a small bundle of cloth inadvertently. The finding of civilian cloth was no proof of the prisoners' guilt."

"Mr. Frey claimed that one of the guards reported to him that the prisoners wanted to escape," snapped Mr. Klein.

"I am not sure that it is true. I am inclined not to believe the Nazis in general and him in particular. Experience showed me the opposite. But, let's assume that it was true, and that one of the guards found the clothing and reported to Alois Frey. As an old Nazi, who was in service of the SS, SD, and concentration camps, he knew exactly, without any shadow of a doubt, that any report to Auschwitz about a possible attempt to escape spelled a death sentence for the prisoners, regardless of the merit of the case.

"If the defendant possessed a little bit of humanity in himself, a tiny, small palpitating human heart, he would have investigated it before sending in his report. He could have called the prisoners and confronted them with the guard. Maybe it was a misunderstanding and everything would have been straightened out. The fact that he did not investigate speaks for itself. He did not want to find out the truth, which weighed very heavily against the defendant, because a report to escape, as I said, meant death."

"Why didn't the defendant report other similar cases of attempting to escape?"

"He did. I know of another case in which the defendant reported an attempt to escape."

"How do you know it? Maybe you are mistaken. You are not sure of it. This is only your personal opinion."

"I am sure of it, because the prisoner was suddenly forbidden from going to work and was kept inside under strict supervision. In addition, the report was sent to Auschwitz by letter, which was dictated by the defendant to Mr. Pastel, a prisoner of the accounting division in Günthergrube who told us about it. Frey's writing abilities and his spelling were evidently very poor and all his letters were written by Mr. Pastel."

Later, I was cross-examined by the lawyer of the defendant.

"You wrote to the minister of justice that at the time of the hanging Dr. Fischer was present, who was tried in another country outside West Germany. Do you know that Dr. Fischer was sentenced to death?"

"The crimes committed by Alois Frey, which I myself witnessed with my own eyes, were definitely not less than those committed by Dr. Fischer, and can be compared equally to those of the commandant of Auschwitz, Rudolf Hoess, and to those of the commandant of Treblinka, Franz Staengl. As chiefs of Nazi extermination camps they committed many crimes.

"Secondly, I wrote not to any foreign department of justice but to a German ministry of justice because the prosecutors delayed, procrastinated, vacillated and hesitated with the trial. I demanded only that the commandant of Günthergrube should be put on trial. It would have been a humiliation and a disgrace to the future history of the German people to prolong the starting of the trial any longer."

On this note, my testimony was ended. The judge wanted to know only the number which was engraved on my left forearm in Auschwitz.

I replied that my number was 94430 and showed it to the judges.

On the way back to my hotel, Judith asked me, "What do you think is going to be the sentence?"

"I don't know," I answered, "but seeing how Prosecutor Klein behaved in the case of the commandant of Günthergrube, and noticing how the court insisted at the beginning that I testify only about the time after the evacuation of Auschwitz, I doubt now whether the punishment will fit the crimes. He might get off very lightly, maybe only a few years of imprisonment."

I returned to New York broken-hearted, feeling very disappointed. I realized that it didn't make sense at all to come to Germany and testify. It was a waste of time, energy and resources.

Heniek Ehrenfield! I know that you were hanged by Alois Frey for no reason at all.

I did my best to bring the criminal to justice. The Nazi trials in Germany are not to distribute justice, but to cover up justice.

Your face, when you stood on the gallows with the rope over your neck, stands vividly before my eyes. I will never forget it! If there is a G-d, high up in the skies, go there. Take with you the souls of thousand and thousands of little children and present your case. Demand justice!

Half a year later, on 6/25/74, I sent the following letter to the court in Germany.

"To the Chairman of the Regional Court, Frankfurt, Germany.

"On February 4, 1974, I was a witness for the prosecution in the case of Alois Frey, commandant of Günthergrube (Auschwitz III), Case No. 4Ks 2/73.

"As you know from my testimony, I am writing a book about the Second World War, about the concentration camps, particularly about Auschwitz and Günthergrube and also about Germany of today.

"Therefore I would like to ask you, to send me the following:

"1. The verdict of the court in the case of Alois Frey.

"2. The finding of the jury and the explanation of their decision.

"I am sure, that you'll comply with my request, because:

"a. The trial was open to the public and so was the verdict and decision of the jury.

"b. I was a witness in the case and helped the court in its proceedings.

"c. I complied with the request of the court, and in spite of many difficulties, like closing my medical office for the time of the trial, and the accrued expense, I traveled to Germany in order to tell the court what I had seen with my own eyes.

"Therefore, I do strongly believe that I am entitled to this courtesy.

"Thank you, and am expecting your reply, as soon as possible."

On July 9, 1974, I received the following reply.

"Dear Doctor.

"I received your letter of June 25, 74. In which you asked for the verdict of the court in the case of Alois Frey. I believe that the President of the court will grant your request. We don't know as yet when the verdict will be pronounced. Definitely, not before spring time of the year 1975. It is very difficult to get the witnesses to come to Frankfurt, Germany, to testify, and therefore their testimony must take place in other countries like U.S.A. Israel, Poland, etc.

"In view of the above, I would like to ask you to repeat your request again in the early months of 1975.

"Thomas
Judge of the Regional Court."

Many survivors, evidently, were already acquainted with the German trials and refused to participate in any of those theatrical performances. I regret that I was not aware of it before going to Germany.

On April 25, 1975, I received another letter from Mr. Thomas, chairman of the jury trial.

"Dear Doctor.

"I confirm herewith your letter dated March 10, 1975, to transfer to you the verdict of the court and its reasons. I am afraid that it will not be possible to comply with your request. The consent of the prosecutor is necessary, and not that of the President of the court. In my previous letter to you, July 9, 1974, I made a mistake by telling you that the President of the court has to give his permission.

"The prosecutor refused to grant your request. I regret not being able to send you another decision.

"Very truly yours,
Thomas
Chairman of the court (trial by jury)."

Naturally, I didn't like the refusal to send me the verdict because it was *promised to me previously*. It was unbelievable that the chairman of the court, Mr. Thomas, didn't know the normal and regular proceedings regarding sending an extract of the verdict of the jury.

Therefore, on June 3, 1975 I sent a reply to Mr. Thomas.

"To the Chairman of the trial by jury, Frankfurt/Main, Germany.

"Dear Mr. Thomas.

"I was surprised and deeply shocked on receiving your letter dated April 25, 1975, in which you refused to send me the decision of the court regarding the case of Alois Frey, Commandant of Günthergrube (Auschwitz III).

"Therefore I would like to state the following:

"1. The prosecutor has no right to keep secret the verdict of the court and the decision of the jury, because the trial was *open to the public*!

"2. If the decision was right and based on German law, the prosecutor should not keep the proceedings secret.

"3. I was promised by you, Mr. Chairman, that you would inform me of the verdict and the explanation of the jury. In your letter of July 9, 1974 you wrote, 'The President of the court will grant your request.'

"4. My consent to travel to Germany and to testify in this case was based on this assumption and belief.

"In view of the above, I am asking you to reconsider your decision and to keep your original promise."

In view of the refusal it became clear to me that the verdict would be very mild, or even acquittal.

Everything was possible in the German courts.

It was a repetition of the old Nazi methods of acquittal of bloodthirsty murderers. It had happened before and it is happening now. It is the same animal with another fur coat.

It is a tragedy to the history of the world, because such methods carry the seeds of another holocaust. Only fools can make the same mistake twice, three times. . . .

On August 19, 1975, I received a reply from Mr. Thomas.

"Dear Doctor.

"In reply to your letter of June 3, 1975, I would like to state the following:

It is true that the court proceedings were open freely to the public. But for the sending of the verdict to a third party the consent of the prosecutor is necessary. . . .

"You don't have to feel displeased.

"Thomas
Judge of the regional court."

My G-d, how in the world, could I not feel displeased.

The Germans murdered millions of innocent human beings. They murdered all the members of my family. They kept me in the inferno of the concentration camp for two long years, which I survived thanks to miracles. I saw the commandant of Günthergrube, Alois Frey, hanging four innocent young men, which I could never forget. I see their sad faces in the day time and I dream about it at night.

How could I not feel displeased?

How? How? Please tell me. . . .

On June 6, 1975, I wrote to the Justice Minister of Hessen, Germany, 62 Wiesbaden, Wilhelmstrasse 24.

"Dear Minister.

"I would like to inform you the following:

"On February 1974, I was a witness at the regional court in Frankfurt (Germany) in the case of Alois Frey.

"I was very much amazed, mystified and shocked that prosecutor Klein, instead of working for the prosecution, acted entirely in the defense of the defendant.

"*Here is the evidence*.

"1. A few months before the trial took place, Prosecutor Klein was in my office in New York. He showed me many pictures and asked me to identify the commandant of Günthergrube (Auschwitz III), Alois Frey. I could not identify him in any one of the pictures shown to me. Mr. Klein then took out one of the pictures of a man completely bald and told me, 'This is Mr. Frey, as he looks today.' I saw Frey later, at the trial in Frankfurt, whom I recognized and who had hair on his scalp. I can, categorically, state now that the picture shown to me by the prosecutor Klein was not of Alois Frey. It was a way of *misleading the witness*.

"2. Mr. Klein told me in my office, in New York, that Mr. Frey speaks a very pleasant German dialect and that his face is round, nice, and doesn't look like a killer, and therefore it *will be difficult* to indict him. Prosecutor Klein tried here to influence the witness.

"I was very much amazed to hear these words coming from the prosecutor himself. I told Mr. Klein that Himmler had a nice round face also, and his dialect was pleasant to certain ears too. Yet Himmler was confirmed to be the greatest criminal in the history of the world, not only toward the other nationals but towards the German people as well.

"I had seen Frey committing many crimes in Günthergrube, and I witnessed his hanging of four young men (one was killed on the transport) for no reason at all.

"Finally, Prosecutor Klein acknowledged that he had witnesses, who saw with their own eyes how Alois Frey also murdered five Gypsies in the Gypsy camp.

"It is clear that Alois Frey was not nominated to his position as a commandant of a concentration camp without distinguishing himself in the field of atrocities.

"In view of the above, it is clear that Mr. Klein disqualified himself as a prosecutor in the Nazi trials. Therefore the trial may be considered a mistrial and should be tried again.

"The above facts, I am bringing to you, Mr. Minister, as the highest representative of German justice, and not to any international authority as yet.

"I was promised by Mr. Thomas, the judge of the regional court, Frankfurt, that he would send me the verdict of the court and the decision of the jury. Therefore I was amazed when I received a letter from Mr. Thomas saying that the Prosecutor rejected my demand to send me the verdict of the court.

"Is the prosecutor ashamed to send me the decision of the court? I understood that the trial was *open to the public* and not a secret one.

"In view of the above, and in the name of the numerous innocent people murdered by Alois Frey, I am asking you, Mr. Minister, the following:

"1. To see, that justice should be fullfilled in the case of the commandant of the concentration camp Günthergrube. It is a mistrial and the case should be tried again with another prosecutor.

"2. To send me the verdict of the court.

"I hope to hear from you very soon. Thank you."

On June 16, 1975, I received a reply from the Justice Minister, Germany.

"Dear Doctor.

"I confirm the receipt of your letter of 6/6/75 and would like to inform you that I couldn't do anything regarding the proceedings of the court. Regarding Prosecutor Klein, I asked for additional information. After receiving the latter, I'll inform you about my decision. . . .

"Very truly yours,
Rothenberger."

As of today, 11/15/77, I still have not received the promised answer and decision of the German Minister of Justice.

I believe that the German prosecutor and the judges were acquainted and completely familiar with all the crimes committed by the commandants of the Nazi extermination camps, and particularly with those perpetrated by Alois Frey. They understood it the same as I and all the other survivors perceived it, although they were not incarcerated themselves. They learned it by hearing from hundreds of eyewitnesses, by the proceedings of the international tribunals, by visiting the concentration camps like, Auschwitz, Maidanek, Treblinka, and others. I assume that many of them were acquainted with the atrocities which occurred before and especially during the war. Yet, the postwar German Governments (except the late President Adenauer) made all kinds of difficulties and obstacles to punish the criminals in a way that the same atrocities and genocide would not be repeated again. The system of justice in Germany today, as far as the Nazi trials are concerned, has been changed to some kind of a performance and not to justice suitable to the crimes committed.

It has become unrealistic, bordering on absurdity and ludicrousness. Some of the prosecutors and the judges are ashamed of their own performances.

How could one explain otherwise the adamant refusal of prosecutor Klein to send me the verdict and the excerpts of the decision of the jury?

I would like here to recapitulate the above Nazi trial and to sum it up, as follows:

It was proven, in my opinion, without a shadow of a doubt that Alois Frey, the commandant of the Auschwitz concentration camp (Günthergrube), committed the following crimes:

1. He hanged four young innocent prisoners in the camp.
2. He selected prisoners for the gas chambers, where they perished.
3. He created conditions in the camp which caused the death of many prisoners.
4. He shot prisoners on the road after the evacuation of Auschwitz.
5. Prosecutor Klein himself told me in my office that he had eyewitnesses who saw him shooting Gypsies.

On December 26, 1975, I received from the World Jewish Congress an excerpt of an issue, "Algemeine Jüdische Wochenzeitung No. 29, 1974," in which the result of the Nazi trial of Alois Frey was published, which I am quoting in the original language of the paper.

"Der Ehemalige Komandoführer des zum konzentrationslager Auschwitz Gehörenden nebenlagers Günthersgrube, und SS-Oberscharfuhrer Alois Frey (63) ist von einem Frankfurter Schwurgericht . . . *Freigesprochen worden.*"

English translation.

"The ex-commandant of the camp Günthergrube, which belonged to the Auschwitz concentration camp, Alois Frey, was found *not guilty* by the court of Frankfurt."

Unbelievable! Shocking! A travesty of justice! . . .

The same publication reported further, "Die Auklagevertretung und die verteidigung hatten aus den gleichen grunden auf freisprach pladiert."

English translation.

"The prosecutor and the defense asked the defendant be freed."

It means that Prosecutor Klein acted not as a prosecutor but as a defender of the criminal Alois Frey in order to free him, in spite of all the crimes that he knew Frey committed, and like the defense he asked for acquittal.

It is incredible, inconceivable, untenable, but it is the truth.

A question arises here:

What was the purpose of creating Nazi trials if the courts and the prosecutors free the perpetrators? What was the aim and meaning of conducting such trials?

One Example of a Nazi Trial

It is to be assumed that the Germans believed that the publicity of the Nazi trials would rehabilitate them in the eyes of the world, and that the majority of the people would not follow the decisions and the verdicts of the courts. It was partially true and was confirmed by the fact that even Dr. Harsaw himself did not realize it and did not know, before his testimony on the Nazi trial of Frankfort, about the *real nature* of these Nazi trials.

The resulting verdicts amounted to very little or to nothing at all.

It still sounds very strange to me, how Prosecutor Klein defended the Nazi Alois Frey in my office because "He spoke with a pleasant German dialect and he had a nice round face."

The many young lives which Alois Frey took away and murdered in cold blood were forgotten by Prosecutor Klein, and he asked the court to free the criminal.

Does the action of Prosecutor Klein and the verdicts of the court of Frankfurt reflect the thinking and the policy of the postwar German Governments?

I must answer this question in an affirmative way, because too many criminals are walking freely on the streets of Germany today. I assume that those criminals are scoffing, jeering and mocking the mild sentences, strengthening their belief in atrocities and mass torture.

In view of the above, I believe that another Hitler will arise in the future who might even not be an anti-Semite, but who will build again gas chambers and Krematoria in order to repeat another genocide.

Taking into consideration the new and modern techniques of conducting wars, the atomic and hydrogen weapons, our planet will be destroyed.

Maybe this constitutes the way planets disappear in the universe, manifested by appearances of many scattered meteors.

When we see a flash and streak of light high up in the sky, an ionized trail of fire, it may be a sign of a blasted world like ours destroyed by a maniac.

If the freeing of Nazi criminals doesn't constitute a permanent and perpetual policy of the present German government, but rather a conduct and artificial scheme of certain courts, then the following legislation is presented for passage, by the German authorities.

1. The Nazi trials should be conducted like any other trial. In view of the enormity of the unheard-of crimes the mitigating circumstances should be abolished, because they establish a tragedy to the future history of Germany and constitute an offense to the memory of the millions of innocent people massacred.

The authorities in Germany should also remember that the crimes committed by the Nazis were not known on our planet previously, and therefore mitigating circumstances cannot be applied.

2. To treat the few remaining victims of Nazi bestiality with compassion and not with hatred. To eliminate the officials of the Wiedergutmachung offices, who are acting against the spirit of this law.

The above two requests must be fulfilled if Germany of today is to be rehabilitated in the eyes of the survivors and the world at large.

It should be noticed that the trial and the sentencing of the Nazis is not an internal and domestic matter, but constitutes a grave international problem. Most of the victims were not Germans: but Russians, Jews, French, British, and others.

The postwar German Chancellors, with exception of Konrad Adenauer, were indifferent in my opinion to the fate of the survivors, and very tolerant and permissive of the verdicts of the Nazi courts, which reached their peak at the time of Chancellor Brandt. The later, although himself a fugitive of Nazi Germany, or maybe because of it, did not stop the hatred of some officials of the Wiedergutmachung offices towards the survivors. He did not protest either the mild sentences in the Nazi trials and looked unconcerned upon the freeing of Nazi criminals.

I express my hope that Chancellor Schmidt will follow in the footsteps of the late Konrad Adenauer and will rehabilitate the German people in the eyes of the world from the irony, cynicism and sarcasm of the Nazi trials and will defend the few survivors from the clutches of hatred of some German officials.

ONE EXAMPLE OF A NAZI TRIAL

Only time will show whether the present leader of Germany is a truly big man, or a simple German politician.

I related in this book the complete proceedings of one Nazi trial. All the other Nazi trials were more or less the same.

This explains why so many Nazi criminals, who committed atrocities unheard of in the past history of mankind, are freed by the German courts.

The millions of innocent people murdered by the Germans expressed in the last minutes of their lives their hopes and prayers "That the perpetrators will pay for their crimes and that another genocide will thus be avoided."

Those wishes and calls for justice were lost in the chimneys of the Krematoria and spread by the winds to all the corners of the world.

They were lost in the Nazi trials of today's Germany.

Their bodies were destroyed by the Nazis and their hopes were dissolved and doomed by the judicial system of present-day Germany.

The danger of a repetition of the same crimes is here and real.

The reason why life has become so defenseless in the world today lies partially in the German courts, whose light is being reflected on the criminals and potential desperadoes, hoodlums and cutthroats of today.

The first Chancellor of postwar Germany was an outstanding, decent and compassionate man whose name was *Konrad Adenauer*.

He deplored deeply and sincerely the crimes committed by the Nazis. He was instrumental in forming the "*Law of Wiedergutmachung*," which compensated in a very small way the survivors of Nazi bestialities.

He realized that no compensation was possible for lost lives. for terror and atrocities perpetrated for many years over innocent people.

No life could be restituted and no chronic disease, physical or spiritual, could be restored.

It was an expression of atonement and expiation on behalf of himself and some of his compassionate co-workers.

What amends could be offered to a survivor who lost all the members of his family, for no reason at all, and who remained all by himself in this world?

What reparation could be offered to a person for the enormous sufferings sustained in the ghettos and the concentration camps?

What indemnities could be submitted to a survivor, broken up physically and mentally, whose infirmities could never be cured by the best physicians and best medical remedies available?

Who will take away the sufferings of the daytime and the terrible, constant nightmares which accompany him from the day of liberation till the day he departs from this world?

It was expected that the German people, who were responsible for the crimes, by freely electing Hitler and the Nazis, by tolerating the atrocities for many years thereafter, by cheering the Nazis during the first years of victories, would show sympathy toward the survivors.

The world anticipated from the German people deep gratitude for the ways they were treated after the war, especially by the Americans, for the Marshall Plan, and for other help which brought a prosperity to Germany which never existed before.

It was assumed that the Wiedergutmachung offices, whose task was to compensate slightly the survivors of Nazi bestialities, would exceed each other in politeness, courteousness understanding and compassion towards the very few remaining individuals left over after the massacre.

Some of the officials of the "Wiedergutmachung," to the amazement, flabbergastation and bewilderment of the world, have no compassion at all towards the survivors.

They deliberately put obstacles and many difficulties in their ways. Often they exhibited hatred, enmity, arrogance and contemptuousness. Many pensions were taken away from the survivors for no reason at all, causing unnecessary aggravation and sufferings and which could be surpassed only by those caused during the Nazi regime.

One Example of a Nazi Trial

I'll relate here the authentic story of one survivor, Mr. Dig.

The story of the survivor Mr. Dig.

I declare under oath, that I was incarcerated in Auschwitz for two years by the Nazis, and that everything which I am going to relate here, including all the details corresponding to the "Wiedergutmachung offices," are true and represent only the truth.

The following decision in my case was rendered by the Civilsenat of Koblenz, Germany, on 11/11/1965.

1. Disability of 30%, which meant a weekly pension of about $25.00.

2. Reimbursement for the cost of treatment for ailments contracted in the German concentration camp, which were:

   a. Peptic Ulcer,
   b. Left Inguinal Hernia,
   c. Meralgia Paresthetica.

Note: In order to receive the small pension ($25.00 per week), the disability should be at least 25%.

A disability of any survivor, which did not reach 25%, is not entitled to any compensation.

In the year 1969, I was operated on for the hernia and so informed the Wiedergutmachung office in Trier (Germany).

Here started the abuses, arrogance and contemptuousness exhibited by the German officials of the "Wiedergutmachung."

In 1970, I received a letter from Trier (Germany) informing me that my pension would be taken away from me, because after the operation my disability is less than 25%.

This was a flagrant misrepresentation of the facts and a desire to take away my pension and to act against the decision of the court in Koblenz.

They knew perfectly clearly that my disability was 30% *plus* reimbursement for the cost of the operation. It was a deliberate act of adding additional injury to my previous torment and torture. I hired a lawyer in Germany and asked him to intervene in my case. Naturally I had to pay him in advance for this intervention.

One year passed and I didn't hear anything more from Germany.

In 1971, I received a letter from my lawyer in Trier, Mr. Schöllendorf, in which he wrote that he was able to prove on the basis of the decision rendered in Koblenz that I was entitled to the pension, which will be returned to me as before. It was.

The German officials knew it long ago, but their desire to annoy and aggravate the survivors evidently took priority over any decency and correctness.

I hoped that the officials would be ashamed and embarassed by the detection of their tricks and deliberate falsehood.

But I was wrong in assuming so.

In 1973, I was informed by the same German officials that my pension was taken away again. I was very much astonished and amazed. Why now?—Why?—What do they want from me, the Germans, again?

The German officials knew that they were wrong. All that they desired was to continue to annoy me and to persecute me, as in the old Nazi days.

It was terrible and very tragic. I felt like being in Auschwitz again. My anxieties and painful emotions, which I have been experiencing in my dreams only, became real again, caused by the actions of the Wiedergutmachung officials. They kept me constantly under threat of taking away my pension, by malicious and unjust motives and designs, which caused a further deterioration of my health.

I decided to give the case to the lawyer in Germany, Mr. Schöllendorf, and asked him the names of the German officials who were embittering my life.

I received an answer, that the name of the official who has been handling my case was *Mr. Momper* and his superior, the chief on the Wiedergutmachung office of Trier, was *Mr. Bellersheim*.

At the same time he informed me that my case will come up for trial in the court of Trier on January 29, 1974.

I decided to travel to Germany, and to defend my own case in court, because of the following:

1. The accusations of Mr. Bellersheim and Mr. Momper had

no foundation at all. In fact they made no sense. I wanted to observe the faces of the judges, when they heard the accusations.

2. I wanted to see Mr. Bellersheim and Mr. Momper, because their ruthlessness and intense hatred, which they exhibited towards the survivors of the terrible gas chambers and Krematoria, were incomprehensible to me and constituted a complete surprise to me.

3. Rumors were spreading in New York that the Germans were taking away many pensions given previously to the survivors. I didn't want to believe it and decided to go to Germany, in order to find out the truth.

4. My personal appearance was important also because the above named officials dug up, all the time, new senseless accusations which, although worthless, were intended to confuse the judges and Mr. Schöllendorf.

I believed at that time that Germany was a democratic country, free, liberal and just. I based my assumption on the fact that the leaders of postwar German government expressed their anger and regret on finding out the truth about the Nazi atrocities committed by their countrymen. I remembered the words of Chancellor Brandt in front of Auschwitz and in front of the memorial in Warsaw (Poland) and also in "Yad Vashem" of Jerusalem.

Was all this a facade, a comedy for the outside world?

Impossible! Unimaginable! Behind the bounds of reason!

When I arrived in Germany, I received the shock of my life. The trial which I expected and desired was postponed. Nobody let me know in advance. I traveled 3,000 miles for nothing, wasting my time, energy, money, etc.

Why didn't they inform me?

They certainly could have sent me a telegram not to come. Evidently, they didn't care about the subhumans, and I still was a subhuman in their eyes.

Mr. Bellersheim and Mr. Momper did not want me to appear in the court. They were afraid, because I would have exposed their machinations and their falsehood and proved to the court how they take away unjustly the pensions of the few survivors.

But the courts were supposed to be independent. Why didn't they let me know that the trial was postponed? They probably work together.

This assumption was corroborated later by the statement of the Redaktor of the Newspaper *Frankfurter Rundschau*, Mr. Norbet Leppert, whom I met in Frankfurt/Main. Here are the redactor's own words, as uttered to me and my wife in Hotel Savoy, Frankfurt, at the beginning of 1974.

"The Wiedergutmachung offices in Germany are taking away many pensions of the disabled survivors. The court and the officials work together."

Imagine! Survivors partially or totally disabled—caused by enormous sufferings and persecutions in the Nazi concentration camps—were losing their pensions. This constitutes, if it is true, an enormous injustice. It awakes unnecessarily memories of past atrocities and produces many doubts about the sanity of the world.

I decided to go to Bonn, where the Chancellor had his office, and to find out the truth for myself.

On Thursday, January 31, 1974, I met in Bonn, in the Chancellor's office, two people: one was Dr. Sprenger of the Press Division and the other one was Dr. Schauer of the Foreign Relations Division.

Both of them were shocked and promised to present it to the attention of Chancellor Brandt himself.

In the words of Dr. Sprenger, "It is an explosive story!"

I never heard from Chancellor Brandt's office. It seemed to me that he didn't care much about the injustices in Germany towards the survivors. He was busy with his own affairs.

In order to have a clear picture of the situation, without any shadow of a doubt, I went over to speak to Dr. Ribka, the newly appointed chief of the Wiedergutmachung office of all Rheinland-Pfalz.

Dr. Ribka was very upset about the matter, especially about my coming to Trier for the prearranged trial which did not take place.

"How could the court make an appointment for January 29

and then to postpone it without letting you know in advance?" he asked in anger.

Poor Dr. Ribka, he was new in his post and didn't understand as yet the falsehood and machination of his office.

"Dr. Ribka!" I answered. "I came here from the U.S. of America believing that I'd be able to be at my own trial. I agree to stay here a few days longer in order to have a trial."

"Sure, you are right. The trial has to take place. I'll call one of my officials who has been working here for many years."

The name of the official was, if I am not mistaken, Mr. Mennen or Hennen. But I am not sure of his exact name.

The official came in and said, "It is not our business. The court has to decide about it."

"But this man," insisted Dr. Ribka, "came from the U.S.A. on a court proceeding that had to take place on 1/29/74. He was not informed beforehand about the postponement. Why couldn't it be arranged to have the trial in 2-3 days? It is incomprehensible to me."

The official started to mumble in a low voice, his eyes directed towards the floor.

"Mr. Dig doesn't have to be present at his own trial. We'll take care of everything. Let him return to New York."

Dr. Ribka was not satisfied and said, "I'll call Mr. Bellersheim and ask him to meet you in Trier and to make arrangements for a trial."

He disappeared for a moment, in order to telephone Mr. Bellersheim. In the meantime, I observed the official who was sitting in front of me. He gave an impression of a German who had decided already, way in advance, to take away the pensions regardless of cause and justice. He didn't want me to defend my own case. This would be bad publicity.

In the meantime Dr. Ribka returned and said, "I made arrangement with Mr. Bellersheim to meet you tomorrow in his office in Trier."

Next morning, I went to meet the chief of the Wiedergutmachung office in Trier, Mr. Bellersheim, whose office was one of the most important of this kind in Germany.

I was accompanied by my wife.

When I entered his office, I saw a short fellow standing in front of a huge table.

He started to talk very rapidly.

"I spoke about you with Dr. Ribka and his official. You don't have to be at the trial. We'll take care ourselves. We'll let you know the decision."

"Mr. Bellersheim!" I said. "I came over here from the U.S.A., in order to be present at my own trial, which had to take place on 1/29/74. It was very difficult for me to close my business and to waste time and expenses for nothing. Dr. Ribka told me that it is possible to arrange the trial in a few days."

"We don't want you to be present at the trial," he snapped, "and we'll arrange it in such a way that you will not be able to be present."

I didn't understand the meaning of his last words. Therefore, I asked Mr. Bellersheim:

"What do you mean, that I'll not be able to be on my trial?"

My wife, who was sitting quietly, intervened and said, "Mr. Bellersheim, my husband has a lot of aggravation now, and he suffered, also, much in the last war from the Nazis. I don't want him to worry any more. Please, if possible, arrange a trial within the next few days, as Dr. Ribka suggested, and I would highly appreciate it, because this was the reason for which we came to Germany."

Mr. Bellersheim suddenly jumped from his seat, started to yell and to knock with his fists over the table.

My wife continued, "Dr. Ribka, from the main office, told us yesterday, that everything depends on you. You may proceed in any way that you wish. Let's have a trial now."

"I don't wish to do anything," yelled Mr. Bellersheim.

He became red in his face and wet from perspiration and anger.

He continued to scream and to knock the table with his fists.

It was terrible! Unbelievable behavior from a high official of present day Germany.

I looked at him. Everything in the room started to move in

circles in front of my eyes. Mr. Bellersheim continued to yell and to shout.

I forgot where I was. It seemed to me that I was again in the cellar of the Gestapo being tortured and tormented, agonized and martyrized.

I opened my eyes and couldn't believe it. It was Bellersheim, not the Gestapo, yelling.

We left the office of Bellersheim, the chief of the "Wiedergutmachung" of Trier.

These were the officials in whose hands lay the fate of the unfortunate victims of Nazi bestialities. No wonder that many of the survivors continued to be persecuted with their pensions taken away from them.

I realized now that the rumors in New York regarding Germany were not rumors but the truth.

"He behaved like a real Nazi, a chief of the Gestapo," concluded my wife on the way back.

"Maybe, he passed the Nazi schools in his youth," I answered.

"Then why does the present German government employ people of this kind on such sensitive places?" asked my wife.

When I returned to the U.S.A. I found a letter from my lawyer, Mr. Schöllendorf, in which he informed me that my case instead of one session would have three sessions.

It became clear to me then what Mr. Bellersheim meant when he said, "We'll arrange it in such a way that you will not be able to be present at your trial."

He and Mr. Momper contrived a new scheme, namely:

Normally, this kind of a case lasted 1-2 hours in the German courts.

It was a small case.

Instead of having one session, as previously decided, they decided to have it in three sessions:

April 4, 1974.
April 11, 1974.
April 18, 1974.

In other words, in order to appear at my trial, I had not only to travel from America to Germany one additional time, to waste again money, time and energy and to close my business, but I would have to stay in a hotel in Germany for at least *three weeks*. The hotels in Germany were very expensive and I suspected that the Germans, after seeing me, might postpone my trial again after my arrival to Trier.

Therefore, it was impossible for me to return to Germany and be present at my own trial.

The purpose of my going to Germany was actually, not so much the return of my pension, but to find out whether the survivors were being persecuted again, and whether their pensions were being taken away from them for no reason at all.

My first journey to Germany gave me all the information that I wanted to know. Therefore I did not travel again to Germany.

Later, my lawyer in Trier, Mr. Schöllendorf, informed my that the trial took place in three sessions and the verdict of the court regarding my pension would be announced very shortly.

This was April, 1974.

Up to November of 1977, more than three years later, the court had not announced its verdict regarding the return of my pension.

In the judicial systems of all the nations of the world, it was very rare to encounter a case in which a hearing was completed and the verdict of the court not pronounced after more than three years. Usually it is pronounced in a few days after the hearing.

This is Germany. This is the way the courts operate, especially in relation to the poor survivors of Nazi bestiality. As we can see, the German courts produced many mitigating circumstances for the criminals who committed unheard-of atrocities and who offended the dignity of mankind, and at the same time permitted further persecutions of the Nazi victims.

This is the end of the true story of Mr. Dig.

The case of Mr. Dig is not unique and not uncommon in the "Wiedergutmachung" offices of Germany. Many of the few survivors of Nazi terror are being persecuted again for no reason at all. Many pensions were taken away, and the survivors were brutally offended in the process. For example:

The pension of Mr. Dig was not only taken away but the judge, in the absence of Mr. Dig, called, him *vulgar* ("Grob" in German). The judge didn't know Mr. Dig. He had never seen him.

Imagine, Mr. Dig, whose family was murdered by the Nazis in cold blood, and who suffered two long years in Auschwitz concentration camp—he is "vulgar", but Mr. Bellersheim and Mr. Momper, who continue the old persecution of the Nazi victims, are nice people.

The question arises, why was the law of "Wiedergutmachung" created? Wouldn't it be better not to have such a law at all?

What is the use of continuing persecution of the few poor survivors by giving them, first, a small pension and then taking it away from them?

It is like having a bad incurable wound on the body, which is being constantly jabbed and punched at.

Wouldn't it be better to leave the wound alone and let the forces of nature take over?

Why the continuous jabbing and poking?

The answer lies in two factors:

First, the Germans felt very guilty immediately after the war and something had to be done to demonstrate their dissent towards the Nazi atrocities.

They did not know either what was going to be the world response towards such enormous crimes.

Secondly, it lay in the personality, high statemanship and compassion of the first postwar German Chancellor, Konrad Adenauer.

Later, with passing of time, the sense of guilt diminished. U.S. of America helped to bring a prosperity to Germany which startled and shocked the nation. They never expected it. They enjoyed a thriving condition and wealth not encountered in all the recent German history.

This was the reaction of the Allies, especially of the U.S.A., towards the defeated Germany, which was completely different from the way the officials of the "Wiedergutmachung" offices treated the Nazi victims. These officials, as we had seen, exhibited hatred instead of compassion, and persecution instead of understanding.

I hope that the present German government will stop the further persecution of the survivors and will investigate the so-called "Nazi Trials." If not, then I'll consider this book to be a total failure as far as Germany is concerned, *but a revelation, an eye-opener and a warning to the rest of the world.*

It is well to remember the words of the philosopher Santayana. "Those who do not remember the past are condemned to repeat the same mistakes again."

WINGS TO FLY

Who would give me wings to fly very high up, where the supreme forces of our universe have their quarters. I would reach the kingdom of heaven and put in front of the All-powerful, the Supreme Being, our Lord, the following questions:

1. Do you remember the gas chambers where corpses were standing like columns of stones, being separated with powerful hooks and dragged to the Krematoria?

2. Do you remember the black smoke emanating from the burned human bodies and the nearby tables with alcohol, where Germans were jubilating and shouting, "Heil Hitler"?

3. Do you remember the father hanging his own son and committing suicide soon thereafter because the son had a mark on his face and had to be hacked to death by a shovel next morning?

If you do remember, why then do you permit the postwar German governments to free the bloodthirsty criminals who tortured, tormented, offended and shocked your planet which you created for thousands of years to come?

Please promise that no more gas chambers, nor pits, nor Krematoria to destroy mankind will again be constructed on our earth.

"The rainbow in the clouds should forever remind You, just as the floods of the ancient times, of this everlasting covenant."

Aren't the mild sentences and the freeing of the criminals an invitation to commit more terrible crimes and mass destructions?

Aren't the Nazi trials an encouragement to the hoodlums, ruffians, evildoers all over the world to continue in their wickedness and viciousness?

The wrongdoers contend:
"Our immoralities and iniquities are children's plays in comparison to the Nazi criminals, who brutally murdered thousands of little children, their mothers and fathers. If those criminals were freed and declared to be innocent in the German courts, then our actions may be considered virtues and not faults."

Oh, Allmighty G-d, we plain humble human beings don't understand indeed your ways and modes.

Please, enlighten us. . . .

THE BIBLICAL "JOB" AND THE SURVIVOR.

Most of the well informed people are familiar with the book of "Job" (Eyov).

Therefore, I would like to make a comparison between the biblical "Job" and the contemporary survivor of a concentration camp and to formulate the right equation expressing the ratio between the two.

"Job" was a righteous, rich, virtuous man, who was grateful to G-d, and served the Almighty with all his might, all the time, and in every place.

Once upon a time "Job" lost, in a very short time, all of his wealth. The house where his children gathered for the annual reunion and celebration collapsed, killing all his children, seven boys and three daughters.

He became suddenly very poor and miserable. In addition, he was afflicted at the same time with a severe skin disease, causing a lot of pain, pruritus, and enormous suffering.

Our sages and wise men expressed their doubts of these possible happenings, when such terrible events occurred all at the same time.

Therefore, our learned and profound men concluded that "Job" did not really exist, was not born. It was a legend, a fantasy, a fable. It was too horrible to think otherwise.

Yet, a survivor of a German concentration camp suffered not less, but more than the biblical "Job." His family was murdered, choked in the gas chambers and burned in the Krematoria. He lost all his wealth and contracted different diseases.

The survivor, in differentiation to "Job," lost, also, his freedom. If he survived the starvation, diseases, hard labor and beatings, he was incarcerated in the terrible German concentration camps, where he became a complete slave serving his master under the most inhumane conditions.

"Slave" is not the right word for it. He became subhuman, being treated much worse than an animal. Every hour, every minute of the day, his life was in big jeopardy, being exposed to atrocities unheard of during all the existence of our planet.

Many lost their lives right there. The few who survived remained broken-up human beings, afflicted with physical and mental infirmities which had never been cured. They still suffer now, even after the liberation, from different maladies and ailments during the daytime, and from nightmares during the night, where the dreadful scenes of past atrocities are being revived again and come back to torment them.

"Job" never lost his freedom, hadn't been exposed to atrocities, and his life had never been threatened. He had friends, who came to express their commiseration. He regained his wealth, a lovely family, became healthy again and lived many years thereafter in joy and happiness.

The survivor, in distinction to Job, never regained his health, nor his previous position and standing. He continues to be miserable and cannot forget his past.

The present German officials of the "Wiedergutmachung" offices in Trier don't exhibit compassion or friendship towards the few survivors. They exhibit hatred instead of love, heartlessness instead of compassion, and ruthlessness, cynicism and snubbing, instead of understanding, comprehension sympathy and humanness.

The equation is:

$$SURVIVOR = or > JOB \times 2$$

in terms of suffering and regaining the previous position and status.

The above equation means that the suffering of a survivor of a German concentration camp equals or is more than double the suffering of the Biblical Job.

EPILOGUE

EPILOGUE

The twentieth century was agitated and tormented by world wars prepared, initiated, and organized by one nation, which was Germany.

The First World War, at the beginning of the century (1914-1918).

The Second World War, in the middle of the century, 1939 1945, was unleashed by one man, who was freely elected by one nation, whose ambition and desire was to dominate the world by force and conquest, regardless of cost, means and human sufferings.

The result, in terms of casualties, destruction of cities and wealth, was unparalleled in all the history of mankind.

Special squads (Einsatzgroupen) were created, whose task was *not* to fight the enemy, but to evacuate by force, millions of innocent civilians, including old men, women and children, and to murder them in cold blood, without any reason, without any benefit to the conduct of the war, and without any purpose whatsoever, just for the sake of killing.

This is unique in the history of our world.

So are the erections of factories of death, the gas chambers and Krematoria, utilization of human fat and human hair for the German industry. All these monstrosities constitute something strange, unnatural, queer and unearthly on our planet.

The consequence and outcome of the Second World War was tragic and catastrophic for mankind. It showed how quickly man turns to beast if his actions are approved and promoted by his government.

Ten millions were killed in the German concentration camps alone: Auschwitz, Maidanek, Treblinka, Sobibor, Belzec, Dachau, Mathausen, Janowska, and many more extermination camps.

Fifteen million *civilians* were murdered in cold blood, including small children and even infants, who didn't know what it was all about, who never heard of the name of Germany. Could you imagine one million innocent civilians slaughtered? No! The human mind is not able to comprehend it.

Over six million Jews lost their lives in the most brutal way imaginable. One third of European Jewry disappeared from the surface of the earth.

Nineteen million soldiers were killed on both sides. A total calamity of over 40 million lives.

All this destruction, extermination and slaughter was performed by one nation, which elected freely and fulfilled the most atrocious orders of one man. I repeat, the orders of one man whose name will forever be remembered and connected with the biggest afflictions and curses sent on this earth, Adolf Hitler.

Generation after generation will talk about it, but will never be able to comprehend it.

"How was it possible?" they'll ask. "Why did mankind and the superior forces of our universe permit it to happen?"

The tragedy was largely forgotten because it was too intolerable to remember. It seemed that the world of today has not wakened up as yet from the shock it received after discovering the enormous crimes committed by the Nazis.

Are thirty years not enough to come out from this shock?

Why is the world so indifferent to the travesty of justice in the Nazi courts of today?

Did you know that most of the bloodthirsty criminals who committed unimaginable, inconceivable, unheard-of atrocities are walking freely the streets of Germany today?

They were, to the surprise of the world and even to the astonishment of the evil perpetrators themselves, freed by the

German courts. Sometimes very small sentences were rendered and they were freed shortly thereafter.

It is clear, and without any shadow of a doubt, that the seeds of another, more terrible holocaust are being planted, cultivated and disseminated, because the ground is already prepared.

Taking into consideration the devastating forces of the new atomic arsenal, a Third World War would bring a total destruction of our planet.

The world is indifferent, and the evil forces are being permitted to explode again.

It is dangerous and tragic! The holocaust is not an internal matter of Germany alone. It is international in character, because the victims derived from all the corners of the world and the executions and the massacres took place on territories of other nations.

The twentieth century has an additional twenty-three years to last.

Will a Third World War erupt explode and destroy mankind?

This is the question.

Will Germany be the aggressor as in the preceding two World Wars of the twentieth century?

The Germans say that the atrocities will not be repeated again.

What do they do to prevent such crimes?

Do they really think that by releasing the savages, the hooligans, the larrikins, the barbarians and the beasts who disgraced the image of human species, who shamed and humiliated the history of the German nation, the goal and objective of *"No Repetition"* will be achieved?

It is quite logical to assume that by the continuation of the same postwar policies, the opposite aim will be achieved, because they constitute an encouragement to crime and not a deterrent.

What are the reasons that the German governments permit some of the officials of the so-called "Wiedergutmachung" offices (Compensation of the Nazi Victims) to persecute and to continue to harass and to torment the very few survivors who by miracles were saved from the Nazi fires? Why do these officials exhibit hatred instead of compassion? Why is such conduct and behavior being tolerated and sanctioned?

The murdering of millions of innocent victims by the Hitler regime had never been understood by the world at large. So are the present mild sentences in the Nazi courts and the freeing of the criminals not understood either.

As long as Germany continues the same policy of acquitting the lusty criminals and of exhibiting indifference to further persecution of the survivors, there is a danger of a Third World War at the end of this century, which will surely destroy this time our planet and its inhabitants.

The responsibility lies with the German government, and it is its obligation to remove the sign of Cain, which the Nazis fastened and secured on their foreheads.

I BELIEVE

I BELIEVE that further wars between men and men will stop in view of the destructive powers of our war arsenal and that the atomic and hydrogen energy will be served for peaceful purposes only.

I BELIEVE that nations will not lift up swords against other nations and wars will be eradicated from our earth. The sword and guns will be transformed into plows and spears into pruning knives.

I BELIEVE that the prophecy of Isaiah will be fulfilled. The wolf shall dwell with the lamb, the calf and the young lion and the fatling shall be together. The cow and the bear and lion shall feed jointly by common consent, and a little child shall lead them.

They shall not hurt nor destroy each other, for the earth will be full of knowledge and its inhabitants will be truly cultured and civilized.

I BELIEVE that peace will reign over our planet and the people will enjoy true happiness, the bliss of sunshine and the thrilling delight of living.

I BELIEVE that mankind will soon wake up from the Nazi shock and undertake ways and means to combat evil and make it impossible for a repetition of the same crimes.

I BELIEVE that our planet will not explode by the action of a maniac and will continue to exist for many millions of years to come.

I BELIEVE that justice, fraternity and equality will prevail not only in words but in deeds.

I BELIEVE that human resources and high techniques will overwhelm, defeat and conquer all kind of diseases. Cancer, heart diseases, arteriosclerosis and atheromatosis will disappear from the surface of the earth.

INDEX

INDEX

Action Reinhardt, 226
Action Spare, 240, 241
Auschwitz I, 180, 539
Auschwitz II (*Birkenau*), 181, 186, 188-192
  Children, exterminated, 369
  Diseases, 223
  Evacuation, 468
  Exercises, 336
  Experiments, 339-342
  Organization, 268, 281
  Punishments, 259-263
  Ramp, 182
  Roll call (Apel), 222, 302
Auschwitz III (Buna), 182, 339, 418, 547, 554, 555, 565
Babi Yar, 75-78
Berlin, 468, 506, 509, 510
Berezina River, 43
Bialystok, 137-140, 452
Block Seven, 199-200, 207, 326-331, 336-340
Block Eight, 285-288, 293, 302
Boch-Zalewski (Destroyer of Warsaw), 461
Bologna, 505
Bor-Komorowski, 458-459
Calabria, landing, 364
Chelmno, Extermination Camp, 175-176
Children, selection, 374
Churchill, 9, 460, 524, 537
Ciano (Mussolini's son in law), 363-364
Comintern, dissolution, 323
Crematoria, See Krematoria
Cyclon B (Deadly gas), 225, 369, 385
D-Day, Normandy Landing, 540
Dig, Mr., 573-581
Dixlewanger Brigade (professional criminals), 79
Eichmann, Adolf, 537-538
Epstein, Dr., 233, 234, 267, 270, 277
Extermination groups (Einsatz gruppen), 74
F-Lager, Hospital, 354-356, 386

595

596 INDEX

Fisher, Dr. 421-423
Frank, Hans, 529-530
Frey, Alois, Commandant of
    Gunther-Grube, 400
    Nazi trial, 546-561
    Verdict, 586
Gas Chambers in Birkenau,
    395-397
    Resumption of gassing, 330
    Stopping of gassing, 324-325
Germany
    Capitulation, 468
    Defeat, reasons for, 405-408
    Early victories, 403-404
    Proclamation of war, 7
    Reaction to Hitler's crimes,
    513-515
Gleiwitz, 470-474
Goebbels, 329
Goering, Herman, 346, 527-529
Gorfain, 500
Guntergrube Concentration
    Camp (Lendzin), 416-437
    Escape from, 476-483
    Evacuation from, 468-469
    Forced march, 468
    Hanging of Prisoners,
    443-487
Gypsies in Auschwitz, 296-297,
    326, 353, 400, 546
Greeks, transport of, 297-302,
    330-331, 355
Harsaw, Dr., 21, 415, 416,
    425-426, 476
Heidenfeld, Dr., 386
Himmler, 180, 181, 314, 342,
    346

Hitler, 5-7, 36, 59-61, 89, 186,
    512-525
    Assassination attempt,
    433-434, 505-506, 546
    Atrocities, reasons of, 512,
    520, 521
    Criminal leader, 518-519, 522
    Elections, 513
    Megalomania, 516-517
    Oath of loyalty to, 519
    Suicide, 506
Hoess, Rudolf, Commandant of
    Auschwitz, 181, 226-229,
    532
I.G. Farben Industry, 371
Immortality of Soul, 50-53
Itzkowitz, 337, 387-391
Job, Biblical-Survivor, 583-584
Josselevska, 96
Kalinin, President of Supreme
    Soviet, 87
Kaltenbruner, 530-531
Kaplan, Dr. 149, 244, 273, 470,
    475
Kaplinski, 192, 193, 196, 202
Kattegat, 517
Katyuska, Mortars, 452
Kaufman, Dr., 73
Keitel, German Field Marshal,
    356, 468, 531, 532
Kharkov, 329
Kivorograd, 323, 324, 542, 543
Klein, German Prosecutor,
    548-551, 554, 559, 561
Koniev, Russian Marshal, 462
Konstantinovo, 40-57
Krakow, 495-496
Krematoria, 224, 225, 330

INDEX

Kursk, Salient, 323, 329
Lublin, 497-499
Lyskovo, 84-105, 458
  Deadly march, 109
  Evacuation from, 105
Maidanek Extermination Camp, 365-368, 498
Marcus, Dr., 4
Master, the, 429-443
Mendel (Goldberg), 12, 13, 42, 103, 184
Michla (Pomeraniec-Weissman), 44, 97, 337, 338, 349
Minsk, 75, 450
Miracle #1, 18-19
Miracle #2, 48
Miracle #3, 71
Miracle #4, 106
Miracle #5, 120
Miracle #6, 184
Miracle #7, 241
Miracle #8, 448
Miracle #9, 458
Miracle #10, 477
Miracle #11, 490
Miracle #12, 495
Mohl, 380-382
Molotov, 323
  Speech, 8
Monte Casino, 448-449
Montgomery, 91
Morritz (Goldberg), 32, 33, 84, 111
Moscow conference, 387, 533
Mussolini, 330, 363, 505
Musulman, 374
Nazis, Attempt to create discord, (see also Kovorograd), 539-550
  Offer to exchange lives for trucks, 539-550
Nazis, trials of, 533-537, 546-561, 567
Ohlendorf, Otto, chief of group D (Einsatzgruppen), 78
Operation Anvill-Dragoon, 450
Operation Barbarossa, 6
Operation Citadel, 329
Operation Overlord, 450
Orel, 329
Partisans, 86-89, 99-100
Paulus, German chief at Stalingrad, 92, 186, 323
Peace attempts, 92-99
Pearl Harbor, 65
Piple, the, 269-271
Podorosk, 33, 37, 109-111
Pohl, Oswald, 370
Quackernack, 359-360
Rabinowitz, 274-275
Rokosowski, 462
Rommel, 90, 91, 187
Roosevelt, Franklin, 505
Rovno, 79-80
Rozana, 46, 55-57, 69, 72, 458
Russia, (USSR), 3, 92, 450, 458, 468
  Reasons for German attacks, 403
  Victories, 408-411
Shulman, Dr., 37, 110-111, 167
Sicily, 329, 347
Skagerrak, 517
Slonim, 73-75
Smolensk, 329

Solomon, 134-137
Sonderkommando, Rebellion, 399
Stalin, 3, 5, 33-36, 43, 60, 323-324
Stalingrad, 186
Stein (Kamien),
  Escape from, 475-492
Survivors
  Continuous persecution of, 573-580
Sweden, 517
Szereszewski, 452-456, 475
Theresenstadt, 545
Thomas, Judge of German regional court,
  Correspondence with, 562-564
Timoshenko, Russian General, 8
Treblinka, Extermination Camp, 154-166, 311
Train, Cattle, 474-475
Vistula River, 458
Vlasov, Traitor, 478
Von Bock, 24
Von Runstedt, 24
Von Staufenberg, 433
Warsaw Ghetto, 306
  Rebellion, 305-322

Transports to Treblinka, 155, 156
  Uprising and suppression, 458-461, 499-500
Wiezman, Dr., 542-543
Wolkowysk Concentration Camp, 36, 73-83, 458
  Cattle train (to Auschwitz), 171-177
  Doctors, massacre, 100-101
  Koszary, 121-145
  Transports to the gas chambers:
  First, November 1942, 132
  Second, December 3, 1942, 132
  Third, December 10, 1942, 133
  Fourth, December 20, 1942, 140-143
  Last, January 26, 1943, 170
  Typhus, outbreak of, 131-133
Yanowska extermination camp, 438-443
Yodl, 468
Zapolanski, 293-294
Zenkteller, 212-214, 272-274, 350, 414-415
Zukov, 60, 467
Zollman, 283-284